France

France

A History: From Gaul to de Gaulle

JOHN JULIUS NORWICH

JOHN MURRAY

First published in Great Britain in 2018 by John Murray (Publishers)
An Hachette UK Company

1

© John Julius Norwich 2018

The right of John Julius Norwich to be identified as the Author of the Work has been
asserted by him in accordance with the Copyright, Designs and Patents Act 1988.

Maps drawn by Rosie Collins

'Ballade of Unsuccssful Men' from *Complete Verse* by Hilaire Belloc reprinted by permission
of Peters Fraser & Dunlop (www.petersfraserdunlop.com) on behalf of the Estate of
Hilaire Belloc.

A CIP catalogue record for this title is available from the British Library

Hardback ISBN 978-1-47366-383-1
Trade paperback ISBN 978-1-47367-963-4
Ebook ISBN 978-1-47366-382-4

Typeset in Bembo MT 11.5/14 pt by Palimpsest Book Production Limited,
Falkirk, Stirlingshire

Printed and bound by Clays Ltd, St Ives plc

John Murray policy is to use papers that are natural,
renewable and recyclable products and made from wood grown in
sustainable forests. The logging and manufacturing processes are expected to
conform to the environmental regulations of the country of origin.

John Murray (Publishers)
Carmelite House
50 Victoria Embankment
London EC4Y 0DZ

www.johnmurray.co.uk

To the memory of my mother
who first took me to France
and taught me to love it as she did.

Contents

Preface

'*TOUTE MA VIE, je me suis fait une certaine idée de la France.*'[*] The opening words of General de Gaulle's memoirs have become world famous. I too, in my own infinitely humbler way, have always cherished just such a conception. It stems, I suppose, from my first visit, as a child of nearly seven in September 1936, when my mother took me for a fortnight to Aix-les-Bains, largely in an attempt to wean me from my English nanny. I can still feel, as if it were yesterday, the excitement of the Channel crossing; the regiment of porters, smelling asphyxiatingly of garlic in their blue-green blousons; the raucous sound all around me of spoken French (which I already understood quite well, having had twice-weekly French lessons since the age of five); the immense fields of Normandy, strangely devoid of hedges; then the Gare du Nord at twilight, the policemen with their *képis* and their little snow-white batons; and my first sight of the Eiffel Tower. We fetched up at Aix in a modest pension with a pretty garden, and a young girl called Simone[†] looked after me while my mother was doing the cure and talked French to me from morning till night.

There were two more pre-war trips, one with both my parents for a week in Paris during which we did all the usual things. We took a *bateau mouche* down the Seine, went to the Louvre which bored me stiff and to the sewers which I found fascinating, climbed on to the roof of the Arc de Triomphe, where you get a far better view of Paris than you do from the Eiffel Tower, which is like looking at it from an aeroplane. Of course we did the Eiffel Tower as well, not only going

[*] 'All my life, I have had a certain conception of France.'
[†] Later she had a baby (I think by an American GI) whom she called 'Diana Welcome' after my mother.

up to the top but having lunch in its extremely smart restaurant, which my father claimed was his favourite in Paris because it was the only place you couldn't see it from. I remember being astonished at the number of restaurants all over the city, at many of which people were eating outside; in pre-war London there were comparatively few, and tables on the pavement were almost unheard-of. My other memory is that almost every teenage boy wore a beret and plus fours, hundreds of them meeting regularly at a huge market for collectors of postage stamps at the Rond-Point des Champs-Elysées.★ Eight years later, when my father became ambassador, we led a very different sort of life. I was still at school, but now holidays were always spent in France – including Christmas 1944, when the war was still on – and in a palace. The Hôtel de Charost (to give it its proper name) on the Rue du Faubourg Saint-Honoré is, I believe, the most beautiful embassy of any country in the world. Previously owned by Napoleon's sister Pauline Borghese, it was bought by the Duke of Wellington when he was briefly ambassador after Waterloo and has been the British Embassy for the past two hundred years. The weather that winter was bitterly cold, and it was one of the few warm places; it could also provide limitless quantities of whisky and gin, which had been non-existent in France since the war began, it was full every night with the Parisian *beau monde* from Jean Cocteau down. Soon it became a sort of institution, known as the *Salon Vert*. The queen of it was the poetess – and my father's mistress – Louise de Vilmorin, who would stay in the embassy sometimes for weeks at a time. (My mother, who had no conception of jealousy, loved her almost as much as my father did, which was no surprise: she was one of the most fascinating women I have ever known. We became great friends, and she taught me lots of lovely old French songs, which I would sing to the guitar after dinner.) There were very few politicians, but writers, painters and actors in plenty. I remember the stage designer Christian Bérard, always known as Bébé, another regular attender. One evening he brought his little pug, which instantly deposited a small dry turd on the carpet. Without hesitation he picked it up and put it in his pocket; my mother said afterwards that it was the best manners she

---

★ I used to be an avid collector myself, until a Chinese friend pointed out that philately would get me nowhere.

had ever seen. But the company was by no means only French; there were visiting English, and Americans, and anyone whom my parents knew and happened to be passing through.

Looking back on those days, I have only one regret: I was two or three years too young. I was, I think, moderately precocious for my age, but all these celebrities were only names to me; I called Jean Cocteau Jean and mixed him dry martinis, but I had never read a word he had written. Had I been eighteen in 1944 instead of fifteen I would have known – and learnt – so much more. But there: no complaints. I was lucky to have been there at all.

My father deliberately scheduled his official tours to coincide with my holidays, so we visited every corner of the country. At Easter 1945, just as the war was about to end, we drove south – past the occasional rusting and burnt-out tank – for my first sight of the Mediterranean, the blueness of which – after the green-grey Channel – I shall never forget. In 1946, with a school friend, I bicycled through Provence from Avignon to Nice; but the combination of the intense heat, the battle-pitted roads and the endless punctures (thanks to synthetic rubber inner tubes) made the journey only a partial success. In 1947, while waiting to join the navy, I also spent six months living with a delightful Alsatian family in Strasbourg, attending lectures in German and Russian (which I had begun with a Linguaphone course at the age of twelve) at the university. I enjoyed Strasbourg enormously, apart from the hideous embarrassment caused by my landlady's constant attempt to de-virginise me, often five minutes before her husband was due home. (Now I come to think of it, she probably told him all about it every night in bed, to their combined chuckles.) When we left the embassy at the end of that year, we lived permanently in a lovely house on the lake just outside Chantilly. By this time, France had become my permanent home, the only one I had; and I grew to love it more and more.

It was during those embassy days that I had my first and last meeting with General de Gaulle. On 6 June 1947, the third anniversary of the D-Day landings, a commemorative service on one of the beaches was followed by a huge buffet lunch in an adjacent hotel. For some reason I could not get there, as my parents had, the night before; I therefore drove up on the morning of the day itself. I was seventeen, and it was my first long solo car journey. I had been hoping to arrive in time for lunch; but I got hopelessly lost among the narrow, unmarked lanes of Normandy and arrived only as the meal was ending. On my arrival my father introduced me to the general, who, much to my surprise, stood up to greet me, unwinding all six foot five of him. I was deeply honoured, but also ravenously hungry and all the food seemed to have been cleared away. One plate only remained: the general's, on which lay a large slice of apparently untouched apple pie. I was transfixed by the sight of it. 'Do you think he's going to eat it?' I asked my mother. 'How should I know?' she replied, 'you'd better ask him.' There followed a short battle between hunger and shyness; hunger won, and I went up to his table. '*Excusez-moi, mon général,*' I said, '*mais est-ce que vous allez manger votre tarte aux pommes?*' He immediately pushed the plate over, with a faint smile and an apology that he had spilt his cigarette ash all over it. Realising, I think, that I might be going a little too far, I said that it would be an honour to eat the general's ash – a remark that proved a distinct success. It was my only conversation with the great man; unlike most of those he had with my father or Winston Churchill it could hardly have been more friendly.*

This book is not written for professional historians, who will find nothing in it that they do not know already. It is intended only for the general reader, to whom the French rather charmingly refer as *l'homme moyen sensuel*, and is written in the belief that the average English-speaking man or woman has remarkably little knowledge of French history. We may know a bit about Napoleon or Joan of Arc or Louis XIV, but for most of us that's about it. In my own three schools we were taught only about the battles we won: Crécy and Poitiers, Agincourt and Waterloo.

So here is my attempt to fill in the blanks. I want to talk about the fate of the poor Templars at the hands of the odious Philip the Fair, and what happened to his daughters in the Tour de Nesle; about the wonderful Madame de Pompadour and the odious Madame de Maintenon; about Louis-Philippe, almost forgotten today but probably the best king France ever had; and that's just for a start. Chapter 1

---

* My father used to say that talking to de Gaulle was exactly like talking to the Eiffel Tower.

covers the ground pretty fast, taking us from the Gauls and Julius Caesar to Charlemagne, about eight centuries. But as we continue the pace inevitably slackens. Chapter 21 deals only with the five years of the Second World War. And with that we stop. All history books must have a clearly defined stopping place; if they do not, they drag on until they become works on current affairs, and though I might possibly have gone on to cover Vietnam and Algeria, nothing would have induced me to take on the European Union. No: the year 1945 closed one era and started a new one. The Fourth and Fifth Republics must find another chronicler. (Indeed, they have found several already.)

In introductions like this one, the author is generally allowed to include a personal note; such liberties are not however normally expected in the book itself. I have to admit that in my last two chapters I have occasionally broken this rule. In 1937 my father, Duff Cooper, was appointed First Lord of the Admiralty – the splendid name then given to the Minister for the Navy – an office which he resigned in protest against Neville Chamberlain's agreement with Hitler at Munich; in 1940 he joined Winston Churchill's cabinet as Minister of Information; then, after a period first in the Far East and then later doing secret work in London, in January 1944 he became British representative to General de Gaulle's French Committee in Algiers – going on immediately after the liberation of Paris in August to be Britain's first post-war ambassador there. In all these positions, in one way or another, he comes into our story. I could hardly leave him out.

I have transgressed in other ways too, notably in the matter of consistency, a virtue I have always deplored. In the pages that follow the reader will find dukes and ducs, counts and comtes, Johns and Jeans, Henrys and Henris. The choice has been dictated occasionally by risks of confusion, but more often by simple euphony – and I am well aware that names that sound right to my ear may well sound hideously wrong to others. If they do, I can only apologise.

I know I have said it before, but this is almost certainly the last book that I shall ever write. I have loved every moment of the work on it, and see it as a sort of thank-offering to France for all the happiness that glorious country has given me over the years.

John Julius Norwich
London, March 2018

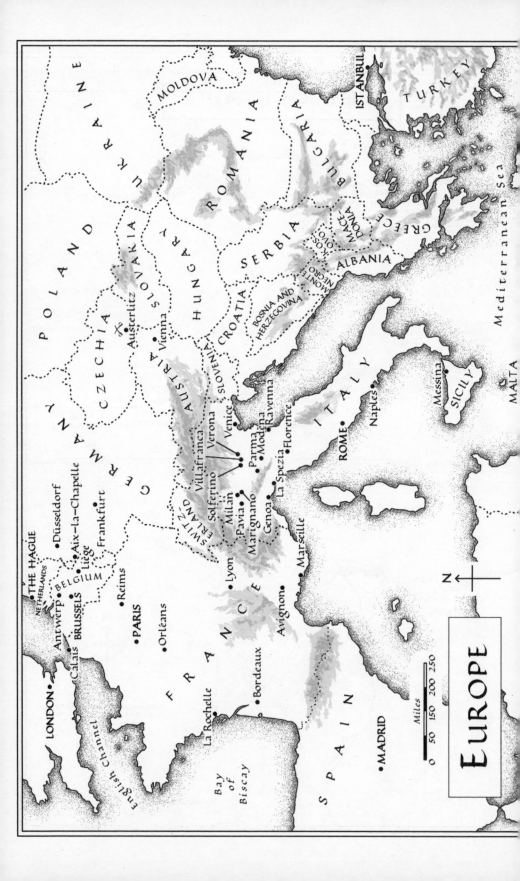

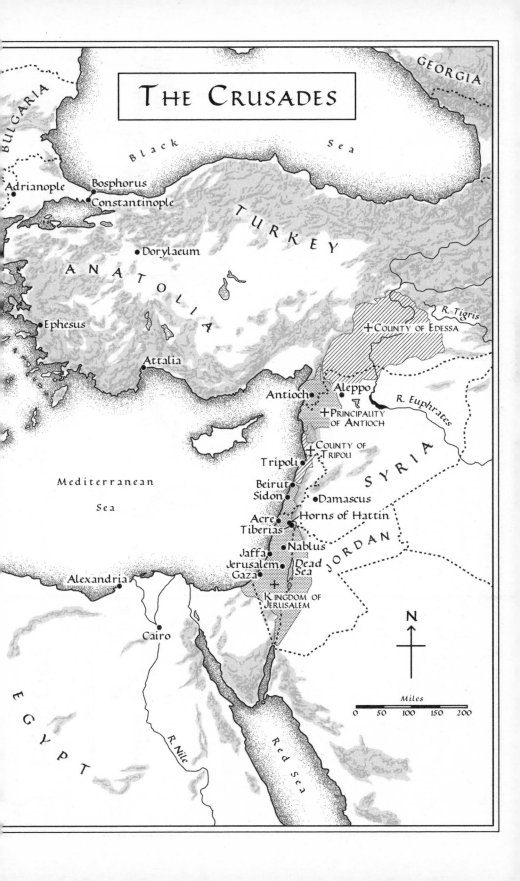

I

Very Dark Indeed

58 BC–843

La Gaule unie
Formant une seule nation
Animée d'un même esprit
Peut défier l'Univers.*
Inscription on Vercingetorix monument

THE FRENCH, LIKE the English, are a racial cocktail: Ligurians, Iberians, Phoenicians and Celts just for a start, not to mention the five hundred-odd different tribes of ancient Gaul. Prehistory, however – as I think I may have mentioned before – is best left to the prehistorians. It is perhaps worth recording that a party of adventurous Greeks from Phocaea on the Aegean coast of Asia Minor founded Marseille around 600 BC; but they left, alas, no surviving monuments behind them, and not much of their culture either. Our story really begins towards the end of the second century BC, when the Romans conquered the south-east corner of what is now France and made it their first province (hence the name it still bears), founding as its capital their new town of Aquae Sextiae, later to become Aix-en-Provence. Other splendid cities – Nîmes, Arles and Orange for a start – followed. Pliny the Elder thought it to be 'more like Italy than a province'. It must, in those days, have been a wonderful place to live.

When asked to name France's first hero, few outside the country would go further back than Charlemagne. But to the French, their

* A united Gaul/ Forming a single nation/ Animated by a common spirit/ Can defy the universe.

I

earliest important leader is Vercingetorix, whose name means either 'great warrior king' or 'king of great warriors'. This is all the more impressive since all the written accounts of him come from the Romans, the people with the most to gain from diminishing his reputation. The South of France was the Roman Empire's first and most profitable province – so profitable, indeed, that they were keen to expand. Seeing that neighbouring Gaul was, to quote Caesar's famous opening line 'divided in three parts', the wily Romans decided to manipulate the perpetual tensions between the three mutually hostile tribes. Caesar always claimed that his reasons for the invasion of Gaul in 58 BC were primarily defensive and pre-emptive; the Roman province had suffered countless raids – and several quite serious attacks – from the Gallic tribes to the north, and he was determined to prevent any further trouble. This may have been partly true, and the war certainly enabled Rome to establish its natural frontier on the Rhine. But Caesar was, as we know, ambitious. The Roman Republic was rapidly becoming a dictatorship, with more and more power being concentrated in fewer and fewer hands. If, as he hoped, he was ultimately to gather it all into his own, he would need an army; and a major campaign in Gaul would provide one.

Though a number of their tribes had attained a moderate degree of civilisation, the Gauls who opposed him were still essentially barbarians. They had no towns worthy of the name; their villages were often little more than clusters of mud-and-wattle huts, thatched with straw and surrounded with primitive stockades. Of agriculture they knew – or cared – practically nothing. They were herdsmen rather than farmers; they kept sheep and pigs, and they hunted the always plentiful deer. They were carnivores through and through. And they loved fighting. Their horsemanship probably outclassed even that of the Romans, and though they lacked the more sophisticated Roman weaponry their courage and determination, combined with the sheer weight of their numbers, made them formidable enemies. In several of their bloodiest encounters they were victorious; their ultimate defeat was probably due to the simple fact that their tribal society prevented them from achieving any degree of political unity.

Largely for this reason, during the first half of the war they produced no outstanding leaders; but early in 52 BC, when Caesar was away raising troops in Cisalpine Gaul,★ the thirty-year-old Vercingetorix became chieftain of the Arverni, who inhabited what is now the Auvergne. Immediately he began forging alliances with the neighbouring tribes, and soon acquired a sizeable army. The first step was to convince the Gauls that it was the Romans, not their own neighbours, who were the enemies. He proved an inspired strategist. His first encounter with the invaders, at Gergovia in the Massif Central, was a decisive victory; according to Caesar himself, the Romans lost some 750 legionaries, including 46 centurions. This brilliant young general represented the most serious threat that he had so far faced. Determined to force the Romans out at all costs, Vercingetorix set up a scorched earth policy. Every village that could offer food or shelter was destroyed: this guerrilla war, however, proved as costly to the inhabitants as the invaders. The tide turned when the tribes baulked at torching the wealthy settlement of Avaricum, arguing that its natural defences (it was built on a hillock and surrounded by marshland) would protect it. Vercingetorix reluctantly agreed, but was proved right when the Roman siege was successful. The following September at Alesia,† Caesar won the deciding victory. The Gauls, fleeing from the field, were intercepted by the Roman cavalry and slaughtered almost to a man. Among the few survivors was their leader himself, who made his formal surrender on the following day. The great Graeco-Roman historian Plutarch, writing around 100 AD, tells how Vercingetorix, 'the chief spring of all the war', put on his finest armour and fitted out his horse in its finest trappings before riding out of the gates. He then made a ceremonial turn around the enthroned Caesar, dismounted, threw off his armour and remained quietly sitting at Caesar's feet until he was led away to prison.

The temptation must have been to commit suicide, as Queen

★ 'Gaul on the hither (i.e. Italian) side of the Alps', a territory conquered by the Romans in the second century BC.

† Alesia has now vanished without trace, and there is much discussion about where it actually was. The most likely site is the hill known as Mont Auxois, which rises above the village of Alise-Sainte-Reine in Burgundy – even though historians have some difficulty in reconciling Caesar's account of the battle with the local geography.

Boadicea is believed to have done after her defeat in the following century. Instead, Vercingetorix was imprisoned for five years before being paraded, as part of Caesar's triumph, through the streets of Rome and finally meeting the customary death by strangulation. In the nineteenth century, thanks largely to Napoleon III, he was celebrated as the first of the great French nationalists. In Clermont-Ferrand there is a marvellous equestrian statue of the young general, his horse at full gallop; while on the supposed site of his last magnificent battle there stands another, its cylindrical plinth bearing the inscription quoted at the beginning of this chapter and endowing its subject with a wonderfully luxuriant walrus moustache, seldom rivalled until the days of Georges Clemenceau.

The war dragged on for another year or two, but after Alesia Gaul became to all intents and purposes Roman. The Gauls, heaven knows, had little reason to love their conquerors: Caesar had treated them harshly – often cruelly – and had shown them little respect. He had looted and plundered without mercy, had seized their gold and silver and had sold thousands of prisoners into slavery. But, as the years went by, they began to see that there were, after all, compensations. Nothing unites peoples like a common enemy, and under Roman governorship they became united as never before; their tribal system simply withered away. Three Roman governments were established, for the provinces of Gallia Celtica (with the headquarters of the Governor General in Lyon), Gallia Belgica, corresponding roughly to what is now Belgium, and Aquitania in the south-west corner; and at once they settled down to work. Within fifty years, the Gallic landscape was transformed just as Provence had been the best part of a century before – with new roads, cities, country villas, theatres, public baths and – for the first time – properly ploughed fields. Now, with a little effort, an educated Gaul might obtain Roman citizenship, with all the privileges that it entailed: as a *civis romanus*, he might even be entrusted with the command of an army, or the administration of a province.

Gaul was to remain Roman for some five hundred years – roughly the same period of time that separates us from the reign of King

Henry VIII. By the beginning of the second century, men had begun to talk of a new religion – one that had its origin in the far-distant province of Asia but was set to inaugurate profound changes across Europe and beyond. Like Roman civilisation itself, Christianity spread slowly northward from the Mediterranean. By 100 AD the first missionaries had reached Marseille; it was the best part of another century before the message got as far as Lyon. The Roman Empire – for an empire it had now become – was surprisingly relaxed where religion was concerned: so long as lip-service was paid to the cult of the emperor, people were free to believe more or less what they liked. The Christians, however, were not prepared to go even that far. Persecution was therefore inevitable. It began under Nero in 64, after the Great Fire of Rome, and continued spasmodically for the next 250 years, reaching its darkest hour in the reign of Diocletian at the turn of the third and fourth centuries. Martyrs were innumerable – among them Saint Denis, third-century Bishop of Paris, who when beheaded calmly picked up his severed head and walked several miles⋆ to the site of the abbey that bears his name while preaching a sermon on repentance.

But then came the dawn: in February 313 the two emperors Constantine the Great and Licinius published the Edict of Milan, which permanently established toleration for Christians throughout the empire; and twenty-five years later – though admittedly only when on his deathbed† – Constantine himself was baptised. In the centuries to come, though France would suffer more than her full share of religious wars, the sway of Christianity would not again be threatened until the Revolution.

By the beginning of the fifth century the Roman Empire was on its last legs, almost defenceless against the barbarians – Goths, Huns and Vandals – who swept down from the north-east, ever in search of warmer climates and more fertile lands. These were

⋆ But, as Madame du Deffand pointed out, *c'est le premier pas qui coûte* – it's the first step that counts.

† Cynics were not slow to point out the advantage of deathbed baptisms: they washed away all sins, but left you no time to commit any more; you therefore ascended to heaven pure as the driven snow.

not invading armies; they were migrations of whole peoples – men, women and children. The eastern Goths (Ostrogoths), the western Goths (Visigoths) and the Vandals were at least semi-civilised; they were all of Germanic origin and were Christians. Unfortunately they were also Arian heretics, steadfastly maintaining that Jesus Christ was not, as the orthodox believed, co-eternal and of one substance with God the Father, but that he had been created by Him at a specific time and for a specific purpose, as His chosen instrument for the salvation of the world. This put them at loggerheads with the Church; but they had no desire to destroy the empire, for which they had nothing but admiration. All they asked was *Lebensraum*, somewhere to settle; and settle they did.

The Huns, on the other hand, were Mongols, and barbarians through and through. Most of them still lived and slept in the open, disdaining all agriculture and even cooked food – though legend has it that they softened raw meat by massaging it between their thighs and the flanks of their horses as they rode. For clothing they favoured tunics made either from linen or, rather surprisingly, from the skins of field mice crudely stitched together; these they wore continuously, without ever removing them, until they dropped off of their own accord. (A law was passed in 416 banning anyone dressed in animal skins or with long hair from coming within the walls of Rome.) The leader of the Huns, Attila, was short, swarthy and snub-nosed, with a thin, straggling beard and beady little eyes set in a head too big for his body. Within the space of a few years he had made himself feared throughout Europe: more feared, perhaps, than any other single man – with the possible exception of Napoleon – before or since.

These were the people who crossed the Rhine early in 451 and smashed their way through France as far as Orléans, before being defeated on 20 June by a combined Roman and Visigothic force on the Catalaunian Plains, just outside Châlons-sur-Marne. Had Attila continued his advance, French history might have been very different; but the situation was quite bad enough without him. As the whole machinery of the empire began to crumble, even communications across the Alps were broken; orders from Rome simply failed to arrive. The abdication in 476 of the last Emperor of the West, the pathetic child Romulus Augustulus – his very name a double-diminutive – is no surprise.

With the Roman Empire effectively gone – though the Byzantine emperor in Constantinople continued to claim authority – Gaul disintegrated into a mass of small barbarian states under so-called kings, dukes and counts. As we know, however, nature abhors a vacuum; sooner or later one state becomes stronger than the rest and ultimately achieves domination. This time it was the Salian Franks. Relatively recent arrivals, they first appeared in the area in the second century, and over the next three hundred years gradually merged with the Gallo-Roman populations, giving their name to modern France in the process. In the later fourth century their kingdom had been founded by a certain Childeric, son of Merovech, and was consequently known as the Merovingian; and it was Childeric's son Clovis who became King of the Franks in 481. Uniting as he did nearly all Gaul under Merovingian rule, Clovis has a serious claim to have been the first King of France. His name, in its later version of 'Louis', was to be given to eighteen successors before the French monarchy ended.

It would be pleasant indeed if we could look upon Clovis in a heroic light, as we can Vercingetorix. Alas, we cannot. He was a monster. He eliminated his enemies occasionally in a legitimate battle – as he did in 486 at Soissons, when he effectively put an end to all Western Roman authority outside Italy – but far more frequently by cold-blooded murder, cheerfully assassinating all potential threats, Frankish and otherwise. It worked. By the time of his death around 513 – the precise date is uncertain – his rule extended over the greater part of modern France, Belgium and, to the east, a considerable distance into northern Germany. He had also reluctantly abandoned his initial Arianism – largely at the instigation of his Burgundian wife Clotilde – and on Christmas Day 496 had been received into the Catholic faith. On that day the fate of Arianism in France was sealed. Over the coming years more and more of his people were to follow his example, leading eventually to the religious unification of France and Germany, which was to endure for the next millennium. And it was thanks to that same baptism that, three hundred years later, Charlemagne and Pope Leo III could forge the alliance that gave birth to the Holy Roman Empire.

Throughout some two hundred and fifty of those years, the Merovingian dynasty ruled France – and came dangerously near to destroying it. The good old days of settled government were over; cities and towns were left to fall into ruin. The Frankish kings, immediately distinguishable from their subjects by their shoulder-length blondish hair – said to represent the sun's rays – journeyed endlessly from one village to the next with their officials and their men-at-arms, carrying with them their huge triple-sealed coffers of treasure and cheerfully waging countless and pointless little family wars. Even when they were not so engaged, violence was never far away. For an example we have to look no further than Clovis's son Chilperic, whom the later French chronicler Gregory of Tours dubbed 'the Nero and Herod of his time' and who took as his second wife Galswintha, daughter of the Visigothic King of Spain. The marriage was not a success, and one morning Galswintha was found strangled in her bed. This seems to have been the work of a serving-maid called Fredegund, who had long been the king's mistress and whom he married a short time later. Now it happened that Galswintha had a sister, Brunhilda, who was the wife of Chilperic's brother Sigebert. The murder caused a series of fearsome wars between the two brothers, until in 575, just when he had Chilperic at his mercy, Sigebert was murdered by Fredegund. Chilperic lived on for another nine years – during which time he introduced eye-gouging as a new sort of punishment – before being stabbed to death in 584 by an unknown assailant, probably one of Brunhilda's men; but he was posthumously avenged when his son Chlothar II seized Brunhilda and had her lashed to the tail of a horse, which was then sent off at a gallop.

There were in theory twenty-seven Merovingian kings, but it will be a relief to the reader that their detailed history will play no part in this book. In fact even this figure can be only a very conservative estimate, since for much of the time France was once again broken up into an infinity of minor kingdoms; frequently there were several kings reigning at the same time. Mention must be made, however, of one, simply since he is the most famous of them all: Dagobert I who, as every French schoolboy knows, put on his trousers inside out.* But he also did a good deal more. In 630 or thereabouts he annexed Alsace, the Vosges and the Ardennes, creating a new duchy, and he made Paris his capital. Though his debaucheries were famous – hence the perfectly idiotic little song – he was deeply religious and founded the Basilica of Saint-Denis, in which he was the first French king to be buried. From the tenth century onwards all but three were to join him there.

These were the dark ages; and in France they were very dark indeed. The only glimmering of light came from the Church which, unlike the State, remained firm and well organised. By this time the ecclesiastical hierarchy had been securely established, with a bishop in every diocese and a conscientious if largely uneducated priesthood. Meanwhile, thanks to the benefactions of the faithful and the efficient exaction of tithes, church property was steadily increasing – as indeed was church power: every ruler knew all too well that he was in constant danger of excommunication or even of an interdict, which would condemn not only himself, but all his subjects as well. The monasteries too were beginning to make their presence felt. They had long flourished in the east, where there was only one monastic order, that of St Basil; but the Basilians were essentially contemplatives and hermits. St Benedict, the sixth-century father of monasticism in the west, had very different ideas. The black-robed Benedictines were communities in the fullest sense of the word, dedicated to total obedience and hard physical labour, principally agricultural. But they also found time to study, to copy manuscripts – immensely important in the centuries before the invention of printing – and generally to keep alive a little spark of learning and humanity in the bleak, depressing world in which they lived.

---

* *Le bon roi Dagobert/ A mis sa culotte à l'envers./ Le grand saint Eloi/ Lui dit: 'Ô mon roi/ Votre Majesté/ Est mal culottée.'/ 'C'est vrai,' lui dit le roi,/ Je vais la remettre à l'endroit.'* Good King Dagobert/ put on his trousers inside out./ Great saint Eligius/ said: 'Oh, sire,/ Your Majesty/ Is badly trousered.'/ ''Tis true,' replied the king,/ 'I'll put them on properly.' The tune is regularly played to this day by the bells of the Hôtel de Ville at Saint-Denis.

Then the Muslims arrived. In 633 – just a year after the Prophet's death – they had burst out of Arabia. The speed of their advance was astonishing. Within thirty years they had captured not only Syria and Palestine, but also most of the Persian Empire, Afghanistan and part of the Punjab. They next turned their attention to the west. Constantinople looked too tough a nut to crack, so they swung to the left and headed along the shores of North Africa. At this point their pace became slower; it was not before the end of the century that they reached the Atlantic, and not till 711 that they were ready to cross the Straits of Gibraltar into Spain. But by 732, still less than a century after their eruption from their desert homeland, they had made their way over the Pyrenees and, according to tradition, pressed on as far as Tours – where, only 150 miles from Paris, they were checked at last by the Frankish king Charles Martel in an engagement which inspired Edward Gibbon to one of his most celebrated flights of fancy:

> A victorious line of march had been prolonged above a thousand miles from the Rock of Gibraltar to the banks of the Loire; the repetition of an equal space would have carried the Saracens to the confines of Poland and the Highlands of Scotland; the Rhine is not more impassable than the Nile or the Euphrates, and the Arabian fleet might have sailed without a naval combat into the mouth of the Thames. Perhaps the interpretation of the Koran would now be taught in the schools of Oxford, and her pupils might demonstrate to a circumcised people the sanctity and truth of the Revelation of Mahomet.

Modern historians are quick to point out that the Battle of Tours is scarcely mentioned by contemporary or near-contemporary Arab historians, and then only as a comparatively insignificant episode. The evidence of these writers strongly suggests that the troops encountered by Charles Martel were simply members of a raiding party who had ventured perhaps hundreds of miles in advance of the main army, and that the so-called battle was little more than a protracted skirmish; but we shall never know for sure. More important for us is Charles Martel himself. By the seventh and eighth centuries the Merovingian kings had descended so far into dissipation and debauchery that they had effectively ceased to rule. The real power of the kingdom now rested with a distinguished head official known as the Mayor of the Palace, a post that had by now become hereditary, and was held by succeeding members of the house of Pepin. Charles Martel – 'the Hammer' – had succeeded his father in 715, and was de facto ruler of France for the next quarter of a century until he was succeeded by his son Pepin the Short. Not a moment too soon, this spelt the end of the Merovingians. In 751 Pepin forced the last king, Childeric III, into a monastery and had himself proclaimed King of the Franks by the Pope. In doing so he founded a new royal dynasty, named after his father, the Carolingian.

Pepin was by far the greatest European ruler of his time; it was, however, his misfortune to be overshadowed by one greater still – his son Charles, better known as Charlemagne, who came to the throne on Pepin's death in 768. Thanks to his immense size, his energy, his health and his prodigious vigour – he had five legitimate wives and four supplementary spouses – and the simplicity of his life, wearing as he did (except on state occasions) the linen tunic, scarlet breeches and cross-gartering of his Frankish subjects, Charlemagne was to become an almost legendary figure, whose authority was to spread far more widely than that of his predecessors. In 774 he captured Pavia and proclaimed himself King of the Lombards; returning to Germany, he next subdued the heathen Saxons and converted them en masse to Christianity before going on to annex already-Christian Bavaria. An invasion of Spain was less successful – though it provided the inspiration for the first great epic ballad of western Europe, the '*Chanson de Roland*' – but Charles's subsequent campaign against the Avars in Hungary and Upper Austria resulted in the destruction of their kingdom as an independent state and its absorption within his own dominions. Thus, in little more than a generation, he had raised the kingdom of the Franks from being just one of the many semi-tribal European states to a single political unit of vast extent, unparalleled since the days of imperial Rome.

And he had done so, for most of the time at least, with the enthusiastic approval of the papacy. It was nearly half a century since Pope Stephen II had struggled across the Alps to seek help against the Lombards from Charles's father Pepin; Charles himself had been in Rome on a state visit in 774 when, as a young man of thirty-two, he had been welcomed by Pope Hadrian I and, deeply impressed by all he saw, had confirmed his father's donation of that central Italian territory which was to form the nucleus of the Papal States. And in 800 he came again, this time on more serious business. Pope Leo III, ever since his accession four years before, had been the victim of incessant intrigue on the part of a body of young Roman noblemen who were determined to remove him; and on 25 April he had actually been set upon in the street and beaten unconscious. Only by the greatest good fortune was he rescued by friends and removed to recover at Charles's court at Paderborn. Under the protection of Frankish agents he returned to Rome a few months later, only to find himself facing a number of serious charges fabricated by his enemies, including simony, perjury and adultery.

By whom, however, could he be tried? Who was qualified to pass judgement on the Vicar of Christ on Earth? In normal circumstances the only conceivable answer to that question would have been the emperor at Constantinople; but the imperial throne was at that time occupied by a woman, the Empress Irene. The fact that Irene had blinded and murdered her own son was, in the minds of both Leo and Charles, almost immaterial; it was enough that she was a woman. The female sex was believed to be incapable of governing, and by the old Salic tradition was debarred from doing so. As far as western Europe was concerned, the throne of the emperors was vacant.

Charles was fully aware, when he travelled to Rome towards the end of 800, that he had no more authority than Irene to sit in judgement at St Peter's; but he also knew that while the accusations remained unrefuted Christendom lacked not only an emperor but a pope as well, and he was determined to do all he could to clear Leo's name. As to the precise nature of his testimony, we can only guess; but on 23 December, at the high altar, the Pope swore a solemn oath on the Gospels that he was innocent of all the charges levelled against him – and the assembled synod accepted his word. Two days later, as Charles rose from his knees at the conclusion of the Christmas Mass, Leo laid the imperial crown upon his head, and the whole congregation cheered him to the echo. He had received, as his enemies were quick to point out, only a title: the crown brought with it not a single new subject or soldier, nor an acre of new territory. But that title was of more lasting significance than any number of conquests; it meant that, after more than four hundred years, there was once again an emperor in western Europe.

Historians have long debated whether the imperial coronation had been jointly planned by Leo and Charles or whether, as appeared at the time, the King of the Franks was taken completely by surprise. Of the two possibilities, the latter seems a good deal more likely. Charles had never shown the faintest interest in claiming imperial status, and for the rest of his life continued to style himself *Rex Francorum et Langobardorum* – King of the Franks and Lombards. Nor, above all, did he wish to owe any obligation to the Pope; there is every reason to believe that he was in fact extremely angry when he found such an obligation thrust upon him. Leo, on the other hand, was creating an all-important precedent. By crowning Charles as he did, he was emphasising that both the empire and Charles at its head were his creations. The world could make no mistake: it was to the Pope, and to the Pope only, that the emperor owed his title.

Although Charlemagne is credited with what is known as the Carolingian Renaissance, vastly increasing the numbers of monastic schools and scriptoria in his dominions, he himself was almost certainly illiterate. There is a theory that he could read a bit; but his biographer Einhard writes rather touchingly about the emperor's attempts to master the art of writing, telling us of the wax tablets he kept under his pillow to practise on when he could not sleep. He tried hard; 'but', wrote Einhard, 'his effort came too late in life and achieved little success'. In the words of Sir Kenneth Clark, he simply couldn't get the hang of it. It hardly mattered: this astonishing figure, more than half barbarian, kept his newly forged empire together by the strength of his personality alone; after his death in 814 its story is one of steady decline, first by family partitioning and finally with virtual disintegration following the extinction of his line in 888. It was probably inevitable: like, ultimately, its Roman predecessor, the Carolingian Empire carried with it the seeds of its own destruction. It was simply too big: proper communication across its length and breadth was impossible.

By his only son, Louis I the Pious, Charlemagne had three grandsons, who after much strife reached an agreement on the division of their territories in 843 at Verdun. Charles the Bald received, very roughly, all France west of the Rhône and the Saône; to Louis II the German went Austrasia (most of north-east France, Belgium and western Germany), Bavaria, Swabia and Saxony; while the youngest, Lothair, had to be content with a long strip of land running from the North Sea, along the valleys of the Meuse, the Rhine and the Rhône, then southwards through the length of Italy into Calabria. It was the partition at Verdun that created the modern countries of France and Germany, together with that territory between them, Alsace-Lorraine, that has bedevilled their relations ever since.

Furthermore, although Charlemagne's empire perished, his ideas did not. Henceforth, the western Europeans were almost able to forget about Constantinople. Before 800, there was only one empire in the Christian world – the empire of Augustus, Trajan and Hadrian, which was not a jot less Roman for having had its capital transferred to the Bosphorus. But the Bosphorus was nearly 1500 miles from Paris; the West now had an emperor of its own, on its very doorstep. And that emperor had been crowned by the Pope in Rome. In Merovingian days most of the kings had been little more than the leaders of bands of thugs; the Carolingians and their successors would be the Lord's anointed. Emperor and Pope would rule jointly, hand in hand, the former physically protecting the latter, the latter ensuring not only the spiritual but also the cultural well-being of his flock. To be sure, later centuries would see this system break down on countless occasions, but the thought was always there. After Charlemagne, Europe would never be the same again.

2

Their Own Destruction Sure

843–1151

If the Lord has called little worms like yourselves to the defence
of His heritage, do not conclude that His arm has grown shorter
or that His hand has lost its power . . . What is it, if not a
most perfect and direct intervention of the Almighty, that He
should admit murderers, ravishers, adulterers, perjurers and other
criminals for His service and for their salvation?

St Bernard of Clairvaux, to the Church in Germany,
The Letters of St Bernard of Clairvaux

SOON AFTER THE beginning of the tenth century a fair-haired
young Viking named Rollo led his fleet of longboats up the
Seine, to be enfeoffed in 911 by the Carolingian King Charles III
the Simple with most of the eastern half of modern Normandy.
He was not the earliest of the Norman invaders; the first wave had
descended from the Scandinavian forests and fjords over half a
century before, in 885 even attempting a siege of Paris. Since then
the migration had persisted at a fairly steady rate; but it was Rollo
above all who focused the energies and aspirations of his countrymen
and set them on the path of amalgamation and identification with
their new homeland. Already in 912 he and many of his followers
had received Christian baptism. (Some, according to Gibbon,
received it 'ten or twelve times, for the sake of the white garment
usually given at this ceremony'.) But within a generation or two
the Normans had become Frenchmen. The same was true of their
language. By 940 the old Norse tongue, while still spoken at Bayeux
and on the coast – where the newer immigrants presumably kept
it alive – was already forgotten at Rouen; and before the end of

the century it had died out altogether, leaving barely a trace behind.

Rollo and his friends were just the men to shake France out of her lethargy and end the chaos into which she had sunk. The later Carolingian kings had been no better than their Merovingian predecessors, and were further weakened by formidable rivals, members of the house of Robert the Strong, Count of Anjou and Blois and one of the greatest magnates in the country. This 'Robertian' house – later to be known as the Capetian – had produced elected kings* who had often alternated with the Carolingians. But with the country still so unclearly defined and communications still rudimentary – far worse than they had been in Roman days – government, such as it was, was largely local and lay principally in hands of the stronger, richer landowners, those who were later to crystallise into the aristocracy, who gathered their followers around them and slowly evolved what we now know as the feudal system. The local lord would build himself a castle, the village would cluster round it, the villagers taking refuge inside it when necessary. Each would swear an oath of fealty to the lord, to fight for him when summoned to do so. As a system it may have been far from perfect, but it was a lot better than anarchy.

The Carolingians limped on until the death, in May 987 as the result of an accident while hunting in the forest of Senlis, of Louis V the Lazy – or, as the French call him when they mention him at all, le Fainéant, the do-nothing. Since he left no legitimate offspring, the lords of France met to elect his successor. There were two candidates for the crown. The first was the Carolingian Duke Charles of Lower Lorraine; the second was Hugh Capet,[†] a great-grandson of Robert the Strong. According to the principle of heredity, Charles was obviously the legitimate king; but at an early stage of the proceedings the Archbishop of Rouen made his preference clear: 'The throne', he thundered, 'is not acquired by hereditary right; he

---

* The monarchy – it was really more of a polyarchy – was sometimes hereditary, sometimes elected: a recipe for chaos if ever there was one.

† The name Capet sounds remarkably plebeian, as indeed it is. It comes from the Latin capatus, which simply means 'wearing a cloak'. It seems to have been first attached to Hugh as a nickname; it is surprising indeed that it should be now applied to his dynasty.

who is elected to it should be distinguished not merely by the nobility of his birth but by the wisdom of his mind.' His words were heeded, and Hugh Capet was awarded the crown of France.

It was, as he must have known perfectly well, a poisoned chalice. For a start, he was surrounded by a number of great feudal lords – the Dukes of Anjou, Aquitaine and (more recently) Normandy, the Counts of Flanders and Blois – who had risen up over the past century and who considered themselves every bit as worthy of the supreme power as he was himself. Had they combined against him he could not have raised a finger in his own defence. In the south, the crown was hardly recognised at all; there the Count of Toulouse was far more respected than the king could ever be. Hugh's subjects did not even share a common language; Celtic was spoken in Brittany, German along his eastern borders, Flemish to the north, the *langue d'oc* in Provence and Aquitaine, to say nothing of at least a dozen dialects across the country.

What did the king have on his side? It helped, of course, to have been unanimously elected; but above all he had the Church. And the Church gave him all it had got, including probably the most elaborate and impressive coronation service it had ever mounted. The oil with which Hugh was anointed – not just on the forehead but on various other parts of his body as well – was, it was claimed, the same as used by St Remigius to anoint Clovis five centuries before, when it had been brought down by a dove from heaven. After his consecration the king took communion in both kinds, and when he stepped out of the Cathedral of Noyon★ into the sunshine, the crown radiant on his head, he must have seemed to many of those present a semi-divine being. He was almost certainly the first of the French kings to be credited with the power of curing scrofula ('the king's evil') – a miracle which he is said to have performed on many occasions.

Yet never for a minute could Hugh Capet have felt like a king. Between Paris and Orléans he possessed towns and estates extending over four hundred square miles; there were also a couple of small properties near Angers and Chartres. But nowhere else in France

---

★ Where Charlemagne had been crowned co-King of the Franks in 768.

was it safe for him to travel; to do so would have been to risk almost certain capture, and though his life might perhaps have been spared he was sure to be held to ransom – quite probably in extremely unpleasant conditions. 'Charlemagne's successor', remarked a contemporary, 'did not dare leave home.' It was doubtless this uncertainty, this constant feeling of living a lie, that prevented him from ever calling himself King of France; nor indeed did any of his successors do so until Philip Augustus at the end of the twelfth century. 'King of the Franks' – *Roi des Francs* – was the title with which he was crowned; and King of the Franks he remained.

But he worked hard all his life to make France a true nation – although, inevitably, he left the job unfinished. He died on 24 October 996 in Paris, which he had made his permanent capital, and was buried in the Abbey of Saint-Denis. He was succeeded by his son Robert, whom he had very sensibly arranged to have anointed in his own lifetime. Although he was not the first of his family to reign, he is rightly regarded as the founder of the Capetian dynasty, which was to rule France directly until the death of Charles the Fair in 1328. In fact the House of Valois which followed it and the House of Bourbon which followed Valois were both cadet branches of the Capetian line; that line could thus be said to have lasted for over eight and a half centuries, until the abdication in 1848 of France's last king.

The tenth century had seen eight French monarchs. The eleventh saw only three: Hugh Capet's son Robert the Pious, who reigned till 1031, his grandson Henry I who died in 1060 and his great-grandson Philip I, known to his subjects as *L'Amoureux*, the Amorous, who was to occupy the throne for the next forty-eight years, a remarkable feat of endurance for the time. This says much for the stability that France had achieved in a hundred years. Succession was now virtually undisputed, the royal authority was much extended and France was well on the way to becoming a nation. Two other events marked the century. One was the Norman Conquest of Britain; the other was the First Crusade.

The recently arrived Normans were a people very different from

the subjects of the Capetian kings. They had quickly shown themselves to be anything but the Viking savages that the French had
originally supposed; on the contrary, they had absorbed the Latin
culture, language and religion of their hosts with astonishing speed.
They had moreover demonstrated qualities not normally associated
with early medieval France: an extraordinary degree of energy and
vigour, combined with that characteristic love of travel and adventure without which they would never have left their homes. They
administered their lands with great efficiency; they showed a deep
knowledge and respect for the law; and they had already begun to
build cathedrals and churches far more beautiful – and more technically advanced – than those of their French hosts. Their historic
conquest of 1066 affected France almost as much as it did Britain;
Duke William the Bastard was no longer simply one of the king's
leading vassals, he was now a powerful sovereign in his own right,
and a serious rival to the King of France.

And then there was the Crusade. On Tuesday 27 November 1095
Pope Urban II addressed the Council of Clermont (now Clermont-
Ferrand), concluding his speech with an impassioned appeal. The
continued occupation of the Holy Places – and above all of Jerusalem
itself – by the infidel was, he declared, an affront to Christendom;
he had been informed that pilgrims were being subjected to every
kind of humiliation and indignity. It was now the duty of all good
Christians to take up arms against those who had desecrated the
ground on which Jesus Christ had trod and to recover it for their
own true faith. In the months that followed, the Pope's words were
carried by Urban himself through France and Italy and by a whole
army of preachers to every corner of western Europe. The response
was tremendous; from as far afield as Scotland men hastened to take
up the Cross. Neither the Emperor Henry IV nor King Philip the
Amorous – who, not altogether surprisingly, had recently been excommunicated by the Pope for adultery – were on sufficiently good terms
with Rome to join the Crusade, but this was perhaps just as well:
Urban was determined that the great enterprise should be under
ecclesiastical control, and nominated as leader and as his official legate
one of the relatively few French churchmen to have already made
the pilgrimage to Jerusalem, Bishop Adhemar of Le Puy. The bishop

was to be accompanied, however, by several powerful magnates: Raymond of Saint-Gilles, Count of Toulouse, the oldest, richest and most distinguished of them all; the French king's brother Count Hugh of Vermandois, who arrived severely shaken after a disastrous shipwreck in the Adriatic; Count Robert II of Flanders; Duke Robert of Normandy, son of the Conqueror, and his cousin Count Stephen of Blois; and Godfrey of Bouillon, Duke of Lower Lorraine. With Godfrey came his brother Baldwin of Boulogne who, as a younger son without a patrimony, had brought along his wife and children and was determined to carve out a kingdom for himself in the east.

Urban himself was a Frenchman; France already had its ideals of chivalry, and it was clearly an overwhelmingly French crusade. The French knights took to it with enthusiasm and, contrary to the expectations of many, it turned out to be a resounding, if undeserved, success. On 3 June 1098 the Crusaders recovered Antioch; and finally, on Friday 15 July 1099, amid scenes of hideous carnage, the soldiers of Christ battered their way into Jerusalem, where they celebrated their victory by slaughtering all the Muslims in the city and burning all the Jews alive in the main synagogue. An election was immediately held to decide upon the future ruler. Raymond of Toulouse was the obvious candidate, but he refused. He was too unpopular, and he knew it; he would never have been able to count on his colleagues for their obedience and support. The choice eventually fell on Godfrey of Bouillon, less for his military or diplomatic abilities than for his genuine piety and irreproachable private life. He accepted, declining only – in the city where Christ had worn the Crown of Thorns – to bear the title of King. Instead, he took that of *Advocatus Sancti Sepulchri*, Defender of the Holy Sepulchre, and was always addressed as *dux* or *princeps*, never as *rex*. But Godfrey lived for only a year after the capture of the city, and his successors were less punctilious; they were all crowned kings, of the Latin Kingdom of Jerusalem.

The Crusader kingdom was of course entirely independent of France; but since nearly all its most powerful lords were French and with French its official language, it was inevitably France that derived the greatest advantage. From a commercial point of view, a French presence in the Levant was invaluable as new routes and markets were opened up; economically France profited – at least indirectly – by a vast increase in the pilgrim traffic; meanwhile at home the French monarchy became appreciably more secure, since many of the more dangerous feudal lords had felt it incumbent upon them to go to the Holy Land, whence a good many of them never returned.

Philip the Amorous died at last, on 29 July 1108, to be succeeded by his son Louis VI, the Fat. Louis was well-named – by the end of his reign he was barely able to rise from his throne without help – but until his increasing weight made it impossible he was essentially a warrior king, the strongest since Charlemagne, who devoted his life to the consolidation of Capetian supremacy throughout his domains. His predecessors had done their best; but at the time of his accession the leading dukes and counts of the realm – to say nothing of William of Normandy – were still so powerful that the king had little real authority beyond the confines of the Ile de France, the region immediately surrounding Paris. Nor were the great noblemen the only problem; more troublesome still were the lesser fry, who can best be described as robber barons. They lived, quite simply, by brigandage, charging illegal tolls on passing merchants and pilgrims and looting churches and abbeys, with perhaps occasionally a little mild kidnapping on the side.

Thanks to his loyal adviser, biographer and friend the Abbot Suger of Saint-Denis, we have detailed accounts of all Louis's many campaigns, which also included encounters with two English kings: William Rufus, the Conqueror's son and successor, and William's younger brother Henry I, who soundly defeated Louis at Brémule in 1119. But defeats in Louis's military career were a good deal less frequent than victories, and when he died in 1137 he left behind him a France which, if not yet completely tranquil, was at least to a very large extent subdued. One of his greatest gifts to his kingdom was, however, not political or administrative but dynastic. Only a few weeks before his death, he married his son and heir, another Louis, to the greatest heiress in France, Eleanor of Aquitaine, who brought as her dowry the whole of the south-west as far as the Pyrenees.

They were, alas, an ill-assorted couple. Louis VII, his father's second son, had originally been determined to enter the Church; it was only after the accidental death of his older brother that he had been obliged to change his plans. Deeply – almost fanatically – religious, he radiated an aura of lugubrious piety which depressed everyone around him and drove his young wife to distraction. 'I have married a monk', she complained, 'not a king.' She herself was an outstandingly beautiful, high-spirited girl who hated the frosty, austere life of her husband's court, and made no secret of her longing to be back in the relaxed, freewheeling, troubadour life of the court of Aquitaine. And things got rapidly worse. In 1142 Louis, most uncharacteristically, allowed Raoul of Vermandois, Seneschal of France, to repudiate his wife, Eléonore, sister of Count Theobald II of Champagne – and to marry Petronilla of Aquitaine, Eleanor's younger sister. This so angered Theobald that he declared war. The fighting went on for two years, and in 1143 Louis's army had set fire to the little town of Vitry – now Vitry-le-François – on the Marne; its inhabitants – more than a thousand men, women and children – were burnt alive in the church where they had taken refuge. Louis had watched the conflagration from a distance, power-less to prevent it. Ever since, the memory of that dreadful day had haunted him. The responsibility he knew to be his; nothing less than a Crusade, with its promise of a plenary indulgence for all sins, could be sufficient atonement.

Nearly half a century before, in the year 1098, Count Baldwin of Boulogne had left the main army of the First Crusade as it advanced into the Holy Land and had struck off to the east, there to found a principality of his own at Edessa on the banks of the Euphrates. He had not stayed there long; two years later he had succeeded his brother as King of Jerusalem. But Edessa had continued as a semi-independent Christian state, under the theoretical suzerainty of the main kingdom, until 1144, when it fell after a twenty-five-day siege to an Arab army under Imad-ed-Din Zengi, Atabeg of Mosul.

The news of its fall horrified all Christendom. To the peoples of western Europe, who had seen the initial success of the First Crusade as an obvious mark of divine favour, it called into question all their comfortably held opinions. After less than half a century the Cross had once again given way to the Crescent. How had it happened? Was it not a manifestation of the wrath of God? Travellers to the east had for some time been returning with reports of a widespread degeneracy among the Franks of Outremer. Could it be that they were no longer deemed worthy to guard the Holy Places against the infidel?

Whatever those Franks may have thought about their spiritual worth, their military weakness was beyond dispute. The first great wave of crusading enthusiasm was now spent. Immigration from the west had slowed to a trickle; many of the pilgrims still arrived, according to the ancient tradition, unarmed; and even for those who came prepared to wield a sword, a single summer campaign usually proved more than enough. The only permanent standing army – if such it could be called – was formed by the two military orders, the Templars and the Hospitallers; but they alone could not hope to hold out against Muslim leaders like Zengi. Reinforcements were desperately needed. There was nothing for it: the Pope must declare another Crusade.

Pope Eugenius III – who was at that time in exile in France* – readily agreed. This time he decided on secular leadership; and when he came to consider the princes of the West, he could see only one suitable candidate. Ideally, the honour should have fallen to the Holy Roman Emperor Conrad of Hohenstaufen, but Conrad was beset with his own difficulties in Germany. King Stephen of England had had a civil war on his hands for six years already. King Roger of Sicily was, for any number of reasons, out of the question. The only possible choice was Louis VII of France.

Louis asked nothing better. At Christmas 1145 he informed his assembled tenants-in-chief of his determination to take the Cross and called upon them to follow him. Odo of Deuil, who was to be his chaplain on the expedition, reports that 'the King blazed and shone with the zeal of faith and his contempt for earthly pleasures and temporal glories, so that his person was an example more

---

* Rome was at that time in the hands of a fanatical monk, Arnold of Brescia, who cherished a passionate hatred for the temporal power of the Church.

persuasive than any speech could be'. It was not, however, persuasive enough. His vassals' reaction was disappointing. They had their responsibilities at home to consider. Besides, the reports they had heard about life in Outremer suggested that their dissolute compatriots had probably brought the disaster on themselves; let them work out their own salvation. That hard-headed churchman Abbot Suger, former guardian and tutor to the king, also turned his face firmly against the proposal. But Louis had made up his mind. If he himself could not fill the hearts of his vassals with crusading fire, he must find someone who could. He wrote to the Pope, accepting his invitation. Then he sent for St Bernard of Clairvaux.

St Bernard was by now in his middle fifties, and far and away the most powerful spiritual force in Europe. To an objective observer of our own day, safely out of range of that astonishing personal magnetism with which he effortlessly dominated all those with whom he came in contact, he is not an attractive figure. Tall and haggard, his features clouded by the constant pain that resulted from a lifetime of fasting, he was consumed by a blazing religious zeal that left no room for tolerance or moderation. His public life had begun in 1115 when the Abbot of Cîteaux, the Englishman Stephen Harding, had effectively released him from monastic discipline by sending him off to found a daughter house at Clairvaux in Champagne. From that moment on, almost despite himself, his influence spread; and for the last twenty-five years of his life he was constantly on the move, preaching, persuading, arguing, writing innumerable letters and compulsively plunging into the thick of every controversy in which he believed the basic principles of Christianity to be involved.

To Bernard, here was a cause after his own heart. Exhausted as he was, broken in health and by now genuinely longing for retirement in the peace of his abbey, he responded to the call with all that extraordinary fervour that had made him, for over a quarter of a century, the dominant spiritual voice of Christendom. Willingly he agreed to launch the Crusade in France, and to address the assembly that the king had summoned for the following Easter at Vézelay. At once the magic of his name began to do its work, and as the appointed day approached men and women from every corner of France poured into the city; since there were far too many to be packed into the cathedral, a great wooden platform was hastily erected on the hillside.★ Here, on Palm Sunday morning, 31 March 1146, Bernard appeared before the multitude to make one of the most fateful speeches of his career. His body, writes Odo, was so frail that it seemed already to be touched by death. At his side was the king, already displaying on his breast the cross which the Pope had sent him in token of his decision. Together the two mounted the platform; and Bernard began to speak.

The text of the exhortation which followed has not come down to us; but with Bernard it was the manner of his delivery rather than the words themselves that made the real impact on his hearers. All we know is that his voice rang out across the meadow 'like a celestial organ', and that as he spoke the crowd, silent at first, began to cry out for crosses of their own. Bundles of these, cut in rough cloth, had already been prepared for distribution; when the supply was exhausted, the abbot flung off his own robe and began tearing it into strips to make more. Others followed his example, and he and his helpers were still stitching as night fell.

His success at Vézelay acted on St Bernard like a tonic. No longer did he contemplate a return to Clairvaux. Instead, he swept through Burgundy, Lorraine and Flanders to Germany, preaching the Crusade to packed churches wherever he went. His line of approach, always direct, was at times alarmingly so. By autumn Germany too was aflame; even the Emperor Conrad, who had at first predictably refused to have any part in the Crusade, repented after a Christmas castigation from Bernard and agreed to take the Cross.

Pope Eugenius received this last news with alarm. Not for the first time, the Abbot of Clairvaux had exceeded his brief. His instructions had been to preach the Crusade in France; no one had said anything about Germany. The Germans and the French were bound to squabble – they always did – and their inevitable jockey-ings for position might easily lead to the foundering of the whole enterprise. But it was too late to change things now. The oaths had been sworn, the vows taken. Eugenius could hardly start discouraging would-be Crusaders before the movement was even on its way.

★ It stood until 1789, when it was destroyed by the Revolution.

St Bernard's letter to the German clergy had been, perhaps, more prophetic than he knew. Largely because of the promise of plenary absolution which accompanied all crusades, their armies tended to be even more disreputable than most others of the Middle Ages; and the German host that set off, about twenty thousand strong, from Ratisbon at the end of May 1147, seems to have contained more than the usual quota of undesirables, ranging from the occasional religious maniac to the usual collection of footloose ne'er-do-wells and fugitives from justice. Hardly had they entered Byzantine territory than they began pillaging the countryside, raping, ravaging and even murdering as the mood took them. Often the leaders themselves set a poor example to those that followed behind. At Adrianople (now Edirne) Conrad's nephew and second-in-command, the young Duke Frederick of Swabia – better known to history by his subsequent nickname of Barbarossa – burnt down a whole monastery in reprisal for an attack by local brigands, slaughtering all the perfectly innocent monks.

Even before the populations along the route had recovered from the shock, the French army appeared on the western horizon. It was a rather smaller force than that of the Germans, and on the whole more seemly. Discipline was better, and the presence of many distinguished ladies – including Queen Eleanor herself – accompanying their husbands doubtless exercised a further moderating influence. Yet their progress was still far from smooth. The Balkan peasantry by now showed itself frankly hostile – and no wonder – asking ridiculous prices for what little food it had left to sell. Mistrust soon became mutual, leading to sharp practices on both sides. Thus, long before they reached Constantinople, the French had begun to feel resentment against Germans and Greeks alike; and when they finally arrived on 4 October they were scandalised to hear that the Byzantine emperor, Manuel, had chosen that moment to conclude a truce with the Seljuk Turks.

Although Louis could not have been expected to appreciate the fact, it was a sensible precaution for Manuel to take. The presence of the French and German armies at the very gates of his capital constituted a far more serious immediate danger than the Turks in Asia. The emperor knew that in both camps, French and German, there were extreme elements pressing for a combined western attack on Constantinople; and indeed just a few days later St Bernard's cousin Geoffrey, Bishop of Langres, was formally to propose such a course to the king. Only by deliberately spreading reports of a huge Turkish army massing in Anatolia, and implying that if the Franks did not make haste to pass through the hostile territory they might never manage to do so, could Manuel succeed in saving the situation. Meanwhile he flattered Louis – and kept him occupied – with a constant round of banquets and lavish entertainments, while arranging passage for the king and his army across the Bosphorus into Asia at the earliest possible moment.

As he bade farewell to his unwelcome guests and watched the ferry boats, laden to the gunwales with men and animals, shuttling across the Bosphorus, the emperor foresaw better than anyone the dangers that awaited the Franks on the second stage of their journey. He himself had only recently returned from an Anatolian campaign; and though his stories of the gathering Turkish hordes had been exaggerated, he had seen the Crusaders for himself and he must have known that their shambling forces, already lacking in morale and discipline, would stand little chance if attacked by the Seljuk cavalry. He had equipped them with provisions and guides; he had warned them about the scarcity of water; and he had advised them not to take the direct route through the hinterland but to keep to the coast, which was still largely under Byzantine control. He could do no more. If, after all these precautions, those idiots still persisted in getting themselves slaughtered, they would have only themselves to blame. He, for his part, would be sorry – but not, perhaps, inconsolable.

It cannot have been more than a few days after bidding them farewell that Manuel received a report, carried by swift messengers from Asia Minor. The German army had been taken by surprise by the Turks near Dorylaeum (now Eskişehir) and massacred. Conrad himself had escaped, and had returned to join the French at Nicaea, but nine-tenths of his men now lay dead amid the wreckage of their camp.

★

The Second Crusade had not got off to a good start. Conrad, with such of his Germans as remained after the slaughter at Dorylaeum, had marched on with the French as far as Ephesus, where the army had stopped to celebrate Christmas. There he had fallen gravely ill. Leaving his compatriots to continue the journey without him, he had returned to Constantinople to recover, and there he had stayed as a guest in the imperial palace till March 1148, when Manuel had put ships at his disposal to take him to Palestine. The French and their ladies, meanwhile, though they had fared rather better than the Germans, had nevertheless had a terrifying passage through Anatolia and had suffered considerably at Turkish hands. Although this was largely the fault of King Louis himself, who had ignored Manuel's warnings to keep to the coast, he persisted in attributing almost every encounter with the enemy to Byzantine carelessness or treachery or both, and rapidly built up an almost psychopathic resentment against the Greeks. At last, in despair, he, his household and as much of his cavalry as could be accommodated had sailed from Attalia (Antalya), leaving the rest of his army and all the pilgrims to struggle on by land as best they might. It was late in the spring before the remnant of the great host that had set out so confidently the previous year dragged itself miserably into Antioch.

And that was only the beginning of the trouble. The mighty Zengi was dead, but his mantle had passed to his still greater son Nur-ed-Din, whose stronghold at Aleppo had now become the focus of Muslim opposition to the Franks. Aleppo should therefore have been the Crusaders' first objective, and within days of his arrival in Antioch Louis found himself under pressure from Prince Raymond to mount an immediate attack on the city. He had refused – typically – on the grounds that he must first pray at the Holy Sepulchre; whereat Queen Eleanor, whose affection for her husband had not been increased by the dangers and discomforts of the journey from France and whose relations with Raymond were already suspected of having passed some way beyond the strictly avuncular, announced her intention of remaining at Antioch and suing for divorce. She and her husband were distant cousins; the question of consanguinity had been conveniently overlooked at the time of their marriage, but if resurrected could still prove embarrassing – and Eleanor knew it.

Louis, who for all his moroseness was not without spirit in moments of crisis, ignored his wife's protests and dragged her forcibly on to Jerusalem – though not before he had succeeded in so antagonising Raymond that the latter henceforth refused to play any further part in the Crusade. No one doubted that the king had carried off the situation with what dignity he could; but the effect on his reputation, particularly at such a moment, had certainly been unfortunate to say the least. He and a tight-lipped Eleanor arrived at the Holy City in May, soon after Conrad. They were welcomed with due ceremony by Queen Melisande and her son Baldwin III, now eighteen; and there they remained until, on 24 June, all the Crusaders were invited to Acre to discuss their plan of action. It did not take them long to reach a decision: every man and beast available must be immediately mobilised for a concerted attack on Damascus.

Why Damascus was chosen as their first objective we shall never understand. It was the only important Arab state in all the Levant to continue hostile to Nur-ed-Din; as such it could, and should, have been an invaluable ally. By attacking it, the Franks drove the city against its will into Nur-ed-Din's Muslim confederation, and in doing so made their own destruction sure. They arrived to find the city walls strong, the defenders determined. On the second day the besieging army, after yet another of those disastrous decisions that characterised the whole Crusade, moved its camp to an area along the south-eastern section of the walls, devoid alike of shade and water. The Palestinian barons, already at loggerheads over the future of the city when captured, suddenly lost their nerve and began to urge retreat. There were dark rumours of bribery and treason. Louis and Conrad were shocked and disgusted, but soon they too were made to understand the facts of the situation. To continue the siege would mean not only the passing of Damascus into the hands of Nur-ed-Din but also, given the universal breakdown of morale, the almost certain annihilation of their entire army. On 28 July, just five days after beginning the campaign, they ordered withdrawal.

There is no part of the Syrian desert more shattering to the spirit than that dark grey, featureless expanse of sand and basalt that lies between Damascus and Tiberias. Retreating across it in the height of the Arabian summer, the remorseless sun and scorching desert wind full in their faces, harried incessantly by mounted Arab archers and leaving a stinking trail of dead men and horses in their wake, the Crusaders must have felt despair heavy upon them. This was the end. Their losses, both in material and human life, had been immense. They had neither the will nor the wherewithal to continue. Worst of all was the shame. Having travelled for the best part of a year, often in conditions of mortal danger, having suffered agonies of thirst, hunger and sickness and the bitterest extremes of heat and cold, this once-glorious army that had purported to enshrine all the ideals of the Christian West had given up the whole thing after just four days' fighting, having regained not one inch of Muslim territory. It was the ultimate of humiliations – one that neither they nor their enemies would forget.

Much as he longed to put his disastrous Crusade behind him, King Louis was in no hurry to leave Outremer. Like so many travellers before and since, he may have been reluctant to exchange the gentle sunshine of a Palestinian winter for the stormy seas and snowbound roads which lay between himself and his kingdom. He knew, too, that his marriage was past redemption. Once back in Paris he would have to face all the unpleasantness of a divorce and the political repercussions that could not but follow. Not till the spring of 1149 did he set his face reluctantly for home. This time he and Eleanor had resolved to travel by sea, but had been unwise enough to entrust themselves to Sicilian transport – dangerous craft in which to brave Byzantine waters.* Somewhere in the southern Aegean they encountered a Greek fleet, which turned at once to the attack. Louis managed to escape by hastily running up a French flag; but one of his escort vessels, containing several members of his suite and nearly all his baggage, was captured and borne off in triumph to Constantinople. Queen Eleanor, whose relations with her husband were now such that she was travelling in a separate vessel, narrowly avoided a similar fate; she was rescued by Sicilian warships just in time.

Finally, on 29 July 1149, Louis landed in Sicily, where Eleanor

---

* Sicily at this time was ruled by the Norman King Roger II, a mortal enemy of Byzantium.

was obliged to join him and where they stayed a few days as guests of King Roger. They then moved on to Tusculum, the nearest town to Rome in which Pope Eugenius, still in exile, could safely install himself. A gentle, kind-hearted man, he hated to see people unhappy; and the sight of Louis and Eleanor, oppressed by the double failure of the Crusade and of their marriage, seems to have caused him genuine distress. John of Salisbury, who was employed in the Curia at that time, has left us a curiously touching account of the Pope's attempts at reconciliation:

> He commanded, under pain of anathema, that no word should be spoken against their marriage and that it should not be dissolved under any pretext whatever. This ruling plainly delighted the King, for he loved the Queen passionately, in an almost childish way. The Pope made them sleep in the same bed, which he had decked with priceless hangings of his own; and daily during their brief visit he strove by friendly converse to restore the love between them. He heaped gifts upon them; and when the time for their departure came he could not hold back his tears.

Those tears were perhaps made all the more copious by the knowledge that his efforts had been in vain. Eleanor's mind was made up and neither he nor anyone else could change it. For the time being, however, she was prepared to keep up appearances, accompanying her husband to Rome where they were cordially received by the Senate and where Louis prostrated himself as usual at all the principal shrines; and so back across the Alps to Paris. It was to be another two and a half years before the marriage was finally dissolved on grounds of consanguinity; but the queen was still young, and still on the threshold of that astonishing career in which, as wife of one of England's greatest kings and mother of two of its worst, she was to continue to influence European history for over half a century.

3

The Gift of *Excalibur*

1151–1223

> When the King of France was known to be entering the port
> of Messina, the natives of every age and sex rushed forth to
> see so celebrated a king; but he, content with a single ship,
> entered the port of the citadel privately, so that those who
> awaited him along the shore saw this as a proof of his weakness;
> such a man, they said, was not likely to be the performer of
> any great matter, shrinking in such fashion from the eye of his
> fellows . . .
>
> > Geoffrey of Vinsauf, *Itinerary of Richard I*
> > *and Others to the Holy Land*

A T THE AGE of thirteen, while hunting in the forest of
Compiègne, Louis VII's son Philip became separated from the
rest of the party and was soon hopelessly lost. Exhausted by cold
and hunger, he was eventually discovered by a local charcoal-burner,
but not before he had contracted an alarmingly high fever. King
Louis went on a pilgrimage to Canterbury to pray – successfully
– for his son's recovery, but suffered a paralytic stroke on his way
back to Paris. On 1 November 1179, according to the old Capetian
tradition, he had Philip crowned in Reims Cathedral by its cardinal
archbishop, the delightfully named Guillaume aux Blanches Mains,
but was, alas, too ill to attend the ceremony himself. He died less
than a year later.

He had been a good king on the whole, although never a happy
one. The Second Crusade had been a humiliation from which he
never fully recovered; but it was not the last. On 18 May 1152, barely
eight weeks after her divorce, Eleanor married – this time for love

– the future King Henry II of England. For poor Louis, here was yet another blow. Henry was technically his vassal and should have asked his permission before marrying – even though in the circumstances such a formality would have been embarrassing for all concerned. Worse still was the fact that the bride delivered all Aquitaine to her new husband. Henry had already inherited the Duchy of Normandy from his mother, Matilda, and Maine and Anjou from his father Count Geoffrey; with the addition of Aquitaine, he now ruled from Scotland to the Pyrenees and was far more powerful in France than Louis himself. But Louis was young – he was still only thirty-two – and there was plenty of spirit left in him. He was deeply conscious, too, that he still lacked an heir. Eleanor had borne him two daughters; his second wife, Constance of Castile, was to provide him with two more before dying in childbirth; only his third, Adela of Champagne, finally produced a boy, who was baptised Philip.

Louis left two magnificent monuments behind him, although to what extent he was personally responsible for them it is not easy to say. The first was the Cathedral of Notre-Dame, begun in 1163; its foundation stone is said to have been laid by Pope Alexander III, to whom he gave refuge during the Pope's long struggle with the Emperor Frederick Barbarossa. The second was the University of Paris, which originated with the cathedral school and has a good claim, after Bologna,* to be the oldest university in the world. For the rest, his reign was principally marked by recurrent but ultimately profitless warfare with Henry, and his consequent support of Archbishop Thomas Becket – whom, like almost everyone else who knew the man, he found insufferable. He reigned for forty-three years, on the whole wisely and well, concentrating – as his father had before him – on consolidating the royal authority across that part of the country where his writ still ran. He died on 18 September 1180 and was buried in the Cistercian Abbey of Barbeau; only in 1817 were his remains taken to Saint-Denis.

Philip Augustus – the imperial title was bestowed on him by his

---

* It owes its name, the Sorbonne, to Robert de Sorbon, who founded its associated theological college in c.1257.

chronicler Rigord, but it stuck – proved to be one of the greatest kings of France. It could even be argued that he was the first of them; all his predecessors had been content to call themselves Kings of the Franks.* He found France in a parlous situation. To the west, Henry II of England was ruling over nearly half the territory that was rightfully Philip's; to the east, the Holy Roman Emperor Frederick Barbarossa was at the height of his power, which extended not only throughout what is now Germany and Austria but also across the Alps into Italy. Between these two giants, France cut a fairly abject figure. During the next forty years, however, Philip conquered both his enemies. The greater of the two was of course Henry, an occupying power whom he hated in much the same way as, nearly eight centuries later, the French were to hate the Nazis in the Second World War. Here he had the Church, which had never forgotten Becket's murder, actively on his side; he was also helped by the constant quarrels between Henry and his four appalling sons. Together they could easily have destroyed him; but for the Plantagenets to act in concert was unthinkable.

The serious trouble began with the death in 1183 of Henry's second son (but the first to survive infancy), also named Henry.† In a vain attempt to heal the breach with France, he had been betrothed as a child and later married to Philip's sister Margaret, who had brought as her dowry the small but important county of Vexin north-west of Paris. Philip now demanded that this should be returned; Henry refused. The two held several meetings beneath an elm tree near Gisors, which stood on the border of their respective domains, but it was only when King Bela III of Hungary demanded the widow's hand in marriage that Henry reluctantly agreed. Then in 1186 came another death – that of Henry's fourth son, Geoffrey Duke of Brittany, who left a pregnant wife behind him. Henry maintained that he should retain the guardianship of the duchy on behalf of the unborn child; Philip, as liege lord, objected. There

---

* He remains, too, the only French monarch to have a station named after him on the Paris Metro.
† He was known as 'the Young King', since he had been crowned in 1170, while his father was still very much alive.

followed two years of inconclusive fighting, during which Henry's surviving sons, Richard and John, rebelled against their father. Philip joined them, and at last he and Richard forced Henry into submission. On 4 July 1189, at Azay-le-Rideau, Henry renewed his homage to Philip and renounced his claim to Auvergne. It was his last political action. Within two days he was dead.

But, suddenly, the temper of the world had changed. Exactly two years before, on 4 July 1187, the entire army of the Christian East had been destroyed by the forces of Islam. As usual, the West had had plenty of warning, but had reacted far too late. To most Europeans, the Crusader states were remote to the point of unreality – exotic, egregious outposts of Christendom in which austerity alternated with sybaritic luxury, where *douceur* and danger walked hand in hand; magnificent in their way, but somehow more suited to the lays of troubadour romance than to the damp and unheroic struggle that was the common lot at home. Even to the well-informed, Levantine politics were hard to follow, the names largely unpronounceable, the news when it did arrive hopelessly distorted and out of date. Only when disaster had actually struck did the knights of western Christendom spring, with exclamations of mingled rage and horror, to their swords.

So it had been forty years before, when the news of the fall of Edessa and the fire of St Bernard's oratory had quickened the pulse of the continent and launched the grotesque disaster that was the Second Crusade. And so it was now. To any dispassionate observer, European or Levantine, who had followed the march of events for the past fifteen years, the capture of Jerusalem must have seemed inevitable. On the Muslim side there had been the steady rise of Saladin, a leader of genius who had vowed to recover the Holy City for his faith; on the Christian, nothing but the sad spectacle of the three remaining Frankish states – Jerusalem, Tripoli and Antioch – all governed by mediocrities and torn apart by internal struggles for power. Jerusalem itself was further burdened, throughout the crucial period of Saladin's ascendancy, by the decline of its leper King Baldwin IV. When he came to the throne in 1174 at the age of thirteen, the disease was already upon him; eleven years later he died. Not surprisingly, he left no issue. At the one moment when wise and resolute leadership was essential if the kingdom were to be saved, the crown of Jerusalem devolved upon Baldwin's nephew, a child of eight.

The death of this new infant king, Baldwin V, in the following year might have been considered a blessing in disguise; but the opportunity of finding a true leader was thrown away and the throne passed to his stepfather, Guy of Lusignan, a weak, querulous figure with a record of incapacity which fully merited the scorn in which he was held by most of his compatriots. Jerusalem was thus in a state bordering on civil war when, in May 1187, Saladin declared his long-awaited jihad and crossed the Jordan into Frankish territory. Under the miserable Guy, the Christian defeat was assured. On 3 July he led the largest army his kingdom had ever assembled across the Galilean mountains towards Tiberias, where Saladin was laying siege to the castle. After a long day's march in the most torrid season of the year, the Christians were forced to camp on a waterless plateau; and the next day, exhausted by the heat and half-mad with thirst, beneath the little double-summited hill known as the Horns of Hattin, they were surrounded by the Muslim army and cut to pieces.

It remained for the Saracens only to mop up the isolated Christian fortresses one by one. Tiberias fell on the day after Hattin; Acre followed; Nablus, Jaffa, Sidon and Beirut capitulated in quick succession. Wheeling south, Saladin took Ascalon by storm and received the surrender of Gaza without a struggle. Now he was ready for Jerusalem. The city's defenders resisted heroically for twelve days; but on 2 October, with the walls already breached by Muslim sappers, they knew that the end was near. Their leader, Balian of Ibelin – King Guy having been taken prisoner after Hattin – went personally to Saladin to discuss terms for surrender.

Saladin was neither bloodthirsty nor vindictive. After some negotiation he agreed that every Christian in Jerusalem be allowed to redeem himself by payment of the appropriate ransom. Of the twenty thousand poor who had no means of raising the money, seven thousand would be freed on payment of a lump sum by the various Christian authorities. That same day the conqueror led his army into the city; and for the first time in eighty-eight years, on the anniversary of the day on which the Prophet was carried in his sleep from Jerusalem to Paradise, his green banners fluttered over the Temple Mount from which he had been gathered up, and the sacred imprint of his foot was once again exposed to the adoration of the faithful.

Everywhere, order was preserved. In contrast to the events following the Crusaders' capture of the city, there was no murder, no bloodshed, no looting. The thirteen thousand people for whom the ransom money could not be raised remained in the city; but Saladin's brother and lieutenant al-Adil asked for a thousand of them as a reward for his services and immediately set them free. Another seven hundred were given to the Patriarch of Jerusalem, and five hundred to Balian; then Saladin himself spontaneously liberated all the old, all the husbands whose wives had been ransomed and finally all the widows and children. Few Christians ultimately found their way to captivity. This was not the first time that Saladin had shown that magnanimity for which he would soon be famous through East and West alike;* but never before had he done so on such a scale. Here was an example of chivalry which was to have an effect on the forthcoming Crusade.

The recently elected Pope, Gregory VIII, lost no time in calling upon Christendom to take the Cross; and in the high summer of 1190 Philip Augustus and Henry II's son and successor Richard Coeur-de-Lion, with their armies behind them, met together at Vézelay – perhaps in the circumstances an unfortunate choice of rendezvous. The two kings agreed to set off on their journey together less for reasons of companionship than because neither trusted the other an inch; and indeed no two men could have been more dissimilar. The King of France was still only twenty-five; but he was already a widower† and apart from a shock of wild, uncontrollable hair there was nothing youthful about him. Never handsome, he had now lost the sight of one eye, giving his face an asymmetrical look. His ten years on the throne of France had brought him unusual

---

* In 1183, when he laid siege to the castle of Kerak during the wedding celebrations of its heir, Humphrey of Toron, to Princess Isabella of Jerusalem, he had carefully enquired which tower contained the bridal chamber and had given orders that it was to be left undisturbed.

† His first wife, Isabelle of Hainaut, had died in childbirth a few months before.

wisdom and experience for one so young, but had made him permanently suspicious and had taught him to conceal his thoughts and emotions behind a veil of taciturn moroseness. Though brave enough on the battlefield, he is thought to have lacked outstanding courage; in society he was strangely wanting in charm. But beneath his drab exterior there lay a searching intelligence, coupled with a strong sense of both the moral and the political responsibilities of kingship. It was easy to underestimate him. It was also unwise.

He cannot have looked upon his fellow-ruler without envy. Richard had succeeded his father, Henry, just a year before. At thirty-three, he was now in his prime. Though his health was often poor, his magnificent physique and volcanic energy gave the impression of a man to whom illness was unknown. His good looks were famous, his powers of leadership no less so, his courage already a legend across two continents. From his mother, Eleanor, he had inherited the Poitevin love of literature and poetry, and to many people he must have seemed like some glittering figure from the troubadour epics he loved so much. One element only was lacking to complete the picture: however sweetly Richard might sing of the joys and pains of love, he had left no trail of betrayed or broken-hearted damsels behind him. But if his tastes ran in other directions they never appreciably affected the shining reputation, burnished as his breastplate, which remained with him till the day of his death.

Those who knew Richard better, on the other hand, soon became aware of his other, less admirable qualities. Even more impetuous and hot-tempered than the father he had so hated, he altogether lacked that capacity for sustained administrative effort that had enabled Henry II, for all his faults, to weld England almost single-handedly into a nation. His ambition was boundless, and nearly always destructive. Himself incapable of love, he could be faithless, disloyal, even treacherous, in the pursuit of his ends. No English king had fought harder or more unscrupulously for the throne; none was readier to ignore the responsibilities of kingship for the sake of personal glory. In the nine years of life left to him, the total time he was to spend in England was just two months.

The hills round Vézelay, wrote an eyewitness, were so spread with tents and pavilions that the fields looked like a great multicoloured city. The two kings solemnly reaffirmed their crusading vows and sealed a further treaty of alliance; then, followed by their respective armies and a huge multitude of pilgrims, they moved off together to the south. It was only at Lyon, where the collapse of the bridge across the Rhône under the weight of the crowds was interpreted as a bad augury for the future, that the French and English parted company. Philip turned south-east towards Genoa, where a chartered fleet was awaiting him; it must have been considerable, since the army to be transported amounted to 650 knights, each with two squires, and 1,300 horses. Richard continued down the Rhône valley to join his fleet at Marseille. The two kings, it was agreed, would meet again at Messina, whence their combined army would sail for the Holy Land.

Philip arrived at Messina first, on 14 September, Richard nine days later. Nothing was more typical of the two than the manner of their disembarkation. A description of Philip's arrival will be found at the head of this chapter; Richard's made an interesting contrast:

> When Richard was about to land, the people rushed down in crowds towards the beach; and behold, from a distance the sea seemed cleft with innumerable oars, and the loud voices of the trumpets and the horns sounded clear and shrill over the water. Approaching nearer, the galleys could be seen rowing in order, emblazoned with divers coats of arms, and with pennons and banners innumerable floating from the points of the spears . . . The sea was boiling with the multitude of oars, the air trembling with the blasts of the trumpets and the tumultuous shouts of the delighted crowds. The magnificent King, loftier and more splendid than all his train, stood erect on the prow, as one expecting alike to see and be seen . . . And as the trumpets rang out with discordant yet harmonious sounds, the people whispered together: 'He is indeed worthy of empire; he is rightly made King over peoples and kingdoms; what we heard of him at a distance falls far short of what we now see.'*

★ Geoffrey de Vinsauf, *Itinerary of Richard I and Others to the Holy Land.*

Not all the king's admirers on that memorable day may have been aware that that superb figure had preferred, through fear of seasickness, to take the land route down the peninsula; and that this mighty landfall was in fact the culmination of a sea journey that had brought him only the few miles from Calabria. Fewer still could have guessed that, for all the golden splendour of his arrival, Richard was in a black and dangerous mood. A few days before, passing through Mileto, he had been caught in the act of stealing a hawk from a peasant's cottage and had narrowly escaped death at the hands of the owner and his friends; worse still, on landing at Messina, was his discovery that the royal palace in the centre of the city had already been put at the disposal of the King of France, and that he had been allotted rather more modest quarters outside the walls.

Why, we may ask, was the royal palace not occupied by the King of Sicily himself? Because Sicily was in turmoil. Its last legitimate king, William II, had died childless the previous year, leaving as his widow Joanna, daughter of Henry II and consequently Richard's sister. The throne was now occupied by Tancred of Lecce, William's bastard cousin, who – Richard had good reason to believe – was treating the young queen disgracefully, keeping her under distraint and withholding from her certain revenues that were properly part of her marriage settlement. How far these suspicions were justified it was not easy to say, but Richard's subsequent behaviour suggests that he saw Sicily as a potential new jewel in his own crown, and that he was already on the lookout for any excuse to make trouble. Settling Joanna in the Abbey of Bagnara on the Calabrian coast, he returned to Messina, where he fell on the city's own most venerable religious foundation, the Basilian monastery of the Saviour. The monks were forcibly and unceremoniously evicted and Richard's army moved into its new barracks.

And what, it may be asked, was the reaction of Philip Augustus to such shenanigans? He had seen Sicily simply as a staging post, from which he was anxious to move on as quickly as possible to the Holy Land. Shocked and shamed by the conduct of his fellow-monarch, he had offered to mediate, but his proposals had been coldly rejected. Meanwhile, day by day, the situation in Messina was growing more threatening. It was many years since any Sicilian city had been called upon to accommodate a foreign army, and the predominantly Greek population had already been scandalised by the barbarous behaviour of the English. Their free and easy ways with the local women, in particular, were not what might have been expected of men who bore the Cross of Christ on their shoulders. The occupation of the monastery came as the final outrage, and on 3 October serious rioting broke out. Fearing – with good reason – that the King of England might take possession of their city and even of the whole island, the Messinans rushed to the gates and bolted them; others barred the harbour entrance. Preliminary attempts by the English to force an entry failed; but no one believed that they could be held in check for long. The sun set that evening on an anxious city.

Early the following day Philip Augustus appeared at Richard's headquarters outside the walls. He was accompanied by his cousin Hugh, Duke of Burgundy, the Count of Poitiers and the other leaders of the French army, together with a similarly high-ranking Sicilian delegation, including the archbishops of Monreale, Reggio and Messina itself. The ensuing discussions went surprisingly well. The parties seemed on the point of agreement when suddenly the noise of further tumult was heard. A crowd of Messinans, gathered outside the building, were shouting imprecations against the English and their king. Richard seized his sword and ran from the hall; summoning his troops, he gave the order for immediate attack. This time it was the Messinans who were taken by surprise. The English soldiers burst into the city, ravaging and plundering it as they went. Within hours – 'less time than it took to say matins', wrote a contemporary chronicler – Messina was in flames.

> All the gold and silver, and whatsoever precious thing was found, became the property of the victors. They set fire to the enemy's galleys and burnt them to ashes, lest any citizen should escape and recover strength to resist. The victors also carried off their noblest women. And lo! When it was done, the French suddenly beheld the ensigns and standards of King Richard floating above the walls of the city; at which the King of France was so mortified that he conceived that hatred against King Richard that lasted all his life.

Geoffrey de Vinsauf goes on to describe how Philip insisted, and Richard finally agreed, that the French banners should be flown alongside the English; he does not mention how the citizens of Messina felt about this new insult to their pride. Just whom, they must have asked themselves, was the King of England supposed to be fighting? Did he intend to remain permanently in Sicily? It seemed a curious way to conduct a Crusade.

To Philip Augustus, the incident over the flags seemed to confirm his worst suspicions. Within a fortnight of his arrival as an honoured guest, Richard was in undisputed control of the second city of the island; and King Tancred, though not far away at Catania, had made not the slightest effort to oppose him. To Catania therefore Philip now despatched the Duke of Burgundy, charging him to warn Tancred of the gravity of the situation and to offer the support of the French army if Richard were to press his claims any further. Tancred, however, needed no warning. He was well aware of the danger of leaving Messina in Richard's hands. But a new idea was taking shape in his brain. The legitimate heir to the throne of Sicily was Constance, the posthumous daughter of King Roger II; and she – unaccountably and unforgivably – had been married off by William to Henry of Hohenstaufen, the son of Frederick Barbarossa. Frederick was now dead – he had been drowned in a river in Asia Minor on his way to the Crusade – and Henry, now the Emperor Henry VI – would shortly be making his way to Sicily to claim the crown on behalf of his wife. If Tancred were to resist – which he had every intention of doing – he would need allies; and as allies the English would be vastly preferable to the French. Crude and uncivilised they might be – and their king, for all his glamorous reputation, was as bad as any of them – but at least he had no love for the Hohenstaufens. Philip Augustus, on the other hand, had been on excellent terms with Barbarossa; if the Germans were to invade now, while the Crusaders were still in Sicily, French sympathies would be to say the least uncertain. Tancred therefore returned the Duke of Burgundy to Philip with suitably lavish presents but not much else, and sent an envoy of his own to negotiate directly with Richard at Messina.

This time the financial inducements were more than the king

could resist. Tancred offered Richard and Joanna 20,000 ounces of gold each, and agreed that Richard's heir, his nephew Duke Arthur of Brittany, should be betrothed to one of his own daughters. In return Richard promised to give the King of Sicily full military assistance for as long as he and his men should remain in the kingdom, and undertook to restore to its rightful owners all the plunder he had taken during the disturbances of the previous month. On 11 November, with due ceremony, the resulting treaty was signed at Messina.

The reaction of Philip Augustus to this sudden rapprochement between the two monarchs can well be imagined. As usual, however, he concealed his resentment. Outwardly his relations with Richard remained cordial. The two of them had plenty to discuss before they set off again. Rules of conduct must be drawn up, for soldiers and pilgrims alike; there were endless logistical problems still to be solved; it was vital, too, that they should reach agreement in advance about the distribution of conquests and the division of spoils. On all these matters Richard proved surprisingly amenable; on one point only, unconnected with the Crusade, did he refuse to be moved. It concerned Philip's sister Alys, who had been sent to England more than twenty years before as a bride for one of Henry II's sons. She had been offered to Richard who, predictably, would have nothing to do with her; but instead of returning her to France Henry had kept her at his court together with her substantial dowry, later making her his own mistress and, almost certainly, the mother of his child. Now Henry was dead and Alys, at thirty, was still in England and as far away from marriage as ever.

Philip was in no way concerned for her happiness; he had never lifted a finger to help his other even more pathetic sister Agnes-Anna of Byzantium, twice widowed in hideous circumstances before she was sixteen. But this treatment of a princess of France was an insult that he could not allow to pass. He found Richard just as adamant as Henry had been. Not only did he refuse once again, point-blank, to consider marrying Alys himself, he had the effrontery to try to justify his attitude on the grounds of her besmirched reputation. Here indeed was a test of Philip's sangfroid; and when Richard went on to inform him that his mother Eleanor was at that very moment on her way to Sicily with another bride intended for him in the shape of Berengaria, Princess of Navarre, relations between the two monarchs came near breaking point.

On 3 March 1191 the King of England rode down in state to Catania to call on the King of Sicily. The two reaffirmed their friendship and exchanged presents – five galleys and four horse transports for Richard who, according to at least two authorities, gave Tancred in return a still more precious token of his affection – King Arthur's own sword, Excalibur itself, which had been supposedly found, only a short time before, lying beside the old king's body at Glastonbury. The meeting over, the two returned together as far as Taormina, where a deeply disgruntled Philip was waiting. A new crisis seemed inescapable when Tancred, for reasons which can only be guessed, showed Richard the letters he had received from Philip the previous October, warning him of English machinations. Yet by the end of the month the allies were again reconciled, and relations seem to have been comparatively cordial all round when, on 30 March, Philip sailed with his army to Palestine.

He had timed his departure well; or, perhaps more likely, it was Eleanor and Berengaria who had timed their arrival. Scarcely had the French fleet disappeared over the horizon when their convoy dropped anchor in the harbour of Messina. It was forty-four years since the old queen had last seen Sicily, when she and her detested husband had called on Roger II on their way back from the Holy Land. On this second visit she had hoped to witness the marriage of her favourite son to the wife she had chosen for him; but Lent had begun, and a Lenten marriage was out of the question. Despite a recent prohibition of women from going on the Crusade, it was therefore decided that Berengaria should accompany her future husband to the East; young Queen Joanna, who could obviously not be left on the island, would make a perfect chaperone for her. Once everything was settled, Eleanor saw no reason to delay any longer. After only three days in Messina, with that energy for which she was famous throughout Europe – she was now sixty-nine and had been travelling uninterruptedly for over three months – she left again for England. The day after bidding her mother goodbye for the last time, Joanna herself set off with Berengaria for the Holy Land. Richard remained for one more week, organising the embarkation of his army. Finally, on 10 April, he too sailed away. The people of Messina cannot have been sorry to see him go.

Philip arrived in Palestine on 20 May 1191; he was not to stay there long. He marched straight to Acre, which was already under siege. Richard arrived on 8 June, having captured Cyprus – and incidentally married the unfortunate Berengaria – on the way. Acre held out until 12 July, but by that time the French camp had suffered a serious outbreak of dysentery. Philip had succumbed, and was lying miserably on his sickbed when he received a report of the death – due to the same epidemic – of Philip of Alsace, Count of Flanders. This was grave news indeed, since it threw into doubt the whole question of the Flemish succession, essential if Philip was to keep his north-eastern border under control. One suspects that the king felt nothing but relief to have such a cast-iron excuse to return to France; in any case the moment he was well enough to travel, return he did. He left Palestine on 31 July with his cousin Peter of Courtenay, having been there a little over ten weeks – a period which had seen several more bitter quarrels with Richard, with whom he was now once again barely on speaking terms. His army meanwhile remained in the Holy Land, under the command of the Duke of Burgundy.

Richard, as might be expected, made several snide remarks about Philip's premature departure before returning to the campaign. On 20 August he destroyed his chivalric reputation for ever by ordering the massacre of all his Muslim prisoners of war, some three thousand of them, together with a number of women and children; but he failed altogether to destroy Saladin. It was not until the summer of 1192 that it dawned on him that Philip and his brother John might well be taking advantage of his absence. At last he realised that he must return to England and finally reached a settlement with a thoroughly disgusted Saladin on a three-year truce, during which Christian pilgrims and merchants would have free access to Jerusalem and the Holy Places. A few days later he took ship from Acre. His journey home was delayed, first by bad weather, then by shipwreck and finally by imprisonment at the hands of Duke Leopold of Austria, from which he was released only on the payment of 100,000 pounds of silver – between two and three times the annual income of the English crown. In February 1194, on hearing that, thanks largely to Queen Eleanor, the money had at last been raised, Philip – who had tried unsuccessfully to bribe the Emperor Henry VI to keep his prisoner a few months longer – sent Richard's brother, Prince John, a message: 'Look to yourself – the devil is loose!' A little over a month later Richard was back on English soil.

Until now, Philip Augustus has come out of our story a good deal better than Richard the Lionheart; but as soon as he returned to France he began to level the score. He knew that he would never be happy until he had driven the English out of France. Before leaving on the Crusade, he and Richard had each taken an oath not to attack each other's lands during their absence; but he now began a campaign to blacken Richard's name, accusing him of having been involved in treacherous communications with Saladin; of having conspired with him to cause the fall of several Crusader cities; and, finally, for having been responsible for the assassination in April 1192 of Conrad, Marquis of Montferrat, husband of Queen Isabella of Jerusalem.* But none of this really mattered: nine months later, Richard himself was back – and on the warpath. Soon all Normandy was aflame – at one moment Philip narrowly escaped drowning, when a bridge collapsed just as he and his army were crossing it – and the fighting continued for the next five years. The two kings met for the last time in January 1199, with Philip standing on the bank of the Seine, Richard on a boat a little way offshore. Somehow the pair of them managed to agree on further talks between their respective ambassadors, and these were eventually to result in a five-year truce, which mercifully held. Three months later, during a minor campaign in the Limousin to suppress a mutinous vassal, Richard was struck by a bolt from a crossbow. The wound quickly became gangrenous, and on 6 April 1199 he died at the age of forty-one.

Philip Augustus, however, still had work to do. His chief enemy now was his former ally John of England. One or two modern

---

* It was in fact an empty title, since Jerusalem was no longer in Christian hands.

historians have tried to defend John, blaming much of his deplorable reputation on two chroniclers, Roger of Wendover and Matthew Paris, both of whom were writing after his death. He may not, as Paris suggests, have offered to convert to Islam in exchange for military aid from the Almohad rulers in southern Spain; but he was very probably responsible for the murder of his nephew Prince Arthur of Brittany – providing Shakespeare with one of his most poignant scenes – and there is no doubt whatever that he was lecherous, duplicitous, faithless and cruel – worse even than his brother, the worst king England ever had. After a short-lived treaty of peace, fighting between Philip and John began in earnest in 1202. Thanks largely to John's treatment of his allies, over the next two years more and more of them deserted him, and by August 1204 Philip had recovered all Normandy, Anjou and Poitou. John's only remaining dominion on the continent was Aquitaine; but Queen Eleanor had died in April at the age of eighty-two, and once deprived of his mother's support he managed to hold it for only two more years.

In 1209 John acquired a powerful new ally: his nephew Otto,* now the Emperor Otto IV. Otto had promised to help his uncle to regain his lost territories, but had never found the opportunity to do so. The two remained, as may be imagined, a permanent anxiety for Philip – who, seeing them both enmeshed in power struggles with the Pope, decided to strike. On 27 July 1214, he met the combined forces of John, Otto and Count Ferdinand of Flanders near the village of Bouvines in Picardy. Their army numbered some 25,000 men, compared with Philip's 15,000. In the middle of the battle Philip was unhorsed by Flemish pikemen and saved only by his armour; but soon afterwards, when Otto was carried off the field by his wounded and terrified horse and Count Ferdinand, also seriously wounded, was taken prisoner, the imperial troops saw that the battle was lost, turned tail and fled. The French began to pursue them, but night was falling and Philip called them back. He returned triumphantly to Paris, followed by a seemingly interminable line of prisoners, and on his arrival the whole city erupted in celebration.

* He was the son of John's sister Matilda, who married Henry the Lion, Duke of Saxony.

There was dancing in the flower-strewn streets, and the students of the embryonic university caroused for a week. His fellow-monarchs, by contrast, had little to celebrate except their survival. Otto returned to Germany, where he was soon obliged to abdicate. John returned disgraced and discredited to England, where in the following year he signed Magna Carta and in 1216 he died – though not before seeing his country once again invaded by the French. As for Ferdinand of Flanders, he was to remain in prison for the next twelve years.

The reign of Philip Augustus also witnessed one of the blackest episodes in French history: what is ridiculously known as the Albigensian Crusade. It was launched in 1209, and was directed against as pure and harmless a group of innocents as ever existed. The Cathars – who became known as the Albigensians simply because they were vaguely centred on the city of Albi – had first appeared in the Languedoc around the beginning of the eleventh century. Essentially, they maintained the Manichaean doctrine that good and evil constituted two distinct spheres – that of the good, spiritual God and that of the Devil, creator of the material world – and that the Earth was a constant battleground between them. The leaders, known as the *perfecti*, abstained from meat and from sex; they also rejected saints, holy images and relics, together with all the sacraments of the Church, particularly baptism and marriage. To Pope Innocent III, such departures from orthodoxy could not be tolerated. At first he hoped for peaceable conversion, sending a Cistercian mission headed by a legate, Peter of Castelnau, and subsequently joined by the Spaniard Domingo de Guzmán, better known as St Dominic; but in 1208 Peter was murdered by a henchman of Count Raymond of Toulouse, and Innocent proclaimed a Crusade.

That Crusade was to continue for the next twenty years, pitting the northern barons, led by Simon de Montfort, against those of the south. It led to several hideous massacres – the worst of them in the town of Monségur – and it utterly destroyed the dazzling Provençal civilisation of the early Middle Ages. Even when the war ended in 1229 with the Treaty of Paris, the heresy refused to die. It was another hundred years before the Inquisition, unleashed on the region with all its terrifying efficiency, succeeded in crushing it.

Philip himself took little interest in the Crusade, preferring to remain in Paris to oversee his favourite projects: the paving of the principal streets; the provision of a central market, Les Halles;* the building of a great fortress on the Seine, later to become the Louvre; and the continuation of his father's work on the Cathedral of Notre-Dame. He established the Royal Archives, together with the city's first police force, consisting of twenty men mounted and forty on foot. He lived on until 1223, when he died at the age of fifty-four. The one stain on his record was his periodic persecution of the Jews, whom he bled white; but he left a France no longer threatened by the Germans, and no longer half-occupied by the English: a France happier, almost certainly, than it had ever been.

* It lasted for seven and a half centuries, until its demolition in 1971.

4

The Fatal Tower

1223–1326

He is neither a man nor a beast, but a statue.

Bernard Saisset, Bishop of Pamiers, on Philip IV

FOR ABOUT A year, Philip Augustus's son Louis VIII claimed the title of King of England. He landed on the Isle of Thanet in Kent on 21 May 1216, was welcomed by the barons, marched to London and was proclaimed king in St Paul's Cathedral. Three weeks later he had taken Winchester and soon controlled more than half the kingdom. He would doubtless have gone a good deal further – and perhaps even been crowned – had not John died of dysentery on 18 October, leaving a nine-year-old son, Henry. Thinking, presumably, that the son could not possibly be as bad as the father, many of the barons transferred their allegiance to the infant Henry III, and it was agreed to crown him immediately to reinforce his claim to the throne. The coronation ceremony, using his mother's necklace – John having lost the crown jewels,* which had travelled with him on campaign – was held in Gloucester Cathedral on the 28th, and for Louis the tide suddenly turned. His army was beaten at Lincoln the following May, his navy off Sandwich in August, and he was forced to come to terms. He got off lightly. The Treaty of Lambeth awarded him 10,000 marks, in return for a promise never to attack England again and an admission that he had never been its legitimate king.

His claim to the English throne had been slight indeed, but there

* Tradition says that they were lost while the royal baggage train was negotiating the treacherous tidal mudflats around the Wash.

is reason to suppose that had he lived he might have been an excellent King of France. Alas, the dread dysentery was once again to do its work, and he died in November 1226, leaving a son of twelve – another Louis – with his widow, Blanche of Castile, to act as regent. Blanche – she was the granddaughter of Henry II by his daughter Eleanor, and hence the niece of Richard Coeur-de-Lion and John – was passionately devoted to her eldest son, and insanely jealous when he married Margaret of Provence. After their marriage, he and Margaret were given apartments one above the other, and it was said that both bedrooms were so closely watched that the couple, who were deeply in love, had to meet on the staircase between them to avoid the prying eyes of Blanche. They managed none the less to have eleven children.

It was Blanche, too, who was almost certainly responsible for Louis IX's excessive piety. Every morning he heard Mass, every afternoon the office of the dead. At regular intervals he washed the feet of the poor. He also took part in two further Crusades. The first of these – it was actually the Seventh, and it deprived France of her ruler for six years – was like almost all the Crusades after the First, a succession of disasters. The royal fleet, commanded by the king's brothers Charles of Anjou and Robert of Artois, sailed from Aigues-Mortes during the autumn of 1248 for Egypt, to which the base of Muslim power had now shifted. Louis's attempted march from Damietta to Cairo in the high summer of 1249 was made almost impossible by the appalling heat and the annual flooding of the Nile, which seems to have taken him completely by surprise; then in April 1250, at the three-day Battle of Al-Mansura, he lost his entire army of some 20,000 men. He himself was captured and, after swearing an oath never to return to Egypt, was finally ransomed for 400,000 dinars. Now would surely have been a sensible time for him to return to France; instead, he spent four more years in what was left of Outremer – limited now to Acre, Jaffa and Caesarea – helping the remaining Crusaders to rebuild their defences and holding fruitless negotiations with the Muslim authorities in Syria. Not till the spring of 1254 did he take ship for home.

Once returned to France, Louis cannot have been altogether surprised to find a new coalition of the barons – including, inevitably, the King of England – arrayed against him. He dealt with it in the most unusual fashion; to the surprise of everyone and to the horror of many, he cheerfully granted Poitou, Guienne and Gascony to the English king – for, he explained, 'we have two sisters to wife* and our children are first cousins, wherefore it is surely fitting that peace be between us'. He asked in return only that Henry do him homage for these lands, and that he should abandon all other continental claims. The gesture was in fact typical of him: peace among Christians was his first priority, and he was prepared to go to almost any lengths to secure it. Never had a united Christendom come closer to realisation.

Within France itself, Louis continued where his father had stopped, doing his best to put an end to the innumerable little wars between the barons that were plaguing the country. He also radically revised the judicial system, banning trial by ordeal and, even more important, introducing the principle of presumption of innocence. (He himself would dispense justice, we are told, sitting under an old oak tree in the Forest of Vincennes.) Characteristically, he was an ardent collector of relics of Christ's Passion; and to house the holiest item in his entire collection, the Crown of Thorns – which had been given to him by Baldwin II, the Latin Emperor of Constantinople† – he built the loveliest early Gothic building in all France, the Sainte-Chapelle.‡

But not even the Sainte-Chapelle was enough to satisfy Louis's Christian zeal. There was more crusading to be done. The Eighth Crusade was his own idea. The catastrophic Seventh and his consequent imprisonment had continued to rankle, and twenty years later in 1267, when he was already in his fifty-fourth year, he decided to make one more attempt to restore Christian rule to the Holy Land. This time, on the advice of his brother Charles of Anjou, he decided that the new Crusade should begin with an attack on Tunis. He took three years to prepare a suitable fleet for the operation, but one wonders whether he had learnt anything from his previous

* Henry III was married to Queen Margaret's sister Eleanor.
† The Greek emperors had been replaced by Franks after the Fourth Crusade (1204–5). They were to recapture Constantinople in 1261.
‡ The Crown of Thorns, however, is now kept at Notre-Dame.

experience in the tropics. It seems on the whole not, because the fleet chose to land on the African coast in July 1270. There was little water available and nearly all of it was filthy. Within days most of his men had fallen sick, and a month later the king himself was dead. Charles of Anjou took over the leadership, but without Louis the heart had gone out of the expedition and the survivors soon returned home.

Saint Louis – he was canonised in 1297, barely a quarter-century after his death – left a France very different from the one he had inherited. Henceforth the head of the Capetian line would be accepted everywhere as the legitimate sovereign chosen by God – a quite unprecedented move towards absolute monarchy – while his kingdom acquired a moral authority unlike anything it had known before. This made him, it need hardly be said, a difficult act to follow. His son Philip III was known as Philip the Bold (in French, *le Hardi*), but for no very good reason. He had accompanied his father on the Eighth Crusade, but had not particularly distinguished himself; and on his return to Paris after his father's death he had proved timid, submissive and strangely colourless – crushed, probably, by the domineering personalities of both his parents, and especially his mother. It was typical of the formidable Queen Margaret, during her husband's lifetime, to make her son swear to remain under her tutelage until he was thirty; and although the Pope technically released him from this oath when he was only eighteen he was never to escape from her shadow. He died at Perpignon in 1285 and was soon forgotten.

After Philip Augustus and Saint Louis, the third and last member of the great Capetian trinity was King Philip IV, the Fair; and King Philip was always a bit of a puzzle. He gave nothing away and no one could be quite sure what made him tick. The popular image of the handsome young king, swaggering and debonair, could hardly be more misleading. He was, as far as we can make out, only moderately good-looking; the eldest son of Philip the Bold and Isabella of Aragon, he was taciturn and surly, passionately acquisitive, and capable on occasion of appalling cruelty. And yet he was, unquestionably, a great king. A serious-minded and hard-working professional, he governed not with barons but with lawyers and bureaucrats, his object not by any means that of his grandfather – to raise France to be a virtuous, peaceful and above all a Christian monarchy – but rather to make it strong, efficient and influential. Thanks to his marriage (to Queen Joan I of Navarre) and to other inheritances, his dominions steadily increased, and with them his expenditure. Throughout his reign he was desperate for money, and he did not much care how he got it. This attitude was to make him many enemies, among whom none was more implacable than Pope Boniface VIII.

Boniface was the epitome of the worldly cleric. Born between 1220 and 1230, a man of huge intelligence and a first-class legist and scholar, he founded Rome University, codified the canon law and re-established the Vatican Library and Archive. But there was little of the spiritual in his nature. For him the great sanctions of the Church existed only to further his own temporal ends and to enrich his family. Foreign rulers he treated less as his subjects than as his menials. As for his office, he saw it in exclusively political terms, determined as he was to reassert the supremacy of the Apostolic See over the emerging nations of Europe. For this task he possessed abundant energy, self-confidence and strength of will; what he lacked was the slightest sense of diplomacy or finesse. Concepts such as conciliation or compromise simply did not interest him; he charged forward regardless – and ultimately he paid the price.

The mutual hostility that existed between himself and King Philip had begun in 1296, when Philip imposed a heavy tax on French churchmen. Furious, the Pope had replied with a bull, formally prohibiting the taxation of clergy or church property without express authorisation from Rome. Had he given the matter any serious consideration, he would have seen in an instant just how short-sighted this action was: Philip simply forbade the export of currency and valuables, simultaneously barring the entry of Roman tax collectors into the country. Since the papal exchequer relied heavily on income from France, Boniface had no alternative but to climb down – attempting to recover some of his lost prestige by formally canonising Philip's grandfather Louis IX.

Then, in the autumn of 1301, Philip summarily imprisoned the obscure but contumacious Bishop of Pamiers, charging him with treason and insulting behaviour.* The Pope, without having troubled even to look into the case, angrily demanded the bishop's release; Philip refused; and the battle entered its final phase. Boniface, in yet another bull – *ausculta fili* ('listen, son') – loftily summoned the king himself, together with his senior clergy, to a synod in Rome to be held in November 1302. Philip of course refused; but thirty-nine French bishops somewhat surprisingly found the courage to attend. It was after this that Boniface fired his last broadside, *unam sanctam*, in which he claimed in so many words that 'it is altogether necessary for salvation for every human creature to be subject to the Roman Pontiff'. There was nothing particularly new in this; similar claims had been made by Innocent III and several other popes. None the less, papal absolutism could scarcely go further, and there was no question that it was King Philip whom Boniface had principally in mind.

Probably on the advice of his new minister, Guillaume de Nogaret – whose Albigensian† grandfather had been burnt at the stake, and who consequently had no love for the papacy – Philip now returned to his former tactic of all-out personal attack. All the old charges – together with several new ones, such as illegitimacy and heresy – were repeated, and an insistent demand made for a general council at which the Supreme Pontiff should be made to answer for his crimes. An army of 1,600 under de Nogaret was despatched to Italy with orders to seize the Pope and bring him, by force if necessary, to France. Boniface was meanwhile in his palace at Anagni, putting the finishing touches to a bull excommunicating Philip and releasing his subjects from their allegiance. He was due to publish it on 8 September; but on the previous afternoon de Nogaret and his troops arrived. The Pope – by this time he cannot have been far short of eighty – donned his full papal regalia and faced them with courage, challenging them to kill him. They briefly took him prisoner, but he was rescued by the people of Anagni and spirited away. De

* He had a point. The bishop had called him 'a useless owl'.
† See Chapter 3, p.48.

Nogaret, seeing that there was no way of laying hands on him short of a massacre, wisely decided to retire.

His mission, however, had not been in vain. The old Pope's pride had suffered a mortal blow. After a few days' rest he was escorted back to Rome, but he never recovered from the shock. He died less than a month later, on 12 October 1303. Dante, by anticipation – since the Pope's death occurred just three years after the poet's visit to hell – places him in the eighth circle, upside down in a furnace. The judgement may be thought a trifle harsh; but one sees, perhaps, what he meant.

Boniface's successor, Benedict XI, lived for only a year after his election and can safely be ignored. The subsequent conclave that opened in 1304 was split down the middle, and the deadlock continued for eleven months; it was finally agreed that if a new pope were ever to be elected he would have to come from outside the College of Cardinals. The choice finally fell on Bertrand de Got, Archbishop of Bordeaux, who took the name of Clement V. Had he been an Italian, elected and crowned in Rome, he might well have proved himself, if not a great pope, at least a strong one. Being, however, a subject of King Philip, from the moment of his election he found himself under almost intolerable pressure from his sovereign. Philip began as he meant to go on, insisting first of all that, since the new Pope was already in France, he should be crowned there.

There is no reason to believe that Clement did not intend to move to Rome in due course. For the following four years he had no fixed abode and moved constantly between Lyon, Poitiers and Bordeaux, his cardinals following as best they could. (By now they were mostly Frenchmen: of the ten he created in December 1305, nine were French – four of them his nephews – and the French element was to be increased still further in 1310 and again in 1312.) Philip meanwhile maintained the pressure to keep him in France; but in 1309 Clement decided to settle in Avignon – which, lying as it did on the east bank of the Rhône, was at that time the property of Philip's cousin and vassal Charles II of Anjou. The little town – it was with some five thousand inhabitants scarcely more than a village – was to be the home of six more popes after him, and the seat of the papacy for the next sixty-eight years.

Those years are often referred to as the 'Babylonian captivity'; but the popes' residence in Avignon was nothing of the kind; they were there only because they wanted to be. None the less, early fourteenth-century Avignon was not a comfortable place. The poet Petrarch described it as 'a disgusting city', battered by the mistral, 'a sewer where all the filth of the universe is collected'. The Aragonese ambassador was so nauseated by the stench of the streets that he had to return home. As papal territory, it was also a place of refuge for criminals of every description, and its taverns and brothels were notorious. Nor was it designed to accommodate a papal court. The Pope and his immediate entourage moved into the local Dominican priory; a few fortunate cardinals managed to requisition the larger houses; the rest found a roof wherever they could.*

The move to Avignon should at least have allowed Pope Clement a degree of independence; but Philip was too strong for him. The Pope was a sick man – he is said to have suffered from stomach cancer throughout his pontificate – and he soon showed himself to be little more than a puppet of the French king. Determined as he was to bring Boniface to justice, in 1309 Philip obliged him to open a full enquiry into the late Pope's record. Delays and various complications ensued, and in April 1311 the proceedings were suspended. Clement, however, had to pay a heavy price: the annulment of all Boniface's actions that were prejudicial to French interests and the absolution of his attacker Guillaume de Nogaret. And a still greater humiliation was in store: Philip now involved him in what was to be the most shameful crime of his life: the elimination of the Knights Templar.

It is difficult for us nowadays to understand – even to believe – the influence of the Templars in the later Middle Ages. Founded in the early twelfth century to protect the pilgrims flocking to the Holy Places after the First Crusade, within fifty years they were firmly established in almost every kingdom of Christendom, from Denmark to Spain, from Ireland to Armenia; within a century 'the

---

* The present papal palace was not built until the reign of Benedict XII, the third of the Avignon popes.

poor fellow-soldiers of Jesus Christ' were – despite their Benedictine vows of poverty, chastity and obedience – financing half Europe, the most powerful international bankers of the civilised world. By 1250 they were thought to possess some nine thousand landed properties; in Paris and London their houses were used as strongholds for royal treasure. From the English Templars Henry III borrowed the purchase money for the island of Oléron in 1235; from the French, Philip the Fair extracted the dowry of his daughter Isabella on her marriage to Edward II of England. For Louis IX they provided the greater part of his ransom, while to Edward I they advanced no less than 25,000 livres. They were most powerful of all in France, where they effectively constituted a state within a state; and as their influence increased it was hardly surprising that Philip should have become uneasy. But that was not the reason for the action which he now took against them.

He wanted their money. He had already dealt with the Jews; in 1306 he had seized all their assets and expelled them from France.* Now it was the turn of the Templars. Similar action against them would secure all the Templar wealth and property in his kingdom, and should solve his financial problems for years to come. The Order would, he knew, prove a formidable adversary; fortunately he had a weapon ready to hand. For many years there had been rumours circulating about the secret rites practised at its midnight meetings. All he needed to do was institute an official enquiry; it would not be hard to find witnesses who – in return for a small consideration – would be prepared to give the evidence required. And that evidence, when extracted, was all he could have dared to hope. The Templars, he now claimed, were Satanists who at their initiation denied Jesus Christ and trampled on the crucifix. Sodomy was not only permitted but actively encouraged. Such illegitimate children as were nevertheless engendered were disposed of by being roasted alive.

On Friday 13 October 1307, the Grand Master of the Temple, Jacques de Molay, was arrested in Paris with sixty of his leading brethren. To force them to confess, they were first tortured by the palace authorities and then handed over to the official inquisitors

---

* Edward I of England had already done much the same in 1290.

to be tortured again. Over the next six weeks no fewer than 138 knights were subjected to examination, of whom – hardly surprisingly – 123, including the Grand Master himself, finally confessed to at least some of the charges levelled against them. Philip, meanwhile, wrote to his fellow-monarchs urging them to follow his example. Edward II of England – who probably felt on somewhat shaky ground himself – was initially inclined to argue with his father-in-law, but when firm instructions arrived from Pope Clement V – as always, only too happy to assist the French king in any way he could – he hesitated no longer. The English Grand Master was taken into custody on 9 January 1308. All his knights followed him soon afterwards.

The public trial of the Order opened in Paris on 11 April 1310, when it was announced that any of the accused who attempted to retract an earlier confession would be burned at the stake. On 12 May fifty-four knights suffered this fate, and in the next two weeks nine others followed them. The whole contemptible affair dragged on for another four years, during which Pope and King continued to confer – a sure sign of the doubts that refused to go away – and to discuss the disposition of the Order's enormous wealth. Meanwhile the Grand Master languished in prison until his fate could be decided. Not until 14 March 1314 did the authorities bring him out on to the scaffold that had been erected in front of Notre-Dame, there to repeat his confession for the last time.

They had reason to regret their decision. De Molay can hardly be said to have distinguished himself over the previous seven years. He had confessed, retracted and confessed again; he had shown little courage, and few qualities even of leadership. But now he was an old man, in his middle seventies and about to meet his God: he had nothing more to lose. And so, supported by his colleague Geoffroy de Charnay, he spoke out loud and clear: as the Lord was his witness he and his Order were totally innocent of all the charges of which they had been accused. At once he and de Charnay were hurried away by the royal marshals, while messengers hastened to Philip. The king delayed his decision no longer. That same evening the two old knights were rowed out to a small island in the Seine, where the fires had been prepared.

It was later rumoured that with his last words de Molay had predicted that both Pope Clement and King Philip would appear at the judgement seat of God before the year was out, and had further pronounced that the royal line should be accursed to the thirteenth generation; it did not pass unnoticed that the Pope was dead in little more than a month, and the king, who was only forty-six, suffered a fatal stroke while hunting towards the end of November.* The two old knights faced the flames with courage and died nobly. After night had fallen, the monks of the Augustinian monastery on the further shore came to collect their bones, to be revered as those of saints and martyrs.

A great pope – Gregory VII for example, or Innocent III – could and would have saved the Templars; Clement V, alas, fell a long way short of greatness. His craven subservience to Philip in the most shameful chapter of the king's reign constitutes an indelible stain on his memory. In one instance only did he show any inclination to go his own way: Philip – who had instituted the campaign solely to get his hands on the Templars' money – cannot have welcomed the bull by which, on 2 May 1312, the Pope decreed that all their properties (outside the kingdoms of Castile, Aragon, Portugal and Majorca, on which he deferred his decision) should devolve upon their brethren the Knights Hospitallers, who suddenly found themselves richer than they had ever dreamed.

Anglo-French relations, meanwhile, continued to be an open sore. In England, Edward I had succeeded his father Henry III in 1272. At six foot two he towered over those around him, though a drooping left eyelid and a lisp slightly spoiled the general effect. Fortunately for King Philip much of his campaigning life was taken up, first with the Ninth Crusade and later with baronial wars in England, Wales and Scotland; but in 1293 matters came to a head when a

* The second part of the curse also seems to have had some effect. Philip and his five predecessors had reigned for a total of 177 years; his three sons, succeeding each other, reigned less than six years each, dying aged respectively twenty-seven, twenty-eight and thirty-three, with none of them leaving a male successor despite a total of six wives between them.

number of French sailors were violently attacked while ashore in British-held Gascony. Philip somewhat high-handedly summoned Edward, in his capacity as Duke of Aquitaine, to appear before the *Parlement** of Paris to answer the charges.

Edward of course had no intention of doing any such thing. First he sent ambassadors to Paris, who were instantly expelled. He then despatched his brother, Edmund Crouchback, Earl of Lancaster – who was both Philip's cousin and stepfather-in-law – to speak on his behalf, not only about the troubles in Gascony but about the king's own remarriage. He was still heartbroken after the death in 1290 of his beloved wife Eleanor of Castile (one of the happiest marriages in English history) but he had reluctantly agreed – entirely for diplomatic reasons – to marry Philip's half-sister Blanche. In the event of the negotiations being successful, Lancaster was also bidden to bring her to England. Unfortunately they were not: Philip was to reveal somewhat to his embarrassment that Blanche was in fact already engaged to Rudolph III of Habsburg. Furious, Edward once again declared war; and it was only five years later that a distinctly shaky truce was agreed. Finally, in 1299, a series of treaties provided for a double marriage: first, Edward to Blanche's sister Margaret; second, Edward's son, the future Edward II, to Philip's daughter Isabella. The first of these two marriages certainly helped to keep the peace between the two countries, though it cannot have been much fun for poor Margaret, forty years younger than her husband; the second was a disaster, since it led, as we shall shortly see, to the Hundred Years' War.

Philip the Fair died in 1314; but the last year of his life was over-shadowed by the worst scandal the House of Capet was ever called upon to face – when his daughter Isabella, Queen of England, publicly accused his three daughters-in-law of adultery, most of which she claimed had taken place in the dark and mysterious Tour de Nesle, a guard-tower of the old city wall on the left bank of the Seine. The king had three sons, all three of whom were to be kings of France. The eldest, the future Louis X, had married Margaret,

---

* The French *Parlement* should never be confused with the English Parliament. It was more like a permanent court of justice.

daughter of Robert II, Duke of Burgundy. Their marriage was not happy; Louis is said to have neglected his wife, 'feisty and shapely' as she was, far preferring to play tennis with his friends. The second son, Philip, was married to Joan, eldest daughter of Count Otto IV of Burgundy. This alliance seems to have been a lot more successful: the pair had four children in quick succession, and Philip's passionate love letters have come down to us. Charles, the third son, from all we hear sounds a crashing bore, and his marriage to Joan's sister Blanche was boring too.

The story begins in 1313, when Edward II and Queen Isabella came on a visit to her father in Paris. Their marriage was certainly not going well. Edward was flagrantly homosexual, and spent far more time with his favourite, Piers Gaveston, than he did with his wife. While in Paris, however, the two were on their best behaviour, and Isabella presented embroidered purses to her brothers- and sisters-in-law. A few months later, back in London, when the royal couple gave a dinner to celebrate their return Isabella noticed that two of the purses she had presented to her sisters-in-law were being carried by two young knights, the brothers Gautier and Philippe* d'Aunay. She immediately drew her own conclusions, and informed her father.

The king put the two men under surveillance, and gradually the facts became clear. It appeared that Gautier and Philippe were enjoying regular encounters in the Tour de Nesle with Margaret and Blanche. The third of the three ladies, Joan, was believed to have preferred watching. At any rate Philip decided to make the matter public and had all five arrested. The d'Aunay brothers were interrogated under torture; both confessed and were found guilty. They were first castrated, then drawn and quartered, and finally hanged. Blanche and Margaret, tried before the *Parlement* in Paris, were also convicted. Their heads were shaven and both were sentenced to imprisonment for life. They were sent to the dungeons

---

* I use the French version of his name here to avoid confusion. Maurice Druon's *Les rois maudits* provides a splendid version of the story. There is also a play by Alexandre Dumas, *La Tour de Nesle*, which I have not seen, and a highly enjoyable film made by Abel Gance in 1954 which I have.

of the castle of Château-Gaillard, where Margaret was smothered as soon as her husband succeeded to the throne so that he could marry again. Blanche remained in the dungeons for eight years, and was then sent to a nunnery. Joan was also tried, but found innocent.

Were the findings against the three princesses and their lovers justified? Probably yes – though Isabella had recently given birth to her son Edward, and there is no doubt that the removal of all three of her sisters-in-law would have substantially increased his prospects for the throne of France. Her own marriage was to fail catastrophically in a few years, and it is widely believed that she may have been indirectly responsible for the hideous murder of her husband Edward II, after she and her lover Roger Mortimer had seized power in England in 1326. She was not known as the 'She-Wolf of France' for nothing.

5

A Captured King

1326–80

Tell him, the crown, that he usurps, is mine,
And where he sets his foot, he ought to kneel;
'Tis not a petty dukedom that I claim,
But all the whole dominions of the realm;
Which if with grudging he refuse to yield,
I'll take away those borrow'd plumes of his
And send him naked to the wilderness.

Shakespeare, *Edward III*, Act I, Scene I★

T HE CAPETIAN LINE ended with something of a whimper: the three brothers – plus, if we are to be strictly accurate, a week-old baby – reigned altogether for only fourteen years. Louis X – known as *le Hutin*, the Quarrelsome, though several other kings might have had a better claim to the title – had in fact been King of Navarre since the death in 1305 of his mother, Queen Joan, but was to occupy the French throne for little more than eighteen months. His apologists give him credit for abolishing serfdom and for readmitting the Jews to France; but neither concession proved quite as good as it might have seemed. First of all, it was announced that each serf would have to pay for his freedom; if he could not or would not, his possessions – such as they were – would be seized anyway, to pay for what seemed an almost perpetual war in Flanders. As for

---

★ Most scholars now believe that at least the major part of this play is by Shakespeare. It has been included in both the Arden and the New Cambridge collections. This seems, incidentally, to be the first appearance in English of the phrase 'borrow'd plumes'; the *Oxford English Dictionary* dates it no earlier than 1802.

the Jews (whom his father had expelled) they were indeed allowed back, but only for twelve years, on approval. During that time they were obliged always to wear an armband and to live in ghettos. After that time, they risked being expelled again.

The darkest stain on Louis's character is the murder of his wife, Margaret, who, whatever she had been up to in the Tour de Nesle, certainly did not deserve death by suffocation. It was only five days later, on 19 August 1315, that her husband married Princess Clementia of Hungary.* Less than a year later he was dead, after a particularly exhausting game of tennis,† leaving Clementia pregnant. Here was a problem indeed, for this was the first time that a Capetian king had died without a male heir. Louis already had a daughter, Joan. If Clementia were to produce a son, he would inherit the throne; if a daughter, she and Joan would have roughly equal claims. Joan was older; on the other hand she was the daughter of Margaret, and after the affair of the Tour de Nesle no one could be sure by whom. Louis's brother Philip took over the regency until finally, on 15 November 1316, Clementia gave birth to a boy. Unfortunately he is known as John I the Posthumous, for he lived for just five days, until the 20th: the youngest king of France with the shortest reign, and the only king to have borne the title through his entire lifetime. He was succeeded – though only after a good deal of opposition – by his uncle Philip, who now became Philip V – thus reaffirming the old Salic law which excluded women from the line of succession.

There can be little doubt that Philip was the ablest of the three brothers. He was also the nicest. While Louis and Charles showed no mercy to their errant wives after the great scandal, Philip stood by Joan of Burgundy – whose implication in the affair was admittedly a good deal less certain – through thick and thin, until her name was finally cleared by the *Parlement* in Paris and she was allowed to return to court. Cynics have suggested that he refused to abandon

---

* Her claim to the title is too long and complicated to go into here. She was born and brought up in Naples, and never set foot in Hungary in her life.
† He is the first person whose name we know to have played the game, and its first fatal casualty. See also p.193, fn.

Joan because if he did he might also lose Burgundy, but such a consequence would have been highly unlikely: their surviving letters suggest a far more probable reason: that the two were deeply in love.

Politically and diplomatically, Philip's principal achievement was to come to an agreement with Count Robert of Flanders, whereby Robert would formally recognise Philip's young grandson Louis as his heir, in return for Louis being pledged in marriage to Robert's second daughter, Margaret. He was, however, rather less successful with his infinitely trickier neighbour Edward II of England. The difficulty was the province of Gascony. Here Edward was technically Philip's vassal; but he had avoided doing homage to Louis X and was clearly just as unwilling to show proper recognition to his brother. At last he most reluctantly consented – but on his arrival at Amiens was horrified to discover that Philip was now insisting on something more – a further oath of personal fealty to himself. This he very understandably refused; but the consequence was that relations between the two kings became worse instead of better.

Philip V reigned for a little over five years, dying – of sundry natural causes – in January 1322, and was succeeded by the youngest of the brothers, Charles IV, who reigned for six and despite three wives produced no male issue. Charles had difficulties, as had Philip, with the Count of Flanders and Edward of England, but those with Edward were soon overtaken by events – when in 1326 Queen Isabella and her lover Roger Mortimer seized the country with a small mercenary army, forced her husband to abdicate and the following year had him hideously murdered in Berkeley Castle. Her son Edward was thus a little over fourteen years old when he found himself the richest and most powerful ruler in Europe. True, English possessions beyond the Channel were no longer what they had once been. Two centuries before, Edward's great-great-great-grandfather Henry II had claimed, either as fiefs by inheritance or through marriage with Eleanor of Aquitaine, almost half the area of the France we know today. Since Henry's time, however, nearly all this had fallen away; and Edward wanted it back. On his mother's instructions – but against every instinct of his own – he concluded a peace treaty with Charles. He would take back Aquitaine, but

Charles would receive considerable territory in exchange, including the rich provinces of Limousin, Quercy and Périgord.

Charles himself died on 1 February 1328 in the Château de Vincennes. Like his brothers before him, he had produced no surviving male heir, but history strangely repeated itself. He left – just as Louis had left – a pregnant wife, and a regency under his cousin Philip of Valois was declared until she should produce her child. After two months, however, she gave birth to a girl; and so, owing to the Salic law, the direct branch of the Capetian line was extinct. There were now three possible candidates for the throne: Edward III of England, son of Isabella and grandson of Philip the Fair; Philip of Evreux, son-in-law of Louis X; and Philip of Valois, nephew of Philip IV and grandson of Philip III by his third son, Charles. Once again the Salic law became an issue, but the fact was that the French did not want a foreigner; they certainly had no wish to see themselves united with England under a single crown. Edward was still hardly more than a child – though he was already married, to Princess Philippa of Hainaut – lived across the sea and was the senior representative of that House of Plantagenet that for two centuries had caused them nothing but trouble. Philip was, moreover, already regent. They wanted a French king; and they got one. On 29 May 1328 King Philip VI was crowned at Reims.

And so, with Philip VI, 'the Fortunate', began the House of Valois. It was not a particularly promising start. The Capetians had been on the whole excellent kings. They had steadily built up France, transforming it from a Carolingian custard into a nation. Philip, however, perhaps conscious that he was not of royal birth – his father Charles of Valois, a younger brother of Philip IV, had striven all his life to gain a throne for himself but had never succeeded – seemed principally interested in matters of feudal prestige, particularly where they concerned the young Edward III who was, curiously enough, his nearest male relative. One of his first actions after his coronation was to summon Edward to pay homage for Aquitaine. Edward complied, but took his time; and when he eventually met Philip in Amiens Cathedral thirteen months later, he worded his vows so ambiguously that they were the cause of arguments between the two kings for years to come. But such arguments were inevitable, simply because Edward was convinced that it was he who had the strongest claim to the French throne. Even if the Salic law were upheld, he maintained, he himself as the late king's nephew was a closer relation than Philip, who was merely a cousin; and from the moment of his own coronation he began to prepare for war.

Until the middle of the thirteenth century bows and arrows had been considered inferior weapons, with too short a range and insufficient penetrating power to be of much use against armoured cavalry; but Edward's grandfather Edward I had, in the course of his campaigns in Wales, discovered the qualities of the Welsh longbow:

> In the war against the Welsh, one of the men at arms was struck by an arrow shot at him by a Welshman. It went right through his thigh, high up, where it was protected inside and outside the leg by his iron chausses, and then through the skirt of his leather tunic; next it penetrated that part of the saddle which is called the alva or seat; finally it lodged in the horse, driving so deep that it killed the animal.*

Edward had decreed that archery should be regularly practised by all his subjects 'who were not lame or decrepit', and the decree was theoretically still in force: his grandson thus had at his command, potentially at least, the most formidable army in Europe. But he was not yet ready to move against France. First he must deal with Mortimer, who was using his power simply to enrich himself and acquiring castles and titles all over the country. Eventually in 1330 the king ran him to earth at Nottingham Castle. Despite Isabella's famous entreaty, 'Fair son, have pity on the gentle Mortimer', her odious lover was hanged at Tyburn, his immense estates forfeited to the crown and his body left swinging on the gallows for two full days in public view.

For these first years of Philip's reign his relations with Edward were cordial enough; in 1332 the two even planned a joint Crusade, though it never came to anything. But Aquitaine remained a sore point, and Flanders was another, simply because the economies of England and Flanders were interdependent: England's principal product was wool, the Flemish were a nation of weavers. The

---

* *Itinerarium Cambriae*, 1191.

effective ruler of Flanders, Louis de Nevers, was Philip's vassal, but his subjects were anglophiles to a man and Edward knew he could count on them when necessary. Then in 1336 there came the problem of Count Robert of Artois. Robert claimed that he had been unjustly dispossessed of his estates, and in attempting to recover them had resorted to forgery. His guilt had been discovered, and he had sought refuge in England. Philip had demanded his extradition; Edward – to whom Robert, as a former adviser to the king, was extremely useful – had refused. Philip in return declared Aquitaine confiscated, accusing Edward of 'the many excesses, rebellions and acts of disobedience committed against us' and of 'sheltering the King's mortal enemy'. That, for Edward, was the last straw. He denied Philip's legitimacy and summoned him to surrender the throne of France.

The Hundred Years' War had begun.

There is no reason for us to trace the course of the war in any great detail. It was not in fact a single confrontation; rather was it a series of conflicts waged between 1337 and 1453 by the House of Plantagenet against that of Valois for the control of the Kingdom of France. Although at an early stage Edward had established himself with his family at Antwerp as a forward base, he did not invade French territory until the autumn of 1339. Invading armies seldom behave well towards local populations, but the English army seems to have been worse than most. The countryside was ravaged, villages laid waste. At Origny the local convent was burnt to the ground, the nuns subjected to wholesale rape. Such conduct may have been deliberately intended to provoke the King of France to battle; if so, it very nearly succeeded. When the French army finally caught up with the English near Saint-Quentin, Philip proposed a formal encounter in single combat – the old chivalric tradition was dying hard – at a site to be chosen by Edward; he stipulated only that the field should have neither trees, ditches nor marsh.

Edward asked nothing better. He was twenty-five years old, at the peak of his health and vigour, with a passion for war in all its aspects. He was a regular participant at tournaments; and what, after all, was his cousin proposing but a glorified joust? No sooner had the challenge been accepted, however, than Philip had second thoughts. The chronicler Froissart suggests that he listened to the advice of his uncle Robert of Anjou, King of Naples and a noted astrologer; more probably his scouts simply reported that the English king was a good deal stronger than he had been led to expect. At all events he returned to Paris. The English, grumbling loudly about French cowardice, retired to Brussels for the winter.

Edward's temper was considerably improved when, in January 1340, the people of Flanders recognised his claim to the French crown. He immediately quartered the arms of France with his own, ordered a new seal complete with fleurs-de-lys and adopted a surcoat of scarlet and blue, embroidered with the leopards and lilies that remain to this day on the royal escutcheon. But the Flemings, happy as they were to be an English rather than a French dependency, were men of business first and foremost, with a clear understanding of the value of money. When the king returned to England soon afterwards to hasten the delivery of the provisions he needed, they politely insisted that his wife and children should be left behind as security for the payment of his debts, Queen Philippa's own crown being put in pawn to the merchants of Cologne.

Meanwhile the French navy had entered the Channel, where they were giving increasing trouble. Already in 1338 their privateers had raided Portsmouth and Southampton; that October, Edward had ordered a line of stakes to be driven across the Thames to prevent similar assaults on London. The following year it had been the turn of Dover and Folkestone. Finally, by midsummer 1340, the king was ready to sail from the Thames estuary with the navy that he had long been preparing: some two hundred vessels, carrying perhaps five thousand archers and men-at-arms, together with horses and stores. Also accompanying him were what a contemporary described as 'a large number of English ladies, countesses, baronesses, knights' ladies and wives of London burgesses, who were on their way to visit the Queen of England at Ghent'. But just before they sailed came ominous news: scouts who had been patrolling the Channel reported that a French fleet at least twice the size of the English was awaiting them at the mouth of the River Zwin near the little town of Sluys – in those days the port of nearby Bruges. Edward's chancellor, the Archbishop of Canterbury John Stratford, urged him even at this late stage to cancel the whole expedition: in such conditions, he argued, to continue would be suicide. But the king remained firm – whereupon Stratford resigned his seal of office on the spot – and, shortly after midnight on 22 June, gave the order to weigh anchor.

On the afternoon of the day following, as his fleet approached the Flemish coast, Edward saw for himself the strength of the huge armada that Philip had drawn up: four hundred sail or more – 'so many', writes Froissart, 'that their masts resembled a forest'. Nineteen of them were larger than any that the English had ever seen. Characteristically, however, the king decided to attack at once. Pausing only to ensure the protection of the ladies, he spent what remained of the day deploying his ships, one with men-at-arms between every two carrying archers. Then, early in the morning of Midsummer Day, he led his fleet straight into the harbour mouth.

What followed was a massacre. The French fought valiantly, but were so tightly crowded together in the narrow inlet that they could barely move. Edward bore down upon them with the wind behind him, his archers – operating from platforms or 'castles' mounted high above the decks – loosing volleys of arrows high into the air to rain down on the enemy ships, while the sharp English prows shattered the motionless French hulls like matchwood. Only when sufficient damage had been done did the longbowmen pause in their work, to allow the men-at-arms to grapple, board and fight to the death. For nine hours the battle continued. When it was finished 230 French ships, including the flagship, had been captured and the rest destroyed, the two admirals dead among the wreckage. The fish in the harbour drank so much French blood, it was said afterwards, that had God given them the power of speech they would have spoken in French.

The Battle of Sluys – the first great naval victory in English history – gave Edward command of the Channel and ensured a moderately satisfactory bridgehead for his expeditionary armies for several years to come. The French army, however – in marked contrast to its navy – remained unscathed, still refusing to fight; the Flemish allies, bored with the war, were growing ever more obstreperous; and when, at the approach of autumn, the elderly Countess of Hainaut – Edward's mother-in-law and Philip's sister – emerged from the convent to which she had retired and proposed a truce, the two monarchs willingly agreed. It was signed on 23 September 1340 and lasted until midsummer the following year.

The next five years saw a good deal of inconclusive fighting in Brittany and Gascony. In 1346, however, King Philip received disturbing news. The English were preparing a considerable army – reports spoke of 10,000 archers and 4,000 men-at-arms – while a fleet estimated at 700 sail was assembling at Portsmouth. Their destination remained a close secret; even the captains, it was said, were given their orders under seal, to be opened only when they had left harbour. This meant that Philip had to keep his own ships widely dispersed, ready for any eventuality. Froissart tells us that the English fleet was originally bound for Gascony; but at the last moment Edward changed his entire plan: it landed instead in Normandy, at the little port of Saint-Vaast-la-Hougue on the eastern side of the Cotentin peninsula,* on 12 July.

For reasons not entirely clear, the army encamped for thirty-six hours on the beach before it advanced,† burning and plundering as it went. The unwalled towns of Barfleur, Carentan and the city of Caen were taken and sacked, and Rouen would have suffered the same fate – leaving the English in uncontested control of the lower Seine – had not the French army arrived just in time to save it. Edward had neither the time nor the money for a long siege; instead he wheeled to his right and crossed the river at Poissy, birthplace of Saint Louis and site of one of Philip's favourite palaces, in which he celebrated the Feast of the Assumption, making free with his

* Just ten miles to the north of Utah beach, where the American 4th Division landed on D-Day, 6 June 1944.

† Possibly because the king had injured himself on landing. Froissart reports that 'he stumbled, and fell so heavily that blood gushed from his nose. The knights surrounding him took this for a bad omen and begged him to go back on board for that day. "Why?" retorted the king without hesitation. "It is a very good sign: it shows that the land is thirsty to receive me."' The story would be more credible if it were not also told of William the Conqueror – and, I seem to remember, Julius Caesar.

cousin's best wines. Then he set off again towards Picardy and the Low Countries. He had a stroke of luck when he reached the Somme: the bridges were down, but it was low tide and his army was able to cross at a shallow ford just before the waters rose to block off the pursuing French. This twelve-hour respite was a godsend, giving him time to find a suitable defensive position and to rest his men before the confrontation he had long been awaiting. He found it on 26 August at Crécy, twelve miles north of Abbeville on the little River Maye, with a valley in front of him and thick woods behind.

The French cavalry of 8,000, supplemented by 4,000 hired Genoese crossbowmen and other mercenaries from Poland and Denmark, arrived in the late afternoon of Saturday 26 August, following a heavy shower of rain. The infantry was still some way behind. For that reason alone an immediate engagement was not to be thought of, and after a brief reconnaissance Philip ordered the attack deferred till the following day; but the knights in his vanguard ignored him, continuing to press forward up the hill until the English archers, no longer able to resist the temptation, loosed their first volley. By then it was too late to retire: the whole army was committed and the battle had begun. The Genoese advanced with their cross-bows, the strings of which were soaking wet after the rain; but the evening sun was full in their eyes, and the English longbowmen – who had protected their own bowstrings by removing them and putting them inside their helmets – could shoot six arrows in the time it took the Italians to deliver a single bolt. The latter turned tail and fled – straight into the charging French cavalry, which mowed them down by the hundred before itself falling under the relentless hail from the archers. Pressed hard from behind, the French attacked again and again, but – at least where the English centre and left flank were concerned – with no greater success.

The principal threat was to the right wing, commanded by the young Prince of Wales,★ where a number of French knights, together with a few Germans and Savoyards, had braved the arrows and were

★ There is no reason to think that his sobriquet, the Black Prince, probably occasioned by his black armour, was ever attached to him during his lifetime.

now grappling hand-to-hand with the English men-at-arms. The fighting was fierce and protracted, but they were finally routed by the prince and his companions. Meanwhile, in the gathering twilight, King Philip lost all control of the battle and his army lapsed into confusion. The fighting continued until long after dark; by morning, more than a third of the French army lay dead on the field. Among them – together with the king's brother the Duke of Alençon, his nephew Guy of Blois, the Duke of Lorraine, the Count of Flanders, nine French counts and over fifteen hundred knights – was the stone-blind John of Luxembourg, King of Bohemia, who had insisted on being led into the fray to strike at least one blow with his sword. His entourage, in order not to lose him, had tied his horse's bridle to their own. Not one of them escaped alive. They were found the next day, the knights lying round their leader, their horses still fastened together. The king's body was washed in warm water and wrapped in a clean linen shroud, and a solemn Mass was celebrated by the Bishop of Durham for the repose of his soul. The Prince of Wales there and then appropriated his badge of the three ostrich feathers and the motto *Ich Dien* – 'I Serve' – which his distant successor still bears to this day. English losses were less than a hundred.

Dawn brought a heavy fog – not unusual in Picardy in late August – and the earls of Arundel, Northampton and Suffolk set off with a force of mounted knights to look for King Philip and any other important Frenchmen who might be trying to escape. They failed to find the king, but came instead upon the bulk of the French infantry, together with a number of leading church dignitaries, including the Archbishop of Rouen and the Grand Prior of the Order of St John of Jerusalem. None of them had heard anything of the battle, and at first assumed that these new arrivals were their own compatriots. They were soon disillusioned. The English were in no mood for mercy. All the churchmen were killed in cold blood, as were the majority of the infantry – four times as many, according to one report, as lost their lives in the main encounter.

King Edward, Froissart tells us, had remained at the windmill he had chosen for his command post and had not once donned his helmet throughout the battle. Yet it was to him, rather than to his son, that the victory truly belonged. His alone was the strategy that had made it possible, while his coolness and shrewd tactical sense stood out in marked contrast to the impetuousness and lack of control shown by his adversary.* It was clear, too, that he better than anyone else understood the way in which warfare was evolving. The development of the longbow, capable in skilled hands of penetrating chain mail – or even a steel breastplate – from a range of a hundred yards or more, meant that henceforth any cavalry charge could be stopped in its tracks. As for artillery, such primitive devices as then existed were used exclusively for siege warfare; it would be well over a century before cannon and musketry proved their supremacy over the drawn bowstring, and the balance swung once again in favour of the aggressor rather than the defence.

And what, finally, of King Philip? He may have been a hopeless general; nevertheless he had been twice unhorsed and twice wounded, he had seen his standard-bearer killed in front of him and he had fought as valiantly as any of his men. With the help of Count John of Hainaut he managed to escape from the battlefield and rode under cover of darkness to the castle of Labroye, whose seneschal, roused in the small hours, demanded to know who so insistently sought admittance. 'Open quickly', answered Philip, 'for I am the fortune of France.' He was indeed. As his son was to prove ten years later at Poitiers, France could ill afford the cost of a captured king.

As soon as he had buried his dead, Edward advanced to Calais. He had no legal claim to the city: it had never been English. Even the French had been put off by its marshy approaches and general difficulty of access; it was only in the past century or so that the counts of Boulogne had recognised its strategic importance and developed it into the prosperous and strongly fortified city it had now become. But to Edward, too, its advantages were clear. Standing at the point

---

* The chronicler of the Abbey of Saint-Denis suggests another reason for the French defeat: 'The common soldiers wore tight shirts, so short that they exposed their private parts every time they bent over. The noblemen, on the other hand, wore hauberks extravagantly decorated and surmounted by vainglorious feathery crests. The Lord God, offended by so much obscenity and vanity, decided to use the King of England as His flail, to beat the French host into the ground.'

where the Channel was at its narrowest, only some twenty miles from the English shore, Calais promised not only a far more convenient bridgehead than the ports of Flanders, but the all-important control of the eastern approach to the straits. It would not, however, be easy in the taking. Behind its formidable walls, protected by a double ditch fed by the sea itself, there waited a strong and determined garrison under an outstandingly able commander – even though he was a martyr to gout – named Jean de Vienne. A direct assault was obviously out of the question; the only hope lay in a blockade. And so, early in September, the English pitched their camp on the flat and windy marshes and built what was in effect a small wooden village, which Edward named Villeneuve-le-Hardi. (French was still the language of the English court.) The siege threatened to be long; it was only sensible to make themselves as comfortable as possible.

Winter came, and spring, and summer – and still Calais held out. Finally, at the end of July 1347, King Philip appeared with his army on the cliff at Sangatte, a mile or so to the west. He was horrified by what he saw. Villeneuve-le-Hardi had become a veritable town. A network of well-laid-out streets surrounded a marketplace, where regular markets were held on Wednesdays and Saturdays. There were, writes Froissart, 'haberdashers' and butchers' shops, stalls selling cloth and bread and other necessities, so that almost anything could be bought there. All these things were brought over daily by sea from England, and goods and foodstuffs were also supplied from Flanders.' This prosperous little community could of course have been easily destroyed, had Philip been able to reach it; but Edward, forewarned, had made the necessary dispositions. Loading his ships with archers, catapults and bombards, he had drawn them up in the shallow water along the whole length of coast between Sangatte and Calais, making any advance along the shore impossible. The only other route, through the swampy ground behind the dunes, depended on a bridge at Nieulay where he had posted his cousin the Earl of Derby with the remaining archers and men-at-arms. The most cursory reconnaissance – effected with the full cooperation of the English – was enough to convince Philip that the situation was hopeless. The next morning he and his army were gone.

The departure of his sovereign told Jean de Vienne all he needed to know. Further resistance was pointless. He now signalled his readiness to surrender, provided only that the king would promise safe conduct for all the citizens. Edward at first refused point-blank. Calais had cost him vast quantities of money and countless men, together with almost a year of his own life. But when his envoy, Sir Walter Manny, returned to report that without the assurance of safety the city would continue to resist he relented. Manny was sent back to de Vienne with new conditions: six of the principal citizens must present themselves before the king, barefoot and bare-headed, with halters around their necks and the keys of the city and castle in their hands. With them he would do as he pleased; the rest of the population would be spared.

The English terms were proclaimed in the marketplace, and immediately the richest of all the burghers, Master Eustache de Saint-Pierre, stepped forward. Before long five others joined him. There and then the six stripped to their shirts and breeches, donned the halters, took the keys and made their way to the gates, led by Jean de Vienne himself on a pony, his sword reversed in token of submission. On their arrival before the king they knelt before him, presented him with the keys and begged for mercy. Edward refused to listen, and ordered their immediate execution; Sir Walter pleaded with him in vain. Only when Queen Philippa, then heavily pregnant, threw herself with some difficulty on her knees before her husband and begged him to spare them did he finally relent.* On Saturday 4 August 1347, Edward III entered Calais in triumph and gave orders that the entire city be evacuated. The miserable citizens were permitted to take nothing with them: houses and estates, furniture and possessions, all were left behind for the use of English colonists whom the king brought in to take their places. The descendants of those colonists were to remain there for over two centuries until, on 7 January 1558, the city was recaptured at last.

---

* Auguste Rodin's magnificent sculpture *The Burghers of Calais*, commissioned by the city in 1884, stands in front of the Hôtel de Ville. Another of the twelve original casts can be seen in Victoria Tower Gardens, London, in the shadow of the Houses of Parliament. McDonald's, in the city centre, has not changed its name as I suggested.

For nine years after the fall of Calais, the war was largely forgotten. The Black Death struck France in January 1348; within ten years it had killed an estimated one-third of the people living between India and Iceland. Of those who survived, the majority had other, more pressing anxieties. There were a few minor skirmishes in Gascony and Brittany, and towards the end of 1355 Edward even landed at Calais with another army. He seems, however, to have thought better of the operation: he and his men were back in England little more than a month later. But he remained as determined as ever; he would be satisfied with nothing less than the throne of France. Philip's son John II – John the Good, as he was later called – who had succeeded his father in 1350, was an incorrigible and impecunious romantic, whose dreams of chivalric derring-do were to betray him again and again. Fighting was in his blood, just as it was in Edward's. For the time being, both monarchs had other business on their minds; but when the moment came, both would show themselves only too keen to continue the struggle.

In the same year as Edward's abortive Calais expedition the Black Prince, now twenty-five and his father's lieutenant in Gascony, took an army to the south-west, failing to capture Narbonne and Carcassonne but causing appalling devastation in the surrounding country. In 1356 he was more ambitious still, launching raids up and down the Loire to the point where John II determined to teach him a lesson, summoning all the nobles and knights to assemble with their retinues at Chartres in the first week of September. The response was almost universal; by the time the army was ready it included the king's four sons, none of them yet out of their teens; the Constable of France, Gauthier de Brienne; two marshals; twenty-six dukes and counts; and lesser lords and knights without number, all bringing their own troops. Holinshed refers to three 'battles' (battalions) of 16,000 men each, making a total of 48,000, but he is almost certainly exaggerating. Whatever the precise figure, it was by any account a fairly impressive force that crossed the Loire at various points and then pressed south with all speed in pursuit of the English, catching up with them on the morning of Sunday 18 September, in the valley of the little River Moisson, seven miles south-east of Poitiers.

The French were in confident mood. For one thing, they comfortably outnumbered the English, who were probably no more than ten or twelve thousand at most; they also had reason to believe that the invaders were seriously short of food. For the rest of that day the two sides reconnoitred each other's positions and prepared for battle, while the Cardinal Talleyrand de Périgord, who had been sent by the Pope to attempt to negotiate a peace, shuttled fruitlessly backwards and forwards between the two sides. The Black Prince, who would certainly have avoided the battle if he could, offered to restore all his prisoners without ransom and to return all the castles that he had occupied; but John would accept nothing less than his own personal surrender, with a hundred of his knights – a demand that the prince refused to contemplate. As a result, soon after sunrise on the following day, the attack began.

It seems extraordinary that since their defeat at Crécy the French had taken no steps to raise and train enough longbowmen to pay back the English in their own coin, particularly since John was fully conscious of the danger presented by the English archers. His plan seems to have been to send a small force of some 300 mounted knights to charge into their midst and scatter them, before following with the main body of his army – on foot, because the marshy ground and the countless hedges and ditches were impossible for the cavalry to negotiate. The tactic proved disastrous. The knights – who represented the flower of his army, and included the Constable of France and both marshals – succumbed to the usual hail of arrows, and after this initial massacre the battle was as good as won. The French fought valiantly but were overwhelmed; and when the fighting was over their king himself was among the prisoners. The Black Prince treated him with elaborate courtesy. Froissart tells of how, the evening after the battle, he gave a supper in his honour, to which he also invited the other noble captives – including thirteen counts, an archbishop and sixty-six barons. 'He himself served in all humility both at the King's table and at the others . . . insisting that he was not worthy to sit himself at the table of so mighty a prince and so brave a soldier.' Seven months later he personally escorted John to London.

The capture of John II, leaving France in the hands of a nineteen-year-old dauphin,* might well have signalled the end of the war. King Edward, however, saw it differently. To him it seemed the perfect opportunity for the final decisive thrust that would win him the French crown. For the next four years he fought hard, often brilliantly; but contrary to his expectations he made no real headway, and early in 1360 he agreed to peace negotiations. On 8 May, in the little village of Brétigny near Chartres, the Black Prince and the dauphin, Charles, agreed to the terms of a treaty, subject to confirmation by their respective fathers. The French would recognise Edward's claim to Gascony and Poitou, together with various counties and towns in northern France, including Calais. They would also surrender the city of La Rochelle, which was of vital importance to England as the centre of the salt trade. King John's ransom was fixed at 3 million gold crowns: he was to be released on payment of the first instalment, which was to be one-fifth of the total. No fewer than forty noble hostages would be given as security for the remainder, which would be paid in six more annual instalments. Edward, for his part, would agree to renounce his claim to the throne of France and to all other regions of the country.

When the two kings met at Calais in October, however, Edward insisted that he would make his renunciations only after the transfer to him of all the lands ceded at Brétigny, with a proviso that this should be complete by 1 November 1361. It was a deeply disingenuous stipulation, and both sides knew it. Such transfers were long and complicated: they could not possibly be completed in a single year. The fact of the matter was that Edward was determined to leave his options open. He willingly agreed to easier terms for the payment of the ransom – but, as things turned out, it would have been better if the money had not been paid at all. In the summer of 1363 one of the hostages, John's second son, the Duke of Anjou, broke his parole and fled. His father, horrified, declared his intention of returning voluntarily to his captivity in London.

* He was the first heir presumptive to bear the title of Dauphin. In 1349, when Humbert II of Viennois sold the Dauphiné to Philip VI, he made a condition of the sale that the title would always be borne by France's sovereign or his heir.

His advisers did everything they could to dissuade him, but he remained firm. 'If good faith and honour are to be banished from the rest of the world,' he is quoted as saying, 'they should still be found in the hearts and words of princes.' He left Paris the week after Christmas, crossed the Channel in midwinter, and arrived in January 1364. Four months later he was dead, 'of an unknown illness'. Edward ordered him a magnificent funeral service at St Paul's before returning the body to France, where it was buried at Saint-Denis.

The former dauphin, now Charles V, may not have possessed all his father's sense of honour, but he was a far more intelligent man and a far better king. He saw, as clearly as any of his subjects, that his army was hopelessly outmoded. Its radical remodelling he entrusted to a minor Breton nobleman named Bertrand du Guesclin, who had shown consistent courage in innumerable skirmishes and whom he now made his commander-in-chief. The result was the first permanent army paid with regular wages – an immense relief to the peasantry, who were no longer regularly robbed and plundered by companies of unemployed soldiers. For the rest of the century there were no more major battles; the policy instead was to keep up a steady pressure on the English, to harry them remorselessly and to allow them to tire themselves out. It worked remarkably well: by the time Charles VI succeeded his father in 1380 they had lost interest and enthusiasm and most of them had returned home.

Alas, it proved to be a false dawn. The Hundred Years' War was not over yet, and the new King of France was revealed, all too soon, to be hopelessly insane.

6

A Foregone Conclusion

1380–1453

The cause of all the poor in '93:
The Cause of all the world at Waterloo;
The shouts of what was terrible and free
Behind the guns of *Vengeance* and her crew;
The Maid that rode so straightly and so true
And broke the line to pieces in her pride –
They had to chuck it up; it wouldn't do;
The Devil didn't like them, and they died.

'Ballade of Unsuccessful Men', Hilaire Belloc

THE NEW REIGN started well enough. Charles VI was only eleven years old; the government was consequently entrusted to a Council of Regency, which comprised perhaps half a dozen of the leading nobles, led by the king's uncles Philip ('the Bold') Duke of Burgundy and Louis Duke of Orléans. There was no love lost between the brothers, but they concealed their mutual hostility as best they could; only after the regency ended did their fateful struggle for power begin.

The first sign of trouble came in August 1392, when the king – now twenty-three – was riding through a forest with a group of knights; a young page, overcome by sleep, dropped the royal lance. Charles suddenly went berserk, drawing his sword and shouting: 'Forward against the traitors! They want to deliver me to the enemy!' whereat he laid about him indiscriminately to left and right. At last he was unhorsed and disarmed, but not before several of his own knights lay dead at his feet. From that time forward he was regularly visited by fits of insanity. The symptoms varied; sometimes he forgot who he was and had no idea that he was king, sometimes he believed he was St George, sometimes he was convinced that he was made of glass and would shatter at the slightest impact. He could not legitimately be removed from the throne, since there were prolonged periods when he appeared perfectly sane; but it was obvious that there must be a new regency – one which would have to continue, in all probability, for the rest of his reign.

The new council was presided over by the queen, Isabeau of Bavaria. Once again it inevitably included the dukes of Orléans and Burgundy, but this time their relative positions had changed. Whereas the earlier council during the king's minority had been dominated by Philip of Burgundy, his influence had decreased; it was now Louis of Orléans who was the driving force. Married to Valentina Visconti, daughter of Gian Galeazzo Duke of Milan, Louis was highly intelligent and deeply versed in the arts and culture of Italy; but his debauches were notorious and he was almost certainly the lover of the queen; it may well be that some of her twelve children were his. After a few years he was given the official guardianship of the dauphin and his siblings, a post which still further increased his power at court. Duke Philip, as may easily be imagined, watched these developments with mounting fury; but matters finally came to a head only after his death in 1404 and his succession by his son John, generally known as the Fearless. Relations between the houses of Burgundy and Orléans now broke down altogether, and the two entered into open conflict. The king's uncle, John Duke of Berry, persuaded them on 20 November 1407 to make a solemn vow of reconciliation, but just three days later Louis of Orléans was struck down by a bunch of assassins in a Paris street. John the Fearless made no attempt to deny responsibility; the murder, he claimed, was a totally justifiable act of 'tyrannicide'. He wisely slipped out of Paris for a short spell until the fuss died down, but only sixteen months later, by the Treaty of Chartres, he was officially absolved of the crime and restored to royal favour, his guardianship of the royal children confirmed.

By then, however, there had broken out what amounted to a civil war between the two rival houses. At the time of the assassination Louis's heir Charles of Orléans, though only fourteen, was determined to recover all the properties that the Burgundians had managed to confiscate from his father over the past years. To do this he needed powerful allies, chief among whom was his future father-in-law, Bernard VII Count of Armagnac.* Thus it was that the Orléans party came to be known as the Armagnacs. France was again deeply and dangerously divided.

All this was welcome news to the young Henry V of England when in 1413 he succeeded his father Henry IV as king. It seemed that France, torn apart by civil strife, headed by a mad monarch and governed by a young and friendless dauphin, was his for the taking. In fact, as the son of a usurper – Henry IV had deposed his predecessor, Richard II – he had little enough claim to the French throne, but he hoped to strengthen his case by marrying the king's daughter Princess Catherine. Early in 1415 he sent his uncle Thomas Beaufort to the French court, at the head of an impressive company of high ecclesiastics and noblemen and armed with a list of formidable demands. It was a tactic as old as diplomacy itself: deliberately to ask of a weaker nation more than it could possibly perform, and then to use its inevitable refusal as an excuse for war. First on the list was the crown of France. When this was denied – as it clearly would be – Beaufort was to demand Normandy, Maine, Anjou, Touraine and all the territories ceded to France by the Treaty of Brétigny in 1360. Next he was to claim half of Provence, with the castles of Beaufort and Nogent, as being part of the Lancastrian inheritance through Henry's grandfather John of Gaunt. These demands accounted for much of the French kingdom; but they were not all. Henry further insisted on the immediate payment of all the arrears of the ransom of John II – 1.6 million gold crowns. Finally he required the hand of the Princess Catherine, for whom he would be ready to accept a dowry of 2 million crowns.

France was not ready for war and was willing to pay heavily to avoid it; but such demands were beyond the bounds of reason. The French negotiators, led by the Duke of Berry, offered a considerable territorial addition to the English Duchy of Aquitaine and, for

---

* Charles of Orléans was to marry Bernard's daughter Bonne in 1410. Meanwhile Valentina's brother Carlo had married Bernard's sister Beatrice.

Catherine, an unprecedented dowry of 600,000 crowns, later increased to 800,000; but beyond that they could not go. Unhesitatingly Beaufort rejected the offer and returned to England to inform his master. Henry could not conceal his satisfaction. It was exactly what he had expected. Diplomacy could have gained him valuable territory, but only war could win him a crown. He now began his preparations in earnest. In less than six months he had some 1,500 vessels lying at anchor along the coast between Southampton and Portsmouth. Meanwhile he contracted for about 2,500 fully armoured knights with their attendant esquires, pages and horses, and some 8,000 archers, together with gunners, sappers, armourers, grooms, surgeons, cooks, saddlers, smiths, fletchers, chaplains and even minstrels. The cost, inevitably, was enormous: huge cash loans were raised from the wealthier private citizens, with virtually everything of value that the king possessed – including most of the crown jewels – being offered as security.

While this immense force was assembling, Henry set off on a pilgrimage to the shrine of St Winifred at Holywell in Wales – a return journey of some 400 miles – before making his way to the south coast, stopping briefly at Winchester to receive a delegation from the French court, sent in a desperate last-minute attempt to avert the coming invasion. He received the ambassadors with all the honour due to their high rank and loaded them with presents; but he rejected their improved offer of 900,000 crowns for Catherine's dowry. The expedition, he explained, was on the point of departure; there could be no turning back now. And so, on Sunday 11 August 1415, carrying such of the crown jewels not in pawn together with a hefty piece of the True Cross, he boarded *La Trinité Royale* and crossed the Channel to Harfleur.

Harfleur, lying on the estuary of the Seine a mile or two to the east of Le Havre, was generally believed to be impregnable. Its walls ran for two and a half miles, protected by a broad, deep moat and twenty-six towers. The fleet anchored in the estuary safely out of range of its cannon, while the army landed on the soft, marshy terrain a little to the east of the town and trundled its siege engines into position. On the following day the operation began. It was to continue for the next five weeks – weeks which, to the besieging

85

army, rapidly became a nightmare. The marshes, unhealthy at the best of times, swarmed with flies in the August heat; and the only available food supplies, consisting largely of rotten fruit and dubious shellfish washed down with raw Normandy cider, led to fever and dysentery which quickly spread through the whole army. Within a month the Bishop of Norwich and the Earl of Suffolk were both dead, together with many of the leading knights and some two thousand men; another five thousand, including the king's brother the Duke of Clarence, were sent back to England on stretchers.

But life was no easier for the people of Harfleur. They were by now running seriously short of food; and on 18 September the commander of the garrison sent a messenger to the king asking for terms. Henry's first reaction was to insist on unconditional surrender; then, realising that his own army could not continue in its present condition, he relented and gave permission for a delegation from the town to appeal for help to the dauphin in Rouen, on the understanding that if this were not forthcoming within four days Harfleur would capitulate. The delegation set off, only to be informed that the French army was nowhere near ready for action; and on the 22nd, as promised, the garrison surrendered. There followed a ceremonial entry into the town, with all the pomp and panoply that the king could muster; however, he dismounted at the gates, removed his shoes and went barefoot into the church of St Martin to give thanks.

His treatment of the townspeople was severe rather than savage. Harfleur was not put to the sack, as it might easily have been. The chief citizens were captured and held to ransom. For the rest, those who agreed to swear allegiance to the English crown were allowed to remain; those who refused – numbering perhaps two thousand, including women and children – were driven out. (Most of them were later picked up by the French army and resettled in Rouen.) Henry meanwhile sent an envoy to the dauphin bearing a challenge to single combat, the crown of France to go to the winner after the death of Charles VI; but this was rather a matter of form than anything else. The nineteen-year-old dauphin, a confirmed debauchee who had already contracted the disease that was to kill him within the year, was hardly likely to measure himself against a professional soldier eight years his senior, in the prime of life and the pink of condition.

Harfleur had been, in a sense, a victory; but it had also been a catastrophe. Death or disease had deprived the king of almost a third of his men. Of the 2,500 men-at-arms who had sailed with him to France, only 900 remained, together with perhaps 5,000 archers. The planned advance on Paris was now plainly out of the question; the only sensible course for Henry would have been to return directly to England, leaving a strong garrison in the conquered town. But for him the adventure was not yet over. He now announced to his surviving captains his intention of marching on Calais.

To most of them, such a plan must have seemed little short of insane. Calais was separated from Harfleur by 150 miles of difficult country, studded with hostile castles and fortified towns and crossed by a number of rivers, many of which might soon be flooded by the autumn rains. The French army, meanwhile, was known to have received the Armagnac reinforcements it had long been expecting; it now easily outnumbered the sadly depleted English force and could confidently be expected to block its path. Of all this the king was well aware, but his mind was made up. On 8 October he gave the order to march.

The army had not gone far beyond the River Somme when the French heralds rode up and informed the king that their army was only a short distance ahead; the English must prepare to face it in pitched battle, on ground – for such were the rules of medieval chivalry – equally favourable to both sides. In fact the expected encounter did not occur for another three days; but at last, on the morning of 24 October, the coming of dawn revealed the French army encamped on the opposite bank of the little River Ternoise. After some difficulty in securing the existing bridge, the English crossed in safety; but the king knew that he would not get much further without a fight, and it soon became clear just where the battle was to be fought – in the open country some thirty miles north-west of Arras, between the neighbouring villages of Tramecourt and Agincourt.* As he watched the French army preparing for the

---

* The village is now known as Azincourt.

fray, Henry at last seems to have realised the gravity of his situation. He was, first of all, overwhelmingly outnumbered – perhaps by as many as five or six to one. Moreover the enemy was fresh and rested, while his own men were near exhaustion after two weeks on the march. And so he took a decision that has usually been overlooked by British historians (and of course by Shakespeare): he sued for peace, offering the restoration of Harfleur and all his other gains, with full compensation for all the damage caused by his troops, in return for their safe passage to Calais. There was little hope, as he well knew, that his offer would be accepted; but at least it might delay the start of the battle, giving his soldiers the night's rest they so desperately needed.

For a week there had been almost incessant rain. All day the storm clouds had been gathering again, and as evening fell there came yet another downpour, which continued for much of the night. Lying – as most of the English were – out in the open, few of them could have got much sleep. Fewer still could have realised, however, that where the coming battle was concerned this almost unremitting rain was the best thing that could possibly have happened and would be seen, in retrospect, as a gift from God.

By the morning of Friday 25 October – it was the Feast of St Crispin and St Crispinian – the rain had stopped, leaving the recently ploughed meadows between the woods of Tramecourt to the east and Agincourt to the west a waterlogged morass; but there had been no reply to Henry's offer of terms, and both sides now prepared for battle. The king drew up his army in three divisions, line abreast. He himself, wearing his surcoat on which the three leopards of England were quartered with the fleur-de-lys of France, his helmet encircled by a thin gold crown, took command of the centre. All three divisions, in which the men-at-arms fought dismounted, were supported on each flank by companies of archers.

The French commanders, the Constable of France Charles d'Albret and Marshal Jean Boucicault, followed a different plan. For an army as large as theirs, the limited space between the two woods on each side – some 1,200 yards – made a line formation impossible:

they accordingly formed a column deployed in three ranks one behind the other, similarly dismounted but with a body of heavy cavalry on each side of the front rank. Between the three were companies of crossbowmen; despite the lessons of the previous century, the longbow had still not been generally adopted in France. Basically the French were putting their trust in their far superior strength, and in the impetus of the outflanking cavalry attack with which they intended to open the battle.

Oddly, they seem to have taken no account of the recent weather. A knight in full armour imposes a formidable weight on the strongest of horses, and for a successful cavalry charge hard ground was essential. At eleven o'clock d'Albret gave the signal for the attack and the chargers moved forward; but they soon sank up to their fetlocks in the soft mud, and the dismounted men-at-arms did very little better. Meanwhile the English archers loosed deluges of arrows and took a fearsome toll of cavalry and infantry alike, before exchanging their bows for short swords, axes and clubs, with which they quickly accounted for the relatively few Frenchmen who managed to reach the English line. The second wave of the attack, under the Duke of Alençon, was no more successful than the first, the English scrambling over the piles of dead and wounded to continue the slaughter. The third wave, seeing the fate of its predecessors, turned tail and fled.

It was at this point, with victory already assured, that the king gave the order which in the eyes of posterity has constituted the darkest stain on his reputation. Only the highest-ranking noblemen – for whom valuable ransoms could be expected – were to be spared; all other prisoners, he ordered, were to be instantly put to death. What prompted such a reaction, utterly contrary as it was to all the traditions of warfare? Was there, as it was later claimed, some sudden movement on the part of the French cavalry that led Henry to suspect an attack from the rear? It is possible, though no such attack was ever made. Many of his men refused point-blank to obey the order, even after he had threatened to hang all those who held back; at last he was obliged to designate two hundred of his own archers specifically for the task. Such, alas, was the aftermath of the victory that has gone down as one of the most glorious in English history.

By mid-afternoon there was nothing to do but to count and where possible to identify the dead. The French losses were enormous: out of some 20,000 men, well over a third – some 7,000 – were gone, including d'Albret, the dukes of Alençon and Bar, and two brothers of the Duke of Burgundy, Anthony Duke of Brabant and Philip Count of Nevers. With them were 1,560 knights, perhaps 5,000 men-at-arms and an unknown number of irregulars. Marshal Boucicault, with the dukes of Bourbon and Orléans, was a prisoner. By contrast the English losses were at the most 1,600, probably a good deal fewer. Only two English noblemen lost their lives: the young Earl of Suffolk – whose father had died at Harfleur – and the forty-two-year-old Duke of York, who was seriously overweight and whose heavy armour seems to have brought on a heart attack.

Given the state of the ground and the tactics chosen by the French, the victory of Agincourt was a foregone conclusion; but there were other reasons too why the battle ended as it did. The English army was united under a single commander, who had already proved himself a superb leader of men and who himself fought like a tiger throughout the battle, personally saving the life of his brother the Duke of Gloucester. The French on the other hand were split, with none of their generals in undisputed control and their command structure, such as it was, riven by divided loyalties. Moreover – and this must be repeated, since to us in retrospect it seems well-nigh inexplicable – despite their experience at Crécy and Poitiers they had still not accepted the superiority of the longbow and were consequently powerless against the English archers. For this alone they deserved to lose – though they certainly did not deserve the unspeakable brutality they suffered after their defeat.

Agincourt added fuel to the flames of the hatred – for it was nothing less – which now existed between the Burgundians and the Armagnacs. In May 1418 John the Fearless – who had kept his troops well clear of the battle – captured Paris and proclaimed himself protector of the mad king; the dauphin was forced to flee for his life. John was careful not to ally himself openly with the English for fear of losing his immense popularity among the common people of France, but it was by this time obvious where his sympathies lay: when the English took Rouen in 1419 he did not lift a finger to defend it. With almost the whole of northern France in English hands and Paris in Burgundian, the dauphin saw that his only hope lay in reconciliation, and it was agreed that he and the Duke of Burgundy should meet on 10 September 1419 on the bridge at Montereau, at the confluence of the Seine and the Yonne. John arrived in all good faith, but within minutes of his arrival was assassinated by a misguided friend of the dauphin.* His son and successor, to be known as Philip the Good, stepped up the civil war and in 1420, by the Treaty of Troyes, allied himself with England – an alliance which was to be confirmed three years later after Henry's death when Philip's sister Anne was married to John Duke of Bedford, Henry's brother and regent for the infant Henry VI. But the treaty had another consequence, far more immediate and important: Henry's marriage to Charles VI's daughter Catherine and his recognition by her poor, mad father as the legitimate successor to the French throne.

France's situation had never been more desperate. As a free nation, she had almost ceased to exist. The civil war showed no sign of stopping: Burgundians and Armagnacs were still at each other's throats. Through his marriage, Henry had become not only regent, but heir to the throne. The dauphin was effectively in exile at Bourges; Bedford was governor in Paris. And when, in 1422, Henry and Charles died within three months of each other, it was the eight-month-old Henry VI of England who was proclaimed King of France. Certainly the country still had a French king: young Charles VII, now nineteen. He was deeply pious, always firmly maintaining his innocence over Duke John's assassination, but tormented always by doubt: was he truly the heir to the House of Valois? His mother Isabeau had – perhaps forgivably – been serially unfaithful to her husband. He knew that the vast majority of his subjects – if subjects they were – would welcome him; they had no desire to be ruled by a foreigner. But how was he to make good

---

* Many years later a monk in Dijon showed Francis I the hole in John's skull. 'Here, sire,' he said, 'is the hole through which the English entered France.'

his claim? The English, already masters of northern France, were now laying siege to Orléans, which was resisting bravely but had little hope of defeating them.

At this point, in March 1429, there appeared on the scene France's beloved heroine, Joan of Arc. Born of peasant stock at Domrémy in Lorraine, she had first heard her 'voices' at the age of thirteen; and four years later, in the early spring of 1429, she left her home village, against formidable opposition, for the court of the dauphin★ at Chinon. On 8 March, having been instantly identified by her as he hid among a group of courtiers, he granted her an audience – in the course of which she reassured him 'that he was the true heir of France and son of the King' and informed him of her divine mission: to raise the siege of Orléans and to escort him to his coronation at Reims. Still unconvinced, he sent her to Poitiers for examination by a body of ecclesiastics; only after they had given their unqualified approval did he despatch her to Orléans.

The city had been under siege since the previous October by an English army initially under the command of Thomas Montagu Earl of Salisbury, who had recently returned to France with a private army of 2,700 men raised at his own expense. In November, however, Salisbury had been killed by a French cannonball as he stood at a window; his place had been taken by two joint commanders, William de la Pole Earl of Suffolk and John Talbot Earl of Shrewsbury, who had determined to starve out the city. The winter that followed had not been uneventful. An armed convoy of provisions had been attacked on 12 February by 4,000 French and Scots. The assailants had been repelled, but not before their cannon had shattered the supply casks, which had spewed vast quantities of salted fish all over the field. Shortly after this 'Battle of the Herrings' the defenders of Orléans, now running seriously short of food, suggested the surrender of the city to the Duke of Burgundy, who had joined the siege with an army of his own. Bedford – who had remained so far in his

---

★ Though Charles VI had now been seven years in his grave, Charles VII was still known as the dauphin, not yet having been consecrated or crowned.

headquarters at Chartres – naturally refused,★ but the duke took grave offence and immediately withdrew with all his men.

It was at this point that Joan arrived in the city. Her appearance put new spirit into the citizens, and on 4 May the counter-attack began. She herself, though wounded in the neck by an arrow, refused to leave the battle till it was won. A day or two later the English were in full retreat, the French in pursuit. During the fierce street fighting Suffolk and Talbot were both taken prisoner. Joan, now believed on all sides to be invincible, met Charles at Tours and pressed him no longer to delay his coronation at Reims. The ceremony took place, in her presence, on 17 July 1429. Her work done, her voices now silent, her mission accomplished, she longed to return to her village. Had she been allowed to do so, it would have saved her life; but the people refused to let her go and she bowed, disastrously, to their will, urging Charles now to march on Paris. He did so in September, but his attempt to capture the city was unsuccessful and Joan was once again wounded, this time in the thigh.

All was not yet lost: the English, still in retreat, had already evacuated the Loire valley, most of the Ile-de-France and virtually all Champagne; a concerted French push into Picardy might have driven them back to Calais. But the chance was thrown away. The French commander George de la Trémoille – who detested Joan – now took it upon himself to disband the army, giving Bedford the perfect opportunity to regroup and recover, and to bring his young sovereign over to France for his coronation. Henry, by now nine years old, reached Calais in April 1430 in the company of Cardinal Beaufort, Bishop of Winchester and 10,000 men, but such was the prevailing anarchy that he had to remain there for another three months; not till the end of July was he able to travel, and then only as far as Rouen. He was lodged in the castle, and was still there five months later when Joan arrived, in chains. She had been taken prisoner on 23 May during an attempt to relieve Compiègne, which

---

★ Bedford answered the duke's ambassadors that 'it was not honourable nor yet consonante to reason, that the kyng of England should beate the bushe and the duke of Burgoyne should haue the birdes'; (Edward Hall).

was under siege by the Burgundians; but she had spent the interim in several other prisons while her captor John of Luxembourg haggled over her price with Philip of Burgundy and the Duke of Bedford. Finally she had been handed over to the English for 10,000 francs. Did she and Henry ever meet? They certainly could have; but Richard Beauchamp, Earl of Warwick – the king's guardian and tutor, who happened also to be governor of the castle – kept her guarded day and night by five English soldiers. He is unlikely, to say the least, to have permitted his young guest to come in contact with a woman whom he believed to be an evil witch, 'the disciple and limb of the Fiend'.

Joan's examination began on 21 February 1431. Five weeks later, on 27 March, she appeared at her trial, during which she was allowed no defence counsel or spiritual adviser; and on Wednesday 30 May, excommunicated and declared a heretic, she was burned at the stake in the marketplace of Rouen – the pyre having been prepared well in advance of the sentence. Her ashes were cast into the Seine. She was only nineteen, but she had done her work well. She had delivered Orléans; she had seen the dauphin crowned, as his ancestors had been crowned before him, in the cathedral at Reims; from the moment of her first appearance, English fortunes had begun to decline. They were never to recover. True, the ten-year-old Henry VI finally reached Paris where, on 26 December, alone of all the English monarchs, he was crowned in Notre-Dame – by Cardinal Beaufort, and according to the English liturgy; but if Bedford had hoped to impress the French by this ceremony, he failed. The service was poorly attended, the subsequent banquet proved a fiasco, no amnesty was declared, no alms were distributed to the poor, and two days after Christmas the king was slipped almost furtively out of Paris to return to England.

By now there were few people on either side of the Channel who had much stomach for the war. To the pious young king, hostility between fellow-Christians was a cause of continual grief; Bedford, knowing that the cause was hopeless, longed to put an end to the fighting and found strong support in Parliament, which actually presented a petition to that effect. Burgundy, too, was increasingly eager for peace. Only Humphrey Duke of Gloucester

– another brother of Henry V – continued to argue fiercely for a continuation of the war, sabotaging every attempt at negotiation. Finally in 1435 Philip of Burgundy lost patience and convened, on his own initiative, a peace conference at Arras.

The English, whose delegation was strongly influenced by Duke Humphrey, refused to renounce the royal title to France and ultimately withdrew altogether from the negotiations. Almost at once they had reason to regret their departure. A week later, on 21 September, they were horrified to learn that France and Burgundy had effected a reconciliation. King Charles had agreed to make a public apology for the assassination of John the Fearless and to surrender those responsible; Philip had then been formally absolved by the attendant cardinals from his oath of allegiance to the English king. When young Henry heard the news, he wept; for Humphrey and his militants, on the other hand, there was a great wave of support as the people of London expressed their anger at the Burgundian betrayal by looting and firing the houses of all the Flemish merchants in the city.

Bedford, too, would have shed tears to see much of his life's work brought to nothing; but a week before the Franco-Burgundian peace, on 14 September 1435, he had died aged forty-six at Rouen and been buried in the cathedral. He had served his father, his elder brother and his nephew with unswerving loyalty, never once – in marked distinction to his brother Humphrey – putting his own interests before his duty. If his life ultimately ended in failure, it was no fault of his. His wisdom and selflessness were sorely to be missed in the years that followed.

In 1436 King Charles VII made his solemn entry into Paris. Normandy was recovered in 1450, Guienne in 1453. The English retained Calais, and nothing more. The Hundred Years' War had been a heavy price to pay for it.

7

The Universal Spider

1453–83

Of all pleasures he loved hunting and hawking, but nothing pleased him more than dogs. As for ladies, he never got involved with them whilst I was with him, for about the time of my arrival he lost a son which caused him great grief, and he swore an oath to God, in my presence, to touch no other woman but the Queen, his wife.* And although this is no more than he ought to have done according to the laws of marriage, it was a considerable achievement, seeing that he had so many at his command, to persevere in this resolution, since the Queen, though a good woman, was not one of those in whom men take great pleasure . . .

Philippe de Commines

WITH THE WAR out of the way, France flourished. By 1440, and perhaps even a little before, King Charles VII had become the most influential ruler in Europe. 'He is the King of Kings,' wrote the Doge of Venice, 'nothing is possible without him.' He was lucky, too, to have at his court one of the most brilliant merchants of all time. Jacques Coeur had made his way in about 1430 to the Levant, basing himself in Damascus; and within a few years he had established France firmly in the Middle East to the point where it became a serious rival to the great trading republics of Italy. In 1436 Charles summoned him back to Paris and made him Master of the Mint; then in 1448 he travelled to Rome as the king's ambassador to Pope Nicholas V, and from about that time

* Charlotte of Savoy.

made his master regular financial advances with which to carry on Charles's wars when necessary. By now he was the richest private citizen in French history. He probably possessed more ships than the king, he employed three hundred managers and had business houses all over western Europe. His house in Bourges remains one of the finest secular monuments of the late Middle Ages to be found anywhere. He gave the cathedral its exquisite sanctuary, and his son Jean became its archbishop.

But it was too good to last. In February 1450, Agnès Sorel, the king's ravishingly beautiful mistress – she was known as *la Dame de Beauté* and was the first officially recognised royal mistress in history – died mysteriously at twenty-eight, and one of the court ladies, deeply in debt to Jacques Coeur, formally accused him of having poisoned her. There was not a shred of evidence against him, but in July 1451 Charles bowed to the increasing pressure, giving orders for his arrest and for the confiscation of his goods. Accusations rained down: he had paid French gold to the infidel, he had kidnapped oarsmen for his galleys, he had sent back a Christian slave who had sought refuge in one of his ships, he had been guilty of sharp practice in Languedoc. Everyone knew he was innocent, but it made no difference: he was held for nearly two years in five different prisons, after which he was obliged to do public penance and to pay the king a vast additional sum, while the rest of his property was forfeited and he was exiled for an indefinite period. In 1455 he managed to get to Rome, where Pope Nicholas – who remembered him with affection – welcomed him warmly. On Nicholas's death in 1455 his successor Calixtus III gave Coeur the command of a fleet of sixteen ships he was sending to Rhodes, which was suffering one of its periodic sieges by the Mameluke Sultan of Egypt. Coeur was taken ill on the way, and died soon after his arrival.

Did Charles have a guilty conscience over the fate of Jacques Coeur? He certainly should have, but in his last years there were two greater anxieties on his mind: the Duchy of Burgundy and his son Louis, the dauphin. The dukes of Burgundy, technically vassals of France, had – like Coeur – grown too rich and too powerful; but – being by now kings in all but name – they were a good deal less easily dealt with. Besides Burgundy – which Philip the Bold had received as an appanage from his father, John the Good – they had acquired Flanders through marriage and now controlled all the Low Countries as far west as the mouth of the Somme. Their duchy extended from the North Sea to the Jura, the foothills of the Alps. They had long since ceased to pay homage to the King of France – indeed, they had gone so far as to ally themselves with the English during the Hundred Years' War. (It was they, far more than the English, who had been responsible for the capture and burning of Joan of Arc.) Their court at Dijon was every bit as cultivated as that of Paris; their architecture was superb, their sculpture – inspired by the astonishing genius of Claus Sluter – still more so. As early as 1429 Duke Philip the Good had founded the Order of the Golden Fleece, which was to become perhaps the highest and most-sought-after decoration in all Europe.

The other problem was the dauphin. Almost from the day of his birth in 1423, young Louis had been a problem. Eldest of the fourteen children borne to Charles VII by Marie of Anjou, as a boy he had shown himself to be fearsomely intelligent – a good deal more so than his father, whom he disliked and despised. Before long he was demanding real power, but Charles – who fully recip-rocated his son's feelings – always refused. Louis consequently did everything he could to destabilise his father's reign. As early as 1440, when he was only seventeen, he had joined a vassals' rebellion against the king known as the *Praguerie*,* and was soon obliged first to retire to his province of Dauphiné, and then in 1456 to seek refuge with Philip of Burgundy. 'My cousin of Burgundy knows not what he does,' said Charles with feeling. 'He is suckling the fox who will eat his hens.' Louis also showed particular animosity against his father's mistress Agnès Sorel, on one occasion driving her with a drawn sword into Charles's bed. It was almost certainly he who was responsible for her murder – now thought to be by mercury poisoning – for which the innocent Jacques Coeur paid so heavy a price.

* It was connected with the contemporary Hussite uprisings in Prague, in which he was also involved.

In 1458 the king fell seriously ill. The disease began with an ulcer on his leg which refused to heal and began to suppurate; soon afterwards the infection spread to his jaw, where it caused a huge and painful abscess. This continued to grow in size until he could no longer swallow. Realising that he had probably only a few days to live, he summoned the dauphin to his bedside; but Louis predictably refused to come. It was his last disobedience, his last betrayal. Charles died on 21 July 1461, and was buried next to his parents in Saint-Denis. He had been a good king, if not perhaps a great one. The first part of his reign had been inevitably overshadowed by Joan of Arc and her martyrdom; but in the second he succeeded in doing something that his four predecessors had all failed to do – he had driven the English out of France, leaving only their last toehold in Calais. Finally, he had provided France with a standing army, her first since the days of the Romans. His subjects had good cause to be grateful.

With Louis XI it can safely be said that the age of chivalry was gone for ever. His character failed utterly to improve. He cared little for honour, breaking his word again and again, and fully expecting others to break theirs. Having been a consistently disobedient son, he expected his own children to behave in much the same manner and never trusted them an inch. And yet, in his own rather dreadful way, he was a greater king than his father, one who worked extremely hard, if never entirely selflessly, to create a strong, centralised monarchy in which the nobility would know its place. That last qualification was important: Louis had always been fearful of the great, whose power and influence he strove all his life to diminish. He infinitely preferred to employ the bourgeoisie and those of humble origins, raising them regularly to the highest offices of state, while he himself travelled constantly through his kingdom, taking provincial officials and local governments off their guard and instituting ruthless investigations if he was dissatisfied – which he very often was.

When he left the Burgundian court to receive the crown of France

at Reims he was already thirty-eight years old and a widower:* now
at last he could give free rein to the planning and plotting for which
he was to become famous. Intrigue was in his blood. Before very
long he had earned the sobriquet *le Rusé* – the Cunning – and
before much longer he was being described as *l'araignée universelle*,
'the universal spider', spinning intricate webs of conspiracy, enmeshing
his enemies one by one and slowly pulling them in. His principal
enemy, not unnaturally, was Burgundy. The fact that the Burgundian
court had given him refuge for five years mattered not a jot to him;
his father's prophecy was proved right, and once back in France he
was resolved to do all he could to destroy it – a resolution which
became even more determined after the succession in 1467 of Duke
Charles the Bold, whom he knew to be planning to raise Burgundy
into an independent kingdom. He had already found some unexpected allies in 1465, when the people of Liège first rose up against
Duke Charles's father Philip, and had immediately joined them.†
This turned out to be a serious mistake. The rebels were defeated
and Louis was forced into a humiliating treaty, giving up much of
the territory that he had acquired from Philip. His subsequent
conduct, however, was entirely typical of him. First he turned on
the Liègeois, giving his support to Duke Charles in a siege of the
city in which hundreds of his former allies were massacred; then he
returned to France, whereupon he instantly repudiated the treaty
and set about building up his forces for a full-scale war. This broke
out in 1472, when Charles laid siege to Beauvais and several other
towns; but he got nowhere and finally had to sue for peace.

Burgundy continued as a European power for another two years.
It was finally defeated not by Louis but by the army of the Duke
of Lorraine and the Swiss. The Battle of Nancy was fought on 5
January 1477. Duke Charles's naked body was found several days
later, locked into a frozen river, his head split almost in two, his
face so badly mutilated that his physician was able to identify him

---

* His first wife, Margaret of Scotland (daughter of King James I), had died,
childless and miserable, in 1445 at the age of twenty. In 1451, without his father's
consent, Louis had taken as his second wife Charlotte of Savoy; he was twenty-
seven, she was nine.
† The story is told in Sir Walter Scott's *Quentin Durward*.

only from his old battle scars and his curiously long fingernails. Here was a piece of luck for Louis, for Charles had no male heirs; Burgundy and Picardy accordingly reverted to the French crown, and the King of France could congratulate himself that he no longer had to endure a serious and troublesome rival on his north-eastern frontier.

It was only unfortunate that the duke had left a daughter, Mary, who inherited his personal fortune and all those territories that had previously belonged to the empire. To get his hands on these, Louis made a determined effort to arrange for her to marry his eldest son, but here again there was a problem: Mary was twenty, the dauphin was nine. Unsurprisingly she preferred Maximilian of Austria, who many years later was to become Holy Roman Emperor – bringing him, incidentally, as her dowry the entire territory of Flanders, including the city of Brussels which her family had made its capital. Mary herself never became empress; in 1482 she fell from her horse and was killed. She left a son – confusingly, another Philip the Fair, of whom we shall be hearing more later – and a daughter, Margaret; and it was Margaret rather than her mother who was eventually betrothed to the dauphin, bringing to France as her dowry Artois and the Franche-Comté on the Swiss border. She came to Paris as a child of three and grew up at the French court as a *fille de France*. Here for Louis was another bloodless victory.

While the French and the Burgundians were at each other's throats, the English were fully occupied with a civil war of their own: that bitter struggle between the houses of York and Lancaster known as the Wars of the Roses. Louis, it need hardly be said, kept a watchful eye on its progress. The weak – some said half-witted – King Henry VI of Lancaster had been deposed in 1461 and succeeded on the throne by the Yorkist Edward IV, thanks largely to the machinations of Richard, Earl of Warwick ('the King-maker'); and Duke Philip of Burgundy had made no secret of his support for the Yorkists. On the other hand King Henry's queen, Margaret of Anjou, was Louis's cousin.[*] Later that year she crossed to France and persuaded him to lend her money and send an expeditionary force to restore her husband, promising him Calais in return. In fact Duke Philip refused point-blank

[*] Louis's mother, Marie of Anjou, was the sister of Margaret's father René.

to allow French troops to cross his territory, so the whole scheme came to nothing; but Queen Margaret remained at the French court, and was still there when Warwick, having fallen out with King Edward, now arrived in France and made a formal request to Louis for protection.

Louis was only too pleased to agree. By this time Edward had succeeded in antagonising almost all of his most important erstwhile supporters, and there seemed at last to be a chance of restoring Henry VI and cementing an Anglo-French alliance against the Duke of Burgundy. The principal stumbling block was Queen Margaret. Could she ever be persuaded to overcome her hatred for Warwick – who had after all been responsible for her husband's deposition – and ally herself with him? Louis prepared his ground carefully; and at last, on 22 July 1470, the Earl of Warwick presented himself before Margaret and flung himself at her feet. She left him, we are told, lying prone for some considerable time before agreeing to forgive him, and even then insisted on a further public act of contrition at Westminster after her husband had been restored. But Warwick was finally permitted to rise to his feet and, to celebrate their reconciliation, Margaret's son Richard Prince of Wales was formally betrothed in the church of St Mary in Angers to his daughter Anne Neville, while all those present swore on a relic of the True Cross to remain faithful to Henry VI.

But this is a history of France, not of England. Let it be said simply that King Edward, having fled briefly to the Low Countries, returned shortly afterwards to destroy the Lancastrians at Tewkesbury in May 1471. Queen Margaret had meanwhile retired with her ladies to a 'poor religious place' on the Worcester road, and was still there three days later when she was taken prisoner. For the next four years she was under what might be called house arrest, being constantly transferred from place to place, and this might well have been the pattern for the rest of her life had Edward not decided, in 1475, to assert his claim – such as it was – to the throne of France.

Having as he thought concluded a profitable alliance with the Duke of Burgundy, Edward crossed the Channel in June, with an invasion force of some 16,000 men. His intention was to march through Burgundian territory to Reims, but to his astonishment he soon found that Burgundian troops were barring his way and Burgundian towns refusing him entry. Louis, characteristically, now sent word to him that he could offer better terms than his so-called allies. Edward accepted and on Louis's suggestion, made his way to Amiens.

For Edward's expedition – and for much of the reign of Louis XI – we have a fascinating contemporary source. Philippe de Commines was a writer and diplomat in the courts of France and Burgundy; he has been described as 'the first critical and philosophical historian since classical times'★ and he gives a meticulously detailed account of all that took place. 'The King of England', he writes,

> camped half a league from Amiens . . . The King sent the King of England three hundred wagons loaded with the best wine it was possible to find and this supply train appeared to be an army almost as large as the English one . . . He had ordered two large tables to be set up at the entrance to the gate of the town, one on either side, laden with all kinds of foodstuffs which would make them want to drink the wine. Men stood by to serve it, and not a drop of water could be seen . . . As soon as the English approached the gate they saw this arrangement . . . They took it all in very good part. When they were in the town, they paid for nothing wherever they went. There were nine or ten taverns fully stocked with everything they needed where they could eat and drink. They asked for whatever they wanted and paid nothing; this lasted for three or four days.

The two monarchs finally met at Picquigny, a little village on the Somme just outside Amiens, on a specially constructed bridge with a wooden grille at its centre. Such conditions seemed hardly favourable for serious negotiations affecting the future of both countries; yet somehow they proved successful. In an agreement signed by the two monarchs on 29 August 1475, they agreed to a seven-year truce, with free trade between them. Louis was to pay Edward 75,000 crowns, essentially a bribe never again to pursue his claim to the French throne. This would be followed by an annual payment of

---

★ *Oxford Companion to English Literature.*

50,000 crowns. Another 50,000 provided a ransom for Queen Margaret. It was settled that Edward's daughter Elizabeth was to marry the dauphin, Charles, when she came of age.

Here now was the real end of the Hundred Years' War. It was entirely due to Louis, and was in every way typical of him. He believed that every man had his price, and when necessary he was perfectly happy to pay it. Of course the whole Picquigny adventure was bribery, and not only of the king; half a dozen of his leading advisers were also granted generous pensions. There were those on both sides – Richard of Gloucester among them – who denounced it as dishonourable; Louis de Bretaylle, English envoy to Spain, remarked that this one shady deal had taken away the honour of all King Edward's previous military victories. But Louis XI was not bothered by such considerations; he had got what he wanted, and without a drop of blood being shed. As he put it, his father might have driven out the English by force of arms; he had been equally successful with pâté, venison and good French wine.

And not only had he driven out the English; he had freed his cousin Margaret from what would otherwise have been life-long captivity. He regretted only that he had been less successful with her husband, Henry, who had died on the night of 21 May 1471 in the Tower of London. The circumstances of his death are not absolutely clear. According to the subsequent proclamation it was the result of 'pure displeasure and melancholy'; but both in England and in France it was an open secret that he had been murdered, almost certainly by Edward's brother Richard, Duke of Gloucester, the future King Richard III. When his coffin was opened in 1910, the skull was found to be 'much broken'. It was a sad end indeed for the only English king who had also been crowned King of France in Notre-Dame.

Louis XI was never popular; he made not the slightest effort to be loved by his subjects, whom he taxed mercilessly and to whom he frequently showed appalling cruelty: Philippe de Commines described the wooden cages, only eight feet square, in which he kept his enemies, sometimes for years. In 1481, however, there came at least partial deliverance. Louis suffered the first of a series of strokes, which utterly unhinged him: he became dangerously paranoid and no longer capable of governing. He died at eight o'clock in the evening on Saturday 30 August 1483, at the age of sixty-one. He was not, by any standards, a good man; but he left France as she emerged from the Middle Ages stronger, safer and better governed than she had ever been throughout her history.

8

A Warm, Sunlit Land

1483–1515

His Majesty is small, ill-formed and ugly of countenance, with pale, short-sighted eyes, nose far too large and abnormally thick lips which are always apart. He makes spasmodic movements with his hands that are most unpleasant to look upon, and his speech is extremely slow.*

The Venetian ambassador to Charles VIII

THE DAUPHIN WHO, in 1483 at the age of thirteen, became King Charles VIII did not initially impress. His head seemed too big for his body, which was weak and distinctly undersized. There was nothing royal about him; he struck people as a perfectly nice boy, with excellent manners perhaps but frankly pretty dull. 'Affable' – it has the same meaning in French as in English – was the word that sprang to mind, and it stuck. Brought up at Amboise, he seldom saw his father – which, from the point of view of his own character, was probably just as well. The regency was put in the hands of his elder sister, Anne de Beaujeu.

The year 1488 saw the death of Francis II, Duke of Brittany, which resulted in something of a crisis. The duke's heir was his eleven-year-old daughter, another Anne, who would clearly be bringing the duchy as a dowry to her husband, whoever he might be. Among her suitors was Maximilian of Austria, whose first wife, Mary of Burgundy, had died in that riding accident six years before. Maximilian already controlled Flanders; if he became master of

* The historian H. A. L. Fisher calls him 'a young and licentious hunchback of doubtful sanity', but goes, I think, a little too far.

Brittany as well, France would be held in a Habsburg vice. Anne de Beaujeu lost no time. She immediately proposed her brother, backing up the proposal with an army of 40,000 men. It was a curious form of courtship, but one that could hardly be refused. In December 1491 Anne of Brittany, now fourteen, arrived for her wedding to King Charles VIII at the Château de Langeais, somewhat pointedly bringing with her two separate beds.

All this, however, caused another problem: what was to be done about Margaret of Austria? The poor girl was still only eleven; but for the past eight years she had been brought up in the French court as the future Queen of France; she had also grown fond of her prospective husband. She was deeply distressed to be somewhat roughly informed not only that her marriage was off, but that she would nevertheless remain in France until she could be usefully married to someone else. She wrote to her father that if it brought her freedom, she would willingly flee Paris in her nightgown. At last, in 1493, she was allowed to return, carrying with her, as it were, Flanders and Artois.★

Anne of Brittany, unlike Margaret, soon became reconciled to her new position; and she too grew to love Charles. He was not what most people would have considered attractive, but then she was no beauty herself, and quite severely lame into the bargain. She soon settled at Amboise, where she occupied the Clos Lucé, the future home of Leonardo da Vinci; and despite those two beds and the fact that they lived mostly apart, she and Charles had seven children and seem to have been remarkably happy together. She was highly educated, an intellectual and a generous patron of the arts; and in Brittany in particular she has never been forgotten.

In 1492 Charles at last managed to shake off his sister Anne, who would never have countenanced an adventure of the kind on which

---

★ She subsequently married, first the Prince of Asturias and after his early death Duke Philibert II of Savoy; but he too died young. Her father Maximilian then appointed her Governor of the Low Countries and guardian of her nephew Charles – the future Emperor Charles V.

he was now determined to embark. His ministers had done their best to dissuade him, but in vain; he believed himself to be abundantly justified. He had no wish, he protested, to conquer the territory of others, only to claim such lands as belonged to him by right – which for him unquestionably included the Kingdom of Naples.* And there was a further consideration: with this kingdom for the past three centuries there had been associated the style of King of Jerusalem – a title which, empty as it was, would give him the additional prestige necessary to lead the long-overdue crusade of which he dreamed.

The moment seemed auspicious. That year had seen the death of Lorenzo de' Medici and, just three months later, of Pope Innocent VIII. Lorenzo, now remembered principally for his patronage of the arts, had also been largely responsible for preserving the always tenuous balance of the Italian states. By maintaining the alliance of Florence, Milan and Naples he had provided a fixed background for the smaller powers such as Mantua, Ferrara and some of the Papal States, and had also kept in check the dangerous ambitions of Venice. With his death and the succession of his feckless son Piero that moderating influence was gone. Pope Innocent too, for all his corruption and nepotism, had been a force for peace; Rodrigo Borgia, the Spaniard who succeeded him as Pope Alexander VI, was quite simply out for what he could get. Italy lay once again open to attack, and that attack was not long in coming.

The expedition began promisingly enough. In September 1494, Charles, with his cousin the Duke of Orléans and his army of some 25,000 – his cavalry drawn from the high nobility and gentry of France, his Swiss halberdiers and his German pikemen, his Gascon archers and his quick-firing light artillery – crossed the Alps without incident over the Montgenèvre Pass, his heavy cannon having been shipped separately to Genoa. Milan, under its brilliant and all-powerful ruler Ludovico Sforza, received him with warmth; so too did Lucca and Pisa; in Florence, he was welcomed as a liberator by the Dominican preacher Girolamo Savonarola. On 31 December, Rome opened her

---

* He was descended from Charles of Anjou, brother of Saint Louis, who had been King of Naples and Sicily in the thirteenth century.

gates, while a terrified Pope Alexander briefly sought refuge in the Castel Sant'Angelo before sullenly coming to terms. Finally, on 22 February 1495, Charles entered Naples, while its people – who had never looked on the rival house of Aragon as anything other than foreign oppressors – cheered him to the echo. The Aragonese king Alfonso II fled to Sicily, and on 12 May Charles was, for the second time, crowned a king.

But he did not remain long in his new kingdom. Soon, inevitably, his success began to turn sour. The Neapolitans, delighted as they had been to get rid of the Spaniards, quickly discovered that one foreign occupier was very much like another. Unrest also grew among the populations of many smaller towns, who found themselves having to support, for no good reason that they could understand, discontented and frequently licentious French garrisons. Beyond the Kingdom of Naples, too, men were beginning to feel alarm. Even those states, Italian and foreign, who had previously looked benignly upon Charles's advances were asking themselves just how much further the young conqueror might be intending to go. In Spain, Ferdinand and Isabella decided to send a fleet to Sicily; the Holy Roman Emperor-elect Maximilian, terrified that Charles's successes might lead him in his turn to claim the imperial crown, also made his preparations; Pope Alexander, never happy about Charles, was becoming increasingly nervous; and even Ludovico Sforza of Milan, by now as alarmed as anyone, was further disconcerted by the continued presence at nearby Asti of Charles's cousin Duke Louis of Orléans – whose claims to Milan through his grandmother, the Duchess Valentina Visconti, he knew to be no less strong than those of Charles to Naples. The result was the formation of what was known as the Holy League, ostensibly pacific but in fact with one single objective: to send the King of France packing.

When news of the League was brought to Charles at Naples, he flew into a fury; but he did not underestimate the danger he was facing. Only a week after his coronation, he left his new kingdom for ever and headed for home. Following the west coast of the peninsula up to La Spezia, he then branched right along the mountain road that would bring him across the northern range of the Apennines and down again into Lombardy. Even in midsummer, the task of dragging heavy artillery over a high mountain pass must have been a nightmare. The ascent was bad enough, but the journey down was infinitely worse; it sometimes needed as many as a hundred already exhausted men, lashed together in pairs, to restrain a single heavy cannon from careering over a precipice – and, if they did not act very quickly, carrying them with it. At last, on 5 July, the king was able to look down on the little town of Fornovo, twenty miles south-west of Parma – and, deployed just behind it, on some thirty thousand soldiers of the League under the command of the Marquis of Mantua, Francesco Gonzaga.

Gonzaga's army had every advantage. It outnumbered the French by three – possibly four – to one; it was fully rested and provisioned; and it had had plenty of time to choose its position and prepare for the coming encounter. The French, by contrast, were exhausted, hungry and disinclined to fight. But fight they did, the king himself as bravely as any; the battle that followed was the bloodiest that Italy had seen for two hundred years. When at last it was over and the field was thick with bodies, the difficulty was to establish who had won. Gonzaga built a *chiesetta di vittoria* – a little church of victory – with a specially commissioned altarpiece by Mantegna; not everyone, however, would have agreed with him. The French had admittedly forfeited their baggage train; on the other hand their losses had been negligible compared with those of the Italians, who had utterly failed to stop them – as was seen when Charles and his men continued their march that same night, reaching Asti unmolested only a few days later.

But there was bad news awaiting them. A French naval expedition against Genoa had failed, resulting in the capture of most of the fleet. Louis of Orléans was being besieged in Novara by a Milanese army and unlikely to hold out much longer. King Alfonso's son Ferrantino had landed in Calabria where, supported by Spanish troops from Sicily, he was rapidly advancing on Naples. On 7 July 1495 he re-occupied the city. Suddenly, all the French successes of the past year had evaporated. In October Charles managed to come to an agreement with Sforza which ended the effectiveness of the League; a week or two later he led his army back across the Alps, leaving Orléans behind to maintain a French presence as best he could.

Vercingetorix, 'great warrior king'.
Statue erected in 1865 on Mont
Auxois, the supposed site of his last
battle against the Romans.

Charlemagne was crowned Holy Roman
Emperor in 800 AD. Reliquary bust,
fourteenth century.

The Pont du Gard, Roman aqueduct over the River Gardon
near Nîmes, first century AD.

Pope Urban II addressing the Council of Clermont and calling for a Crusade to the Holy Land, 1095. Fifteenth-century manuscript.

Eleanor of Aquitaine and King Henry II. Her marriage to Louis VII was annulled in 1152; later she married Henry. Her influence on European history continued for over half a century. Tombs at the Abbey of Fontevraud.

Philip Augustus, one of the greatest kings of France, makes peace with King John. By his death in 1223, he left a France no longer half-occupied by the English. Fourteenth-century manuscript.

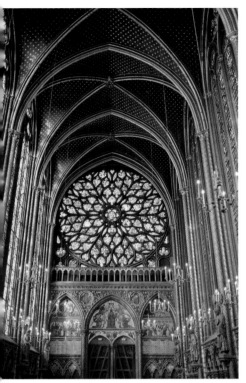

Paris, the Sainte-Chapelle,
consecrated in 1248 by St Louis
to house the Crown of Thorns.

St Louis (Louis IX) embarks
on the Seventh Crusade, 1248.
Fifteenth-century manuscript.

Four Knights Templar on their
way to execution, while Philip IV
looks on. Early fourteenth-
century manuscript.

The sea battle of Sluys, 1340, one of the opening conflicts of the Hundred Years' War between England and France. Fifteenth-century manuscript.

Battle of Crécy, 1346, won thanks to the superiority of the English longbow. Fifteenth-century manuscript.

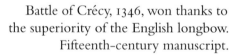

The Black Death struck France in January 1348. Mid fourteenth-century illustration.

Joan of Arc. From the moment of her first appearance English fortunes were to decline, never to recover. Portrait, c.1605.

In 1429 King Charles VII was crowned in Reims Cathedral; within ten years he had become the most influential ruler in Europe. Portrait by Jean Fouquet.

Philip the Good, Duke of Burgundy, founded the Order of the Golden Fleece in 1429. Portrait after Rogier van der Weyden.

Louis XI, known to his enemies as 'the universal spider'. In his own dreadful way he was a greater king than his father Charles VII, whom he succeeded in 1461. Seventeenth-century portrait.

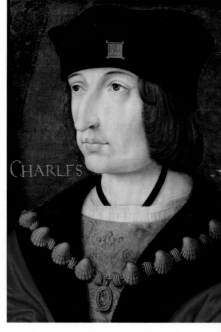

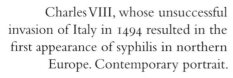

Charles VIII, whose unsuccessful invasion of Italy in 1494 resulted in the first appearance of syphilis in northern Europe. Contemporary portrait.

Francis I, in a portrait by Jean Clouet. More than any other single figure, he personified the French Renaissance.

Château de Chambord, Loire Valley. Begun by Francis I in 1519 as a hunting lodge, it was still unfinished at the time of his death.

Catherine de' Medici (left), who became the wife of Henry II in 1533; the marriage produced ten children. Not entirely surprisingly, however, Henry preferred Diane de Poitiers (right), twenty years older, who became a power second only to the king himself. Portrait by François Clouet, *c.*1571.

Henry IV, a Protestant, converted to the Church of Rome – 'Paris is well worth a Mass.' In 1598 he signed the Edict of Nantes which put an end to the religious wars that had plagued France for the last half-century. Contemporary portrait.

Equestrian statue of Henry I by Giambologna on the Pont Ne the city's oldest bridge. La seventeenth-century paintir

Louis XIII with Cardinal Richelieu at the Siege of La Rochelle (1627–8), stronghold of the French Huguenots. Contemporary painting.

Paradoxically, Charles's Italian adventure was to have its most lasting effect in northern Europe. When his army was paid off at Lyon in November 1495, it dispersed across the continent with reports of a warm, sunlit land inhabited by a people whose life of cultivated refinement went far beyond anything known in the greyer, chillier climes of the north, but who were too disunited to defend themselves against a determined invader. As the message spread, and as the painters, sculptors, stuccoists and woodcarvers whom Charles had brought back with him began to transform his old castle at Amboise into a Renaissance palace, so Italy became ever more desirable in the eyes of her northern neighbours, presenting them with an invitation and a challenge they were not slow to take up in the years to come.

The disbanded mercenaries carried something else too – something far deadlier than any dream of conquest. Columbus's three ships, returning to Spain from the Caribbean in 1493, had brought with them the first cases of syphilis known to the Old World; through the agency of the Spanish troops sent by Ferdinand and Isabella the disease had quickly spread to Naples, where it was rife by the time Charles arrived. After three months of *dolce far niente* his men must in turn have been thoroughly infected, and all available evidence suggests that it was they who were responsible for introducing the disease north of the Alps. By 1497 cases were being reported as far away as Aberdeen. In that year Vasco da Gama reached India, where the disease was recorded in 1498; seven years later it was in Canton.

But however swift the spread of the *morbo gallico* – the French disease, as the Italians called it – death came to Charles VIII more quickly still. At Amboise on the eve of Palm Sunday 1498, while on his way to watch the *jeu de paume* – an early kind of tennis – being played in the castle ditch, he struck his head on a low lintel. He walked on and saw the game through to its end, but on his way back to his apartments, just as he was passing the place where the accident had occurred, he collapsed. Although it was the most sordid and tumbledown corner of the castle – a place, sniffs de Commines, 'where every man pissed that would' – his attendants for some reason thought it better not to move him. There he lay on a rough pallet for nine hours; and there, shortly before midnight, he died. He was twenty-eight years old.

All four of Charles's children had died before their father; the throne therefore passed to his own father's first cousin and recent companion-in-arms Louis of Orléans, who now became King Louis XII. His father, Charles, had been the greatest poet of his day;* Louis, unfortunately, was not. He had long been in love with the queen, Anne of Brittany, whom, now that she was a widow, he longed to marry. It was unfortunate that he was already married to Jeanne, a daughter of Louis XI, who was described as 'slight, dark and round-shouldered' and was known also to be sterile. But the Pope's son Cesare Borgia† stepped in and – in return for a generous offer of money and lands – had a word with his father. It was pleaded, with some justification, that the marriage had been forced on the groom by his father-in-law,‡ and Louis secured his annulment. Anne grew to love her second husband as she had grown to love her first – and Brittany remained French. As for poor Jeanne, she retired to Bourges, where she founded a religious order of contemplative nuns dedicated to the Annunciation – and, in 1950, was duly made a saint.

To the rulers of Italy, who had had plenty of experience of Louis in recent years, his succession could mean just one thing: another French invasion of the peninsula, this time to vindicate not only the Angevin claim to Naples but the Orléanist one to Milan. They were not in the least surprised to hear that the new king had expressly assumed the title of Duke of Milan at his coronation. The superiority of French arms had been tried and tested at Fornovo, and the army that Louis was said to be preparing bid fair to be larger, better equipped and more efficiently organised than its predecessor. Pope Alexander might have objected, but Louis had managed to buy him off without difficulty by offering to Cesare Borgia – who, bored

---

* Son of the assassinated Duke Louis, he had been taken prisoner at Agincourt and spent the next twenty-five years in captivity in England.

† Pope Alexander VI had at least nine children by various mistresses.

‡ It had indeed; Louis XI had hoped thereby to extinguish the House of Orléans for ever.

with being a cardinal, had decided to abandon the Church in favour of a life of military adventure – the rich duchy of Valentinois (part of the Dauphiné) and the hand in marriage of Charlotte d'Albret, sister of the King of Navarre.

It was in mid-August 1499 that this second invasion was launched. On 2 September Duke Ludovico Sforza fled with his treasure to the Tyrol, and on 6 October King Louis made his solemn entry into Milan. The following April the duke was taken prisoner, never to regain his liberty, and for the next twelve years Milan was to remain the principal French stronghold in Italy. Louis, however, was still not satisfied: Naples beckoned. His cousin Charles had won the city but then lost it again; he himself would be more careful. In November 1500 he concluded with Ferdinand of Aragon the secret Treaty of Granada, in which the two rulers would jointly conquer Naples. In return for his alliance – or at least for his non-intervention – Ferdinand would receive a fair half of the kingdom, including the provinces of Apulia and Calabria. To Louis would go Naples itself, Gaeta and the Abruzzi. The Pope gave his approval, and in May 1501 the French army, supplemented by 4,000 Swiss mercenaries, was on the march. It was not long before French garrisons had occupied the castles of Naples, while other contingents headed north into the Abruzzi.

But the Treaty of Granada had left too many questions unanswered. Nothing had been said about the province of the Capitanata, which lies between the Abruzzi and Apulia, nor about the Basilicata, on the instep of the Italian boot between Apulia and Calabria. One might have thought it possible to settle such bones of contention by amicable means, but no: by July France and Spain were at war. The fighting continued on and off for two years, victory finally going to the Spaniards, who in 1503 smashed the French army at Cerignola. On 16 May they entered Naples, and in the last days of December they fell on the French yet again, by the Garigliano river. This time the battle was decisive, spelling the end of the French presence in Naples. Gaeta, the last French garrison in the kingdom, surrendered to Spanish troops on 1 January 1504. Thenceforth in the mainland kingdom, as well as in Sicily and in Spain, the House of Aragon reigned unchallenged. 'Twice', complained Louis, 'the King of Spain has betrayed me.' 'Ten times', boasted Ferdinand, 'have I deceived him.'

That might have been the end of French ambitions in Italy, but for the death in 1503, in mildly suspicious circumstances, of Pope Alexander VI. His successor, Pius III, died less than month after his election and was followed by perhaps the most redoubtable of all the Renaissance popes, Giuliano della Rovere, who took the name of Julius II. Julius had very decided ideas about Italy. The peninsula, as he saw it, was now divided into three. In the north was French Milan, in the south Spanish Naples. Between the two, there was room for one – and only one – powerful and prosperous state; and that state, he was determined, must be the papacy. The problem, clearly, was Venice. She might, if she wished, survive as a city; as an empire she must be destroyed. In return for their alliance against the Most Serene Republic, he offered the princes of Europe vast rewards. To France, for example, would go the cities of Bergamo and Brescia, Crema and Cremona and all the lands, towns and castles east of the River Adda and as far south as its confluence with the Po.

The European princes had no interest in the Pope's theories. They were, however, well aware that Venice had a perfect legal right to the territories they planned to seize. However much they might try to present their action as a blow struck on behalf of righteousness, they were fully conscious of the fact that their own conduct was far more reprehensible than Venice's had ever been. But the temptation was too great, the promised rewards too high. They accepted. And so it was that on 14 May 1509, just outside the little village of Agnadello between Bergamo and Milan, an army commanded by Louis XII in person destroyed the Venetian mercenary forces. On that one day, wrote Machiavelli, 'the Venetians lost what it had taken them eight hundred years to conquer'.

As it turned out, Machiavelli was wrong: Venice was to recover with astonishing speed. Many of the cities and towns that had surrendered had been perfectly content to live under Venetian rule, and soon came to resent the heavier and far less sympathetic hand of their new masters. Our business, however, is to follow the fortunes of France. Did she draw any long-term benefits from so triumphant a victory? She did not. In February 1510, less than a year after Agnadello, Pope Julius performed a complete volte-face. Having encouraged the French to take up arms against Venice, he now refused to allow them the rewards that he himself had promised, turning against them with all the violence and venom that he had previously displayed towards the Venetians. The Republic – although, to its considerable surprise, it now found itself allied to the papacy – could now withdraw from the centre of the stage. Henceforth the war would be primarily between the Pope and King Louis – together with Louis's ally the Duke of Ferrara – who, as husband of Lucrezia Borgia and son-in-law of Alexander VI, was in the Pope's eyes condemned many times over. Shortly afterwards Julius anathematised and excommunicated the duke with a papal bull, in language that St Peter Martyr said made his hair stand on end.

King Louis, however, now played an important new card. His nephew Gaston de Foix, Duke of Nemours, had at the age of twenty-two already proved himself one of the outstanding commanders of his day. In February 1512 Nemours launched a whirlwind campaign against the papal and Spanish forces, ending on Easter Sunday at Ravenna with the bloodiest battle since Fornovo nearly twenty years before; when it was over, nearly ten thousand Spaniards and Italians lay dead on the field. But, like Fornovo, it had been a pyrrhic victory. The French infantry alone had lost over four thousand men; most of the commanders had also perished, including Nemours himself. Had he lived, he would probably have rallied the remains of his army and marched on Rome and Naples, forcing the Pope to come to terms and restoring King Louis to the Neapolitan throne; and the subsequent history of Italy would have been different indeed.

By this time the three principal protagonists in the war had gone through two permutations in the pattern of their alliances. First France and the papacy had been allied against Venice, then Venice and the papacy had ranged themselves against the French. It remained only for Venice and France to combine against the papacy – which, in March 1513, by the Treaty of Blois, they did. Venice, having re-asserted her position on the mainland, was determined that Pope and emperor should not elbow her aside, and as the French no longer constituted any danger to her they were her obvious allies. But in fact the situation changed again, even before the treaty was signed: on 21 February 1513 the seventy-year-old Julius II died in Rome.

There is a story that when Michelangelo was working on his fourteen-foot bronze statue of Pope Julius and suggested putting a book in his left hand, Julius replied, 'Nay, give me a sword, for I am no scholar!' He spoke no more than the truth; he was indeed a soldier, through and through. No pope for nearly five centuries had led an army into battle;* Julius did so on several occasions, most recently in 1511 at the age of sixty-eight. Had there been a little more of the spiritual in his character he would never, surely, have been guilty of one of the most shameless acts of official vandalism in all Christian history, the demolition of St Peter's. Only one tiny chapel now remained in which the assembled cardinals could elect his successor. Their deliberations were too slow for the organising authorities, who in an effort to speed things up daily reduced the catering, first to a single dish per meal and later to a purely vegetarian diet. Even so, it was a full week before the result was announced: the new Pope was Cardinal Giovanni de' Medici, who took the name of Leo X.

'God has given us the Papacy; now let us enjoy it.' Whether or not the new Pope actually uttered the superbly cynical words ascribed to him, few Italians of the time would have shown much surprise. Leo was thirty-seven. He was immensely rich, immensely powerful – his family had been re-established in Florence in 1512, after an eighteen-year exile – and he showed a far greater penchant for magnificence than his father Lorenzo had ever done. He was also, unlike Julius, a man of peace, and his election was genuinely popular. On the other hand, he was enough of a realist to believe that King Louis would soon be once again on the warpath, and he was determined to protect papal interests wherever necessary.

But Louis's adventures in Italy were over. In June 1513, 10,000 of his men had been routed by Sforza's Swiss mercenaries at Novara, and Sforza was back in Milan. The Emperor Maximilian now decreed that all imperial subjects fighting with the French army should return at once to their homes on pain of death, while the French themselves were hurriedly recalled to their native soil to deal with the English, who had invaded France and had already captured Tournai.

* The last to do so had been Leo IX, at Civitate in 1053.

There were simply no soldiers left to carry on the struggle in Italy; besides, the king no longer had the heart to continue. Worn out at fifty-two and already showing signs of premature senility, in the autumn of 1514 he had taken as his third wife Princess Mary of England, sister of Henry VIII. She was fifteen years old, radiantly beautiful and possessed of all her brother's inexhaustible energy. Louis had done his best: after their wedding night on 9 October he boasted to all who would listen that 'he had performed marvels', but nobody believed him. He died on New Year's Day 1515, less than three months after the marriage – exhausted, it was generally believed, by his bedchamber exertions. Could he perhaps be claimed as the first French victim of the House of Tudor?

9

With His Usual Flourish

1515–47

This monarch is predestined for great things. He is educated
in letters, which is unusual with our kings, and also possesses
a natural eloquence, wit, tact, and an easy pleasant manner;
nature, in short, has endowed him with the rarest gifts of body
and mind. He likes to admire and to praise princes of old who
have distinguished themselves by their lofty intellects and brilliant deeds, and he is fortunate to have as much wealth as any
king in the world, which he gives more liberally than anyone.

Guillaume Budé, the king's librarian,

to Erasmus of Rotterdam

IT MAY OR may not have struck readers of this book that of the
many kings who have succeeded each other over the preceding
pages, few have been particularly colourful characters. There have
been among them some excellent rulers and one or two remarkable
men – Philip Augustus, St Louis, Philip the Fair perhaps, Louis XI
certainly – but few to make the heart beat faster. To some extent
this is obviously due to the period in which they lived: the Middle
Ages, dominated as they were by war and religion, were not, frankly,
very much fun. Even so, it is hard to deny that England did rather
better in this regard: Henry II, Edward II, Edward III, Henry V,
Richard III – the last two admittedly much assisted by Shakespeare
– may not have been better monarchs than their French counterparts,
but as human beings they were a good deal more interesting.

But now we come to Francis I – and Francis I hit France like a
rocket. The country had never seen anything like him before. Nor
had it ever expected him to be king. Louis XII had been called the

Father of his People, but despite three wives he had fathered little else and died without a male heir; it was Francis, his first cousin once removed, who on 25 January 1515 at the age of twenty-one was crowned and anointed in Reims Cathedral as his country's fifty-seventh king. His subjects cheered him to the echo. Here at last was a proper king: a young man of colossal charm, bounding with all the energy of youth. He was not, perhaps, strictly handsome – his perfectly enormous nose was to earn him the name of *le roi grand-nez* – but it hardly seemed to matter: he made up for it with his grace and elegance, and with the glorious silks and velvets that he wore with such swagger. Moreover it was clear from the outset that he really loved being king: loved the hunting, the feasting and jousting, and loved above all the ready availability of beautiful women.

But all that was only the beginning: Francis was, in every fibre of his being, a man of the Renaissance: it could almost be said that in France he *was* the Renaissance. Not only did he show a genuine passion for art; he also possessed the wealth to indulge it. Long before he was thirty, he was famous as the greatest patron of his time. It was entirely typical of him that he should have brought Leonardo da Vinci from Italy, settling him in the magnificent apartments at Amboise in which the great man lived in comfort until his death. He was also a compulsive builder; Amboise was very largely his creation, as were Blois and Chambord and, best-loved of all his châteaux, Fontainebleau, where he gave his favourite painter Francesco Primaticcio a free hand and which still bears his character – as well as his salamander emblem – in every room.

Books, too, he loved and revered. His mother, Louise of Savoy, had seen that he was fluent in Spanish and Italian, both of which he read with ease. He was a personal friend of François Rabelais, for whose happy giant Pantagruel he is said to have provided the inspiration. All over northern Italy he employed special agents to seek out manuscripts and the still relatively rare printed books for his library, which in the fullness of time was to provide the nucleus of the Bibliothèque Nationale; at the time of his death it was to contain over three thousand volumes, and was open to any scholar who wished to use it.

Francis's greatest intellectual triumph came in 1529 when, to the fury of the Sorbonne, he founded the Collège des Lecteurs Royaux, the future Collège de France. In short, it seems hardly too much to say that modern French culture as we know it was virtually his creation. The Middle Ages were past. For a nobleman of the sixteenth century hunting and fighting were no longer enough: education and culture were now equally necessary. War might still be important – Francis himself, as we shall see, was a fearless fighter on the battle-field – but the art of elegant living was more important still. And so it comes as no surprise that, of all their kings, it is Francis whom – with Henry IV – the French most love today. They love him for his swagger and his braggadocio; for his courage in war and his prowess in the bedchamber; for the colour and opulence with which he surrounded himself; and for the whole new civilisation that he left behind. They pass over with a shrug his financial recklessness; only his increasing persecution of the Protestants in the last decade of his reign do they find hard to forgive.

Francis had two wives. His first was Claude, Louis XII's only surviving child, daughter of Anne of Brittany. Her name is still remembered in the Reine Claude plum, or greengage, but in not much else. She did her duty by bearing her husband seven children; but since she was 'very small and strangely corpulent', with a limp and a pronounced squint, she never interested him much. She died in 1524, in her twenty-fifth year. The king's second wife, whom he married after six years of riotous bachelorhood, was Eleanor of Austria, sister of the Emperor Charles V; for three brief years she had been the third wife of King Manuel I of Portugal. Alas, she proved to be no great improvement on her predecessor: tall and sallow, with the jutting Habsburg chin and a curious absence of personality. A lady-in-waiting was subsequently to report that 'when undressed she was seen to have the trunk of a giantess, so long and big was her body, yet going lower she seemed a dwarf, so short were her thighs and legs'. Already four years before her wedding to Francis it was reported that she had grown corpulent, heavy of feature, with red patches on her face. Francis largely ignored her; there were no children. She was certainly no match for her husband's regiment of mistresses – of whom the loveliest of all was Anne, one of the thirty children of Guillaume d'Heilly, Sieur de Pisseleu ('worse than a wolf') in Picardy. Later the king was to make her Duchesse d'Etampes. Highly cultured and ravishingly beautiful, she was, he used to say, '*la plus belle des savants, la plus savante des belles*'.★

Francis was constantly on the move. 'Never,' wrote a Venetian ambassador, 'during the whole of my embassy, was the court in the same place for fifteen consecutive days.' Yet the logistical demands for such mobility were immense. When the court was complete, it took no fewer than 18,000 horses to move it; when the king visited Bordeaux in 1526, stabling was ordered for 22,500 horses and mules. The baggage train normally included furniture, tapestries (for warmth) and silver plate by the ton. And, as may be imagined, the finding of suitable accommodation was a constant nightmare. Often there were rooms only for the king and his ladies; everyone else was obliged to find what shelter they could, often five or six miles away or even under canvas. But whatever hardships the court was called upon to suffer, it was always expected to be ready for the elaborate ceremonies that were staged by the major cities and towns through which it passed. These royal visits did not go without a hitch: in 1518 the captain of Brest was obliged to pay one hundred gold écus 'following artillery accidents during the King's entry . . . as indemnity to the wounded and to the widows of the deceased'.

It would have been an excellent thing for France if the Valois kings had been able to keep their hands off Italy. Alas, they could not. Francis had taken care that his claim to Milan was included in his coronation oath, and the loss of Milan after Novara in 1513 rankled badly. He wasted no time. Less than nine months after his coronation, he took his revenge on Sforza and his Swiss pikemen. He met them on 13 September 1515 at Marignano – now Melegnano – some ten miles south-east of Milan. The battle was long and hard: beginning in mid-afternoon, it raged throughout the night until the morning sun was high in the sky. The king fought with his usual courage, and had himself knighted on the battlefield by Bayard, that almost legendary *chevalier sans peur et sans reproche*. At last, on 11

★ 'The most beautiful of scholars, the most scholarly of beauties'.

October, he rode triumphantly into Milan, beside himself with joy and pride.

But there were other prizes to be won, greater far than Milan; and the greatest of all was the Holy Roman Empire. It was elective; the present emperor, Maximilian of Habsburg, was already in his late fifties, an old man in those days; and the seven Electors – the Archbishops of Mainz, Trier and Cologne, the King of Bohemia, the Duke of Saxony, the Margrave of Brandenburg and the Count Palatine of the Rhine – would, Francis suspected, probably not be averse to a little gentle bribery. There were strategic reasons too: Maximilian's grandson Charles – his principal rival – already had title to Spain, the Low Countries, Austria and Naples; were he to acquire all the imperial territories as well, he would hold France in a vice, virtually surrounding it. The king was well aware, of course, that Charles would be equally determined on his own election, for precisely the converse reason – that were he, Francis, to be successful, the imperial dominions would be split down the middle. Francis did his best, but the odds were stacked against him. The Electors – all German – hated the idea of a French emperor as much as Charles himself; the Fuggers, that colossally rich and influential banking family from Augsburg, lined as many pockets as was necessary; and in 1519 Charles was elected – unanimously.

Although twelve years later Charles and Francis were to find themselves brothers-in-law and there were to be moments of cordiality between them, geography alone meant that they could never be true friends. Friendship, however, seemed a good deal more possible with Francis's neighbour to the north, Henry VIII of England. The two were of much the same age – Henry was just three years older – and of much the same character: they shared the same boisterous energy, the same love of the arts. A degree of jealousy was inevitable; but of mistrust too, because Henry had already shown, with a brief invasion in 1513, that he had not renounced any of his French ambitions. Clearly a meeting between the two could not be long delayed; and so, from 7 to 24 June 1520 they met – at the Field of the Cloth of Gold.

It was a magnificent name and the occasion was more magnificent still, with each of the two protagonists determined to outdo the other in splendour. Henry brought with him a suite of well over five thousand, and employed some six thousand artisans and craftsmen to transform the modest little castle of Guînes and to surround it with temporary structures so elaborate and fantastical they seemed to have come straight out of a fairy tale. At dawn on the appointed day, a great gong was sounded as the two kings spurred on their horses and rode at full gallop towards each other. At the last moment they reined in, embraced, dismounted and walked arm in arm to a sumptuously decorated tent where toasts were drunk and various presentations made. There were no political discussions: that was not the point. The Field of the Cloth of Gold was planned simply so that the two kings should become acquainted with each other; it was the most extravagant getting-to-know-you party in history. Presents were exchanged, in a quantity and of a quality that neither side could afford; there was seemingly endless jousting, banqueting, dancing and mutual embracing. It was all great fun, but when Henry and Francis separated at last, the old suspicions still lingered: they got on well enough together, but neither monarch trusted the other an inch.

For the Emperor Charles V, Francis's seizure of Milan was a serious danger signal; and in 1521, to strengthen his hand against him, he had signed a secret treaty with Pope Leo, as the result of which a combined papal and imperial force had expelled the French once again from Lombardy, restoring the house of Sforza. This had committed the Pope fairly and squarely to the imperial side; and when in 1523 Leo was succeeded* by his cousin – who took the name of Clement VII – the emperor naturally assumed that he would follow the same policy. Instead, Clement tried to make peace between the two parties – an attempt that failed utterly, just as everyone had told him it would. Charles was adamant: he would yield Milan only in exchange for Burgundy. Francis, meanwhile, was determined to return at once to Italy and, with an army even

---

* Clement was in fact Leo's second successor. In between came the mildly ridiculous Adrian VI, but he need not concern us here.

larger than before, to establish his supremacy once and for all. In the absence of any clear papal opposition the way seemed clear for him to go ahead; and in the early summer of 1524, for the second time, he led 20,000 men over the Mont Cenis Pass into Italy. In late October he duly recovered Milan.

He then turned south to Pavia. The city proved a tougher nut to crack than he had expected; its imperial garrison of 6,000 Germans and Spaniards made it clear that they proposed to give as good as they got. With winter approaching, the king's most sensible course would have been to retire to Milan until the spring; but that was not his way. Instead, he and his men besieged Pavia for four unusually cold and uncomfortable months without any apparent effect, and they were still there in late February when an imperial army appeared on the horizon. The two armies met in the great hunting preserve of Mirabello Castle, just outside the walls of Pavia; and on the morning of Tuesday 24 February 1525 – it happened to be the emperor's twenty-fifth birthday – battle was joined. The ensuing engagement was one of the most decisive in European history. It was also the first to prove conclusively the superiority of firearms over pikes. The Swiss pikemen, who were this time fighting for Francis, struggled valiantly; but their weapons, fearsome as they were, were no match for Spanish bullets. When the fighting was over, the French army had been virtually annihilated; some fourteen thousand soldiers – French and Swiss, German and Spanish – lay dead on the field. Francis himself had shown, as always, exemplary courage; after his horse had been killed under him he had continued to fight on foot until at last, overcome by exhaustion, he had allowed himself to be captured. 'All is lost,' he wrote to his mother, 'save honour, and my skin.' Having sustained nothing more than a bruised leg and a scratched hand and cheek, he was indeed lucky: the best estimates suggest that of the fourteen-hundred-odd French men-at-arms on the field, not more than four hundred survived.

Francis was taken first to the castle of Pizzighettone on the Adda river, where he remained for some three months. The emperor, when the news of his capture was brought to him in Madrid, ordered services of thanksgiving for the victory and then withdrew to pray alone. Having decided that his prisoner should be held in Naples, he also – characteristically – sent orders to the imperial viceroy, Charles de Lannoy, ordering him to take good care of him and to send regular reports to his mother on his health and well-being. Francis, however, was so dispirited at the thought of a Neapolitan prison that he begged Lannoy to send him instead to Madrid. One is mildly surprised that the viceroy should have dared to disobey his master's orders; more remarkable still is the fact that he did not even report to Charles that he had done so: it was purely by chance that the emperor heard of his prisoner's arrival in Spain. He showed, however, no sign of anger, simply sending a message of welcome and expressing the hope that peace would soon follow.

Throughout the journey to Madrid, Francis found himself treated like the king he was. In Barcelona he attended Mass at the cathedral and even touched for the king's evil. At Valencia he was so mobbed by the populace that the Spanish captain responsible for his safety had to take him to a comfortable villa outside the city. The last stage of his journey to the capital was more than ever like a royal progress. There were banquets; there were bullfights; there were visits to hospitals and universities. But in Madrid a bitter disappointment awaited him: he was accommodated in the deeply gloomy tower of the Alcázar, standing on the site of the present royal palace. The Duc de Saint-Simon, who visited it two centuries later, describes it in his memoirs:

> The room was not big, and had only one door . . . It was made a little larger by an embrasure on the right as one came in, facing the window. The latter was wide enough to give some daylight, it was glazed and could be opened, but it had a double iron grill, strong and stiff, which was welded into the wall . . . There was enough room for chairs, coffers, a few tables and a bed.

From the window, the duke added, there was a drop of more than a hundred feet, and the tower was guarded day and night by two companies of troops. Here Francis – having made one unsuccessful attempt to escape disguised as a black servant – was made to wait, his only exercise the occasional mule ride under heavy escort, while preparations were begun for peace talks.

These began in Toledo in July 1525, and were attended on the

French side by both Francis's mother – Louise of Savoy, now Regent of France – and by his sister Margaret of Alençon. With Burgundy remaining as always the principal bone of contention, negotiations did not get very far and were still dragging on by 11 September when Francis suddenly fell ill – so ill that his life was despaired of. For twenty-three days he lay inert and for most of the time unconscious; the emperor, who till now had shown no desire to meet his fellow-monarch, came hurrying to his bedside; it was their first encounter. According to the doctors, the root of the trouble was 'an abscess in the head', but sixteenth-century diagnoses were far from reliable. In any event the king eventually began to recover, and as soon as he was well enough was moved to the capital, where he was gradually restored to health.

The first thing to be said about the resulting Treaty of Madrid, which a convalescent Francis signed on 14 January 1526 and by which, in return for his own liberation, he surrendered Burgundy, Naples and Milan, was that he had not the faintest intention of observing it – despite the fact that he had agreed to leave his two sons as hostages for his good behaviour. He had even taken the precaution of signing another, secret, declaration, nullifying the surrender of Burgundy as having been extracted from him by force. He was still far from well: on Sunday 29 January he had to be carried to church on a litter. The next day, however, he was sufficiently recovered to attend a luncheon given in his honour – and even, afterwards, to visit a convent where he touched thirty scrofulous nuns.

On 13 February the emperor joined him in Madrid. It had been arranged as part of the treaty that Francis should marry Charles's sister Eleanor; and Charles now introduced the pair for the first time. She tried to kiss his hand, but he – characteristically – insisted as her husband on a proper kiss on the lips. (All too few, alas, were to follow.) Two days later the two sovereigns separated – Charles to Lisbon, there to marry his own Portuguese princess, King Manuel's daughter (and Eleanor's stepdaughter) Isabella; Francis to return to Paris, whither it was arranged that his new bride should follow him in due course.

But there was one unhappy little ceremony to be completed first. It occurred on the Bidasoa river, which constituted – as it still does

– part of the frontier between France and Spain. There was no bridge; early on the morning of 17 March 1526, two rowing boats made their way from opposite sides to a pontoon in mid-stream. One carried the king, together with the Viceroy of Naples; the other bore two little boys, the eight-year-old dauphin and his brother Henry, Duke of Orléans, aged seven. Both still recovering from serious attacks of measles, they were on their way to Spain for an indefinite period as hostages for their father's good behaviour. When the two boats reached the pontoon they changed passengers, while a tearful Francis made the sign of the cross over his children and promised – with how much hope, one wonders – to send for them as soon as he could. The exchange completed, the boats then returned to their original moorings.

Francis spent a delightful summer riding gently through his realm and arrived in Paris only in the autumn, by which time some of the initial indignation at the terms of the Treaty of Madrid had begun to die down – though the Estates of Burgundy were still vociferously protesting that the king had no right to alienate a province of his kingdom without the consent of its people. Francis replied, quite simply, that he had no intention of doing so: everyone knew, surely, that promises extorted in prison had no binding force. He had no wish to antagonise Charles more than necessary; apart from anything else, he was anxious to recover his sons. At the same time the balance of power had become seriously upset: the emperor was once again too powerful, and it was clear that something must be done to cut him back to size.

News of the treaty had left Pope Clement aghast: without a French presence anywhere in Italy, how could he hope to defend himself against imperial pressure? Hastily he recruited Milan, Venice and Florence to form an anti-imperialist league for the defence of a free and independent Italy – and invited France to join. Though the ink was scarcely dry on the Treaty of Madrid, and though he and the Pope held widely differing views on Milan – the Pope favouring the Sforzas while Francis still wanted the city for himself – on 22 May 1526 the king, with his usual flourish, signed his name to what was to be called the League of Cognac. It meant, he knew, that it would be a long time – perhaps another three or four years, unless he could persuade Charles to accept a cash ransom – before he saw his sons again, but there: they would be well looked after, would learn beautiful Spanish and would doubtless make a number of contacts which might be of use to them in the future.

For the emperor, this was nothing less than a betrayal. There could now be no question of a ransom, if indeed there ever had been. Francis's breach of faith horrified him, and shocked him deeply: crowned heads simply could not behave so shamelessly. He had been planning to go to Italy for his coronation by the Pope; that journey would now have to be indefinitely postponed. 'He is full of dumps', reported an English envoy, 'and solitary, musing sometimes alone three or four hours together. There is no mirth or comfort with him.' To the French ambassador he did not conceal his anger:

> I will not deliver them [the two princes] for money. I refused money for the father; still less will I take money for the sons. I am content to render them upon reasonable treaty; but not for money, nor will I trust any more the King's promise; for he has deceived me, and that like no noble prince. And where he protests that he cannot fulfil some things without grudge of his subjects, let him fulfil that that is in his power, which he promised by the honour of a prince to fulfil; that is to say, that if he could not bring all of his promise to pass he would return again hither into prison.

But Francis still felt threatened. Charles and his brother Ferdinand seemed determined to control the whole of Europe; his own kingdom was already surrounded by potentially hostile territory. If it were to survive unconquered, its best hope lay in finding a new ally to the east – and that could only be the Ottoman Sultan. It was a wild, outlandish idea, unthinkable in former years, but the regent had had it before her son: the first French diplomatic mission to Suleiman the Magnificent had set out early in 1525 – immediately after Pavia, and even before the king's return from captivity.

But how would the news of such an alliance be received? To the rest of Christian Europe, the Sultan was the Antichrist, Satan's representative on earth; one did not form alliances with him, one went on Crusades against him. Did Francis not bear the papal title of 'the Most Christian King'? How then could he contemplate dealings with the infidel personified? But, as Thomas Cromwell once remarked, no Christian scruple would deter the King of France from bringing the Turk and the Devil into the heart of Christendom if this could help him recover Milan. And Francis himself cheerfully admitted as much: 'I cannot deny that I keenly desire the Turk powerful and ready for war, not for himself, because he is an infidel and we are Christians, but to undermine the Emperor's power, to force heavy expenses upon him and to reassure all other governments against so powerful an enemy.'

None the less, he found himself on a tightrope. He was obliged to keep Europe persuaded of his loyalty to the Christian cause; at the same time it was essential that the Sultan should be constantly reassured, and persuaded that such public statements as he was obliged to make from time to time were of no real significance. He knew too that he needed Suleiman far more than Suleiman needed him: without the Sultan's help what hope had he of resisting the immense power of the Empire, which hemmed him in both east and west? And how else was he ever to achieve the old Valois dream of ruling Italy?

Peace between France and the Empire, when it came at last, was the result of negotiations begun during the winter of 1528–9 between Francis's mother, Louise of Savoy, and her sister-in-law (and the emperor's aunt), Margaret of Austria. The two met at Cambrai on 5 July 1529, and the resulting treaty was signed in the first week of August. The Ladies' Peace, as it came to be called, was a surprisingly long and complicated document, but it effectively confirmed imperial rule in Italy. Francis renounced all his claims to Milan, Genoa and Naples, for which he and his predecessors had struggled so hard for the best part of forty years; Charles ransomed the king's sons after all – though he demanded no less than a million ducats – and promised not to press his claims to Burgundy, Provence and the Languedoc. For Francis and his allies in the League of Cognac it was a sad and shameful settlement. But Italy was at peace, and that long and agonising chapter in her history, a chapter that had brought her nothing but devastation and destruction, was over at last.

★

In the autumn of 1532, Francis congratulated himself on something of a diplomatic coup: he had persuaded Pope Clement to give his consent to the marriage between his niece Catherine de' Medici and the king's second son, the Duke of Orléans. What was more, the Pope had agreed to be present in person. And so it was that on 11 October 1533, as the shore batteries cannonaded their welcome, a papal fleet of sixty ships dropped anchor in the harbour of Marseille. On the following morning the Pope entered the city in state, accompanied by fourteen of his cardinals. Francis arrived on the 13th, and on the 28th, in the church of Saint-Ferréol les Augustins, Clement pronounced the pair man and wife. Both bride and groom were fourteen years old. The wedding Mass was interminable and followed by a sumptuous banquet and ball. Then at midnight, when both the children must have been utterly exhausted, they were led to the bridal bedchamber – accompanied by Francis, who is said to have remained there until the marriage was properly consummated, afterwards reporting that 'each had shown valour in the joust'. The next morning, while they were still in bed, they received a visit from the Pope, who added his congratulations and blessings. It was, one feels, all they needed.

Such a ceremony could have been interpreted only as a sign of a Franco–papal alliance; but since no written treaty followed it is impossible to say precisely what it was that Francis and Pope Clement discussed during their many long conversations together. The king would certainly have hammered away at his old obsession of Milan; we know too that the Pope was left in no doubt as to Francis's feelings about the Turks. 'Not only will I not oppose the invasion of Christendom by the Turk', the king allegedly declared, 'but I will favour him as much as I can, in order the more easily to recover that which plainly belongs to me and my children, and has been usurped by the Emperor.'

When Pope Clement returned to Rome at the end of the year he was already a sick man; and on 25 September 1534 he died. To Francis it came as a serious blow. The new entente for which he had worked so hard was now in ruins. The magnificent marriage of which he had been so proud was suddenly seen as a *mésalliance* – since the Medici, for all their magnificence, had always been considered a fundamentally bourgeois family and always would be. Had Clement been succeeded by another member of his clan, all would have been well; but the election of Alexander Farnese on 13 October as Pope Paul III meant a complete reappraisal of French policy towards the Holy See. And – as if that was not enough – only five days later came *l'affaire des placards*.

'ARTICLES VERITABLES SUR LES HORRIBLES, GRANDS ET IMPOR-TABLES ABUZ DE LA MESSE PAPALLE' were the opening words, in large Gothic type, of the *placards*, or broadsheets, that appeared all over Paris on the morning of Sunday 18 October 1534. The four long paragraphs following took the form of a violent attack on the Catholic Mass, expressed in a language that terrified their readers. The city was swept by a wave of hysteria as the rumours quickly spread: all Catholic churches were to be burnt to the ground; all the Catholic faithful were to be massacred in their places of worship. The panic increased further when it was learned that the *placards* had not been confined to Paris; they had also been found in Orléans, Tours, Blois and Rouen. One, it was said, had even been discovered fixed to the door of the king's bedchamber at Amboise, where he was living at the time.

The search for those responsible began at once. Countless arrests were made; several innocent unfortunates were burnt at the stake. And, sadly, Francis seems to have lost his head. What followed was nothing less than an inquisition. All new books were banned. In order, presumably, to defy the terrorists – for it was as such that they were seen – a 'general procession' was summoned for 21 January in Paris. The most sacred relics – they included the Crown of Thorns from the Sainte-Chapelle – were removed from the city's churches and paraded through the streets from Saint-Germain l'Auxerrois to Notre-Dame, the Blessed Sacrament being carried by the Bishop of Paris beneath a canopy borne by the king's three sons and the Duc de Vendôme. Immediately behind it walked Francis himself, dressed entirely in black, bare-headed and carrying a lighted torch. High Mass was celebrated in the cathedral, after which he and Queen Eleanor were entertained at the bishop's palace. The king then addressed a large crowd, encouraging his subjects to denounce all heretics, including families and friends. The day ended with another six burnings.

And so the reign of terror continued. Why, one wonders, was there so wild an over-reaction to what had been in fact fairly slight provocation? The answer usually given is that Francis took the *placard* found at Amboise as a personal affront, but this is not easy to believe.★ The truth, surely, is that he had no choice. The provocation seems slight enough; but it did not seem so at the time. The *placards*, couched as they were in violent and abusive language, attacked the Church, the Mass, the priesthood and, through them, every one of the king's God-fearing Catholic subjects. Francis could not have ignored them, or even passed them over lightly. He may not have instigated the resulting persecutions, which were more probably ordered by the *Parlement*; but he could not possibly have withheld his approval.

What is undeniable is that after the *affaire des placards* France was never – from the religious point of view – the same again. On 1 June 1540 the king issued what was to become known as the Edict of Fontainebleau, which declared that Protestantism was 'high treason against God and mankind', and so deserved the appropriate punishments of torture, loss of property, public humiliation and death. Between 1541 and 1544 six Parisian booksellers or printers were persecuted – one was tortured and two were sent to the stake – and in 1542 the Sorbonne began to compile the first index of forbidden books. Henceforth, Protestantism was to be considered a dangerous threat to the State; French Catholics felt themselves to be under siege, and the wars of religion began to cast their shadow. The worst of the atrocities occurred in the little town of Mérindol in the Vaucluse. The victims on this occasion were not Protestants but Waldensians, a Christian sect of ancient origin still existing today who, despite a number of doctrinal differences, had embraced the Protestant Reformation. Somehow they came under the scrutiny of the authorities in Paris, as a result of which, on 18 November 1541, the *Parlement* issued the so-called *Arrêt de Mérindol*, effectively the town's death warrant. Over the next four years several appeals were

---

★ Less than two years earlier, in January 1533, three armed strangers had been found in the king's chamber in the Louvre; Francis's only reaction had been to ask the *Parlement* to show more vigilance at night.

made, all of them unsuccessful; then, in 1545, there arrived an army of 2,000 men. They showed no mercy, destroying not only the town itself but two dozen neighbouring Waldensian villages. Thousands were killed, thousands more lost their homes, while hundreds of able-bodied men were sent off to the galleys. When it was over, both Francis and Pope Paul announced their enthusiastic approval, the Pope going so far as to decorate the president of the *Parlement* of Provence, who had been principally responsible for the atrocities.

In 1542 Sultan Suleiman was preparing to lead another of his immense expeditions into central Europe. Having no need of his fleet, he offered to lend it to Francis for the following summer for joint operations against the Empire. Some hundred and twenty vessels left Istanbul in April 1543 and ravaged the coasts of Italy and Sicily – at the king's request, carefully avoiding the Papal States. At Gaeta the Sultan's admiral, the former Barbary pirate Kheir-ed-din Barbarossa – now about sixty but obviously feeling a good deal younger – married the governor's eighteen-year-old daughter: a girl, we are told, of quite startling beauty. His passion for her was said to have hastened his death – but, as many people pointed out at the time, what a way to go. After several weeks of cheerful looting and plundering, the fleet at last arrived at Marseille, where a tremendous welcome awaited it. Barbarossa, himself superbly dressed and encrusted with jewels, was received by the twenty-three-year-old François de Bourbon, Count of Enghien, who presented him with a plethora of priceless gifts, including a silver sword of honour. In return the duke received on behalf of the king a small stable of magnificent Arab horses, all superbly accoutred.

Here – if one was needed – was the perfect illustration of the importance that France attached to her friendship with the Turks; but the celebrations ended badly. Barbarossa had expected to discuss plans for the forthcoming campaign against the Emperor Charles V; he soon discovered that the French, for all their promises and solemn undertakings, had made virtually no serious preparations at all. Their ships were completely unprepared for war; few had even been provisioned. Suddenly, protocol was forgotten: Barbarossa lost his temper. 'He became scarlet with anger', wrote an eyewitness, 'and tore at his beard, furious to have made such a long voyage with such a large fleet and to be condemned in advance to inaction.' The news was immediately reported to Francis – who did his best to pacify him, ordering the immediate provisioning of several of the Turkish vessels as well as his own; but even then there was serious disagreement on their joint plan of action. Barbarossa had hoped for a direct attack on the emperor in Spain, but for Francis such an operation was clearly impossible: the reproaches of all Christendom would rain down upon his head. He proposed instead an attack on Nice, which was at that time ruled by the staunchly imperialist Duke of Savoy. This was not by any means the sort of campaign that Barbarossa had in mind; but it was the best that could be hoped for. Reluctantly, he was obliged to agree.

If the siege of Nice in August 1543 is remembered at all in the city today, it is because of the courage of its heroine. Early in the morning of the 15th, heavy bombardment from Barbarossa's galleys opened a breach in the walls near one of the principal towers. The French and Turks poured through it, and a Turkish standard-bearer was about to plant his flag on the tower when a local washerwoman – her name was Catherine Ségurane – seized it from his hands and, with a few brave men whom she had summoned to support her, led a furious counter-attack. The invaders were beaten back, leaving three hundred dead behind them. Nice was saved, temporarily; but for all her heroism Catherine had only delayed the inevitable.* Just a week later, on the 22nd, the governor of the city formally surrendered. In doing so, he was entitled – and doubtless expected – to be offered honourable terms, but over the next two days Nice was sacked and put to the torch. Inevitably the Turks were blamed; in fact it was almost certainly the French who were responsible. Such at least was the opinion of the Marquis de Vieilleville, who dictated

* According to another version of the story, Catherine showed her heroism by turning her back to the Turkish forces and exposing her bare bottom, the sight of which is said to have so shocked the sensibilities of the Muslim infantry that they turned tail and fled. A memorial plaque, with an illustration in bas-relief, was erected in 1923 near the supposed location of her action; regrettably, it illustrates the first version of the story rather than the second.

his memoirs shortly before his death in 1571: 'The city of Nice was plundered and burned, for which neither Barbarossa nor the Saracens can be blamed . . . Responsibility for the outrage was thrown at poor Barbarossa to protect the honour and reputation of France, and indeed of Christianity itself.'

The siege and capture of Nice was the first and last joint operation of the Franco-Turkish alliance. The sight of Christians fighting Christians with the help of infidels left many deeply shocked; but that was only the beginning. Barbarossa now demanded that his entire fleet should be refitted and revictualled, and Francis had no choice but to invite him to occupy Toulon for the winter. Many of the town's inhabitants, brought up on hideous tales of Turkish atrocities, left in terror; to the astonishment, however, of those who remained, Barbarossa imposed an iron discipline and, in the words of a French diplomat, 'never did an army live more strictly or in better order'. The only drawback was the expense: Francis was obliged to pay 30,000 ducats a month; Provence and the whole surrounding area were savagely taxed in consequence. To make matters worse, the old ruffian did not seem in any hurry to leave; nor indeed did his men, who were predictably enchanted by what was, for most of them, their first experience of the Côte d'Azur. Finally, however, it was made clear that they were seriously outstaying their welcome, and in April 1544 Barbarossa – having at the last moment completed his revictualling operations by ransacking five French ships in the harbour – returned to a hero's welcome in Istanbul.

In the first weeks of 1545 Francis fell desperately ill. Already in January he was suffering an agonisingly painful abscess 'in his lower parts'. It was repeatedly opened and drained, and in early February he was sufficiently recovered to leave Paris on a litter for the Loire valley. He was, he told the imperial ambassador, quite restored to health, 'albeit dead in respect of the ladies'. But there was more trouble in March, and as the year went on he grew steadily weaker. Not for a moment did he relax his grip on government, and foreign ambassadors seldom failed to comment on his knowledge and understanding of international affairs; but by the autumn of 1546 it was clear that he had not long to live. At the end of January 1547, when he was at Amboise, there came the news of the death of Henry VIII; Francis tried to return to Paris, where he planned a memorial service at Notre-Dame; but when he reached Rambouillet he found he could go no further. He died there, in the early afternoon of Thursday 31 March. He was fifty-two.

The funeral ceremonies lasted over two months. Perhaps their most curious feature was the continued service, for eleven days from the end of April, of meals for the dead king. While his remarkably life-like effigy – by François Clouet – lay on a bed of state in the great hall of the Château de Saint-Cloud, these were served exactly as if he were still alive: the table was laid, the courses brought in one by one, the wine poured out twice at each meal. At the end, grace was said by a cardinal. Not till 11 May was the king's coffin taken on a wagon to Notre-Dame and thence, after a short service, to its final resting place in the Abbey of Saint-Denis. There the new king, Henry II – whose filial conscientiousness was exemplary, though Francis never liked him much – commissioned an exquisite tomb from the architect Philibert de l'Orme: Francis and Queen Claude lie together, as it were in state, on a high plinth, while their naked and worm-eaten bodies repose below.

10

'Well worth a Mass'
1547–1643

All my shirts are torn, my doublet is worn through at the elbow, often I can entertain no one, and for the last two days I have taken my meals now with one, now with another.

King Henry IV

TENNIS – IN ITS earlier version, *jeu de paume* – was always a dangerous game for the French monarchy. Louis X had died after playing it; Charles VIII had died after going to watch it; and Francis I's eldest son, the Dauphin Louis, had died in August 1536, having drunk a cooling cup of water at the end of a game. It therefore came about that Francis was succeeded by his second son, Henry, the former Duke of Orléans – who, with his brother, had been held hostage in Spain for over four years after the Treaty of Madrid. He had since suffered that most exhausting wedding to Catherine de' Medici in Marseille. The following year, however, when still only fifteen, he had become romantically involved with a thirty-five-year-old widow, Diane de Poitiers, who for the next quarter of a century was a power in France second only to the king himself,★ even on occasion signing royal documents in his name.

Diane had been married at the age of fifteen to a certain Louis de Brézé, Seigneur d'Anet, who was already fifty-four and had died in 1531. In her youth she had served as a lady-in-waiting to Queen Claude, to Louise of Savoy and to Eleanor of Austria. During the early years of Henry II's marriage she had been a good friend of

---

★ A fact that did not prevent her agreeing to be painted by François Clouet, naked in the bath.

Queen Catherine – to whom she was distantly related – nursing her when she was ill and being responsible for the education of the royal children, of whom there were eventually ten. Inevitably, however, as time went on, Catherine grew increasingly jealous – especially when the king remodelled the Château d'Anet★ for Diane's benefit and then, as if that were not enough, gave her that of Chenonceau, which Catherine had coveted for herself. There was clearly nothing to be done during his lifetime; but when Henry lay on his deathbed Catherine refused to allow Diane anywhere near the sickroom, despite his repeated calls for her; nor was she invited to the funeral.

The French writer André Maurois maintained that Henry II was one of France's greatest kings. It is hard to agree with him. Henry was, if anything, still more bigoted than his father, continuing his persecution of the Protestants – or Huguenots, as they were by now generally known – more savagely than ever. If found guilty – which they nearly always were – they could confidently expect to be burned at the stake or, at the very least, to have their tongues cut out. Horrified at developments in England – where, under the boy king Edward VI, Protestantism was becoming more and more extreme – and determined to prevent any Anglo-Scottish reconciliation, he lost no time in marrying off his eldest son, Francis, to Mary Stuart, the child Queen of Scotland. Where Germany was concerned, however, in his detestation of the Emperor Charles – whom he had never forgiven for his four years' captivity – he had no hesitation in encouraging a delegation of the Protestant princes, led by the Elector Maurice of Saxony, to sign the Treaty of Chambord in 1552. This resulted in the cession by the princes of three important bishoprics – those of Toul, Metz and Verdun – vastly strengthening his eastern border – in return for military and economic aid against Charles.† Charles retaliated at once, and

---

★ Anet, the work of Philibert de l'Orme, is one of the loveliest châteaux near Paris. It was used as the chief location in Jean Cocteau's film *La Belle et la Bête*, and also in the James Bond film *Thunderball*.

† In fact the princes had no right to surrender imperial territory in this way; they – and Henry – were lucky to get away with it. The region did not technically become part of France until the Peace of Westphalia in 1648.

put Metz under siege; but thanks largely to the extraordinary courage of Francis, Duke of Guise★ – and also to a sudden outbreak of typhus in the imperial camp – the siege was abandoned.

Henry continued his father's policy, too, by forging even closer links with Sultan Suleiman – to the consternation, as always, of the rest of Christian Europe. There was serious concern, for example, when it was discovered that a French ambassador, Gabriel d'Aramon, had been present with the Turkish fleet during the siege of Tripoli in 1551, when the city was captured from the Knights of St John – and, worse still, had attended the Turkish victory banquet afterwards. But Henry was unrepentant: soon afterwards he ordered all his galleys in the Mediterranean to join the Ottoman fleet. The siege was the beginning of an all-out war between Henry and Charles – a war which lasted throughout the rest of the decade in various theatres: eastern France, the Mediterranean and Italy. The Italian campaign, however, was distinctly half-hearted. Henry never shared the enthusiasm of his predecessors for the peninsula. Italy, he believed, was more trouble than it was worth; and he welcomed the Peace of Cateau-Cambrésis, which on 3 April 1559 brought that whole sad saga – together with a long-drawn-out war, first with Charles and then after his death in 1558 with his son Philip II – to an end.

There was no doubt about it: the Empire had won on points, thanks in large measure to the assistance provided by the House of Savoy. This was one of the oldest ruling families of Europe, having been founded in the year 1003;† by the middle of the

---

★ Francis of Guise was a remarkable man indeed. In 1545, when the French were besieging Boulogne – which had been taken by Henry VIII in the previous year – he had been struck with a lance through the bars of his helmet. The lance had been snapped off leaving six inches of its shaft and the steel tip piercing both his cheeks. However, the duke remained firmly in his saddle, riding back unassisted to his tent. Later, we are told, when the surgeon was operating and thought he might die of pain, 'he bore it as easily as if it had been but the plucking of a hair out of his head'.

† Its members have at various times held the titles of King of Sicily, King of Sardinia, King of Croatia, King of Spain, King of Cyprus, King of Armenia, King of Jerusalem and Emperor of Ethiopia. They were also to provide the four kings of Italy between the country's unification in March 1861 and June 1946, when it became a republic.

sixteenth century it covered the area of the present Italian region of Piedmont, together with the French departments of Savoie and Haute-Savoie, with its capital at Chambéry.* It had been peaceful enough until Francis I had invaded and occupied it in 1536; Duke Charles III ('the Good') and his son Emmanuel Philibert – who succeeded his father in 1553 – were then effectively exiled, and had thus become enthusiastic allies of the Empire. The peace, signed by Henry and Philip II – both by proxy – restored to Savoy all its former territories, while Henry renounced any further claims in Italy. This meant that Philip kept direct control of Milan, Naples, Sicily and Sardinia; it also meant that the only truly independent states in the Italian peninsula were Savoy and the Republic of Venice. To France, on the other hand, went Calais. The English were predictably furious about the latter provision, but there was nothing they could do. Meanwhile the agreement was sealed with the gift, by Henry to Emmanuel Philibert, of the hand of his sister Margaret, Duchess of Berry, now aged thirty-six and described by a contemporary as 'a spinster lady of excellent breeding and lively intellect'.

But Henry did not long survive. On 1 July he was jousting at the Château de Tournelles in Paris – the site is now occupied by the Place des Vosges – during a tournament held to celebrate the peace. His opponent was Gabriel, Comte de Montgomery, a French nobleman who happened to be the captain of his Scottish Guard. During their encounter Montgomery's lance shattered and, by a one-in-a-million chance, a splinter from it slipped under the king's visor, ran through his eye and penetrated deep into his brain. He died of septicaemia ten days later.

The king's accident and death cast a heavy cloud over the wedding celebrations of Emmanuel Philibert and Margaret. Just before he lost consciousness, obviously fearful lest the bridegroom should take advantage of his death to renege on the alliance, the king ordered that the wedding should take place immediately. Plans for an elaborate service at Notre-Dame were scrapped: the two were married in a midnight ceremony in a small church near where Henry lay

* The capital was to be moved to Turin in 1563.

dying. Queen Catherine, the bride's sister-in-law, sat apart from the rest, making no effort to restrain her tears.

The next twenty years – for the second time in French history – saw three successive kings of France, all brothers. First came Francis II, husband of Mary Queen of Scots. Both physically and psychologically frail, he was to reign for only seventeen months. Those months were full of incident, but Francis was to have little control over them: although fifteen years old and not, theoretically, in need of a regent, on his accession he voluntarily delegated his authority to Mary's uncles, Francis, Duke of Guise and Francis's brother Charles, Cardinal of Lorraine.* His mother Queen Catherine, still in deep mourning for her husband, made no objection.

Many others, however, did. They were led by Anthony of Bourbon, who was married to Queen Joan of Navarre. So far as these two were concerned, the Guises were nothing but ambitious upstarts from Lorraine, now French only because their father had been given citizenship by his friend Francis I. They certainly had no right to take advantage of the king's youth, as they were so obviously doing. Their regime of austerity – vitally necessary, since the long wars against the Empire had reduced France to the brink of bankruptcy – had made them more unpopular still. Finally, their accession to power coincided with a further stepping up of Huguenot persecution, every day bringing more house searches and arrests.

It was, more than anything else, this persecution that brought matters to a head. Despite anything the king could do, the fact was that Protestantism in France was rapidly increasing, particularly among the nobility. By the 1560s, it is estimated, more than half of them were Huguenots, constituting a serious potential threat to the monarchy itself. In 1560 a group of provincial Huguenot noblemen planned to seize the king and to arrest the Guises. Word of their plot, it need hardly be said, soon reached the cardinal, who quickly transferred Francis and his court from Blois to the much more easily defensible Amboise. On 17 March the conspirators attempted to

* Mary's father James V had married Mary of Guise as his second wife in 1538.

storm the château; but they were defeated almost before they had begun. Their leader, the Seigneur de la Renaudie of Périgord, was drawn and quartered, what was left of him being displayed at the gates of the town. In the presence of the king and queen, his followers – some twelve to fifteen hundred of them – were also executed, their bodies hung on trees or slung from iron hooks on the walls. The first round, beyond any doubt, had gone to the Guises.

Then, on 5 December 1560, King Francis died of an infection in his ear. A pathetic figure, blown this way and that by others stronger and more intelligent than himself, he had reigned for less than five months, but he had never ruled. His influence on the country had been negligible. His marriage to Mary of Scotland if anything had emphasised his inferiority: he was abnormally short, almost dwarfish; she stood a fraction under six feet. Whether the marriage was ever consummated we cannot tell, but it seems unlikely. Mary as we know was to have two more husbands, neither of them entirely satisfactory; but both, one feels, must have been distinct improvements on her first.

The childlessness of Francis and Mary meant that the throne now devolved on Francis's younger brother Charles, who became King Charles IX. Being only ten, he needed a regency; and his mother, Queen Catherine, by threatening the Guises with the Bourbons and the Bourbons with the Guises, managed without too much difficulty to secure it for herself. The political picture was now completely dominated by the religious wars, and Catherine, though herself always a dedicated Catholic, realised that she must try to steer a middle course. It was easier said than done. With the Edict of Saint-Germain in January 1562 she recognised the existence of Protestantism, guaranteeing freedom of conscience and permitting worship in private – though not of course in public, which would have been asking for trouble. Alas, only two months later Francis, Duke of Guise, returning to his estates, stopped in the village of Vassy to attend Mass. There, in a barn that they were using as their church, he came across a group of Huguenots holding a service of their own. Some of his men tried to push their way inside, but were driven back; one thing led to another, stones were thrown and the

duke was struck on the head. Furious, he ordered his men to set
fire to the barn, killing sixty-three and wounding a hundred.

That was the end of the Edict of Saint-Germain, which was
revoked under pressure from the Guises. The next year saw open
civil war. Louis of Bourbon, Prince of Condé – the suspected architect of the Amboise conspiracy – assumed the role of protector of
Protestantism and began to garrison strategic towns along the valley
of the Loire. Anthony of Bourbon was killed at Rouen, Francis of
Guise at Orléans. Eventually Queen Catherine – who had shown
remarkable courage and wisdom throughout – succeeded in restoring
order by means of another edict, signed at Amboise in March 1563.
Though less permissive than its predecessor, it still allowed Protestant
services in the private houses of nobles, and in one designated suburb
of every principal town. There followed a year of extremely uneasy
peace; Charles declared his majority in August, but was wisely content
to let his mother keep tight hold of the reins. Gradually the tension
lessened, to the point where, in the following spring, the two of
them felt able together to set off from Fontainebleau on a grand tour
of the country; it took them the best part of the next two years.*

The peace endured till 1567, after which there were another three
years of war – which now rapidly escalated, with England, Navarre
and the Dutch Republic coming in on the Protestant side and Spain,
Tuscany and – hardly surprisingly – Pope Pius V supporting the
Catholics. There was an attempt to abduct the king at Meaux, and
a hideous massacre of Catholics at Nîmes; and so the fighting went
on until the conclusion of another truce, the Peace of Saint-Germain-
en-Laye, in 1570. The king meanwhile, much to his mother's anxiety,
was coming increasingly under the influence of Admiral Gaspard de
Coligny, who had succeeded Condé as Huguenot leader and was
suspected by the Guises of having ordered the assassination of Duke
Francis during the fighting at Orléans in 1563. They were determined
on revenge, and it was not long before they got it.

---

* It was when they reached Roussillon in the Auvergne that the king decreed
that the year would begin on 1 January. Previously the calendar had been at the
mercy of individual dioceses: depending on location, the year might begin at
Christmas, Easter, or on Lady Day, the Feast of the Annunciation on 25 March.

During this last truce, the marriage was arranged between the king's sister, Margaret of Valois, and the Huguenot Henry of Navarre, the future Henry IV. The Catholics of course were horrified, and protested with vehemence; the Huguenots on the other hand were delighted, and many of the leading Huguenot nobles flocked to Paris for the ceremony, which was planned for 18 August 1572. But feelings in the city were now running dangerously high. Four days later, Coligny narrowly escaped an attempt on his life. Two days after that he was not so lucky: Duke Henry of Guise and a group of followers burst into his lodgings and ran him through with their swords. The body was thrown out of the window, and decapitated almost before it reached the ground. But Coligny was far from being the only victim. That day – it was the Feast of St Bartholomew, 24 August – and the days following saw a general massacre of the Huguenots – almost certainly planned by the Guises and quite probably backed by Queen Catherine – which spread to many of the other cities and towns of France. Estimates of those who lost their lives vary; the number has been put as high as thirty thousand.

News of the massacre quickly spread across Europe. Reactions differed widely. In England, Queen Elizabeth went into mourning; in Rome, Pope Gregory XIII ordered the singing of a special *Te Deum* in celebration. More enthusiastic still was Philip II, who sent his congratulations from the Escorial (which he was still building). 'This news', he wrote, 'is one of the greatest joys of my whole life.' As for King Charles, he never recovered from the shock. His moods swung alarmingly: he complained that the screams of the murdered Huguenots kept ringing in his ears. Sometimes he blamed himself, sometimes his mother. But Catherine, as always, kept her head; she had, she said, a lunatic for a son, and that was all there was to it. Charles died – almost certainly of tuberculosis – on 30 May 1574, aged twenty-three. He had fathered two children, neither of them unfortunately by his wife, Elisabeth of Austria;* the throne therefore passed to his brother, the third of Henry II's sons.†

---

* She was the daughter of Emperor Maximilian II.
† The fourth, if we count Louis Duke of Orléans who had died in 1550 aged eighteen months.

This time the succession proved rather more complicated than before, since it happened that King Henry III was already King of Poland. With two surviving elder brothers, no one had expected him to be King of France; he had therefore been considered an admirable candidate for the elective Polish throne. He had reigned at the Castle of Wawel in Cracow for six months, but on receiving the news of his brother's death he had returned to France, via Venice, with all possible speed.* Crowned in Reims on 13 February 1575, he was married the very next day to the not-particularly-well-born Louise of Lorraine, whom he had first met on his outward journey to Poland and to whom, we are told, he was immediately attracted.

But was he? It seems unlikely. All the evidence suggests that he was basically – and indeed flagrantly – homosexual. He certainly surrounded himself with a number of effeminate young men – they were known as his *mignons* – who wore enormous earrings and carried very small muffs and accompanied him everywhere. But apart from the absence of an heir, the question of his sexuality hardly matters; and, as things turned out, it was extremely lucky for France that he never produced one.

Meanwhile, the nightmare civil war continued. The Huguenots, much weakened after the St Bartholomew's Day Massacre, were struggling to recover while the two Guises – now the cardinal and his nephew, Duke Henry – were gaining steadily in strength and influence. This they would prove beyond doubt when the king's youngest brother and heir presumptive Francis, Duke of Anjou, died in 1584. The next heir to the throne was, almost unbelievably, his ninth cousin – Henry King of Navarre, son of Anthony of Bourbon and a direct descendant in the male line of Saint-Louis. Unfortunately he was a Protestant; and since they refused absolutely to countenance the idea of a non-Catholic king the Guises forced Henry III to issue an edict annulling his right to the throne. There could be no doubt now that the king was completely, if unwillingly, under their control.

---

* He is credited with bringing back from Poland the first table fork to be seen in western Europe.

But there was, he knew, one way to regain his independence. He bided his time and then, two days before Christmas 1588, he invited the cardinal and the duke to the Château of Blois, where he had them murdered in cold blood by members of the royal guard.

The reaction was immediate. Queen Catherine was predictably appalled – she took to her bed and died three weeks later – and the whole of Catholic France rose in revolt against its king. In Paris, we are told, a procession estimated at a hundred thousand all simultaneously snuffed out the candles they carried, crying: 'Thus does God extinguish the Valois race!' But Henry kept his head. He slipped away to Tours, arranging for the one power on which he could still rely, the King of Navarre (who happened to be his brother-in-law, married to his sister Margaret), to join him there. The two kings planned a joint attack on Paris, but had got no further than Saint-Cloud when on 1 August 1589 a fanatical young Dominican friar, Jacques Clément, stabbed Henry III in the stomach. He died on the following morning, having enjoined all those around him to recognise the King of Navarre as his rightful successor.

The Huguenots were of course only too happy to do so. As might have been expected the Catholics remained adamant, and for two main reasons. Quite apart from his religion, there was the question of his claim to the throne. As a ninth cousin, could he really be the true heir? Surely few kings in history, succeeding legitimately, had been less closely related to their predecessor; was there no Catholic prince anywhere with a stronger claim? Thus it very soon became clear to Henry of Navarre that if he were to rule his new kingdom, he must first of all conquer it. He won two battles against the Catholic League, at Arques in 1589 and at Ivry (now known as Ivry-la-Bataille) in 1590; but an attempt on Paris later that year was beaten back, and he was forced reluctantly to accept the fact that he would never be generally accepted as king for as long as he maintained his Protestant faith. '*Paris vaut bien une messe*':* his words have passed into history. They sound cynical, but they were not intended as such. 'What would those most devoted to the Catholic faith have said about me', he asked, 'if, having lived to the age of

---

* 'Paris is well worth a mass.'

thirty in one condition, they saw me suddenly change my belief under the expectation of thereby winning a kingdom?' He took his time, refusing to allow himself to be converted 'with a dagger at my throat', and finally rejected his Protestant faith four years after his succession, on 25 July 1593, only after long discussions with his long-time mistress, Gabrielle d'Estrées. Now at last he secured the allegiance of the vast majority of his subjects, and now at last he could be crowned king – not according to the old tradition at Reims, which was still firmly in the hands of the Catholic League, but in the Cathedral of Chartres – on 27 February 1594.

But the Catholics, even though they reluctantly came to accept Henry as their rightful king, were still unhappy, and still bitterly hostile to the Huguenots. In many a city and town, life for the latter remained hard indeed; and it was in an effort to improve the lot of his former co-religionists that in April 1598 the king set his signature to the Edict of Nantes. In it he went as far as he dared: the Protestants were no longer to be treated as heretics or schismatics but would be granted all civil rights, including the right to work for the state and to bring any legitimate grievances directly to him. In fact the Edict pleased neither party: the Catholics deeply resented the recognition of Protestantism as a permanent element in French society, while the Protestants still felt themselves to be second-class citizens. None the less it marked a significant step forward, and – most important of all – it achieved its primary purpose: it brought to an end the wars which had plagued France for the best part of half a century.

Only now could Henry concentrate on restoring unity to his country. 'We are all Frenchmen,' he declared, 'and fellow-citizens of the same fatherland; thus we must join together in reason and kindness, and renounce that severity and cruelty which serve only to inflame men.' And he possessed a further trump card: that immense charm for which he was famous and which, together with his broad Gascon accent, his subjects found irresistible. They loved him too, just as they had loved Francis I, for his unconcealed delight in beautiful women.* His first marriage, to Henry III's sister Margaret,

---

* Meticulous research has produced a list of his mistresses, which is not yet complete. The total so far stands at fifty-six.

had not been a success, and the couple had remained childless; he now wanted to have it annulled and to marry instead his beloved Gabrielle, who had already borne him three children. Not surprisingly he encountered fairly strong opposition; but the matter was tragically resolved in April 1599 by her sudden death, after giving birth to a stillborn son. That same year he obtained his annulment and married Marie de' Medici, the sixth daughter of Francesco I, Grand Duke of Tuscany. In her twenty-ninth year, poor corpulent Marie always looked as if she had been painted by Rubens (as indeed she had). She was already seriously overweight and was known to the court as 'the fat banker'. She was to bear him two sons and three daughters (including the future Queen of England, Charles I's wife Henrietta Maria), but he never liked her much; and relations between them were hardly improved by the constant bickering between her and the many other ladies with whom she sulkily shared the royal bed.

Domestic strife, however, did not for a moment deflect Henry from the huge task that lay ahead: to rebuild and re-pacify France. 'There is destruction everywhere,' reported the Venetian ambassador. 'Most of the cattle have disappeared, so that ploughing is no longer possible . . . The people are no longer what they used to be, courteous and honest; war and the sight of blood have made them sly, coarse and barbarous.' He spoke no more than the truth: other witnesses write of peasants who, lacking beasts of burden, drew the plough themselves, with ropes over their shoulders. In the towns the populations had dramatically decreased, sometimes by as much as 60 per cent. Henry was supremely fortunate, on the other hand, with his right-hand man. Maximilien de Béthune, whom in 1606 he created Duc de Sully, would rise at four, breakfast at six-thirty, work till noon, have his lunch and then work on till ten at night. He and Henry together believed that France's wealth lay above all in the land itself; they built bridges and elm-lined highways, drained swamps, dug canals and reforested vast areas left desolate by the wars. To the city of Paris they made two major contributions: first, the Grande Galérie du Louvre, originally some five hundred yards long (it has since been much shortened) running along the right bank of the Seine and connecting the old palace with the new one built by

148

Catherine de' Medici at the Tuileries; second – and more important still – the Pont Neuf, despite its name the oldest of the Seine bridges, now marked by Giambologna's superb equestrian statue of the king, standing at the point where it crosses the Ile de la Cité. Much of Henry's magic was due to the simple fact that he genuinely loved his people; and that love he was to express in his famous dictum: 'If God keeps me alive, I will ensure that no peasant in my kingdom will lack the means to have a chicken in the pot on Sundays.' Alas, God failed to keep His side of the bargain. Henry, now fifty-six, had already survived two assassination attempts; but the third proved fatal. On 14 May 1610, when his coach was held up by traffic congestion in the Rue de la Ferronnerie,★ a Catholic fanatic named François Ravaillac wrenched open the door and plunged a knife into his chest, bringing to an abrupt close the life of one of the greatest kings that France ever produced. Few had been more hated, or more violently attacked, than Henry IV at the beginning of his reign; none, after their death, has been more deeply loved.

The year 1610 marked something of a watershed. For the next 164 years there were to be only three kings of France, all named Louis; over the same period before that date there had been ten. Like so many of his recent predecessors, Henry IV's elder son, Louis XIII, came to the throne as a child, shortly before his ninth birthday; the regency was put in the hands of his mother, Marie de' Medici. Marie was one of those Italians who, regardless of how long they have lived in a foreign country, remain as Italian as ever they were. She kept most of her husband's ministers but herself came to rely increasingly on two somewhat sinister compatriots: Laura Galigai, with whom she had shared the same wet-nurse and whom she had brought with her from Florence, and Laura's husband, Concino Concini, whom she made Marquis of Ancre and who instantly promoted himself to the rank of marshal. These two, it need hardly be said, were deeply disliked by the rest of the court; and they became more unpopular still when – almost certainly at their promptings

★ A plaque in the pavement marks the spot.

– Marie decided to marry her son the king to Anne of Austria, daughter of Philip III of Spain and great-granddaughter of the Emperor Charles V. The Protestants were predictably outraged, while the Catholics – who held no brief for the Habsburgs either, still feeling France to be surrounded – were not all that much happier.

Nor, probably was the young bride, when she first met her prospective husband. Lord Herbert of Cherbury, whom James I appointed his ambassador and who presented his credentials in 1619, reported:

> I presented to the King a letter of credence from the King my master . . . His words were never many, as being so extream a stutterer that he would sometimes hold his tongue out of his mouth a good while before he could speak so much as one word; he had besides a double row of teeth,* and was observed seldom or never to spit or blow his nose, or to sweat much, tho' he were very laborious, and almost indefatigable in his exercises of hunting and hawking, to which he was much addicted.

Theoretically Louis came of age on his thirteenth birthday in 1614, but he seems to have been content for his mother to retain the regency for another three years; until 1617 she and the Concini were the effective rulers of France. Henri, Prince of Condé – who was at the time second in line to the French throne – led two successive attempts against them and was briefly imprisoned by the queen; but this time she went too far. It was the king's oldest friend Charles d'Albert, Grand Falconer of France, who convinced him that the time had come to break permanently with his mother and to support Condé and his followers; and at last Louis took firm action. In April 1617 Concini was assassinated, almost certainly on his orders. Three months later his widow Galigai was tried for witchcraft, condemned, beheaded and finally burned at the stake. The queen was exiled to Blois; d'Albert was made Duke of Luynes and thereafter became the king's chief counsellor.

Louis had flexed his muscles; he had tasted blood. Henceforth he was prepared to rule. But he was still only sixteen; he remained

* What can this mean?

socially inept, taciturn and suspicious. He was probably bisexual; there is no doubt that women terrified him. He took little interest in his wife, not entering her bed until four years after their marriage in 1615, and even then only when Luynes, who continued to be his only friend, practically forced him into it. Politically, however, he was confident, both of himself and of his judgement; he may have stammered, but he knew precisely what he wanted to say. When Luynes died of the 'crimson fever' – whatever that may have been – in 1621, he shed no tears; indeed, those around him were astonished at how little he seemed to mind. He did, however, need another adviser, and before long he found one – the man with whom his name is permanently associated, Armand du Plessis, Cardinal de Richelieu.

Richelieu was not a newcomer to the political scene. He had been employed not only by Queen Marie during her exile at Blois – when he had served as an invaluable go-between with the king – but also by the young Queen Anne as her almoner. In 1616 he had been promoted to what was effectively Foreign Minister. After the king's coup of 1617 he had been dismissed and exiled to Avignon; but he soon returned, and after the death of Luynes had quickly regained power. In 1622 he was made a cardinal by Pope Gregory XV. Two years later he was chief minister to the king.

And he looked the part. Philippe de Champagne, who was the only painter permitted to depict him in his full state robes – and did so eleven times – may have been in part responsible, but descriptions abound by those who knew him and who wrote of his magnificent presence, of that arched nose, goatee beard and those dark-brown eyes. Certainly there is no other French statesman so instantly recognisable or so immediately impressive. He too, even more than his master, radiated confidence.

And it was just as well that he did, because in 1618 there began a war which was to tear apart the whole of central Europe. The Thirty Years' War was the deadliest and most brutal upheaval the continent had ever seen – the French Wars of Religion, now vastly magnified and transferred to the European stage. By its close in 1648, over eight million men lay dead. It began when the Holy Roman Emperor Ferdinand II attempted to force Roman Catholicism on all his subjects. He should have known better. The Protestant princes in northern Germany, whom Ferdinand's great-uncle Charles V had permitted to decide on their own religion at the Peace of Augsburg some sixty years before, banded together to assert their rights. Soon, on one side or the other, Bavaria, Bohemia, England, Hungary, Saxony, Scotland, Sweden, Spain and the Dutch Republic had all joined the fray. France stayed out of it for as long as she could. Neutrality was clearly impossible in the long term, but she was initially undecided which side to choose. She remained in theory a Catholic state. Her king was a Catholic, his queen a Habsburg through and through, and the country might well have been expected to join the imperialists; but France's age-old hostility to the Empire by which she was effectively surrounded was too strong. To the astonishment of many of the combatants, she was finally to join the Protestant cause. The decision was of course in large part due to Richelieu. Though himself a Catholic and a cardinal, he had no quarrel with the Huguenots; he was indeed perfectly willing to accept them, so long as they were prepared to be obedient subjects of the king; he preferred a French Huguenot to a Spanish Catholic any day of the week. At the same time, he accepted that the Huguenots needed firm control, since there was always a danger that they might become a focus of resistance against the central government – as from time to time they did. In the 1620s there were open revolts in Gascony and Béarn, and in 1625 serious trouble broke out at the port of La Rochelle.

For well over half a century already, La Rochelle had been a problem to the French crown. With its population of some twenty-seven thousand, it was not only one of the largest cities in France; it was also the main base of the French Huguenots, for whom it possessed the additional advantage of administrative autonomy; there was no bishop, no *Parlement*, not even a *seigneur*, making it almost a state within a state. It was superbly fortified, with an excellent harbour, and had been a popular place of refuge ever since the St Bartholomew's Day Massacre. In November 1572, when it had refused to accept a royal governor, it had first been put under siege; in the following year it had withstood eight separate assaults, all of them unsuccessful. The inhabitants had then sent an ambassador to Queen

Elizabeth of England with an appeal for help. Seven English ships had arrived in February 1573 and a larger contingent in April, which had been repulsed by the French navy. Fighting had continued until the end of May, when Henry of Anjou – later King Henry III, who was in overall command – heard that he had been elected King of Poland. He at once lost interest, and the siege ended in July.

The problem of La Rochelle, however, had not gone away; and by the 1620s the city was once again seen to constitute a threat, with Duke Henry de Rohan and his brother Duke Benjamin de Soubise clearly planning a major Huguenot rebellion. In 1627 King Charles I of England, growing alarmed by the speed with which Richelieu was building up the strength of the French navy, went so far as to send eighty ships under his favourite George Villiers, Duke of Buckingham, to encourage a major uprising; but this, as anyone could have told him, was a bad idea from the start. Buckingham's reception proved – much to his surprise – far from warm, to the point where his fleet was denied access to the harbour. He was obliged to land with 6,000 men on the Ile de Ré, where he failed even to capture the little town of Saint-Martin. Soon he ran out of money and, realising that he had made a mild fool of himself, returned to England.

Meanwhile, in August 1627, the siege of La Rochelle began in earnest. King Louis had put himself in supreme authority, with Richelieu at his right hand and Charles, Duke of Angoulême as his commanding general. French engineers encircled the city with entrenchments some eight miles around, with forts and redoubts at regular intervals. They also built a 1,500-yard sea wall to block the maritime access to the city. There were two more relief expeditions from England, but neither did much good. The city held out for fourteen months, during which its population was reduced by famine and disease to some five thousand. Finally, on 28 October 1628, it surrendered. The surviving Huguenots retained their religious freedom, as guaranteed by the Edict of Nantes; but they lost their territorial, political and military rights and were left at the mercy of the monarchy. They were also obliged to accept, as a result of their actions, the marked strengthening of central government and the corresponding reduction in the tolerance that it was prepared to show towards any defiance of its rule.

Richelieu was an autocrat to his fingertips. For him, the security of the state was paramount; and the greatest danger to that security was no longer the Huguenots but the nobility, which, led by the two queens and Gaston, Duke of Orléans, the king's brother and heir apparent, was ceaselessly intriguing against him. A few of these were too powerful for him to touch, but further to calm aristocratic spirits, the cardinal also made the noble custom of duelling a capital offence. As to the people, his golden rule was that they must never be allowed to become too prosperous. In such a case 'it would be impossible to keep them within the rules of their duty . . . By losing the mark of their subjection, they would also lose awareness of their condition. They must be likened to mules which, being accustomed to their burdens, are spoiled by long idleness rather than by labour.' No Sunday chicken in the pot for them.

Such a philosophy might ill accord with Christian teaching; but for Richelieu there were more important considerations. France was still a Catholic country, he himself a Prince of the Roman Church; but in his policy towards the rest of Europe he had no hesitation in siding with the Protestant German princes against the forces of the Counter-Reformation as represented by Austria, Spain and the papacy. The emperor, he knew, would not rest until he had brought the princes to heel and re-established Catholicism throughout Europe; were he permitted to do so, France would be crushed and might never recover. During the eleven years between 1624 and 1635 he applied all his diplomatic and financial skills to recruiting or strengthening allies, though still without involving France directly in the war. King Gustavus Adolphus of Sweden, already a firm Lutheran, needed money to continue the fight; Richelieu sent him a million livres a year, much of which went on the hiring of 8,000 Scottish mercenaries.*

---

* The Swedes loved the Scots, and vice versa. There were already some 12,000 Scots, under the command of Colonel Sir James Spens, in the Swedish army before the Swedes entered the war. By its end there were about 30,000, fifteen of whom had the rank of major general or above.

But then the situation took a dangerous turn for the worse. Gustavus Adolphus died in 1632, and two years later the imperial army, bolstered by 18,000 Spanish and Italian troops, won a crushing victory at Nördlingen over the combined armies of Sweden and the princes. Richelieu realised that he could wait no longer, and in August 1636 declared war on the Empire. France was immediately invaded; Spanish troops from the Low Countries advanced as far as Corbie in Picardy, their scouts reaching even further to Pontoise; but they were driven back, and once again the tide turned. French armies found themselves advancing on all fronts, and by 1642 France extended virtually to her natural boundaries: the Scheldt, the Rhine, the Alps and the Pyrenees.

It was during these last victorious years that there occurred another near-miracle: on 5 September 1638, after twenty-three years of marriage and four stillbirths, the thirty-seven-year-old queen at last gave birth to a son, and two years later to another. The Duke of Orléans, previously almost certain of his succession, saw his hopes disappear. Two years later still, however, the pendulum swung back and France was to sustain a grievous blow: the death in December 1642 of Cardinal Richelieu at the age of fifty-seven. Perhaps even more than the king himself, he had personified France. When his confessor was performing the last rites he asked him whether he forgave his enemies. 'I have had none', the cardinal replied, 'save those of the state.' His words may not have been strictly true; none the less, one knows what he meant.*

Louis XIII did not long survive his chief minister. He died in Paris on 14 May 1643, the thirty-third anniversary of the death of his father. He was forty-one. For years he had suffered from digestive problems – after his death his intestines were found to be badly ulcerated – and also very probably from tuberculosis. His personal achievements are hard to define. He was a fine musician and lutenist, and he also seems to have been responsible for the introduction –

---

* Among the cardinal's non-political achievements the most important was the Académie Française, which he founded in 1635 and which still today regulates – or attempts to regulate – every aspect of the French language: its grammar, its spelling, even its literature. It also publishes the official French dictionary, working hard – though largely in vain – to eliminate modern anglicisms.

for the first time in French history – of the wig, which he began to affect when he found himself going prematurely bald in his thirties. His portraits show it to have been quite a luxuriant affair, though not a patch on the tumbling locks which we associate with the following generation. For the rest, it was his fate to be utterly overshadowed – first by the dazzling cardinal who stole so much of his thunder, and second by his son, *le roi soleil*, who was also to overshadow everyone else.

II

'*L'Etat c'est moi*'
1643–1715

Although he has been blamed for meanness, for harshness . . .
for too much arrogance with foreigners in the days of his
success, for his weakness regarding several women . . . for wars
lightly undertaken, for ravaging the Palatinate with fire, for
persecuting the Protestants, nevertheless his great qualities and
achievements are preponderant over his faults. Time, which
ripens men's judgements, has put its seal upon his reputation.

Voltaire, *Le Siècle de Louis XIV*

W AS THE NEW King of France always to be a child? Certainly
it seemed so. Louis XIV came to the throne at the age of
four, and was to be king for the next seventy-two years – the
longest reign of any monarch in European history.* When he was
still only five his mother, Anne, brought him before the *Parlement*
to request the annulment of his father's will. The action was typical
of her. Louis XIII had agreed that Anne should be regent, but
had carefully provided for a regency council of former Richelieu
cronies who would severely limit her powers – an arrangement
that she, proud Spaniard that she was, refused to tolerate. The
Parlement was only too pleased to oblige. It willingly declared that
'the restrictions placed on the Regent were derogatory of the
principles and the unity of the monarchy', leaving Anne unfettered.
She had always detested Richelieu, and it was now generally
expected that she would turn away from all those who had been
connected with him, but no: in fact she chose as her chief minister

* Queen Elizabeth II came to the throne on 6 February 1952.

one of his most trusted associates, Giulio Mazarini, better known as Mazarin.

With both his parents members of the lesser Italian nobility, his father Sicilian, his mother from Umbria, Mazarin had studied at the Jesuit College in Rome, though he had never joined the Order. He had served briefly as a captain of infantry and then, having through a fortunate friendship become canon at Rome without ever having been ordained, was made Papal Nuncio to France. It was not long before he came to the notice of Richelieu, from whom he differed in every possible respect. The cardinal had been imperious, harsh and unbending; his successor was gentle, flexible and dangerously persuasive, and in 1636 entered the service of France, carrying out several delicate missions with outstanding success. These diplomatic skills, however, he combined with a passion for gambling; and on one lucky evening his winnings were so great that a crowd gathered round the table to watch the stacks of golden écus building up before him. Soon the queen appeared. As she watched, Mazarin staked his whole pile on a single throw of the dice – and won. Like the superb courtier that he was, he attributed his success to her presence at his elbow and offered her a commission of 50,000 écus on the spot. She politely demurred – but later changed her mind.

It was the wisest investment Mazarin ever made; thenceforth he was one of the queen's closest advisers, on such intimate terms that it was widely rumoured the two were secretly married and he was the true father of the dauphin. In 1641, on Louis XIII's recommendation, he was made a cardinal; and on the king's death two years later his position – and his future – were assured. Until his own death in 1661, first during the regency and later after the young king had attained his majority, he was effectively the co-ruler of France – and a very necessary one too. Anne, a devout believer in the divine right of kings, tended to overreact whenever she felt her authority threatened. Anyone who challenged her will, be he aristocrat, minister or member of the *Parlement*, she tended to send straight to prison; had it not been for the moderating influence of Mazarin, the coming troubles would have begun a good deal earlier than they did and raged a lot more fiercely.

Louis's early years in power were largely taken up with peace negotiations. The Thirty Years' War was at last drawing to its close, with the defeat of the Empire and its predominantly Catholic allies. The peace conference, which was to settle the future of Europe for a long time to come, began in 1644, though it did not end till 1648, with the signing of the Treaty of Westphalia. This left France as strong as she had ever been, while Germany was quite literally in tatters – reduced to some three hundred and fifty independent states whose collective decisions had to be unanimous, which meant that they took no decisions at all. The overriding principle was that of *cujus regio, ejus religio*, that every man must adopt the religion of his sovereign; if he refused, he must emigrate.

Of all this, the chief architect was Mazarin. Clearly, he had deserved well of his country; yet strangely enough his country did not think so. In that same year of 1648, Paris rose up against its government. The people, it seemed, resented being governed by a Spaniard and an Italian; they were fed up with cardinals; they were disgusted by the amount of money that France had spent on the war, and the taxes which had increased in consequence. Besides, rebellion was in the air: in 1647 the Neapolitans, under the fisherman Masaniello, had overthrown their king; the English were about to decapitate theirs. In France the result was the *fronde*, as it was called – the French for a sling – in essence a succession of extremely unpleasant but ultimately unsuccessful uprisings that occurred between 1648 and 1653 and could be seen as sinister forerunners to the events of the following century.

One of the difficulties in understanding the *fronde* was its curious lack of direction. It was not only the people who were rising up against the government; it was also some of the nobility, of the *haute bourgeoisie* and even of the Church; one of its principal leaders, Jean François de Gondi, was to be yet another cardinal, Cardinal de Retz. There were two main phases: first came the *fronde parlementaire*, which was precipitated by a tax levied on the judicial officers of the Paris *Parlement*. They refused to pay, at which Mazarin, on the queen's insistence, arrested certain members – including their leader, Pierre Broussel – in a show of force. This led to rioting in the streets, so vociferous that Broussel had to be freed before worse befell. That was the moment when a mob of angry Parisians burst into the royal palace and demanded to see their young king. They were led into Louis's bedchamber, where the terrified child – he was still only ten – pretended to be asleep. The sight of him seemed to settle them, and they quietly took their leave; but the incident had left everyone badly shaken, and the court moved for safety to Rueil – then a village, now a western suburb of Paris. At this point the conclusion of the Peace of Westphalia allowed the Duke of Enghien – later known as the Grand Condé – to return to the capital, where he immediately agreed to help Anne to restore the king's authority. Fortunately he still had his army with him. He attacked the rebels, and after a few skirmishes the two sides reached an agreement. The Peace of Rueil was signed and the court returned with relief to Paris.

Condé, however, was not satisfied with his victory. An intensely proud man who had just led a victorious army in a major war, he was now determined to control France – and the first step was to get rid of Mazarin, whom he hated. Anne, who sympathised with neither of these two objectives, ordered his arrest; but the opposition fought back, and created an aristocratic coalition strong enough to unseat and exile Mazarin, liberate the prince and, for a short time, put Anne under effective house arrest. Clearly such a situation could not last, and after not unfriendly negotiations a modus vivendi was reached which saved face on both sides; but far more important was the effect that all these events had on the young king – bringing his childhood to a sudden and painful end. No wonder he was to develop his deep dislike of Paris, and his profound distrust of the high aristocracy. No wonder he decided to move out of the capital as soon as he could – and to keep them out of it too.

But the nightmare was not yet over. In 1650 came what was known as the *fronde des princes*. By this time the *frondeurs* seem to have forgotten the first, constitutional phases of the rising; now the nobility took centre stage in the scramble for power, united only in a hatred of Mazarin: the king's uncle the Duke of Orléans, the great generals Condé and Turenne, and the duke's daughter, Mademoiselle de Montpensier, known as the *Grande Mademoiselle*. She it was who in 1651 – Mazarin having wisely absented himself for a time – took charge of an army, dressed herself in armour, and opened the gates of Paris to the forces of Condé. When the mob rose up again and the Hôtel de Ville was in flames, she ordered the guns of the Bastille to fire on the royal troops in order to cover Condé's retreat.* The court hastily returned to Rueil.

But it was by now perfectly obvious that the *fronde* was going nowhere. Everyone was growing tired: tired of anarchy and disgusted by the conduct of the princes, several of whom seemed almost to have forgotten what they were fighting for. The merchants in particular, for whom the last five years had been disastrous, sent delegations to Rueil imploring the king to return; and in October 1652 he did so, in considerable state. Mazarin joined him four months later, to be welcomed with open arms by those who had been hurling insults at him for years. The *fronde* was over. It had failed because it deserved to fail: it had had no fixed principles. The king was once again seen as standing for order and responsible government – and the way was cleared for the absolutism for which he was to be famous. He had learned several valuable lessons. He had seen for himself the mob surging through the royal palace, and had understood all too well the potential dangers of an unpopular and over-powerful minister. In future he would govern by himself. He kept Mazarin on out of deep friendship and gratitude; but the cardinal's sails had been quietly and drastically trimmed.

Louis XIV was crowned on 7 June 1654. He was soon to be sixteen and was henceforth his own man, determined to govern France as he wished. He worked hard, for at least six hours a day, often for far longer. He may not have been exceptionally intelligent (the Duc de Saint-Simon, who disliked him, said that he was born with a mind below the mediocre, though this is certainly untrue) but he was never inflexible, always ready to listen to the advice of others and, if he thought it desirable, to act on it. Everyone remarked on the perfection of his manners. He was never offensive, seldom raised his voice and never failed to lift his hat on passing a woman – including the palace chambermaids. He was patient, and he was

---

* 'That cannon shot killed her a husband,' said Mazarin later. She never married or, probably, wanted to.

kind; and if he was famously susceptible to flattery, preferably laid on with a trowel – well, there are many worse faults than that.

He remained, however – and let this never be forgotten – an absolute despot. When he remarked that he *was* the State – '*L'Etat, c'est moi*' – he spoke no more than the truth. Ultimate decisions were taken by him, and by him alone. At the beginning of his reign the Treasury was in the hands of the Superintendent of Finance, Nicolas Fouquet, a highly intelligent and cultivated man and one of France's principal patrons of the arts, a close friend of Madame de Sévigné (the greatest letter-writer of her day) and of the fabulist Jean de la Fontaine; alas, he was his own worst enemy. He had recently built a splendid château for himself at Vaux-le-Vicomte, some thirty miles south-east of Paris. Here he gave magnificent receptions and entertainments – to which on one occasion he invited the king. This proved a mistake, first of all because it suggested that he was putting himself on a par with His Majesty, and second because people began asking themselves where all his money had come from – and since the subject of their curiosity was the Superintendent of Finance the conclusion was not difficult to draw. When he went even further by buying – and fortifying – the remote island of Belle-Ile off the coast of Brittany, he was charged with embezzlement, given no means of defending himself, found guilty and condemned to exile – a sentence which the king 'commuted' to imprisonment for life. He was sent to the fortress of Pignerol (Pinerolo) in Piedmont, where he was to remain until his death sixteen years later.

The way was now clear for his successor, a young official from Reims named Jean-Baptiste Colbert. Colbert's job was a permanent challenge: it was not easy to control the finances of an absolute monarch. 'I entreat Your Majesty', he wrote to the king, 'to allow me to say that in war and in peace Your Majesty has never consulted his finances to determine his expenditures.' One can only wonder what suffering he was caused by his master's passion for warfare – or indeed by the building of the Château de Versailles.

There was in fact a small country house in the village already, built by his father; and Louis had adopted the habit of making quite frequent visits there to see a mistress or two. He loved the place above all because of the privacy it afforded. At the Louvre he was never alone; people went in and out as they wished. To enjoy a good love affair in such surroundings was virtually impossible. He slipped off to Versailles more and more often, throwing out wings here and extensions there; until finally in 1682 he made the palace (as it had now become) his principal residence – and, very soon afterwards, that of most of the aristocracy of France. Within a year or two some 5,000 people were living there, more often than not in conditions of considerable squalor – the building was totally without sanitation – but they had no choice. Unlike their British counterparts, who apart from occasional visits to the House of Lords had no reason to leave their country estates, these French noblemen lost all connection with the lands from which they came; if they failed to live at court, they found themselves virtually disowned by the king, deprived of all lucrative positions and benefices. Life at Versailles was ruinously expensive, but that again was deliberate: past experience of what the aristocracy could do had taught Louis to keep their wings severely clipped. For them, everything depended on the king's favour. With the flicker of an eyelash he could grant them a pension or accord them some valuable privilege: with a single word he could raise a man to distinction or dash him to the dust. Another institution that struck fear into the hearts of the nobility – and the bourgeoisie too for that matter – was the *lettre de cachet*. Such a document, sealed with the royal seal and countersigned by a Secretary of State, could send any of the king's subjects, without appeal, to the Bastille for an indefinite period. Louis himself used this weapon sparingly – sometimes even mercifully, to spare a family the shame and notoriety of the law courts; but even the threat of it was usually enough to keep an overambitious nobleman in his place.

Louis XIV, as we know, liked to think of himself as the sun – the dazzling light that irradiated all around him. Light there may have been; but there was very little warmth. Let no one imagine that life at Versailles was *fun*; it was for the most part bitterly cold, desperately uncomfortable, poisonously unhealthy, and of a tedium probably unparalleled. The most prevalent emotion was fear: fear of the king himself, fear of his absolute power, fear of the single thoughtless word or gesture that might destroy one's career or even one's life. And what was one's life anyway? A ceaseless round of empty ceremonial leading absolutely nowhere, offering the occasional mild amusement but no real pleasure; as for happiness, it was not even to be thought of. Of course there were lavish entertainments – balls, masques, operas – how else was morale to be maintained? But absentees were noted at once, and the reasons for their absence made the subject of exhaustive enquiries. Social death – or worse – could easily result.

It was Louis's great misfortune that he never found a queen worthy of the title, or of himself. In 1660 he married Maria Theresa, the eldest daughter of King Philip IV of Spain. She was just about able to get through a royal ceremony when she had to; but she had the mentality of a fifteen-year-old; she liked to play with her little lapdogs and never read a book. According to Nancy Mitford,

> she was not attractive; she had short legs and black teeth from eating too much chocolate and garlic. The King was fond of her and treated her in a fatherly way . . . one kind look from him made her happy all day.
>
> He made love with her at least twice a month. Everybody knew when this had happened because she went to Communion the next day. She also liked to be teased about it, and would rub her little hands and wink with her large blue eyes.

Poor Maria Theresa was not even particularly successful as a mother: her only son, the dauphin, died at fifty, four years before his father. It was no wonder, then, that the king turned his attention elsewhere – in the first instance to Louise de la Vallière. Louise was a maid of honour to the Duchess of Orléans, the daughter of Charles I of England who had married *Monsieur*, as he was always called, the king's openly homosexual brother Philip.* It was to divert attention from the obvious flirtation that was going on between her and Louis that the duchess deliberately selected three beautiful girls to 'set in his path', of whom the seventeen-year-old Louise was one. The Abbé de Choisy reported that she 'had an exquisite complexion, blonde

---

* Despite his proclivities, Philip had two wives, a mistress and six legitimate children. He was in fact the founder of the House of Orléans, a cadet branch of the House of Bourbon, and the direct ancestor of King Louis-Philippe, to whom we shall be coming later.

hair, blue eyes . . . and an expression at once tender and modest'. It was a little unfortunate that one of her legs was shorter than the other, but her specially made shoes concealed the fact and the king cared not a bit: she was a gentle, innocent girl – 'a little violet hiding beneath the grass and ashamed to be a mistress, to be a mother, to be a duchess', as Madame de Sévigné described her – quite uninterested in money or titles, who sought nothing from the relationship but his love, and who bore Louis five children. Perhaps inevitably, the affair came to an end; from 1667 on, she found herself replaced in the king's affections by the Marquise de Montespan, as proud and dominating as she herself was quiet and timid. Overcome by remorse at her sinful life, in 1674 Louise retired to a convent, where she was to spend the next thirty-six years until her death.

At the end of July 1683 Queen Maria Theresa returned to Versailles. She had been with her husband on campaign, a duty she hated because of the long, exhausting days in coaches or on horseback, but upon which he insisted. Clearly unwell, she complained of an abscess under her arm, which was treated by the court doctor, Fagon, first with bleeding and then with a powerful emetic. Suddenly, his attendants saw the king, tears streaming down his face, running to the chapel to fetch the sacraments. Within an hour the queen was dead; she was forty-five. '*Pauvre femme,*' Louis is said to have murmured, '*c'est le premier déplaisir qu'elle m'ait fait.*'* It was probably true enough in its way; but the poor, silly queen had never been a patch on the immensely intelligent and extremely witty Montespan and she knew it.

Françoise-Athénaïs, Marquise de Montespan, began her career like Louise de la Vallière, as maid of honour to *Madame.*† Her affair with the king began in 1667 when she was already twenty-five, a married woman with two children. She was to give Louis seven more, the upbringing of whom was entrusted to one of her friends, a widow named Françoise Scarron. The relationship lasted for ten

* 'Poor woman, it's the first time she has displeased me.'
† Henrietta Anne, the wife of the Duc d'Orlèans (*Monsieur*). She was the sister of Charles II of England.

years, coming to a dramatic end with what became known as *l'affaire des poisons* when, in 1677, there was a major witchcraft scare. The Paris authorities rounded up a number of fortune tellers and alchemists, accusing them of selling poisons, aphrodisiacs and other potions. Some confessed under torture and revealed lists of their clients, which included several members of the aristocracy, Madame de Montespan among them. Rumours quickly spread; there was talk of black Masses, human sacrifices, even the discovery of the bones of 2,500 babies in the garden of 'La Voisin' (*sic*), one of the principal accused. La Voisin was burned at the stake, and before the enquiry was over thirty-four people had been sentenced to death on similar charges. Meanwhile the king's eye had strayed to another of the court's beauties, the Duchess of Fontanges, who was to die in mildly mysterious circumstances in 1681; thanks entirely to her alleged implication in the *affaire*, the Montespan fell under suspicion. By now it was plain that her relationship with the king must end. They continued to see each other, platonically, for a few more years simply because her undoubted brilliance, humour and charm never failed to delight him, despite her occasional bad temper. But in 1691 she too retired to a convent. She died in 1707, aged sixty-six.

And who should succeed her in the king's bed? None other than her children's guardian Madame Scarron – to whom, some years before, he had granted the title of Marquise de Maintenon. She always maintained that she had resisted for a long time before yielding to his advances; but there is no doubt that by the late 1670s the two were seeing a lot of each other, and after the death of Maria Theresa Louis secretly made her his wife. Since their marriage was morganatic she had no official position as queen and consequently played little part in the social life of Versailles; unlike her two predecessors on the other hand, she was to acquire very considerable political influence; indeed after 1700 she acted as her husband's chief minister. Deeply religious, she fought hard against the profligacy of the court. The king no longer flirted openly with the ladies; comedies and masques were henceforth banned during Lent. Madame de Maintenon is no longer suspected, however, of having been chiefly responsible for what was certainly the greatest mistake of Louis's long reign, and the most indelible stain on his international reputation: the revocation of the Edict of Nantes.

The Edict had been signed by Henry IV in 1598 and granted substantial rights to the Huguenots, offering freedom of conscience to individuals and effectively putting an end to the religious wars which had poisoned the second half of the sixteenth century. Its observance had fluctuated; the Huguenots certainly continued to see themselves as second-class citizens. But now, in October 1685, Louis categorically renounced the edict and, with the new Edict of Fontainebleau, simply declared Protestantism illegal. Protestant ministers were given two weeks to leave the country unless they immediately converted to Catholicism. All Protestant churches and religious buildings were to be demolished. The result was a mass exodus of some four hundred thousand French men and women, most of whom fled to England, Switzerland, Prussia and the Dutch Republic. Not only did this irrevocably damage the reputation of Louis abroad; more serious still, it dealt the national economy a serious blow by depriving France of many of her most skilled craftsmen. Freedom of worship and civil rights for non-Catholics were to be restored only in 1787, two months before the end of the *ancien régime*.

In 1688 William of Orange and his queen, Mary Stuart – daughter of James II of England – jointly succeeded to the English throne. In all Europe Louis had no greater enemy than William, who had no difficulty in forming an alliance against him – it was known as the League of Augsburg – consisting of England and Holland, the Empire, Spain and Sweden. The war that followed was to last nine years, on land and sea, in the Atlantic and the Mediterranean. Peace came at last in 1697 at Ryswick, when Louis agreed to return Lorraine to its duke and undertook to recognise William as King of England.

But peace, in the seventeenth and eighteenth centuries, never lasted for long. On Friday 1 November 1700, King Charles II of Spain died in his palace in Madrid. Weak in body as in mind, he had come to the throne at the age of four on the death of his father, Philip IV, and one glance at the luckless child had been enough to convince the court of his total inadequacy for the life that lay ahead of him. He was always ill, to the point where many suspected witchcraft; few of his subjects believed for an instant that he would grow up to assume power over his immense dominions. But grow up he did, and after a ten-year regency he took over, at least in theory, the reins of government. Thus, from the day of his accession in 1665 and for the next thirty-five years Spain was effectively a great monarchy without a monarch.

It came as no surprise that Charles, despite two marriages, had failed to produce any offspring, and as the century drew to its close the question of who should succeed him grew steadily in importance. The Spanish crown was coveted – and indeed claimed – by the two mightiest dynasties of Europe. Of Philip IV's two sisters – Charles's aunts – the elder, Anne, had been married to Louis XIII of France; the younger, Maria, to Emperor Ferdinand III of Austria. Anne had in due course given birth to Louis XIV, Maria to the Emperor Leopold I. Louis might have been thought to have a secondary claim through Maria Theresa, who was Charles II's elder sister; unfortunately she had been obliged on her marriage to renounce all her hereditary rights in the Spanish dominions.

Charles's younger sister Margaret, on the other hand, had made no such renunciation when she had married Emperor Leopold; her small grandson Joseph Ferdinand was consequently the Habsburg claimant, but in February 1699 he unexpectedly died. Once again, intricate diplomatic negotiations began – not only among the three powers directly concerned, but also with the participation of England and Holland. These two maritime countries both carried on immensely profitable trade with Spain, and both now shared a common concern: to keep out the French. If Spain were to pass from the hands of the weakest monarch in Europe into those of the strongest, what chance was there that trade would be allowed to continue?

But poor hopeless Charles had a surprise up his sleeve. By the autumn of 1700 it was plain that he had not long to live, and on 3 October he put his tremulous signature to a new will, by the terms of which he left all his dominions without exception to Louis XIV's seventeen-year-old grandson Philip, Duke of Anjou. A month later he was dead. What caused this sudden change of heart in favour of France? Above all, the Church. The Inquisition, and indeed the whole hierarchy of Spain, had long favoured a French solution, and Pope Innocent XII had himself written to him recommending Philip of Anjou. With the consciousness of approaching death and the voice of his father confessor whispering in his ear, Charles had no strength to argue.

As for King Louis, he – or at least his grandson – had been offered on a plate far more than he could ever have hoped for. Well aware that the Emperor Leopold would not accept this new dispensation without protest, he lost no time in packing Philip off to Madrid to assume his throne, with a bevy of French officials to take over all the key posts of government. Surprisingly, perhaps, Philip was readily accepted in his new kingdom – only Catalonia proving hostile – but the rest of Europe felt very differently. If Louis had only agreed to remove him from the French line of succession he might have avoided a long and desperate war, but this he refused. He could hardly have suspected what a price he would have to pay for his grandson's throne.

On 7 September 1701 at The Hague, representatives of England, Holland and the Empire signed what was to become known as the Grand Alliance. In certain areas its terms were left deliberately vague, but its principal objectives for the coming war – the imminence of which could no longer be in doubt – were plain enough. The imperial aims were frankly political: Leopold was out to recover for the Empire all the Spanish possessions in Italy. Those of England and Holland, on the other hand, were above all to preserve the balance of power in Europe: to prevent Louis from uniting the forces of France and Spain, conceivably under a single monarch. If they could also secure the future of their navigation and trade, so much the better. Then, just nine days after the signature, the exiled Catholic King James II of England died; and Louis, in a deliberately provocative gesture, immediately recognised his son as James III. The English were furious. Now they had yet another reason to stop the King of France in his tracks.

But seven months before, in February of that same year, Philip of Anjou had entered Madrid as Philip V of Spain, and French troops had reoccupied the Spanish Netherlands, effectively the buffer zone between France and the Dutch Republic. The War of the Spanish Succession had already begun.

★

When the king was not with his army in the field, life at Versailles continued much as it always had. It rotated around Louis's invariable schedule, with his morning *lever*, his evening *coucher* and his *débotter* at sundown when he changed after hunting. Mass, with the queen and the whole court, was celebrated at twelve thirty. There followed a brief time alone with Madame de Montespan before two o'clock lunch, which he took formally with the queen. His appetite was prodigious: we read of 'four plates of different soups, a whole pheasant and a whole partridge or chicken or duck stuffed with truffles, a huge quantity of salad, some mutton, two good slices of ham, a dish of pastry, raw fruit, compotes and preserves'. He would then hunt throughout the afternoon before returning to Madame de Montespan, with whom he spent the entire evening apart from a brief supper with the queen.

He was at this time by far the most powerful monarch in Europe. His army, including foreign regiments, amounted to close on a quarter of a million men, while the English, the Dutch and the Empire together could muster little over 104,000; and even though his navy, consisting of 108 ships of the line, was no match for their combined fleets – the English with 127, the Dutch 83, the Empire none – it was already clear that in this new war, as in its predecessors, the bulk of the fighting would be on land. Louis naturally assumed the supreme command, assisted by a small group of trusted advisers of whom the most important was his Foreign Minister, the Marquis de Torcy. As the war progressed and Louis began to age, Torcy came to dominate the Council of State. In the field, the principal general was Louis Joseph, Duc de Vendôme. Vendôme was a seasoned soldier of long experience; unfortunately, as his fellow-commander but technically his superior, the king had appointed his own grandson, Louis, Duke of Burgundy (and later Dauphin of France). The appointment was to prove a disaster: the two were constantly quarrelling over which of them should give the orders. Again and again decisions had to be referred to the king, and the continued indecision allowed the allies to take the initiative.

On their side, the Dutch and the Empire readily accepted John Churchill, Earl of Marlborough – he was made a duke in December 1702 – as commander-in-chief. Alongside him was Prince Eugene of Savoy with whom, in marked contrast to their French opposites, he got on superbly well. Born in Paris, Eugene had spent his early youth around the French court; but after a scandal involving his mother★ he had been rejected by the king and had transferred his loyalty to the Empire. Since then he had been almost constantly at war, and was in fact a good deal more experienced a general than Marlborough. The two fought together at Blenheim in 1704, when they foiled Louis's attempt to seize Vienna and knocked his ally Bavaria out of the war; again in 1708 at Oudenarde, where Burgundy's continued hesitations and misjudgements were largely responsible for the allied victory; and in 1709 at Malplaquet, the bloodiest encounter of the whole war, when the French army under Marshal de Villars cut the Dutch infantry to pieces before Marlborough was able to force his way through and claim the final victory. The fact remained that the allied armies had lost over 21,000 men – almost twice as many as the French. Few victories have been more pyrrhic. As Villars himself, nursing a badly wounded knee, wrote to the king: 'If it please God to give Your Majesty's enemies another such victory, they are ruined.'

The triumphs of the Duke of Marlborough were however only one small part of the war. Apart from the Low Countries, the Rhine and the Danube, there was heavy fighting in Alsace and Lorraine, in Italy, Piedmont and Savoy, in Spain and Portugal – where, in one of the most important naval encounters of the war, the allied navies destroyed the Spanish treasure fleet and its French escorts in Vigo Bay. In the Mediterranean, the year 1704 saw the capture of Gibraltar. The fighting even spread to North America, where the British colonists feared encirclement by the French in Quebec and in Louisiana.† Regular troops were drafted from Flanders for the proposed Quebec operation, but the English naval expedition against the fortress ended in disaster and the campaign never amounted to more than a sideline.

★ Olympia, Countess of Soissons was accused of having plotted to poison the king's mistress, Louise de la Vallière, her own husband and Queen Maria Luisa of Spain. It was all part of *l'affaire des poisons*, described more fully later in this chapter.

† Louisiana was a lot bigger then than it is today. It covered all the land claimed by France south of the Great Lakes, between the Alleghenies and the Rocky Mountains.

This book is not, however, a history of the War of the Spanish Succession. It is concerned with France, which is why we now leap to the year 1711 when, on 17 April, the Emperor Joseph I died of smallpox in Vienna at the age of thirty-three, leaving no male heir – and the entire European political scene was transformed overnight. Joseph had continued the war against France in an attempt to gain the crown of Spain for his younger brother Charles; if Louis XIV were to be defeated, King Philip would be forced to abdicate and Charles would, in Leopold's view at least, be the rightful heir. But Charles was now the obvious successor to his brother on the imperial throne. The Grand Alliance had been formed only in order to prevent a single family, the Bourbons, from becoming too powerful; if Charles were to succeed to the Empire – as he did, being elected in the following year – the Habsburgs threatened to be more powerful than the Bourbons had ever been, with all their dominions once more united as in the days of his great-great-great-great-uncle Charles V. The balance of power would be turned upside down and Spain would be back in the Low Countries – everything in fact that England feared most. The British government did not hesitate: it made a separate peace with France. Inevitably, many months were to pass before the European powers were able to come to terms with the new situation; it was not until New Year's Day 1712 that negotiations began between the allies and France in the Dutch city of Utrecht.

What is generally known as the Treaty of Utrecht was in fact a whole series of treaties in which, after a European upheaval that had lasted for eleven years, France and Spain attempted once again to regulate their relations with their neighbours. The treaty recognised Philip V as king, but in return Philip was obliged to renounce for himself and his descendants any right to the French throne. France retained, more or less, her present European frontiers, but across the Atlantic lost Newfoundland and Nova Scotia. The Emperor Charles fought on until 1714, and the final peace had to be signed without him. It was essentially on his behalf that the great struggle had continued for the past twelve years, and by distancing himself from the peacemakers he did his Empire a lasting disservice. His interests were not altogether ignored during the long negotiations at Utrecht, but since they were fundamentally opposed to those of France,

Bourbon Spain and the United Provinces – as the Dutch now called themselves – while England remained largely indifferent, it was inevitable that they should have been to some degree neglected. He was forced, for example, to give up Spain. Nevertheless, when the negotiators returned to their homes, Charles found himself master not only of the body of his empire but also of the Catholic Netherlands, Milan, Naples and Sardinia. He was hardly in a position to complain, but with a modicum of diplomatic finesse he could probably have done better still.

As for the throne of Spain, this was of course the most important question of all, the original *casus belli*, the reason for the deaths of hundreds of thousands of men across two continents. Of course Philip kept it; King Charles had left it to him. His kingdom had been drastically amputated – though he would certainly not regret the Low Countries, which had long been a millstone around the Spanish neck. Anyway, there were compensations. He kept Spanish America and all the wealth that it brought him, and he was – thenceforth and for the next thirty years – to rule uncontested.

Louis XIV, who was almost certainly diabetic in the last years of his reign, died of gangrene at Versailles on 1 September 1715, four days before his seventy-seventh birthday.* It was the end of an epoch: there can have been few people in France who remembered the reign of his father. It was also, from the cultural point of view, a Golden Age: the age of France's greatest playwrights, Corneille, Racine and Molière; of philosophers like Pascal and moralists like La Rochefoucauld and La Bruyère; of diarists like Saint-Simon and letter-writers like Madame de Sévigné; of painters like Poussin and Claude, of architects like Mansart, of gardeners like Le Nôtre. But there was a downside too: even Louis's younger contemporary the Duc de Saint-Simon wrote that when he died 'the provinces, in despair at their own ruin and

---

* His heart was removed, as was the custom with the French kings, but was somehow lost during the Revolution. It eventually turned up, preserved in a silver casket, at Nuneham House in Oxfordshire where, according to Augustus Hare, it was eaten by the quite literally omnivorous Dr William Buckland. But Dr Buckland – who may be pursued on Google – is another story.

prostration, trembled with joy. The people, bankrupt, overwhelmed, disconsolate, thanked God with scandalous rejoicing for a release for which it had forsworn all hope', and a popular prayer went into circulation: 'Our Father who art in Versailles, thy name is no longer hallowed; thy kingdom is diminished; thy will is no longer done on earth or on the waves. Give us our bread, which is lacking . . .' By the time Voltaire wrote *Le Siècle de Louis XIV*★ in 1751, few historians had a good word to say about the Sun King. Even Versailles itself had been a dangerous mistake: the emasculation of the nobility by bringing it wholesale to the palace and reducing it to impotence had dealt what was almost a death blow to local government in the provinces. Moreover the king's incurable extravagance had twice – for the first time in 1690 and then again in 1709 – reduced his kingdom to the point where he himself had to watch while his gold and silver, his plate and even his throne were melted down into bullion.

But civilisation must, in the long run, be more important than economics; and the civilisation of France in the age of Louis XIV is among the most brilliant that the world has ever known. No civilisation, obviously, can be ascribed to a single man, or even to a single cause; but the fact that France's two highest points to date coincided with its two most dazzling rulers, Francis I and Louis XIV, surely suggests that there may be some connection: that the effulgence of a great monarch may somehow fertilise and irradiate the genius of his subjects. Louis, who owes his fame exclusively to his position, cannot possibly be accounted a great man; neither, however, can there be any doubt that his force of character, his energy and his unshakeable self-confidence made him a great king. He set his stamp on his country in a way that no monarch had ever done before. In all its history Europe had never seen such majesty, such splendour; nor would it ever be seen again.

★ *The Century of Louis XIV.*

12

The Writing on the Wall

1715–89

> Imagine a handful of oiled ivory balls that you are trying to keep together.
>
> The Comte d'Artois (later King Charles X)
> on his brother Louis XVI

IT IS GIVEN to few monarchs to be succeeded by their great-grandson; but such was the fate of King Louis XIV. His son Louis, the *Grand Dauphin*, had died suddenly in 1711, making *his* eldest son, Louis, Duke of Burgundy, the new dauphin. In the following year, however, both the duke and his duchess died within a week of each other of smallpox – as, shortly afterwards, did their elder son – while the duke's younger brother, the Duc de Berry, was killed in a riding accident. The younger son, aged two, survived the smallpox and consequently, just three years later, became King Louis XV.

Yet again there was a regency. Philip of Orléans was the nephew of Louis XIV – son of *Monsieur* – and also his son-in-law, having married Louis's youngest legitimised daughter, Françoise. (He never liked her, and later was to give her the nickname of *Madame Lucifer*, despite the fact that she was to bear him eight children.) He was a highly intelligent man of forty-one who modelled himself on Henry IV, though he beat him hollow in the number of his mistresses, which seems to have been well over a hundred. He drastically reduced court expenses and temporarily abandoned Versailles, moving the young king to the Tuileries and governing from the Palais-Royal. He detested censorship, ordering the reprinting of all books banned during his uncle's reign. He acted in plays of Molière and Racine, composed an opera, and was a talented painter and engraver. Once again reversing his uncle's policies, he made an alliance with Britain, Austria and the Netherlands and fought a successful war against Spain, while in the diplomatic field he opened up relations with Russia – resulting in a state visit by Peter the Great. In short, he served his country well, and left it in distinctly better shape when, on 15 February 1723, young Louis officially came of age and the regency ended. Philip himself was dead by the end of the year, and on the advice of his tutor, the future Cardinal Fleury, the king most unwisely put the government in the hands of his hopelessly incompetent cousin, the Duke of Bourbon.

One of the first problems Bourbon had to deal with was the choice of a queen. Already two years before, it had been decided that the king should marry the Infanta Mariana Victoria of Spain, who was duly packed off to Paris. The only trouble was that she was just three years old; it would be more than a decade before she was of child-bearing age, and who knew whether Louis – who had recently recovered from a serious illness – would still be alive by then? He must clearly produce a male heir as soon as possible, and there was no time to be lost. In March 1725 back went the infanta to Madrid, and Bourbon had to think again.

There was no shortage of eligible princesses – Bourbon's list of possibles numbered ninety-nine – but the final decision seems to have been largely due to the influence of his mistress the Marquise de Prie. She persuaded him to select one of the poorest – and, we are led to believe, one of the ugliest – of all the candidates, Maria Leszczyńska, daughter of the uncrowned King of Poland. Her principal reason seems to have been that she could totally dominate the young queen, who would owe her everything;* but there were other advantages as well: at twenty-two Maria, unlike the infanta, could supply an immediate production line for royal children;† she was also honest, generous and a pious Catholic. She

---

* Unfortunately Madame de Prie never had a chance to do any dominating: the king shortly afterwards dismissed the Duke of Bourbon and exiled her to her estate at Courbépine, where – according to André Maurois – she poisoned herself out of sheer boredom the following year.

† She was ultimately to produce eight daughters, but only two sons.

first met her husband on the eve of their wedding, which took place on 5 September 1725 at Fontainebleau. Despite her appearance the two were reported to have fallen in love at first sight, and Louis seems to have been faithful to her for the first eight years of the marriage, only then embarking on his long career as a womaniser. She herself had difficulties in earning the respect of the court – which tended to ignore her for having brought no dowry and being, as they considered, of relatively humble birth – and became in consequence a stickler for etiquette and protocol; but she punctiliously performed her royal duties and remained on friendly terms with the king, appearing at his side whenever the occasion demanded.

The king, at the time of his marriage, was distinctly unimpressive: handsome enough with a faintly girlish face, but listless, unfeeling and inclined to gloom. Louis XIV had been toughened by the *fronde*; Louis XV had known nothing but adulation and flattery. His former tutor, now effectively his first minister, Cardinal Fleury – described by Jules Michelet as 'an agreeable nobody' – had left virtually no mark upon him at all. In fact, however, though hopeless as a tutor, Fleury proved a rather better minister than might have been expected. Not entirely unlike his contemporary in England, Sir Robert Walpole, he had no grand ideas and no desire for glory; had the two of them had their way, peace in Europe would have probably been assured.

Louis, however, felt somewhat differently; and on the death of the King of Poland (and Elector of Saxony) Augustus II, the Strong, in 1733, he hastened to intervene on behalf of his father-in-law, Stanislas Leszczyński, whom Augustus had dethroned nearly a quarter of a century before. In this he was only moderately successful: Stanislas returned to Poland in disguise and was elected king by an overwhelming majority of the Sejm, or Parliament; but before he could be crowned Russia and Austria, fearing a Franco-Polish alliance, invaded the country and deposed him again, enthroning Augustus's son as Augustus III. Stanislas fled to Danzig, where he awaited French assistance. When it came it proved perfectly useless, but he continued to fight valiantly until he was at last taken prisoner by the Russians. Eventually the Peace of Vienna of 1738 allowed him to keep his royal titles and also made him Duke of Lorraine,* on the understanding that on his death the province would revert to France.

But the Peace of Vienna did not last long. It must be accounted a misfortune for readers – and indeed for writers – of European history in the eighteenth century that the struggle for the throne of Spain should have been followed after only twenty-seven years by another, this time for the throne of Austria. The Austrian Empire, being not so much the successor to as the continuation of the Holy Roman, remained theoretically elective; during the three centuries of Habsburg rule, however, the duties of the Electors had become more ceremonial than anything else, until the throne was to all intents and purposes hereditary. Unfortunately, like their Spanish cousins, the Austrian Habsburgs suffered from an acute shortage of male heirs – to the point where, as early as 1703, Leopold I had decreed that, in default of males, females should be allowed to succeed – the daughters of his elder son, Joseph, naturally enough taking precedence over those of his younger son, Charles. But, as we have seen, everything was changed by Joseph's sudden death in 1711 and Charles's succession the following year. By a secret family arrangement, known for some ridiculous reason as the Pragmatic Sanction, Charles – now the Emperor Charles VI – gave his own daughters priority over those of his brother, insisting at the same time that in future the Habsburg possessions in northern and central Europe should be indivisible.

When his son predeceased him, Charles was the only male Habsburg alive in the senior line; he was therefore determined that his daughter Maria Theresa should succeed. This, according to the Pragmatic Sanction, should have posed no problems, and for the first few months after his death in 1740 all promised well. Charles had taken care to obtain solemn guarantees from all the principal European powers that they would respect his daughter's succession; England and Holland, the papacy and the Republic of Venice all

---

* He is commemorated in the magnificent Place Stanislas in Nancy, one of the loveliest squares in all France.

willingly recognised the twenty-three-year-old queen.* France, though non-committal, was friendly and reassuring; and the new King of Prussia, Frederick II – later to be known as 'the Great' – not only gave her his recognition but even offered military assistance should she ever need it. He spoke, as it happened, with forked tongue; but Maria Theresa was not to know it until, on 16 December 1740, a Prussian army of 30,000 invaded the imperial province of Silesia. This time it was the War of the *Austrian* Succession that had begun.

And France, after some hesitation, sided with Frederick. The king, although he had no quarrel with Austria – apart from the age-old resentment that existed between the Houses of Bourbon and Habsburg – saw no reason to object; Cardinal Fleury disapproved of his decision, but at eighty-six was unable to tip the scales. The fact was that the army wanted war, and public opinion was behind it. Louis was told that by siding with 'liberal' Prussia he would be striking a blow against Austria's ally England – which was becoming too powerful by half – and allowed himself to be persuaded. For France it was a disastrous mistake, unleashing as it did a whole series of wars which were to give England mastery of the seas and Prussia control of Germany. Hostilities were to continue until 1748; particularly noteworthy, perhaps, were the battles of Dettingen in 1743, when George II became the last English king to see action on the battlefield, and Fontenoy two years later, the great triumph of Marshal Maurice de Saxe,† at which King Louis and his son the dauphin and his mistress Marianne de Mailly – newly ennobled as the Duchess of Châteauroux – were all present, if not actually combatant. Fontenoy was the most decisive battle of the war and the bloodiest: casualties were the highest since Malplaquet (in which de Saxe had

---

* She became empress only in 1745, and then only by marriage. On the death of her father the Empire had passed to her distant cousin from the Bavarian side of the family, who became Charles VII; only on *his* death was her husband Francis of Lorraine elected to the imperial throne as the Emperor Francis I. (He had surrendered Lorraine in 1738 to Stanislas Leszczyński, receiving the Grand Duchy of Tuscany in return.)

† He was the first of the illegitimate sons of Augustus the Strong – the list of whose offspring now numbers 356.

fought as a thirteen-year-old) in 1709, the French losing some 7,000 killed or wounded, the allies up to 12,000.

At the Treaty of Aix-la-Chapelle in 1748, Prussia emerged as the principal beneficiary of the war. Maria Theresa remained on her throne, but Frederick the Great kept Silesia, a humiliating defeat for Austria and a crushing blow to her claim for leadership of the German states. Neither of these conclusions caused particular surprise; far more astonishing was the attitude of France. Louis, who did not wish to be seen as a conqueror, voluntarily returned all his conquests to his defeated enemies, arguing that he was 'King of France, not a merchant'. We may imagine the reaction of his generals, as indeed of French public opinion as a whole, among whom the phrase *travailler pour le roi de Prusse* – 'to work for the King of Prussia' – came to mean working for nothing. France had, in short, been ill repaid for her alliance. Twice during the war Frederick had made a temporary peace with Austria without even bothering to inform Louis – who cordially disliked him anyway.

Since we are principally concerned with France, the above very brief account of the war has been confined to the northern European theatre, not even touching the several campaigns in Italy; it was in fact a world war – perhaps the first in history. There was also fighting in North America, in India, in the East Indies, in Sweden and Finland, in the Bay of Bengal, the Mediterranean and the Caribbean. This was, after all, the age of colonisation; wherever in the world one or more of the great powers was struggling to establish dominion, there the war was instantly reflected. Even when there was peace at home, across the seas to east and west England and France were still at loggerheads. Countless adjustments were made: to remove French troops from Flanders, Britain had to evacuate Cape Breton Island in Canada, where the fortress of Louisbourg was exchanged for Madras. But nothing was settled; it sometimes seemed as if the principal purpose of one war was to rearrange the scenery for the next.

The king's popularity after his return to Paris, already at a low ebb after the surrender of his conquests, was not increased when his subjects learned of his private life. Marianne de Mailly was in fact the youngest of four sisters, with all of whom – in strict order of age – he had had affairs. In June 1744, on his way to the front, he had fallen seriously ill at Metz, so ill that his life had been almost despaired of. Public prayers were held across France, but the royal chaplain refused to give him absolution unless he renounced Marianne and Louis at last gave in, signing a personal confession which was later, to his considerable embarrassment, publicly distributed. Although his recovery earned him the epithet 'well-beloved', he was in fact nothing of the kind; his reputation had taken a hard knock and he knew it.

But still the mistresses came and went until, on the night of 25 February 1745, at a masked ball given to celebrate the marriage of the dauphin to yet another infanta of Spain, Louis met the twenty-three-year-old Jeanne-Antoinette Poisson. She was already married, but that did not seem to matter very much: a month later she was installed at Versailles, in the apartment immediately above his own, and in July she was the Marquise de Pompadour, *maîtresse en titre*★ to the king. But she was very unlike her predecessors. First of all, she took care to be on excellent terms with the queen, whom the others had been inclined to snub; secondly she was highly intelligent and extremely well educated, able to hold her own in any conversation with the great *philosophes* of the day, from Voltaire down. None of this of course protected her from those who despised her plebeian origins, deplored her immense influence with the king and attacked her with cruel lies and libels which, inspired by her slightly unfortunate family name, were known as *poissonades*. She was certainly wounded by some of these attacks, but at the same time she was well aware that her position was unassailable. The king, she knew, relied on her absolutely – not only for the pleasures of the bedchamber but for her wise advice and her sparkling wit. She accompanied him everywhere – at the hunt, at the gaming tables, on his frequent travels around the country. She sang him songs at the clavichord, organised plays and operas for his amusement, and gave intimate

---

★ This had been a semi-official position (which came with its own apartments) since the days of Henry IV.

private dinner parties where he could forget his worries and his deeply depressing family. In short, she irradiated his life.

Her political influence too was considerable, particularly in the all-important matter of senior appointments, and she was a major patron of the arts. With her brother the Marquis de Marigny she was involved in the planning of the new Place de la Concorde – known in those days as Place Louis XV – and the Petit Trianon at Versailles; she commissioned portraits from François Boucher and the court painter Jean-Marc Nattier; and she was in a large measure responsible for the setting-up and subsequent development of the porcelain factory at Sèvres, soon to become one of the most famous in Europe. She also vigorously – and, in the end, successfully – defended the *Encyclopédie* and its chief editor Denis Diderot when the *Parlement* of Paris and the city's archbishop sought to have it suppressed. Although the physical side of her relationship with the king seems to have ended around 1750, she is said to have continued to provide mistresses for him at the Parc-aux-Cerfs (Stag Park), a house in the grounds of Versailles. He remained devoted to her, and when she was dying of consumption in 1764 scarcely left her bedside. Voltaire wrote of his own sadness on hearing the news of her death: 'I was indebted to her, and I mourn her out of gratitude. It seems absurd that while an ancient scribbler, hardly able to walk, should still be alive, a beautiful woman at the height of a splendid career should die at the age of forty-two.'

Madame de Pompadour was the most dazzling of Louis's mistresses, but not the last. Four years after her death she was succeeded by a woman of a very different kind. Jeanne Bécu, later known as Mademoiselle Lange and later still, after an extremely dodgy marriage, as the Comtesse du Barry, had for some years been well known in Paris as a high-class courtesan, who counted among her many lovers several members of the high aristocracy. She was no intellectual, and indeed had no pretensions to being other than what she was; but the king was captivated, showering her with dresses and jewels, of which she could never have enough. It need hardly be said that she was detested by the court – far more than the Pompadour had ever been – her greatest enemy of all being the Austrian princess Marie Antoinette, who had married the future

Louis XVI at the age of fourteen in 1770 and who for two years refused to speak to her.

By this time France had survived yet another European conflict. The Seven Years' War lasted in Europe from 1756 to 1763; but like its predecessor it had ramifications across half the world – particularly in America, where the by now very considerable French colonies in Canada, Illinois and Louisiana had almost surrounded the British ones, which were concentrated principally along the east coast. It was there that the war really began, continuing throughout the hostilities in Europe, with Britain steadily gaining ground: capturing Quebec in 1759 (when General James Wolfe was killed at the moment of victory) and, in the Caribbean, the valuable sugar islands of Martinique and Guadeloupe.*

In Europe, France and Britain switched alliances. The French, seriously alarmed by the growing strength of Prussia – which had now, for the first time and thanks entirely to Frederick the Great, become a major European power – realised that the Austria of Maria Theresa no longer represented the danger that it had in the previous century, overcame their long hostility to the Habsburgs and sided with them in an attempt to recover Silesia, while Britain, long Austria's ally, turned towards her former enemy Prussia. Most of the smaller nations, including the Dutch Republic, sensibly stayed out of harm's way. France, with no general to compare with Maurice de Saxe, did not do well. A French invasion of Hanover and Saxony ended in a humiliating defeat by Frederick the Great at Rossbach, while a series of naval defeats prevented Louis from carrying out his plans for an invasion of England.

Where Britain and France were concerned, the war ended with the Peace of Paris in 1763 – 'one of the saddest', writes Maurois, 'in French history. It cost France her empire and created England's.' A slight exaggeration, perhaps; but France lost Canada ('a few acres of snow', sniffed Voltaire),† together with those islands in the

---

* Guadeloupe was returned at the end of the war, but Martinique remained for the most part in British hands until the Congress of Vienna in 1815.

† She was allowed to keep fishing rights off Newfoundland and the two tiny islands of Saint Pierre and Miquelon, so that the fishermen could dry their catch.

Caribbean, and was also obliged to cede the eastern half of what was then Louisiana – virtually the whole area from the Mississippi to the Appalachians.

On 5 January 1757, at around six in the evening, King Louis, who had been visiting his daughter in the palace, left her to return to the Grand Trianon where he was staying at the time. Suddenly, as he was walking across the marble courtyard on the way to his carriage, a young man emerged from the darkness and stabbed him in the side. Fortunately it was mid-winter and he was well wrapped up; his many layers of clothing probably saved his life. The would-be assassin was duly tried, tortured and executed on the Place de Grève.* It was in itself a relatively unimportant incident; the wound, though something a good deal more than the 'pinprick' – as Voltaire dismissed it – never gave cause for serious concern. The king himself seemed bewildered: 'Why try to kill me?' he asked, 'I have done no one any harm.'

But he had – the people of France. He may have been unconscious of the fact, but he had let them down badly. He was weak – perhaps the weakest of the Bourbons – and easily led, by his mistresses and others. He was moreover incurably lazy, and all too ready to leave affairs of state to frequently incompetent ministers while he hunted or womanised. The result was lost wars, continual clashes with the *Parlement*, and, thanks to the incessant fighting, economic stagnation. His later reign was sad, as he faced constant intrigues by his rather unpleasant children, particularly the dauphin who fortunately died of consumption at the age of thirty-six, nine years before his father – and his eldest surviving daughter, Adélaïde. Madame du Barry doubtless gave him consolation of a kind, but he was growing old and she was no substitute for the Pompadour. When in the spring of 1774 he succumbed for the second time to smallpox he hastily dismissed her from his bed, both to avoid infection and also to obtain absolution for both of them – the poor girl had a good deal to absolve. He died on 10 May at Versailles, at the age of sixty-four.

* Now the Place de l'Hôtel-de-Ville.

His son the dauphin having predeceased him, the crown passed to his grandson: three reigns were to cover six generations and a century and a half. Louis XVI was twenty years old – for once, France had been spared a regency – and, as we all know, a tragic figure; he was also a strangely enigmatic one. To begin with, he totally lacked style. He was short – not much more than five foot six – flabby-faced and distinctly overweight, which was not surprising considering his gargantuan appetite.* He was also one of those men whose clothes, despite the efforts of the best tailors, always look ill-fitting; it was said, as he shambled round the palace, that he looked more like a peasant than a king. His manner, too, was unfortunate: although those who knew him well maintained that he was, in his heart, compassionate and tender-hearted, in conversation he was harsh and abrupt, even disagreeable. 'I want to be loved,' he said on his accession to the throne, but he never seemed to try very hard. He may have lacked charm, but he was not stupid: well before he was grown-up he spoke fluent English and Italian, and he had a passion for astronomy. He was also, rather more surprisingly, an expert locksmith. He was pious, and he was also chaste – which, after his grandfather, was something of a relief. Politics, however, bored him stiff – which perhaps explains the almost pathological indecisiveness which, ultimately, did him in.

On 16 May 1770, when he was fifteen, he had married the second youngest of the sixteen children of the Empress Maria Theresa. The given names of the fourteen-year-old archduchess were Maria Antonia, but she is better known to us in their French version: Marie Antoinette. Her parents had taken little trouble over her education, but she was a lot brighter than her husband; and with her deep blue eyes, thick fair hair and flawless complexion she had all the makings of a popular princess. But, alas, she was Austrian; and to the people of France Austria was bad news indeed. The marriage to '*L'Autrichienne*' was deeply unpopular before it had even begun.

---

* It was said that one morning before going down to the stables he consumed 'four cutlets, a chicken, a plateful of ham, half a dozen eggs in sauce and a bottle and a half of champagne' (Christopher Hibbert, *The French Revolution*).

And Louis didn't seem to enjoy her much either. Like Louis XIII, he was terrified of women. His gloomy, excessively pious father had regularly pointed out the countless mistresses of his grandfather Louis XV as an object lesson in depravity, to be avoided at all costs; and he had taken the advice to heart. He had first met his bride only two days before the marriage, when he had greeted her near the forest of Compiègne. They married two days later at Versailles, but the traditional bedding the same night ended in deep embarrassment all round: despite a liberal sprinkling of holy water over the sheets, Louis went straight off to sleep. A successful consummation was not to occur for another seven years – during which time the reputation of both parties suffered considerable damage. Pamphlets began to circulate, claiming that Her Majesty was now seeking her pleasures elsewhere, with women as well as men. Her reported activities with her closest friend, the widowed Princesse de Lamballe, were described in terms of almost unparalleled obscenity, although the princess – so sensitive that she had once fainted dead away at the sight of a lobster in a painting – was, it was said, far more affected by the libels than the queen herself.

But the babies came at last – the first just before Christmas 1778, after eight years of marriage – and there was particular rejoicing in 1781 when the long-awaited dauphin finally made his appearance. The queen pronounced herself blissfully happy; but she was full of energy and vivacity and, having no intellectual resources, dangerously easily bored; the court etiquette drove her to distraction. Besides, life with Louis was hard. 'You know', she somewhat disloyally wrote to the Austrian ambassadress, 'the person with whom I have to deal? The moment you think him persuaded, a word, an objection raised, makes him change his mind without even suspecting it himself.' In Louis's defence it must be said that from the beginning he was torn: torn between the old conservative traditions in which he had been brought up – the benevolent, fatherly monarchy at the top with the nobility, the Church and the ancient constitution beneath it – and the new ideas of the *philosophes*, of which he might not entirely approve but which he knew represented the future. Thus, although his first cabinet was headed by the Comte de Maurepas, a witty, frivolous cynic who had been Minister for the Navy at the age of twenty-two but had subsequently been exiled after writing a bitchy epigram about Madame de Pompadour, it included one of the outstanding ministers of the century, Anne-Robert-Jacques Turgot, who soon became controller-general of finance. Turgot was a man to be reckoned with: a thinker, a philosopher, and a writer whose works are still read today. 'No bankruptcy,' he warned the king, 'no increase of taxation, no borrowing.' Expenditure would be reduced across the board: 'I shall have to struggle against the natural kindness, against the generosity of Your Majesty, and of the persons dearest to Him.' Meanwhile, as an earnest of his intentions, he reduced his own salary from 142,000 livres to 82,000. He expressed his economic philosophy in an essay, 'Reflections on the Formation and Distribution of Wealth'; 'I have just read Monsieur Turgot's masterpiece,' wrote Voltaire; 'It seems to me that here is a new heaven and a new earth.'

Had Louis given Turgot his full confidence and accepted all his advice without question, it is just possible that he might have spared his country a revolution. Alas, Turgot was to remain minister for less than two years. His cold, rather patronising manner often antagonised people. 'Monsieur Turgot', the king remarked sadly, 'causes no one to love him.' He might well have said the same of himself; but there was more to it than that. The queen, first of all, resented the constant curbs that Turgot was putting on her natural extravagance, and was furious at his refusal to make her favourite, the pro-Austrian Duc de Choiseul, a minister. The bankers and tax collectors saw their profits gravely threatened; the nobles and the *Parlement* – which the king had recalled – hated him for his attacks on privilege; the farmers for his attempts to establish free trade in grain. Ministerial jealousy did the rest. On 12 May 1776 he was ordered to resign his office. He lived to see all his work undone, all the abuses against which he had fought deliberately restored, and France set firmly on the road to the greatest catastrophe that she had ever known.

But the year 1776 has gone down in history for more than the fall of Turgot. When we consider all their losses across the Atlantic after the Seven Years' War, it comes as no surprise that the French, from the king down, supported the American Revolution; for some time already they had been secretly sending armaments and supplies to the rebels. Soon after he had signed the Declaration of Independence, Benjamin Franklin arrived in Paris as the first American ambassador to France. His name was already well known; he was given a rapturous welcome and immediately admitted as a member of the Academy of Sciences. He naturally met Voltaire; the two old men publicly embraced, to enthusiastic applause. At first France held back from active participation in the hostilities; but in December 1777, emboldened by the surrender of the British general John Burgoyne with his army of 6,200 men after the two battles of Saratoga, Louis signed a treaty of alliance recognising American independence and officially entered the war. In the two years following, a French army of 7,000 – considerably more than Washington could boast – under the command of General Jean-Baptiste de Rochambeau, ably assisted by the twenty-three-year-old Marquis de Lafayette,★ fought at the future president's side, while a French fleet successfully prevented the British from relieving Lord Cornwallis, who was finally to surrender after the siege of Yorktown.

It seemed as though the tables were turned. Britain no longer absolutely ruled the waves, while the French stood out as champions of liberty. They were, however, more deeply in debt than they had ever been before, to the point where they had to call in a foreigner. It was Jacques Necker, the dreary, capable and immensely rich Swiss banker who now became director general of finance – he could not be controller because he was a Protestant – and who now assumed the mantle of Turgot. His wife and daughter, Suzanne Curchod and Germaine de Staël, were as distinguished as he was, and a great deal more fun – Suzanne for her famous *salon*, Germaine in future years for her remarkable books, her incurable romanticism and her political enthusiasm. For the four years between 1777 and 1781 Necker was in sole charge of the wealth of France, in 1781 publishing what he called the *Compte rendu au roi*, the first-ever public record of national finances. It had a huge and quite unexpected success, introducing many people to economics for the first time in their lives.

★ A statue of Rochambeau – presented by France to the United States – stands in Lafayette Park in Washington DC. That of Lafayette himself can be seen in the square which bears his name.

Unfortunately it lied in its teeth. While there was actually a deficit of some 46 million livres, Necker claimed that the country was 10 million in credit, thereby deliberately lulling the king and his subjects into a false sense of security when he should have been awakening them to danger.

Before very long, he too fell – not because he cooked the books but because he became a victim, as Turgot had been, of court intrigue. In 1787 he was exiled to forty leagues★ from Paris. His successor, Charles Alexandre de Calonne, fared little better: his proposals included a new land tax, which was to be levied on the nobility and clergy and was therefore instantly rejected. Calonne's successor, Loménie de Brienne, Archbishop of Toulouse, was an utterly unprincipled and probably agnostic prelate whom the *Parlement* detested even more than they had the others. In despair, Louis brought back Necker, who at least had the gift of inspiring confidence even when there was nothing to be confident about. Necker began with a generous gesture – by making the Exchequer a gift of two million livres from his personal fortune. This cheered everybody up, and he managed to keep going a little longer. But the writing was on the wall – not just for him, but for France itself.

The Estates General, consisting of the three estates – nobility, clergy and everyone else – had last been convoked 175 years before, in 1614. It had been suspended for so long largely because it possessed no power in its own right. It was essentially little more than an advisory body to the king, and for over a century and a half the king had not required its advice. But now, on 5 May 1789, he did – because decisive action was necessary. It was becoming obvious that something was rotten in the state of France.

What was the trouble? France was still the most powerful nation in Europe, with a population of 26 million (England could boast only 12 million). It had recently contributed in large measure to the victory of the United States in the War of Independence. Its

★ A league originally meant the distance a person could walk in an hour – between three and four miles.

reputation had never been higher, and its cultural influence was rapidly spreading across the continent. Why then was the whole country so seething with dissatisfaction? First, because it felt that the monarchy had let it down. This not to say that the French were anti-monarchist; they were nothing of the kind. But they expected the king to be on their side and to protect them, both from grasping tax-collectors and from groping noblemen. Instead, by deciding to live at Versailles, he had cut himself off from his people; and by gathering the nobility around him he had estranged them from the lands they owned and the peasants for whom they should have been caring. Then there was the Church. Out of a total population of some 26 million, the clergy numbered fewer than 100,000 but owned more than a tenth of the land. It was, in short, a bastion of fabulous wealth – very little of which, however, came down to the parishes. It levied tithes on the harvest – payable by the peasantry – but was itself, like the nobility, largely immune from taxation. There was a voluntary grant to the state every five years, but as the size of this grant was decided by the assemblies of the Church itself it seldom amounted to very much. The cardinals and bishops lived like fighting-cocks and frequently scandalised the faithful, especially the lower clergy; they did not seem to realise that this was the age of Enlightenment, and that they now had to contend with the writings of Voltaire, Rousseau and the *Encyclopédistes*. And meanwhile, in many parts of France, the peasants were cripplingly poor, barefoot and in rags, crippled by taxes from which the nobility were excused, and looking, according to Tobias Smollett, like 'ravenous scarecrows'.

With the revival of the Estates General, the principal question to be discussed was what was known as the third estate. The first two estates – the nobility and the clergy – were still much the same as they had always been; the third, however – which amounted to the rest of France – had changed radically in the past century. On those previous – and distant – occasions when the Estates General had met it had been not only outnumbered and outvoted by the other two; it had also been largely ignored. Now, in recognition of its vastly increased importance, its numbers were doubled – though no one had revealed whether the voting was to be by a count of individuals. (In the latter event it would be no better off than before.) Its importance was further emphasised by the Abbé Sieyès in an enormously influential pamphlet published in January 1789, entitled '*Qu'est-ce que le tiers état?*' – 'What is the third estate?' He answered the question in a word: 'Everything'; but then added, 'What has it been till now in the political order? Nothing. What does it want to be? Something.' The tone was moderate; the Abbé was against attacking the privileged too forcibly. Far better to move forward at a measured pace, to reform taxation and improve justice first; there would be time for further improvements later. But the underlying message was clear enough.

So the French, as the Estates General opened, demanded radical changes; but the last thing they wanted – or expected – was revolution. They had experienced no real violence since the *fronde*; the model before their eyes now was that of America – which, to be sure, had had to fight for its independence, but which without any serious civil unrest had managed to achieve a constitution based on sound philosophical principles. Surely France could do the same? And it probably could have – if Louis XVI had had an ounce of understanding of his country and people. Had he only been able to realise that the bourgeoisie – the third estate – was no longer what it had been a century before, that it had acquired wealth, culture and very considerable power, and that it looked for equal rights and careers open to talent – then he could perhaps have saved the monarchy. Instead, he identified himself with the privileged; and the mistake was fatal.

13

'I am indeed your king'
1789–93

I carry away with me the last shreds of the monarchy.

> Mirabeau, on his deathbed,
> to Talleyrand, 4 April 1791

THE MEETING OF the Estates General was doomed to failure*
– doomed for a start by its location. The king was determined
to continue his hunting in the local forests; it did not occur to him,
or apparently to anyone else, that accommodation at Versailles for
nearly a thousand deputies† would be impossible to find, nor that
the third estate would be shocked and scandalised by the court life
around them. They were humiliated too: they had been instructed
to dress in black, and were quite literally outshone by the church
vestments and dazzling silks and velvets flaunted by the nobility.
Moreover they found themselves penned up in a separate enclosure
away from the king. Then there was the tedium. The king's speech
was turgid and spiritless; Necker's, which followed, was a disaster.
He had been expected to reveal an exciting new economic policy;
instead he quoted facts and figures for a little over three hours and
bored everybody rigid. Spirits revived only when a representative
of the third estate from Provence, Honoré Gabriel Riqueti, Comte
de Mirabeau, rose to his feet.

Mirabeau should by rights have been representing the nobility,

---

* For the whole of this chapter and the next I am much indebted to my friend
the late Christopher Hibbert, whose book *The French Revolution* is by far the most
useful on the subject that I know.

† The precise figures were: nobility, 188; clergy, 247; third estate, 500.

but had been rejected by his fellows by reason of what they considered his dissolute former life, violent disposition and innumerable love affairs. At first sight of him these last would have seemed improbable; he was villainously ugly, with a huge head and a face deeply pitted with the smallpox that he had contracted at the age of three. Typically, he used it as a weapon: 'Ugliness is power,' he was fond of saying. Undeterred by his rejection, he had then addressed the Provençal third estate: 'Granted that I'm a mad dog; all the more reason for electing me. My fangs will make short work of despotism and privilege.' He was elected on the spot, by both Aix-en-Provence and Marseille, and was to show himself by far the most brilliant speaker in the Estates General. It was soon proposed that the third estate should change its name as well as its nature; after a heated debate it was decided to call it the National Assembly – an assembly not of the estates but 'of the people'. In order to broaden its membership the clergy were invited to join, and about a dozen did so.

It was a modest enough gesture; but it frightened the king – and even more so the queen. Left to himself, Louis would probably have acquiesced as he usually did, but his family persuaded him to take a stand. It was accordingly announced that the actions of the third estate had been illegal and that His Majesty had decided to hold a meeting of all three orders, a so-called *séance royale*. Until then, the meeting hall would be closed. Finding the doors locked the next morning, the deputies were for a moment undecided; then, at the suggestion of a certain Dr Joseph-Ignace Guillotin – whose name would later be famous in another connection – they moved to the *jeu de paume*, the large indoor tennis court nearby, where they swore an oath 'never to separate, and to meet in any place that circumstances might require until such time as the constitution should be established on solid foundations'.★

On 23 May Louis took the chair at the *séance royale*. It too was a disaster. The king first made it clear that all future voting would be by orders rather than by individuals, which meant that the third estate was in much the same position as it had always been; he then declared that the Estates General might discuss taxes, but certainly

★ Yet again, tennis plays a significant part in French history.

not privilege. Any future reforms would be granted voluntarily by himself and not because of any popular demand. 'None of your plans or proceedings', he concluded, 'can become law without my express approval.' At which he marched out, nobility and clergy behind him. The third estate stubbornly remained, and when ordered to withdraw, Mirabeau replied: 'Go tell your master that we are here by the will of the people, and that we shall leave only at the point of the bayonet!' One cannot even imagine such a reply being addressed to Louis XIV; Louis XVI simply shrugged. 'Damn them,' he muttered, 'if they want to stay, let them.' Just four days later, most of the clergy and forty-seven of the nobility had joined the National Assembly and the king knew that he could hold out no longer.

But Marie Antoinette, and those who agreed with her – 'the queen's party' they were called – would not give up. On 11 July Necker was dismissed. Despite his poor showing at Versailles he was still regarded as something of a miracle-worker, and the news was received in Paris with consternation: the stock market plunged, the stock exchange was closed, riots broke out across the city. Louis, by now seriously alarmed, called in the army to restore order – sixteen regiments in all, mostly foreign mercenaries – but they were showered with stones on the Place Louis XV; near the Tuileries a regiment of dragoons was bombarded with garden chairs. Meanwhile, outside the Palais-Royal, a young attorney named Camille Desmoulins called the people to arms and the barricades. Twisting a chestnut leaf into a rough cockade, he stuck it into his hat. The gesture quickly became a symbol: thenceforth such cockades had to be worn by all citizens who wished to avoid being spat on in the street. And now, most ominous of all, the mob broke into the gunsmiths' shops and stripped them bare; smashed its way into the Invalides, dragging off at least ten cannon and 28,000 muskets; and, early in the morning of 14 July, headed for the Bastille.

The Bastille had been built in the fourteenth century as a stronghold to protect Paris during the Hundred Years' War, and had been declared a state prison in 1417. Louis XIV had used it to incarcerate upper-class members of society who had been arrested through *lettres de cachet* but were not guilty of any offence punishable by common law, and after the Revocation of the Edict of Nantes had filled it with recalcitrant Huguenots. By now, however, these had all emigrated and the prison catered once again for every type of prisoner – though by the late spring of 1789 it numbered only seven. Conditions within it were not particularly hard; the dreaded dungeons had not been used for years, and those inmates who could afford it might live in considerable comfort, being allotted pleasant rooms with tapestries and carpets and allowed to wear their own clothes. There was even a library. The food was good too, and for the favoured ones there was always the chance of being invited to dinner with the governor. But it remained the Bastille, looming darkly over the centre of Paris like a great thundercloud, a constant reminder of the power and majesty of the king and an awful warning to those who dared to displease him.

By mid-morning, some nine hundred people had gathered outside the fortress. The governor, the Marquis de Launay, had only two days' supply of food and no domestic source of water; he knew that he could not possibly resist a siege, and invited one or two of the assailants to come inside and see for themselves that he had taken no special defensive measures. He refused only to surrender the guns and gunpowder for which he was responsible, pending instructions from Versailles. Unfortunately, as he soon discovered, the mob was not prepared to wait. In the early afternoon it stormed the outer courtyard, and confused firing broke out on both sides. De Launay had no choice but to try to negotiate a surrender, but while he was doing so the drawbridge suddenly crashed down. The crowd burst in, seized him and dragged him out into the street, where he was viciously stabbed in the stomach. Later he was decapitated, and his head paraded around Paris on a pike. There was no more resistance. The Bastille had fallen.

The king, needless to say, had spent the day hunting and on his return to the palace had gone straight to bed. It was only the next morning that he was told the news, and the famous interchange took place: 'Is this a rebellion?' he sleepily asked the Duc de la Rochefoucauld. 'No, sire,' replied the duke, 'it is a revolution.' Suddenly, it seemed, Louis realised the seriousness of the situation. Leaping from his bed, he dressed in unwonted haste, hurried over to the Assembly and informed it that he had ordered the withdrawal of troops from both Paris and Versailles. He was loudly cheered, and a ninety-strong delegation left immediately for Paris with the good news. General de Lafayette, hero of the recent American War of Independence, read out to the crowd gathered at the Hôtel de Ville the text of the speech the king had just made at Versailles. On the spot he was appointed commander of the citizens' militia, shortly to become the National Guard. Its members were instructed to wear cockades of red and blue – the colours of Paris – to which was added a band of white, the colour of the king. The tricolour thus formed, symbolising both the old France and the new, remains the French flag to this day.

Paris, however, was not so easily pleased as was Versailles. Dissatisfaction was centred on King Louis's refusal to recall Necker to the government. Why this condition was insisted upon remains something of a mystery. Necker was no wonder-worker; he had deliberately misled the people of France on the state of their economy, and he had disappointed everyone with his speech at the meeting of the Estates General. For some reason, however, he was seen to be the man of the hour. 'Gentlemen,' declared the Marquis de Lally-Tollendal, 'as we have seen and heard, in the streets and squares, on the *quais* and in the markets, the cry is "Bring back Necker!" The people's request is an order: we must demand his return.'

And so, much to his own embarrassment, the king recalled Necker and travelled the next morning to Paris through excited crowds, to cries of '*Vive la Nation! Vivent les Députés! Vive Monsieur de Lafayette!*' It was noticed that there were very few cries of '*Vive le Roi!*' The British ambassador, the Duke of Dorset, noted that 'His Majesty was treated more like a captive than a king', and that he was being led along 'like a tame bear'. On arrival at the Hôtel de Ville he was offered the tricolour cockade, which he at once accepted and stuck in his hat. After a short and halting speech he then walked out on to the balcony – to be greeted, now that he was wearing the cockade, with wild cheering. Never, one might have thought, had he been more popular.

But it was too good to last. The National Assembly was granted fresh powers to institute reforms and to frame a constitution, but for the urban poor and the peasants across the country life was becoming harder every day. 'A horrible anarchy', reported the Venetian ambassador, 'is the first aspect of the regeneration it is desired to bestow on France . . . There no longer exist either executive power, laws, magistrates or police.' Riots were breaking out all over the country. At Troyes they murdered the mayor; the royal garrison at Rennes deserted en masse, that at Marseille was forcibly disbanded by an armed mob. Prisons were broken into, their prisoners released, arsenals were emptied, *hôtels de ville* taken over. In Paris itself the deputy mayor of Saint-Denis was pursued through the streets to the top of the church tower and there beheaded. It was rumoured that one of the ministers of Louis's government, Foullon de Doué, had said that if people were hungry they should be made to eat hay; a collar of nettles was put round his neck, a bunch of thistles thrust into his hand and a handful of hay stuffed into his mouth. He was then hanged from a lamppost.

On 4 August the young Vicomte de Noailles, who had fought with Lafayette in America, proposed to the Assembly the abolition of all feudal rights. He was supported by the Duc d'Aiguillon, the greatest landowner in France. The proposal was received with enthusiasm; one by one, until late into the night, noblemen and high dignitaries of the Church leaped to their feet and renounced their rights and privileges, until the Marquis de Lally-Tollendal passed a message to the president: 'Suspend the session; they have all gone quite mad.' The next morning, of course, most of them were thinking better of it; and over the next few days the renunciations were drastically modified. They would anyway have been forbidden, for the king withheld his agreement. 'I will never consent to the spoliation of my clergy or my nobility,' he told the Archbishop of Arles, 'and I will not sanction decrees which seek to despoil them.'

A few days later, however, he was to suffer another severe shock. On 5 October, in pouring rain, some six thousand working women – fishwives, cleaners, market-stall holders, prostitutes – marched on Versailles. Their ostensible reason was a rumour that at a welcome banquet given for the Flanders Regiment, newly arrived at the palace, the tricolour cockades had been trampled underfoot; but they would have demonstrated anyway. Armed with scythes, pikes and any other weapons they could lay their hands on, they marched straight to the National Assembly shouting their slogans and screaming for bread. It was two hours before Mirabeau could pacify them and get most – but even then not all – of them out of the building. Eventually the king agreed to receive a delegation of six – very carefully chosen and not at all typical of the rabble majority – whom he beguiled with every sort of promise; but he need not have bothered. The crowds who had remained outside were as angry as ever.

And worse was to come. In the early hours of the next day the king and queen were awakened by furious shouts of '*Mort à l'Autrichienne!*' A gate from the Cour des Princes had apparently been left unlocked, and some of the more violent – and probably by now more drunken – women had burst in and made their way up the staircase leading to the royal apartments. Marie Antoinette, terrified as well she might be, flung on a few clothes and hurried to the king's apartment, where she found Louis standing with the dauphin, now four years old,* in his arms. By now Lafayette – who had arrived some hours before with a delegation of the National Guard – had gone some way towards restoring order, but the air was still loud with shouting and musket-fire and he knew that the demonstrators would never be satisfied until the king and queen had shown themselves on the balcony. To do so required a good deal of courage; but they agreed, the queen standing unflinching for at least two minutes, every second of which might have been her last. Then the king reappeared, to proclaim the inevitable. 'My friends,' he announced, 'I shall now come to Paris with my wife and children.'

They left that same afternoon, with Lafayette riding beside them, the remainder of the market women marching behind in the continuing rain. They went first to the Hôtel de Ville, and then on to their long-abandoned, cheerless apartments at the Tuileries. There they were entrusted to the generally benevolent guardianship of Lafayette. They were never to see Versailles again.

At the Tuileries, the royal family found itself unpleasantly close to the National Assembly, which was meeting in the neighbouring riding school. It was now almost constantly in session, with a dangerous young lawyer from Arras named Maximilien Robespierre

---

* His elder brother had died in June 1789.

attracting considerable attention from the extreme left. The right was still dominated by Mirabeau who, a few days after the king's arrival in Paris, drew up an advisory memorandum for him: he must immediately leave Paris for the provinces, which were far less extremist than the capital and would be sure to respond favourably to an appeal. He should not, on the other hand, cross the frontier: 'a king, who is the only safeguard of his people, does not flee before them'. Finally, His Majesty must accept that the Revolution was here to stay; he must on no account be thought to be making a stand against it. 'The inseparability of monarch and people is lodged in the heart of all Frenchmen.' 'Never, I think, shall we be in such a sorry state as to have to have recourse to Monsieur Mirabeau,' was the queen's first reaction; but she soon changed her tune. Mirabeau himself had only six months to live, but before he died he remarked: 'The King has only one man, and that is his wife.'

Meanwhile, astonishingly, upper-class life in Paris was continuing as heedless and frivolous as ever. The political and literary *salons* went on as they always had, the cafés were as crowded as ever they had been. The Revolution, to be sure, had changed things a little: the theatres no longer played Molière (too aristocratic) or Beaumarchais (whose *Marriage of Figaro* was considered to be 'dangerously reminiscent of anti-social distinctions'). Fashion, too, reflected the troubled times; women wore liberty hats and constitution jewellery, while the primary colours of the tricolour were everywhere in evidence. On 20 June, at the urging of some members of the nobility, the Assembly abolished all titles, armorial bearings and orders of knighthood as symbols of the *ancien régime*. But spirits remained high; even the king seemed to be growing once again in confidence, and was occasionally cheered in the streets.

The first anniversary of the storming of the Bastille, 14 July 1790, saw a nationwide celebration, when thousands of National Guardsmen and soldiers from across the country converged on Paris for what was called the Fête de la Fédération. When the great day came the rain poured down, but at least it was warm and nobody seemed to mind much. The ceremony began with a Mass, celebrated by the Bishop of Autun, Charles Maurice de Talleyrand-Périgord, of whom we shall be hearing a good deal more before our story is told; next the *Te Deum* was sung, accompanied by 1,200 musicians; then a seemingly interminable number of high officials lined up to swear an oath to be true to the nation, the law and the king. Finally Louis himself rose to his feet. 'I, Louis, King of the French', he declared, 'solemnly swear to employ the powers delegated to me in maintaining the constitution, as decreed by the National Assembly and accepted by me.' The queen followed him, holding up the five-year-old dauphin in her arms. 'Here is my son,' she said. 'He and I fully agree with the King.' That concluded the solemnities. The two days following were devoted to parades, reviews and firework displays. Perhaps, people thought, perhaps after all, the bitterness and pain of the past two years might yet be forgotten.

But no. It was not long before a new problem arose: this time it was the Church. Already, as early as November 1789, the Assembly had declared that all church property was 'at the disposal of the nation'. In December it began to sell off church estates, a process which, if it were to continue, threatened to result in a serious fall in the value of land. At about the same time further legislation abolished the validity of monastic vows, and on 13 February 1790 all religious orders were dissolved. Monks and nuns were instructed to return to private life, to marry and, if possible, to have children. Then, on 12 July the Assembly passed what was misleadingly known as the Civil Constitution of the Clergy, which effectively turned all the remaining churchmen into state employees. It also decreed that parish priests and bishops – whose numbers were now drastically reduced – should henceforth be elected by their parishes and dioceses, and that they should no longer accept the authority of the Pope in Rome. Finally it demanded that all clergy should swear an oath of loyalty to the new constitution. A few did so; but the vast majority refused. The result was a disastrous schism. First it was confined to the Church, but before long it spread to the laity, dividing local populations and even families all over France. Poor Louis was, as usual, in agonies of indecision: deeply pious as he was, far more anxious for eternal salvation than for his throne, could he in all conscience accept Holy Communion from a priest who had sworn the oath? Would he not be endangering his immortal soul? Some time before, he had written to Pope Pius VI for guidance, but had received no reply; and so finally, on the advice of most – though not all – his ministers, he put his deeply reluctant signature to the decree. Soon afterwards there arrived the Pope's long-awaited answer, the only one he could possibly have expected: the king must on no account sign. It was followed by a further letter, suspending all clergy who accepted the Civil Constitution and roundly condemning the proposal of clerical election. Louis immediately replaced his confessor, who had sworn the oath, for another who had not; but he remained deeply troubled.

When Pope Pius's second letter was made public it could not fail to arouse the anti-clericalism of the Parisians. Widespread rioting broke out again; in the gardens of the Palais-Royal the Pope was burned in effigy; convents were broken into and nuns assaulted; a severed head was tossed through the window of the coach of the Papal Nuncio; the mob smashed the doors of the church of Saint-Sulpice, forcing the organist to play the revolutionary song 'Ça ira'.* The king was ordered to dismiss his new confessor, and condemned as a traitor for flouting the law of France by receiving communion from a priest whose allegiance was to the Pope rather than to the state. When at Easter he and his family attempted to leave the Tuileries for Mass at Saint-Cloud, he found the palace gates closed against him. Despite the efforts of Lafayette, the mob flatly refused to let his carriage pass. For nearly two hours they were obliged to wait, while the queen did her best to comfort the sobbing dauphin, before they were allowed to return to the palace.

By now Louis XVI knew that he could never accept the Revolution, nor would the Revolution ever accept him. He remembered too Mirabeau's advice: once he could get away to his army on the frontier, he might well be able to persuade the Austrian emperor – who was after all his brother-in-law – to order an invasion of France. The King of Spain, too, would almost certainly help. Marie Antoinette, it need hardly be said, was enthusiastically in

---

* The song was inspired, somewhat surprisingly, by Benjamin Franklin. When asked about the progress of the American War of Independence, he would reply 'Ça ira, ça ira', meaning literally 'It will go', but effectively 'All will be well'. The song first became popular during the preparations for the Fête de la Fédération, but was soon taken up as the anthem of the Revolution.

favour of the idea; the only problem was how to put it into practice. The Tuileries was, as they had seen, closely guarded; several of the servants were suspected of being paid informers. The king had very little available money, and the queen could not sell any of her jewellery without attracting suspicion. If the family – which Louis was determined should not be split up – were to succeed in escaping, it would need all the help it could get.

Then – it seemed almost miraculously – the right man turned up at the right moment. He was Frederik Axel von Fersen, a tall and unusually good-looking Swedish aristocrat who had served under General Rochambeau in America and was now his country's special representative at the French court. He was a close personal friend of the queen, and a regular attender at her Sunday card-parties; inevitably he was said to be her lover, and it may well be that he was. He too saw that the royal family must escape from Paris, and instantly offered to lend them all the money they needed. He also promised to arrange for a carriage large enough to accommodate the king and queen, their children, the king's sister Elizabeth and the Duchesse de Tourzel, the children's governess. The date set was Monday 20 June 1791. At 11.15 that night, just as the guard was changing, five of them slipped out of a side entrance, the dauphin in a long dress disguised as a girl. They were delayed for another half hour while they waited for the queen, but she appeared at last and Fersen, disguised as a common cabman, drove them to the appointed meeting place outside the Porte Saint-Martin, where a heavy coach* was waiting to take them to Montmédy, a strongly fortified royalist stronghold on the north-eastern frontier.

The flight of the royal family was discovered early the next morning when one of the *valets de chambre* went to wake the king, only to find his bed empty. At once the alarm was raised, and search parties were despatched in various directions. Henceforth it was to be first a hunt, and then a race to arrest the party before they reached safety. Unfortunately for the fugitives, their carriage was painfully

---

* It is always referred to as a berlin, but berlins normally carried only two passengers. To carry five, it must have been far bigger, with dimensions more like those of a stagecoach. We know that it needed six horses to draw it.

slow: over the pitted provincial roads they were lucky to average more than five miles per hour, ten at the most. After twenty-four hours of acute discomfort in the hottest season of the year, they reached the little village of Varennes;* but alas, Varennes was expecting them. At their previous stop, Clermont-en-Argonne, where they had changed horses, Louis had been recognised from his portrait on a banknote† by the young postmaster, a certain Jean-Baptiste Drouet. On his wife's advice Drouet had said nothing at the time; but a short while later, feeling ever more certain that he was right, he and a friend had galloped off in pursuit. They had overtaken the royal carriage, and once at Varennes had alerted the local grocer, appropriately named Sauce. The carriage was stopped, and its passengers were led into his shop. He, meanwhile, sent a message to a local judge, Jacques Destez, who had lived at Versailles and had frequently seen both the king and the queen. Destez immediately recognised them and fell to his knees. 'Yes,' said Louis, 'I am indeed your king.' Just before dawn two officers arrived, bearing a decree from the National Assembly ordering the fugitives to return to Paris at once. They could go no further. The attempt had failed.

The journey home was a nightmare. Thanks to the June sun, beating down on the black roof of the carriage, the heat was almost unendurable; but the furious crowds all the way, shouting and spitting, hammering their fists against the sides of the carriage, made it impossible to open a window. When they reached Pont à Binson, two members of the Assembly climbed in with the royal party, obliging the queen to take the dauphin on her knee and increasing the airlessness still further. One of them, Jérôme Pétion, at least partly answered a question that must spring almost unbidden to the mind:

> We stayed for twelve whole hours in the carriage without once getting out. What surprised me particularly was that neither the Queen nor Madame Elizabeth nor Madame de Tourzel showed any sign of wishing to do so. The Dauphin made water two or three

---

* Its population in 2012 was 656.

† These banknotes, or *assignats*, were paper money issued by the National Assembly between 1789 and 1796.

times. The King himself unbuttoned his breeches and made him pass water into a big silver cup.

It was only after five days of this torment that the royal family arrived back in Paris, exhausted and humiliated. The crowds, the hammering, the screaming of abuse were worse than ever until they eventually drove into the Tuileries. There at least they were safe for the moment; but by now they were broken, broken in body and spirit. There was no fight left in them.

Soon after the attempted escape to Varennes, a document was drafted by Jacques Pierre Brissot, the leading light of the diplomatic committee of the Legislative Assembly, suggesting that by his flight Louis had effectively deposed himself from the monarchy; and on Sunday 17 July 1791 vast crowds assembled in the Champ de Mars to sign it – or, in many cases, to append a slightly shaky X. There were of course speeches, first from Camille Desmoulins and then from a burly, pockmarked young revolutionary whose star was rapidly rising, Georges Danton; but the meeting soon got out of hand. The National Guard was called out, and greeted by volleys of stones. In an attempt to restore order, Lafayette commanded his men to fire a few shots into the air, but the mob – for mob it was – took no notice. He then ordered the guard to lower their elevation and fire into the crowd. About fifty of the demonstrators fell dead. Order was quickly restored, but Lafayette was never forgiven. Desmoulins went into hiding. Danton, who had been responsible for much of the trouble, fled to England for the rest of the summer.

Since the start of the Revolution Marie Antoinette's brother, the Emperor Leopold, had been increasingly concerned for the safety of his sister and her family, but worried too lest any intervention in French affairs might not make things worse for them. After the disaster at Varennes, however, he felt that he must show his anxiety. He therefore invited King Frederick William of Prussia and Louis's brother the Comte d'Artois* to the castle of Pillnitz just outside

---

* The future King Charles X.

Dresden, where on 27 August the three issued a joint declaration. The signatories, it proclaimed, regarded the plight of King Louis XVI as 'an object of concern to all the sovereigns of Europe', and would be prepared to restore a true monarchy to France, if – and here lay the rub – the other powers were prepared to cooperate. As Leopold was well aware, in London the government of William Pitt would never support any such action; he hoped, nevertheless, that the declaration might at least give a degree of comfort to his sister and brother-in-law, and to the French émigrés who had escaped across the border. He did not believe that it could have any serious repercussions.

Alas, he was wrong. It proved a catastrophic error of judgement. In France, the National Assembly – unaware of the views of Pitt, of whom most of them had probably never heard – took it as a clear indication that Austria and Prussia were about to declare war. The desirability or otherwise of open hostilities had been endlessly debated among the countless political clubs that had recently sprung up across the country from the late 1780s onwards. Of these the most influential in the early years had been the left-wing Society of the Friends of the Constitution, which met at the Convent of the Jacobins in the Rue Saint-Honoré and whose members were commonly known as Jacobins. Originally founded by anti-royalist deputies from Brittany, it had quickly grown to become a national republican movement. Most of its members were against the idea of war; but it was by no means monolithic, including as it did the Girondins, so-called because most of their leading members were members of the Legislative Assembly of the Gironde in the south-west. The Girondins too supported the abolition of the monarchy, but they were never an organised political group like the Jacobins; they were simply a party of loosely affiliated individuals, who included among their number the influential Jean Marie Roland and his wife Marie-Jeanne, whose *salon* was to become their principal meeting place. They tended to favour war, which they hoped would provide a catalyst by which the Revolution, hitherto dangerously fluid, might be crystallised into a more solid and lasting form. As may well be believed, the news from Pillnitz gave them much additional strength. On 20 April 1792 the king addressed the National Assembly. 'Gentlemen', he said,

You have just heard the result of the negotiations in which I have been engaged with the Court of Vienna. The conclusions of the report have been unanimously approved by my Council, and I myself have adopted them. They are in conformity with the wishes that the Assembly has on several occasions expressed, and with the sentiments communicated to me by a great number of citizens in different parts of the Kingdom. All would prefer to have war than to see the dignity of the French people any longer insulted . . . Having done my best to maintain peace, as I was in duty bound to do, I have now come, in conformity with the terms of the Constitution, to propose war to the Assembly.

There were a few cries of '*Vive le Roi!*' – by this time all too rare – and hostilities began.

With France in its present state of chaos, it was ridiculous even to suppose that its army was in any condition to take on two of the strongest powers of Europe. Over 3,000 officers had resigned, refusing to sign the new oath of loyalty from which the king's name was omitted; supplies of arms and ammunition were short, largely because so much had been stolen; and, in the atmosphere prevailing, mutinies were common. As for discipline, it had long ceased to exist. General Theobald Dillon – Irish born, but one of several in his family who fought in the French army – was murdered by his own troops; General the Duc de Biron was obliged to call off a bayonet charge when his men voted against it. Cries of '*Nous sommes trahis!*' and '*Sauve qui peut!*',* accompanied by the clatter of falling muskets, were all too frequently heard. And of course the king and queen were blamed. *L'Autrichienne* was clearly sending secret military information to Vienna. She and Louis were traitors to their country and could no longer be tolerated.

Tempers reached boiling point when, on the night of 20 June 1792, a vast mob – it was estimated at eight thousand, women as well as men, armed with every weapon they could find or manufacture – marched, by way of the Hôtel de Ville and the Assembly, to the Tuileries, which they reached at about four in the afternoon.

---

* 'We've been betrayed'. 'Each man for himself.'

We are told they found a side door to the palace unlocked, which sounds unlikely; more probably they smashed it down. Then they sought out the king. For the past ten days, we are told by the queen's maid, he had been in deep depression, refusing to utter a word. When the mob burst in, however, he remained calm. 'Here I am,' he said, standing motionlessly before them, the arms of his sister Elizabeth around his shoulders. (The queen and children had been hurried out just in time by one of the courtiers, who had put them into a small room and barricaded it with furniture.) His calm dignity had its effect. The people grew quiet, and moved to a larger room where a new petition was read. The king, wearing a scarlet 'liberty bonnet', was made to drink out of a bottle to 'the Nation'– which had, he claimed, no better friend than himself.

It was a terrifying experience, but it was nothing to what occurred six weeks later, when news reached Paris of a manifesto – almost an ultimatum – drafted by Count Fersen and signed by the Duke of Brunswick. It announced that the allies would soon be entering France to restore the royal authority and that if any further outrage were offered to the king the city of Paris would be 'totally destroyed'. It roused the people to fury. The last time they had confronted Louis they had let him off lightly; they would not make the same mistake again. Delegations were now arriving in Paris from all over France, a contingent of about five hundred of them from Marseille singing a stirring new song, originally written for the army of the Rhine by Rouget de Lisle, a young engineer officer in Strasbourg. '*Aux armes, citoyens!*' they sang; and the Parisians took them at their word.

This time it was twenty thousand who, on the morning of Friday 10 August, marched on the Tuileries. The palace was defended by 950 Swiss Guards, supported by some 2,000 National Guardsmen of dubious loyalty. The king was advised to go out and show himself to them; there were occasions, as on 20 June, when he had impressed everyone by his calmness and his courage. But that was six weeks ago; today it was very different. 'I can see him now as he passed along,' wrote a member of the Swiss Guard. 'He was silent and careworn and, with his swaying walk, he seemed to say to us "All is lost."' Then, as he watched, he had the humiliation of seeing one battalion after another move off to join the demonstrators in the

Place du Carrousel. According to the queen's maid, who was at one of the palace windows, 'some of the gunners quit their posts, went up to the King and thrust their fists into his face'. He returned hurriedly to the palace, to rejoin his family and to decide what was now to be done. The Swiss Guard had shown itself loyal, and the royal family might have done well to remain where they were; but Louis was strongly advised to put himself under the protection of the Legislative Assembly. It was, in a sense, a betrayal of his own cause, and Marie Antoinette had argued strongly against it, saying that she would rather be nailed to the walls of the palace; but Louis had quietly insisted. Two files of Swiss Guards arrived, under whose escort they walked through the year's first fall of leaves to the Assembly, where they were cooped up in a tiny stenographers' box while the Assembly decided their fate.

But the noise of firing was growing louder all the time, and before long a few small cannon balls came hurtling through the open windows. Soon a band of *sans-culottes*★ burst into the hall, demanding that every deputy should swear to maintain liberty and equality, while at the same time some of the rebels from Marseille and Finistère had advanced towards the palace in an effort to persuade the Swiss Guards to lay down their arms. The Swiss bravely refused; a struggle took place, and firing started. The king, realising what was happening, ordered the Guards to do as they were told, but in the confusion the order reached only some of them. In the ensuing *mêlée*, the mob poured into the palace, now in a frenzy of bloodlust; the result was a massacre. Pages, cooks, maidservants, all were slaughtered indiscriminately, as were the Swiss Guards, whether they had laid down their arms or not. One of the servants who was lucky enough to escape recorded:

> Finding the apartments and staircases already strewn with dead bodies, I jumped from one of the windows in the Queen's room on to the terrace . . . I got to my feet and ran to where some Marseillais, who had just butchered several of the Swiss, were stripping them . . . Some of the Swiss who were pursued took refuge in an adjoining

★ Literally 'without trousers'; the common people of the working class.

stable. I concealed myself in the same place. They were soon cut to pieces close to me . . . Some of the men were still continuing the slaughter; others were cutting off the heads of those already slain; while the women, lost to all sense of shame, were committing the most indecent mutilations of the dead bodies, from which they tore pieces of flesh and carried them off in triumph. Towards evening I took the road to Versailles and crossed the Pont Louis Seize, which was covered with naked carcases already in a state of putrefaction from the intense heat of the weather.

Throughout this time Louis and his family were sweltering in the stenographers' box; but they were, in all but name, in the dock. Three days later on 13 August, they were put under arrest and imprisoned in the Temple, where the king was to spend the last five months of his life.

Nothing is left of the Temple today. It was demolished in 1808 by Napoleon, since it was rapidly becoming a place of royalist pilgrimage. At the time of the Revolution, however, it was still a vast fortress, built in the thirteenth century by the Knights Templar as their European headquarters and containing a complex of buildings which included a church and a massive turreted keep known as the *Grosse Tour*. Its interior was not remotely like a prison; it had formerly been occupied by the Comte d'Artois and was certainly not all that uncomfortable. But it was a prison none the less, selected purely because it could be securely guarded. The king would rise at six, pray for five minutes or more and then, after a light breakfast, spend most of the morning giving lessons to the dauphin. Before dinner at two he and his family were allowed out for a walk within the Temple grounds. Afterwards, he would spend much of the rest of the day reading, as many as twelve books a week, many of them by the great Latin authors. For the virtually uneducated Marie Antoinette on the other hand, the days were long indeed. Now just thirty-seven, she already looked at least fifty. Embroidering and knitting were her chief pursuits, and trying to give lessons to her daughter Marie-Thérèse who, at the age of fourteen and having been properly tutored, probably knew a good deal more than her mother.

We cannot tell how much, during their time in the Temple, the royal family knew of what was going on in France and in the outside world. It is certainly to be hoped that they were unaware of the September Massacres – perhaps the ugliest chapter of the whole history of the Revolution – which occurred in the first week of September 1792. These were based on fears that the Duke of Brunswick, who was believed to be advancing on Paris at the head of the Prussian army, would on his arrival free all the inmates of the city's prisons, who would at once rally to his support. The radicals, and particularly the extremist journalist Jean-Paul Marat, called for pre-emptive action, demanding that all the prisoners in the city should be slaughtered at once. Men of the National Guard and others from the *fédérés* set to with a will; by 6 September half the prison population – 1,400 to 1,500 – had been killed. Well over two hundred of them were Catholic priests, whose only crime had been to refuse to submit to the Civil Constitution of the Clergy. Nor were these straight, clean killings; those responsible soon became no better than homicidal lunatics, torturing, amputating, eviscerating their victims in an orgy of bloodlust. Few of these unfortunates suffered more than the queen's greatest friend, the Princesse de Lamballe. She was stripped, raped and savagely mutilated; her heart roasted and eaten; and her head, impaled on another pike, paraded beneath the queen's window at the Temple.

Paris was still recovering its sanity when the revolutionaries welcomed the first piece of genuine good news they had received for some time. Somehow, in recent months, the French army had managed to work itself back into shape. Brunswick's advance had been halted by the French generals François Kellermann and Charles Dumouriez near the village of Valmy in Champagne. Militarily speaking, the victory had been insignificant enough; in the eyes of the National Convention, on the other hand, it was immense – and it emboldened the Convention on 22 September to make a formal declaration of the end of the monarchy and the establishment of the First French Republic.

On 11 December Louis was summoned to the Convention to face his accusers, and to be charged with high treason and crimes against the state. He was ably defended, but the verdict, given on 15 January 1793, was a foregone conclusion: 693 deputies voted guilty, none not guilty and 23 abstained. On the following day the Convention met again, to decide on what was to be done with him. This time the votes were more evenly distributed, but they remained unarguable: 288 called for his imprisonment or exile, 361 for his immediate execution.* A last-minute motion to grant a reprieve was defeated. The king's fate was sealed. He had expected no less, and he took the news calmly enough; he was sound asleep when they woke him on the 20th to tell him that he was to go to the scaffold on the following day. That evening he said goodbye to his family and ate his supper alone. The following morning, 21 January, he was awoken at five, heard Mass and received communion at the hands of an Irish-born priest, Henry Essex Edgeworth, who had become a close friend. It was Edgeworth who accompanied him to the guillotine in what was then known as the Place de la Révolution and is now the Place de la Concorde.

The guillotine owed its name to Dr Joseph-Ignace Guillotin, whose name has already once appeared in these pages.† A kind, well-meaning man, he had suggested that all those convicted of a capital crime should have the right to beheading, a form of execution previously reserved for the nobility only, and that the process should be as swift and painless as possible. The king gazed up at the towering structure, still showing no trace of fear, and walked firmly with Edgeworth up the steps of the scaffold before removing his coat, shirt and collar. Making a sign to the drummers for a moment's silence, he addressed the crowd in a strong, steady voice: 'I forgive those who are guilty of my death, and I pray God that the blood which you are about to shed may never be required of France.' As he laid himself prone on the platform Edgeworth is said to have cried out: '*Digne fils de Saint-Louis, montez au ciel!*'‡ And the great blade crashed down.

---

* These included the king's own cousin, the former Duke of Orléans, now known by his own wish as Philippe Egalité. This was to cause much bitterness among the monarchists; Philippe would himself be guillotined on the same scaffold before the end of the year.

† See p.193.

‡ 'Worthy son of Saint Louis, ascend to heaven!' They are magnificent, moving words, and they would have given the king much courage.

14

'Pas de faiblesse!'

1793–5

Oh Liberty, what crimes are committed in thy name!
Madame Roland, on the scaffold

THE DEATH OF the king did not mean the end of the French
Revolution – far from it. Anyone settling down to study its
history soon discovers that it was of a truly hideous complication
– so hideous that a full account would demand a hundred pages or
more and would throw the present modest volume utterly off balance.
The last chapter was consequently a shameless oversimplification,
and the present one will be another.

On 20 September 1792, the same day as the victory of Valmy,
and while King Louis XVI was whiling away his last months in the
Temple, the long-awaited National Convention was constituted.
On the following day it was to declare the abolition of the monarchy.
It was then unanimously agreed that 22 September should mark
the beginning of Year I of the French Republic; but there was
agreement on very little else. Hostility increased between the
Girondins and the Jacobins, who had become more extremist than
ever, and – occupying as they did the highest and most remote
seats in the hall – became known as the *Montagnards*, or simply the
Mountain. Over all fell the shadow of the king. The Girondins
would have spared him if they could; so initially would Danton, at
first one of their number though he soon changed his mind since,
as he honestly admitted, 'I did not want my head to fall with his.'
His place, he realised, was now with the Mountain, together with
Camille Desmoulins and Pierre Philippeaux, who were his close
friends and collaborators; with Maximilien Robespierre, whom he

disliked but respected; and with Jean-Paul Marat, whose hysterical outpourings he despised.

He himself was bigger than all of them. In some ways he seemed another Mirabeau, with a huge head pitted by smallpox – his was additionally disfigured by several farmyard accidents in his youth – a magnificent voice and a quite extraordinary feeling for the French language. Like Mirabeau, too, he had a distinctly questionable reputation; he certainly lived on a scale wholly disproportionate to his apparent sources of income. Madame Roland, who had always distrusted him, claimed that he once boasted that since the start of the Revolution he had managed to amass no less than 1.5 million livres. Perhaps he had: but as the courts of Europe reacted to the news of the king's execution and one by one severed their diplomatic relations, it was Danton's voice that was heard above all the rest. 'The kings in alliance try to intimidate us,' he thundered. 'We hurl at their feet, as a gage of battle, the head of the King of France.' Since continental war was now inevitable, he ensured that the Convention should take the initiative: it declared war on England and Holland in February 1793, and on Spain early in March.

How, possibly, could the revolutionary armies hold their own against such opposition? Lately, it is true, they had been doing pretty well. After their triumph at Valmy they had occupied Savoy, which also included the city of Nice. Then Dumouriez had advanced into Belgium, defeated the Austrians at Jemappes and proceeded to Brussels, Liège and Antwerp. Meanwhile General Armand-Louis de Custine had entered Germany and threatened Frankfurt. But by now, with the war opening up on several new fronts, it was clear that the Convention had bitten off more than it could hope to chew. Custine was forced to retreat from the Rhineland while Dumouriez, a convinced Girondin, suffered two successive defeats at Neerwinden and Louvain; he then did his best to persuade his men to march on Paris to restore order and overthrow the revolutionary government. When they refused, he knew that he must choose between flight and capture, with an almost certain end on the scaffold. He defected, very sensibly, to the Austrians, taking the young Duke of Chartres – the future King Louis-Philippe – with him.

And worse was to come. In the Vendée* – a region on the west coast just south of Brittany – the peasantry rose in arms against the new order, massacred all the republicans and revolutionaries that they could find and advanced on Rochefort, which they threatened to open to a British invasion fleet. In Bordeaux, Nantes, Lyon and Marseille the situation was only a little better. Desperate to retain control, in March the Convention established first a Revolutionary Tribunal and shortly afterwards what was to be known as the Committee of Public Safety, its nine members headed by Danton, which was gradually to arrogate to itself absolute powers. It began by launching a campaign against the Girondins, who had been greatly embarrassed by the defection of Dumouriez, one of their most distinguished members. But the Girondins fought back, and in a surprise move arraigned Jean-Paul Marat, one of their bitterest enemies, before the Revolutionary Tribunal.

On hearing the news of his arrest, few members of the Convention could have felt deeply upset. Of them all, Marat was one of the most unpopular. Dr John Moore, an English visitor to Paris who heard him speak, left the following description:

> He has a cadaverous complexion and a countenance exceedingly expressive of his disposition . . . So far from ever having the appearance of fear or deference, he seems to me always to contemplate the Assembly from the tribune either with eyes of menace or contempt. He speaks in a hollow, croaking voice, with affected solemnity . . . Marat has carried his calumnies to such a length that even the party which he wishes to support seems to be ashamed of him, and he is shunned and apparently detested by everyone else. When he enters the hall of the Assembly he is avoided on all sides, and when he takes his seat those near him generally rise and change their places.

The Girondins, none the less, had reason to regret their action. Marat may have been detested, but he too had his champions. He was instantly acquitted by the Tribunal and carried back in triumph to the Convention Hall.

---

* The Vendée revolt is the subject of Victor Hugo's last novel, *Quatrevingt-treize*, and also forms the backdrop of Balzac's *Les Chouans*.

Meanwhile the trouble in the provinces continued to spread. Some sixty departments were now affected. Normandy was in chaos; Lyon, Marseille and Toulon were in the throes of civil war. Everywhere, Paris was blamed – for virtually ignoring the situation elsewhere and by its shameless intimidation of an elected assembly. The Committee of Public Safety did what it could, but in the current confusion it was often powerless. And it was ever conscious of the increasing threat of foreign invasion. During the summer of 1793 the Austrians took the key frontier positions of Condé and Valenciennes; Custine was pressed back by the Prussians; Spanish armies were massing around the Pyrenees; Savoy and Nice were once again under threat; British forces were besieging Dunkirk; Toulon was about to surrender arsenal, town and fleet to Britain's Admiral Lord Hood;* while in Lyon, France's second city, the royalists had resumed control and were busy executing every republican in sight. And Danton, the one man who had seemed capable of taking over the government and somehow restoring order, had failed miserably. He and several others were voted off the Committee of Public Safety, and his place was now taken by possibly the ablest, certainly the most sinister of all the grisly figures with whom these chapters have had to deal: Maximilien Robespierre.

Maximilien Robespierre – his name was originally Derobespierre, but he shortened it in 1789 – was as unlike Mirabeau or Danton as it was possible to be. They were both hideous; he was a dandy, always immaculately dressed in clothes of a perfect cut, usually dark green – a colour which seemed to be reflected in his eyes and even in his sallow, pock-marked complexion. His hair was meticulously brushed and powdered. Small and thin, he made himself taller with high-heeled shoes, on which he walked very fast with short, nervous steps. He fully lived up to his nickname, 'the sea-green incorruptible'; incorruptible he certainly was. He spent money on his wardrobe, but on remarkably little else. He had no close friends; women meant nothing to him, nor did food or drink. He lived mainly on bread,

---

* It eventually did so on 27 August.

fruit and coffee. He was never heard to laugh, seldom seen to smile. There was an extraordinary intensity about him. 'That man will go far,' said Mirabeau shortly before he died, 'he believes what he says.'

In March 1790 Robespierre was elected president of the Jacobin Club, and saw it through its most difficult days when many of its members left – in protest against the petition for the king's dethrone-ment – to form another more moderate club, the Feuillants; and his reputation was still further increased by the military disasters of 1792. He had always been against the war – according to his enemies, because he was entirely lacking in physical courage. Certainly he was never to be seen at popular demonstrations; in August, when the mob stormed the Tuileries, the Girondins accused him of hiding in a cellar. Marat, characteristically, did not mince his words. 'Robespierre', he said, 'grows pale at the sight of a sabre.' He may well have been right; but there could be no question that by the summer of 1793, as President of the Committee of Public Safety, Maximilien Robespierre was supreme.

So much blood had already been shed that it might have been thought that one more killing would have been hardly worthy of notice; but in that same summer a murder was committed that set all Paris alight: the killing, by a fanatical young Girondin named Charlotte Corday, of Jean-Paul Marat. Bursting into his apartment, she found him wrapped in towels, lying in a medicinal bath – the only relief he could find for the debilitating skin disease which made his life a misery – and handed him a letter which contained a list of those implicated in a planned uprising in her home city of Caen. Marat copied down the names, murmuring 'they shall all be guillotined' – at which she plunged a six-inch kitchen knife into his chest. He died instantly, she four days later on the scaffold, having succeeded only in making him a martyr – his bust on a pedestal in the Convention Hall, his ashes reverently laid in the Panthéon, streets and squares all over France renamed in his honour. The deed was also commemorated in several paintings, including the famous *Marat assassiné** by Jacques-Louis David,

---

* It now hangs in the Royal Museum of Fine Arts, Brussels. The letter has survived, complete with bloodstains and marks of the bath water, and is now owned by the Earl of Crawford and Balcarres.

himself a convinced Jacobin who had voted for the death of the king.

After the murder of Marat the Committee of Public Safety pursued its ends with ever-greater zeal. General Custine went to the guillotine, to be followed shortly by the Duc de Biron; a force was sent to the Vendée to put down the civil war there, at the cost of nearly a quarter of a million lives; finally, it was decided that the queen herself must go to trial. After the execution of the king his family had been moved to the Conciergerie on the Ile de la Cité. Originally a Merovingian palace, much of it had been a prison for the past four hundred years; infested with rats and smelling strongly of urine, it was a good deal grimmer than the Temple. The queen was obliged to share a cell with a female attendant and two gendarmes who, according to Count Fersen, 'never left her side even when she had to satisfy the needs of nature'. Still worse for her, she had been parted from her son, whom she knew she would never see again.

Her trial, like her husband's, was a formality. She was found guilty on various charges and condemned to death. According to the *Moniteur Universel*, 'having heard the sentence pronounced she left the court without addressing a further word to the judges or the public, no trace of emotion appearing on her face'. The following morning, 16 October, her head was shaved. She climbed unassisted on to the tumbril. Mounting the steps to the scaffold, she stumbled and inadvertently trod on the foot of the executioner. '*Monsieur, je vous demande pardon,*' she said, '*je ne l'ai pas fait exprès.*'★ They were her last words.

By now the Revolution had begun to devour its own children. Before the month was over, twenty-one of the leading Girondins had lost their heads; in November they were followed by the former Duke of Orléans, Philippe Egalité – who asked only for a twenty-four-hour stay of execution in order to enjoy a last hearty meal – and Madame Roland. Even poor, feckless Madame du Barry, in

★ 'I beg your pardon, Monsieur, I did not do it on purpose.'

floods of tears and screaming for mercy, was executed on 8 December. All that autumn and winter, the Terror continued; Paris saw nearly 3,000 executions; the provinces 14,000. Many of the charges verged on the grotesque. According to the Liste Générale des Condamnés, they included 'Henriette Françoise de Marboeuf . . . convicted of having hoped for the arrival of the Austrians and Prussians', 'François Bertrand . . . convicted of having furnished to the defenders of the country sour wine injurious to health', and 'Marie Angélique Plaisant, sempstress at Douai, convicted of having exclaimed that she was an aristocrat and that she cared "not a fig for the nation"'. All were 'condemned to death in Paris and executed the same day'.

The new calendar had already been introduced, with the First Year of the Republic beginning on the day of the abolition of the monarchy, 22 September 1792. The details were put into the hands of a mildly ridiculous, unsuccessful actor, Philippe Fabre, who affected the name of Fabre d'Eglantine – together with a lorgnette, which drove Robespierre wild with irritation. It was he who proposed the idea that the year should be divided into twelve equal months, with the five days left at the end to be known as *sans-culottides* and celebrated as festivals. The months were to be subdivided into three 'decades' and renamed after the seasons: Vendémiaire, Brumaire and Frimaire for the autumn; Nivôse, Pluviôse and Ventôse for the winter; Germinal, Floréal and Prairial for the spring; Messidor, Thermidor and Fructidor for the summer.* This proposal infuriated the working population, who now had to face a ten-day week, and deeply shocked the clergy, many of whom refused to recognise the new Sabbath.

Besides, they had enough problems of their own. The Revolution's campaign against Christianity was steadily gathering momentum. Crucifixes and statues of the Virgin and saints were hacked to pieces (and even occasionally replaced by busts of Marat); services were suppressed; across the country, towns and villages, streets and squares

---

* Grape Harvest, Mist, Frost; Snow, Rain, Wind; Seeds, Flowers, Meadows; Harvest, Heat, Fruit. Or, as a contemporary English wit suggested, Wheezy, Sneezy, Freezy; Slippy, Drippy, Nippy; Showery, Flowery, Bowery; Hoppy, Croppy, Poppy.

changed their names wholesale; in Paris, Grand Festivals of Reason were held in Notre-Dame and Saint-Sulpice – for, said Danton, 'the people will have festivals where they will offer up incense to the Supreme Being, Nature's master; for it was never our intention to destroy religion so that atheism could take its place.'

But Danton's days were numbered. He had been ill, and during a prolonged convalescence he had had second thoughts over the path that France was now taking. 'Perhaps', he declared to the Convention, 'the Terror once served a useful purpose, but it should not hurt innocent people. No one wants to see a person treated as a criminal just because he happens not to have enough revolutionary enthusiasm.' At once, Robespierre saw a red light. He had always been bitterly jealous of Danton, whom he suspected – with good reason – to be more intelligent than himself, besides being a far better speaker. Moreover – and this may have been another form of jealousy – he could never reconcile himself to Danton's blatant and frequently coarse sexuality, which shocked and disturbed him. And now the man had identified himself with the *Indulgents*, the forgiving, and in Robespierre's book the *Indulgents* were agents of counter-revolution.

It was on the evening of 30 March 1794, at a joint meeting of the committees of Public Safety and General Security, that Robespierre's unsmiling lieutenant, Louis de Saint-Just, laid a warrant for Danton's arrest on the table and invited those present to sign it. Two only refused. Three days later the trial began, with Camille Desmoulins, Fabre d'Eglantine and fifteen other *Indulgents* beside him in the dock. As always, Danton dominated the proceedings. He had no doubts as to the outcome, but he was determined to go down fighting. As that tremendous voice echoed across the courtroom, the president had the greatest difficulty in keeping order, ringing his bell in vain. 'Did you not hear my bell?' he asked. 'Bell?' thundered Danton. 'A man who is fighting for his life pays no attention to bells!' But it was no use: on 5 April the eighteen accused were loaded on to three red-painted tumbrils and taken to the guillotine.

Danton was the last to be executed. Looking down from the scaffold, he noticed the painter Jacques-Louis David – who, despite their former friendship, had voted for his death – sketching him from a nearby cafe, and shouted his final obscenity. After that his face clouded, and he was heard to murmur: 'Oh my wife, my dear wife, shall I ever see you again?' Then he pulled himself together: '*Courage, Danton – pas de faiblesse!*'* Those words have passed into history, as have the words to the executioner that followed: 'Above all, don't forget to show my head to the people. It's well worth looking at.'

The steady rhythm of the guillotine continued until the end of July, at the rate of some thirty a day.† By now fewer than 10 per cent of the victims were aristocrats; another 6 per cent were clergy; the remainder – roughly 85 per cent – were members of what had been known as the third estate. Robespierre himself had witnessed not a single execution. In his own curious way he still claimed to deplore the practice, on the grounds that it brutalised the people. But the momentum could not be halted. 'If we stop too soon,' he declared, 'we shall die. If the revolutionary government is destroyed now, freedom will be extinguished tomorrow.' Nor could he forget the words that Danton had shouted – as only Danton could – as the tumbril passed the house where he himself lodged: 'You will follow us, Robespierre!'

Danton had spoken no more than the truth: in the spring and early summer of 1794 Robespierre found the Revolution turning against him. He antagonised the many surviving secret supporters of Danton by reviling him in a public speech as 'the most dangerous of the conspirators, had he not been the most cowardly', while his increasing arrogance suggested that he now regarded himself as a dictator. On 8 June he organised and presided over a national festival in honour of the 'Supreme Being' that many people found perfectly ridiculous, and which did little good to his reputation. Though generally respected and even admired, he had never been a popular figure;

---

* 'Courage, Danton – no weakness!'
† The total number executed by the guillotine was 16,594 – 2,639 of them in Paris. Another 25,000 perished in summary executions across France; 96 per cent occurred in or after November 1793.

now he was openly feared. Under him, France had become a police state. On 10 June, at his instigation, a new and terrifying piece of legislation was passed: the Law of 22 Prairial, which permitted executions on grounds of suspicion only. Defence lawyers and witnesses were dispensed with; so were interrogations of the defendants, which 'merely confused the conscience of the judges'. It was no longer safe to discuss politics in public places. And, people began to ask, was all this really necessary? The danger of foreign invasion had now passed. On 26 June a French army had defeated the Austrians at Fleurus* in the Low Countries, and early in July had occupied Brussels, bringing about the extinction, after over two centuries, of the Dutch Republic. Toulon had been retaken from the British. Why then must France continue to suffer? Could not this relentless pressure now be relaxed?

And there was another question too: was Robespierre entirely sane? His friends were becoming uncertain. Two of them, Paul Barras and Louis Stanislas Fréron, called on him and found him in his dressing gown.

> He did not reply to our greeting. He turned first towards a mirror that hung on the window, then to a smaller mirror, taking his toilet knife, scraping the powder that covered his face and minutely inspecting the arrangement of his hair. He then took off his dressing-gown, putting it on a chair near us so that we were dusted by the powder that flew off it. He did not apologise, nor show any sign that he had even noticed our presence. He washed himself in a bowl that he held in his hand, brushed his teeth, spat several times on the floor by our feet as though we had not been there . . . He remained standing . . . and still said nothing. I have seen no expression as impassive on the icy marble faces of statues or on those of corpses.

On 26 July (8 Thermidor) 1794, dressed in a sky-blue coat and nankeen breeches, Robespierre arrived to address the Convention. He spoke for over two hours, castigating most of the leaders and showing particular bitterness against those who had derided his

---

* The first battle in history in which reconnaissance aircraft – in this case balloons – were successfully used.

Festival of the Supreme Being. He then turned his attention to the superintendent of finance, Pierre Joseph Cambon, whom he accused of destroying the economy and reducing the poor to near-starvation. This proved a mistake. Cambon leaped to his feet. 'Before I am dishonoured,' he declared, 'I will speak to the French nation. It is time to tell the whole truth. One man alone is paralysing the will of the National Convention. And that man is Robespierre.' The ice had been broken. One by one, other deputies rose to defend themselves and to denounce him. By the end of the session there could be little doubt that Robespierre was doomed.

The next day's meeting brought confirmation. From the start tempers ran high; the president found it almost impossible to maintain order. Before the proceedings broke up in confusion, however, Robespierre's immediate arrest was proposed, together with that of Saint-Just, and the proposal carried unanimously. The gendarmerie was summoned and the two were led away, together with several others including Augustin Robespierre, who had nobly insisted on sharing his brother's fate. And that, one feels, should have settled the matter.

Alas, it did not. A new complication was introduced by the Paris Commune, which now met urgently in the Hôtel de Ville and resolved to defy the two committees and the Convention in protest against the arrests. It must have been astonished when shortly afterwards there arrived Robespierre himself. He had first been sent to the Luxembourg Palace – recently converted into an additional prison – but on orders from the Commune had been refused admittance; barred also from the Mairie, his captors had taken him in despair to the Hôtel de Ville, where he was warmly welcomed. Immediately he assumed control, ordering the Commune 'to close the city gates, to shut down all newspapers, and to order the arrest of all journalists and traitorous deputies'.

It was in the early hours of the 28th – 10 Thermidor – that the Convention decided to act: its forces must go straight to the Hôtel de Ville and bring out Robespierre and his friends by force. If we are to believe the far from modest account of the unhappily named General of Gendarmerie Charles André Merda, he was one of the first into the building.

I saw about fifty people inside, in a state of great excitement . . . I recognised Robespierre in the middle. He was sitting in an armchair with his left elbow on his knee and his head supported by his left hand. I leapt at him, pointing my sword at his heart and crying 'Surrender, you traitor!' He raised his head and replied, 'It is you who are the traitor. I shall have you shot.' At these words I reached for one of my pistols . . . and fired. I meant to shoot him in the chest, but the ball struck his chin and smashed his lower jaw. He fell out of his chair.★

By now it was about three in the morning. Robespierre was carried to the offices of the Committee of Public Safety and lay there until six, when a surgeon arrived and dressed the wound with a bandage that covered all the lower part of his face and that was itself soon drenched in blood. A few hours later he, his brother, Saint-Just and twenty others were formally condemned to death and at five o'clock that afternoon carried off to the guillotine, which they reached soon after seven. Lifted down from the cart, Robespierre lay flat on the ground, apparently only semi-conscious; not till he felt himself being carried up to the scaffold did he open his eyes. The executioner then cruelly tore away the bandage and splint that held his upper and lower jaw together; the blood poured out in torrents and he let forth 'a groan like a dying tiger, which was heard all over the square'.

Of all the leaders of the Revolution, Maximilien Robespierre is the most mysterious and the hardest to understand. Certainly, he was the most honest. He was deeply cultivated, an idealist and an eloquent champion of the poor and oppressed. He campaigned for universal male suffrage and the abolition of slavery in the colonies. He consistently opposed war, maintaining that 'the most extravagant idea that can arise in a politician's head is to believe that it is enough for a people to invade a foreign country to make it adopt their laws and constitution. No one loves armed missionaries.' He was a passionate admirer of Jean-Jacques Rousseau and kept a copy of *Le Contrat Social* beside his bed. And it was he who coined the slogan *Liberté, Egalité,*

★ It has been suggested, though on little evidence, that Merda was boasting, and that Robespierre fired the shot himself in an unsuccessful attempt at suicide.

Fraternité, which, until the coming of the euro, was inscribed on all French currency. He had voted for the execution of the king, but only as what he described as 'a cruel exception to ordinary laws'.

How then does it happen that it is he, more than any other of the revolutionaries, whom we associate with the atrocities of the Terror? Probably because he was by this time quite seriously unbalanced, and genuinely paranoid about the future of the Revolution, which dominated his life and which he believed to be threatened. There was little enough foundation for this belief: no one could still seriously fear a foreign invasion, nor at that time was there any possibility of a re-establishment of the monarchy: the dauphin, Louis-Charles, was a child of nine, already suffering from tuberculosis of the bone. On his death in June 1795 his uncle, the Count of Provence – who was then living quietly at Verona – was to proclaim himself King Louis XVIII as he was honour-bound to do, but it was to be another nineteen years before he assumed the throne. The Revolution was almost over. True, it had not fulfilled all its promises; the economy was in a wretched state and the poor were still protesting over the price of food. Still, the king was dead, and France was now a republic.

Robespierre, however, would have none of it. For him the Revolution was still in progress, and such was his power and authority that he was easily able to persuade others. Whatever instincts he may have had to the contrary, he had convinced himself that the ends justified the means. As he told the Convention on 5 February 1794:

> The basis of popular government during a revolution is both virtue and terror; virtue, without which terror is baneful; terror, without which virtue is powerless. Terror is nothing more than justice, prompt, severe and inflexible. It is thus an emanation of virtue; it is less a principle in itself than a consequence of the general principle of democracy, applied to the most pressing needs of the motherland.

And so, despite everything, he stood for terror; indeed, he personified it. And when, finally, it was for him that the bell tolled, his death proved the most terrible of all.

★

It was inevitable that after the removal of Robespierre from the scene there should be a dramatic swing to the right. The Law of 22 Prairial was repealed; it was even proposed that nobles should no longer be condemned because of their birth, or the clergy for their calling. The Jacobin Club was closed; the red caps of liberty were no longer seen in the streets. Many others whose names had been associated with the Terror followed their leader to the scaffold. It was unfortunate only that the winter of 1794–5 should have been the coldest that anyone could remember: the Seine froze over, starving wolves appeared in the towns and villages, and at the first signs of spring a sudden thaw led to disastrous floods. For the *sans-culottes*, the situation was worse than it had been before the Revolution began. There were more revolts, more angry demonstrations, all of which were savagely put down. Before long the guillotine was as busy as it had ever been.

At this point, to the monarchists, a restoration seemed to be after all a possibility – but not for long. Plans for a rising in the south were discovered and quickly dealt with; and a force of émigrés, provided by the British government with money, uniforms and naval support, actually landed on the south coast of Brittany before being destroyed by the twenty-seven-year-old General Lazare Hoche. Over seven hundred of them, mostly members of the nobility, were shot, in their British uniforms, on the charge of high treason. In Paris, however, the spirit of reaction was as strong as ever. In introducing a new constitution, known as the Constitution of the Year III, in August 1795 François Antoine de Boissy d'Anglas spoke words which might cause comment even today:

> Absolute equality is a chimera. If it existed one would have to assume complete equality in intelligence, virtue, physical strength, education and fortune in all men . . . We must be ruled by the best citizens. And the best are the most learned and the most concerned in the maintenance of law and order. Now, with very few exceptions, you will find such men only among those who own property and are thus attached to the land in which it lies, to the laws which protect it and to the public order by which it is maintained . . . You must therefore guarantee the political rights

of the well-to-do . . . and [deny] unreservedly political rights to
men without property, for if such men ever find themselves seated
among the legislators, they will provoke agitations . . . and in the
end precipitate us into those violent convulsions from which we
have scarcely yet emerged.

Considering the events of the previous six years, the Constitution
of the Year III was a remarkable document indeed. Not only did it
include a comprehensive ban on slavery; it also established a liberal
republic with the franchise based on the payment of taxes, a bicameral legislature and a five-man Directory, who were to wear a
magnificent uniform 'as a protest against sans-culottism'.

There was to be one final insurrection, engineered by the royalists, before the Revolution was genuinely over. They had no
difficulty in drumming up popular support – in Paris the cost of
living was about thirty times higher in 1795 than it had been in
1790 – and by the beginning of October the insurgents were some
25,000 strong. Whom, however, could the Convention trust to
deal with them effectively? After an early disastrous choice it
appointed Paul Barras, who had distinguished himself during the
events of Thermidor; but Barras had little military experience and
it was agreed that he should take on one or more experienced
deputies to advise him. Unhesitatingly, he chose a twenty-six-
year-old officer whom he had known during the royalist siege of
Toulon in 1793 and who immediately swung into action. At 1
a.m. on 5 October – 13 Vendémiaire – this officer took over from
Barras, who willingly surrendered his authority, and despatched a
young lieutenant named Joachim Murat* to fetch forty cannon
from the plain of Sablons – the modern Neuilly. Fortunately, these
arrived before the expected royalist attack, and were strategically
placed at key points around the Pont Neuf, the Pont Royal, the
Place de la Révolution and the Place Vendôme. The major assault
began at about ten in the morning. The forces of the Convention
were outnumbered by about six to one, but the insurgents fell
back when the cannon opened fire. This was what Thomas Carlyle

* Later he was to marry Napoleon's sister Caroline and to become King of
Naples.

was to describe as the 'whiff of grapeshot . . . which blew into space the French Revolution'.

It also made a national hero of Napoleon Bonaparte.

15

A Blessing or a Curse?

1795–1815

Ability is nothing without opportunity.

Napoleon Bonaparte

IT IS A great mistake to assume that because Napoleon Bonaparte was born in Corsica he was of relatively humble origins. His family was in fact descended from minor Tuscan nobility who had settled on the island in the sixteenth century. His father was a distinguished attorney who had served as the official representative of Corsica to the court of Louis XVI, and one of his uncles was a cardinal. He was baptised Napoleone di Buonaparte; but though he gallicised the name in his twenties he remained Corsican through and through. His first language was Corsican, which is much closer to Italian than it is to French. He always spoke French with a heavy Corsican accent, and never mastered its spelling. As to his appearance, we have a detailed description by no less a witness than the famous naturalist and explorer Alexander von Humboldt, who met him at the Institut National in 1798:

> He is small and lean, with a small head, hands small and delicate. His face is more oval than round, hair brown and thin . . . The arch of his eyebrows strong and well curved, so that his forehead protrudes above his nose. His eyes are large and deep-set, nose curved but not hooked. Mouth and chin are very masculine, chin especially strong . . . As he is lean his cheekbones are very pronounced, and all the muscles of his face move when he speaks . . .
>
> His physiology has nothing large about it, or heavy or determined, and he seems to exude more intellectual than moral qualities. He

seems calm, pensive, decisive, relaxed, perceptive and very serious, as if he is committed only to his work . . .

In his youth Napoleon was a fervent Corsican nationalist, a Jacobin and a Republican. It was indeed as a member of the Republican army that he had so distinguished himself in 1793 at Toulon, while the town was under siege by French royalists, assisted by the British and Spanish. His commanding officer, General Jacques François Dugommier, wrote: 'I have no words to describe Bonaparte's merit: much technical skill, an equal degree of intelligence, and too much courage.'

He showed these same qualities in the insurrection of Vendémiaire, when he had taken over the command from Barras. Six months later there was a further takeover, this time of Barras's exquisite Creole mistress Josephine de Beauharnais, whom Napoleon married in a civil ceremony in March 1796; and two days later he left Paris to take command of the Army of Italy. The Italian campaign was another triumph. Piedmont was knocked out in the first fortnight. Austria was now the enemy; but after four successive victories – at Castiglione, Bassano, Arcole and Rivoli – the French were the undisputed masters of Italy. Napoleon then advanced into Austria, where his army had reached Leoben, only some sixty miles from Vienna, before the Austrians eventually sued for peace. On 18 April 1797, at the nearby castle of Eckenwald, a provisional treaty was signed between the twenty-seven-year-old general, acting in the name of the French Directory – although in fact he had never bothered to consult it – and the Austrian Empire. By its terms (details of which remained secret until they were confirmed six months later by the Treaty of Campo Formio) Austria was to renounce all claims to Belgium and to Lombardy, in return for which she would receive Istria, Dalmatia and all the Venetian mainland bounded by the Oglio and Po rivers and the Adriatic.

Napoleon, it need hardly be said, had no conceivable right to dispose in such a way of the territory of a neutral state; but he had left the Venetians in no doubt of their future: they would very soon no longer be a state at all. He now demanded nothing less than the abdication of the entire government and the abandonment of a constitution that had lasted more than a thousand years – the suicide, in fact, of the Republic of Venice. It occurred on Friday 12 May 1797, so that at Campo Formio Austria received far more than she had expected: not just the Venetian terra firma, but the city itself.

Now, briefly, there was peace all over continental Europe. Only England remained an enemy, and England must clearly be invaded and destroyed. The Directory appointed Bonaparte to do just that; but after the best part of a year's consideration he reluctantly decided against it. The expense would be great, the necessary manpower not easy to raise; but the real problem was the French navy. It was in a deplorable state, and certainly no match for the British. There was no French commander who could hold a candle to Hood, Rodney or St Vincent – still less to Nelson.

The alternative was Egypt. As early as July 1797 the Foreign Minister, Charles-Maurice de Talleyrand-Périgord – henceforth to be known as Talleyrand – had proposed an Egyptian expedition, and seven months later he had produced a long memorandum on the subject. There was, inevitably, a pious section about delivering the Egyptian people from the oppression that it had so long endured; worthier of attention was the suggestion that with an army of 20,000 to 25,000, which would land at Alexandria and occupy Cairo, a further expedition might be launched against India – possibly even by means of a hastily dug Suez canal. On 2 March 1798 the Directory gave its formal approval. Not only would the proposal keep the army employed and its terrifying young general at a safe distance from Paris; it also offered an opportunity to take over the British role in India, while providing France with an important new colony in the eastern Mediterranean. Finally, if a little more problematically, it would achieve a major diversion of English sea power to the east, which might make the delayed invasion possible after all.

Napoleon of course accepted the command with enthusiasm. Since his childhood he had been fascinated by the Orient, and he was determined that the expedition should have objectives other than the purely political and military. To this end he recruited no fewer than 167 savants to accompany it, including scientists, mathematicians, astronomers, engineers, architects, painters and draughtsmen. Egypt, he believed, had preserved her ancient mysteries for too long; she was a fruit more than ready for the plucking. The country had been effectively under the Mamelukes★ since 1250. In 1517 it had been conquered by the Turks and absorbed into the Ottoman Empire, a part of which it technically still remained; but now the Mameluke Beys were once again in control. A French invasion would doubtless evoke an indignant protest from the Sultan Selim III in Constantinople; but his empire, though not yet known as 'the sick man of Europe', was a decadent and demoralised shadow of its former self and unlikely to represent much of a threat. Unfortunately there were other risks a good deal more serious. The French transports were poorly armed, their crews practically untrained. Admittedly there was a naval escort of twenty-seven ships of the line and frigates, but Nelson was already known to be cruising in the Mediterranean. Were he to intercept them, their chances of escape – and those of the 31,000 men aboard them – would be negligible.

Napoleon left Toulon in his flagship *L'Orient* on 19 May 1798. His first objective was Malta. The island had been in the possession of the Knights of St John since 1530. The Knights had conscientiously maintained their hospital and had heroically withstood the dreadful Turkish siege of 1565, but as fighters for Christendom they had grown soft. When Bonaparte reached the island on 9 June and sent messages ashore to the German Grand Master Ferdinand Hompesch, demanding the admission of all his ships into the harbour to take on water, he received a reply informing him that, according to the regulations of the Order, states that were at war with other Christian countries might send in only four vessels at a time. A message was returned swiftly from *L'Orient*: 'General Bonaparte is resolved to obtain by force that which ought to have been accorded to him by virtue of the principles of hospitality, the fundamental rule of your Order.'

At dawn on 10 June the assault on the island began. The 550 Knights – nearly half of them were French, and many more too old to fight – resisted for only two days. On the evening of the 12th a

---

★ The Arabic word mameluke means 'slave'. The Mameluke dynasty was descended from slaves, but had taken over Egypt after the fall of the Ayubids (the dynasty of Saladin).

delegation came on board the flagship. The Order would surrender Malta and the neighbouring island of Gozo, so long as the French government used its good offices to find Grand Master Hompesch somewhere appropriate to which he could retire, together with a pension of 300,000 francs★ to enable him to live in a style befitting his rank. Napoleon accepted – though he did absolutely nothing on behalf of Hompesch – and immediately set to work on a programme of reform. In less than a week he managed to convert the island into something tolerably like a French *département*. The number of monasteries was reduced and the power of the clergy drastically curtailed. All gold and silver was removed from the churches, and all the treasure from the Palace of the Knights – which included the famous silver service regularly used by the Order to feed the sick in the hospital[†] – was loaded on to the flagship, to be melted down into 3,500 pounds of bullion for Napoleon's war chest. Three thousand French soldiers were left behind under General Claude Vaubois to provide a garrison, and within a week of its arrival the fleet was ready to continue on its journey. On the 19th Napoleon set sail.

France, however, was not to keep the unhappy island for long. On 3 September, enraged by the behaviour of Vaubois, who had even tried to impose French as the official language and who now proposed to auction the entire contents of the Carmelite church in Medina, the Maltese – led by their clergy – rose in revolt, hurling the French commander of militia out of a window. Vaubois quickly ordered all of his men to Valletta, where he locked the city gates. Thenceforth the French found themselves under siege. The Maltese appealed to the Royal Navy for help, and several British ships arrived to blockade any French vessels that might attempt to relieve the garrison. These were followed shortly afterwards by 1,500 English troops. Vaubois held out until, thanks to the blockade, he had only three days' rations left. He was then allowed an honourable surrender and safe repatriation for the garrison, taking with him – to the

---

★ The franc was introduced as the national currency in 1795, and continued until 1999, when it was replaced by the euro.

† This was the reason why infection was so much lower in Malta than in any other hospitals, all of which used wooden platters pullulating with germs.

further fury of the Maltese, who were not consulted – much of the treasure that his men had looted during their stay.

With the departure of both the Knights and the French, the Maltese found themselves under the authority of a British Civil Commissioner until such time as their future could be settled. In 1802 the Treaty of Amiens – which declared peace between Britain and France, although Napoleon intended to observe it only for as long as it suited him – provided for the return of the island to the Order of St John; the Maltese, however, who had no more love for the Knights than they had for the French, let it be known that their own strong preference was for the security promised by the British crown – which, by the Peace of Paris in 1814, they were finally to obtain.

On the night of 1 July 1798, nearly two weeks after its departure from Malta, the French fleet dropped anchor some seven miles west of Alexandria. The landing of so many men and so much equipment in the small boats, which were all that were available, was a long and complicated task. It began only in the late afternoon of the 2nd, when a storm was already brewing. The vice-admiral, François-Paul Brueys d'Aigaïlliers, had advised delaying the operation until morning, but Napoleon had refused to listen. He himself did not disembark until shortly before midnight. Fortunately for him, there was no resistance until the army reached Alexandria, and even there the crumbling walls and the tiny garrison could do little to delay the inevitable. The whole city proved to be in a state of advanced decay, its population now reduced from the 300,000 that it had boasted in Roman times to a sad and apathetic 6,000. Apart from Pompey's Pillar (which had nothing to do with Pompey) and Cleopatra's Needle (which had no association with Cleopatra)★ there was nothing to evoke its days of glory.

★ The pillar dates from the time of Diocletian at the end of the third century. The obelisk, which had been standing for nearly 1,500 years by Cleopatra's day, was given to the British government by Mohammed Ali in 1819, although it did not reach London's Embankment for another fifty-nine years, until 1878.

To the French army, therefore, the capture of Alexandria came as a sad anticlimax. The July heat was demoralising enough, but men who had expected a rich and magnificent city – with commensurate opportunities for pillage – and who found only a heap of pestiferous hovels felt not only disappointed but betrayed. Napoleon saw that they must be given no time to brood, and decided to march at once on Cairo. Advancing along the western side of the Nile delta, his men captured Rosetta without a struggle (discovering the Rosetta Stone in the process) and on 21 July met the main body of the Mameluke army just below Gezira Island. Napoleon's exhortation to his troops, 'Think, my soldiers – from the tops of these pyramids forty centuries look down upon you!' has gone down in history, but – even if uttered – was hardly necessary: the Battle of the Pyramids was a walkover. Mameluke swords, however valiantly wielded, were no match for French musketry. Some two thousand Egyptians were killed, and twenty-nine Frenchmen. The following day Napoleon entered Cairo – to his men a slight improvement on Alexandria, but scarcely a *vaut-le-voyage*.

Nelson had meanwhile been pursuing the French ships across the Mediterranean. Misled by information that Bonaparte had left Malta three days earlier than he actually did, he had hastened to Alexandria; then, finding to his astonishment no sign of the French fleet, he had sailed off again to search for it along the coast of Syria. It was only around 2.30 p.m. on 1 August that he returned to Egypt, to find thirteen French men-of-war – he himself had fourteen – and four frigates anchored in a two-mile line in Aboukir Bay, one of the mouths of the Nile. But they were still nine miles away; it would take at least another two hours to reach them, and a lot longer still to draw up his own ships in a regular line of battle. Night encounters in those days were hazardous; in the absence of charts there was always a danger of running aground in unknown waters, and a worse one of firing into one's fellows by mistake. Most admirals in such circumstances would have elected to wait until morning; but Nelson was Nelson: seeing that the French were unprepared and that there was a favourable north-west wind running, he decided on an immediate attack. He began by sending four ships inshore along one side of the French line, while he himself in his flagship *Vanguard* led a parallel attack down the offshore side. Each French vessel was thus subjected to a furious cannonade from both sides simultaneously. That was at about six o'clock in the evening; the ensuing battle lasted all the next day and through the following night. By dawn on 3 August all the French ships but four had been destroyed or captured, including *L'Orient*, on which Admiral Brueys had been killed by a cannon shot shortly before the powder exploded. The vessel still lies beneath the waters of Aboukir Bay, together with much of the treasure looted from the palaces and churches of Malta.

Nelson had not only destroyed the French fleet, he had severed Napoleon's line of communication with France, leaving him marooned and frustrating all his plans of conquest in the Middle East. His victory also had a serious effect on French morale – though not, apparently, on Bonaparte's. Almost before the ships' guns had cooled, Bonaparte was at work transforming Egypt into a long-term strategic base. He devised new and more efficient systems of administration and taxation; he established land registries, gave orders for hospitals, improved sanitation and even street lighting. Meanwhile the scientists and engineers whom he had brought with him were put to work on such problems as the purification of the Nile water and the local manufacture of gunpowder.

Where he failed, unsurprisingly, was in his attempts to win the trust and support of the Egyptians. He did his best, taking every opportunity to stress his admiration for Islam; the fact remained that he and his men were not only living off the country, they were behaving as if they owned it. Small-scale revolts were constantly breaking out, with attacks on isolated French garrisons or individual Frenchmen in the street. A more serious uprising in October was put down with brutal efficiency; Napoleon decreed that from that day forward any Egyptian found carrying a firearm was to be beheaded and his body thrown into the Nile. It was no wonder that the longer the occupation continued, the more detested it became.

Beyond the Egyptian frontiers, too, enemies were gathering. On 2 September Sultan Selim declared war on France, and the Turkish governor of Syria, Djezzar ('the Butcher') Pasha, began to raise an army. Rather than risk a Syrian invasion, Napoleon decided to act first. Early in February 1799 he marched his men across the Sinai desert and up into Palestine. On 7 March, Jedda fell; 2,000 Turks and Palestinians were put to the sword, another 2,000 taken down to the sea and shot. Plague was rampant, and in an effort to improve his image after these atrocities Napoleon visited a hospital and, we are told, was ill-advised enough to carry one of the victims out to his grave. He fortunately escaped infection; but as an exercise in public relations his action does not seem to have been outstandingly successful.*

Acre was his next objective; but Acre was well defended, the Turkish commander having enlisted additional support from the British navy under the swashbuckling Commodore Sir Sidney Smith, famous for having escaped from the Temple prison in Paris during the Revolution. For two months the French army besieged the city, but Smith managed to capture the eight gunboats carrying their siege artillery, stores and ammunition. On 10 May Napoleon launched his final assault. It was thrown back with heavy losses, and he had no course but to retreat. By this time the plague had taken hold in his own army. He himself advocated killing all the sick with overdoses of opium, but his chief medical officer refused outright. The hundreds of stretchers considerably slowed the return journey; it was a miserable body of men that finally limped back into Cairo.†

As always, Napoleon did his best to dress up defeat as victory. Turkish prisoners were paraded, captured Turkish flags proudly displayed. What was left of the army, cleaned up as far as possible, staged a triumphal march through Cairo. But no one, least of all the Egyptians, was fooled. The Middle Eastern expedition had been a failure, and had done little for Napoleon's reputation. He was alarmed, too, by reports that Europe was once again at war, that the Italian Cisalpine Republic that he had established two years before was now under Austrian occupation, that the Russian army was on the march and that the domestic situation in France itself was once again critical. For the first time in his career – but not

---

* In some British art gallery – I wish I could remember which – there hangs a large oil painting depicting Napoleon standing among a mass of huddled plague victims on the seashore. It bears the label *The Plage* [*sic*] *at Acre*.

† Reminiscing in later life about Smith's activities in Acre, Napoleon is said to have remarked: 'That man made me miss my destiny.'

the last – he left his army to get home as best it could, and at five o'clock in the morning of 22 August 1799 slipped stealthily from his camp and sailed for France. Not even his successor in command, General Jean-Baptiste Kléber, knew of his departure until he was safely away.

In Paris, the coup d'état of 30 Prairial (18 June) 1799 had expelled the moderates from the Directory and brought in men who were generally considered to be Jacobin extremists, but confusion continued to reign and one of the new directors, Emmanuel Sieyès, declared that only a military dictatorship could prevent a return of the monarchy. '*Je cherche un sabre*,' he said, 'I am looking for a sabre.' That sabre was soon to hand, and from the moment Napoleon arrived in Paris on 14 October – having almost miraculously escaped the British fleet – he and Sieyès started planning a coup of their own. It took place on 18–19 Brumaire (9–10 November), abolished the Directory and established a new government, the Consulate. There were technically three consuls, but effectively only one. The first consul, Napoleon Bonaparte, now resident at the Tuileries, was henceforth master of France.

He spent the winter reorganising the army, and – Russia having by now withdrawn from the anti-French coalition – preparing for a campaign against his principal remaining enemy, Austria. At that moment the Austrians were besieging Genoa, capital of one of his more ephemeral creations, the Ligurian Republic. A lesser general would have marched south from Paris and down the valley of the Rhône; Napoleon turned east at the Alps and led his men over the Great St Bernard Pass, taking the Austrians entirely by surprise. The Austrian general Michael von Melas had no alternative but to leave Genoa and regroup, concentrating all his forces on Alessandria. Napoleon followed them, and on the evening of 13 June 1800 reached the village – it was in fact little more than a farm – of Marengo, two and a half miles south-east of the town.

The encounter that followed almost spelled the end of Napoleon's career. Melas did not wait to be attacked; the following morning, with a force of some 31,000, he lashed out at the 23,000 French, pounding them remorselessly with his eighty guns for over five hours. In the early afternoon their line began to give way: they were forced to retreat nearly four miles to the village of San Giuliano. An Austrian victory seemed certain; strangely enough, however – perhaps because the seventy-one-year-old Melas had now retired to Alessandria, leaving the command to some relatively incapable subordinate – their pursuit was slow, giving Napoleon time to regroup and to welcome substantial reinforcements under General Louis Desaix, who had providentially just then arrived from the south-east. As evening drew on he launched a counter-attack. Desaix was killed almost at once, but his 6,000 men, fresh and rested, gave new spirit to their fellows, and by nightfall the Austrians were in full retreat. When the battle ended they had lost 9,500 men, the French less than 6,000.*

Melas had no choice now but to come to terms, withdrawing all his troops east of the River Mincio and north of the Po, giving the French complete control of the Po valley as far as the Adige. Napoleon, his reputation unstained despite the narrowness of his victory, returned to Paris, where he took over both the military and the civil authority. In 1801 Austria was forced to sign the Treaty of Lunéville, whereby France regained the old frontiers that Julius Caesar had given to Gaul – the Rhine, the Alps and the Pyrenees; and in 1802 the Treaty of Amiens briefly – very briefly – put an end to hostilities between France and Great Britain.

Napoleon's star was now high – and was still rising. As indeed was his ambition; for by now he had set his heart on monarchy. Not of course on making himself king; kings were, after all, what the Revolution had been intended to abolish. But emperors were very different. To Frenchmen steeped in classical history, the Roman Empire – if not every individual emperor – had been wholly admirable, and so an emperor he would be. He presented his ideal of empire as being one based on merit, as opposed to the Bourbon monarchy which depended entirely on birth. In November 1804 a

---

* The news of Napoleon's victory at Marengo reached Rome some hours after the reports of his defeat. The sudden change from celebration to lamentation lends additional drama to Act II of Puccini's *Tosca*.

referendum was held, to approve a change in the status of Napoleon
– he was no longer called Bonaparte – from First Consul to Emperor
of the French. The voting was more reminiscent of the twentieth
century than of the nineteenth: 99.93 per cent in favour, 0.07 per
cent against.

Pope Pius VII, invited to the coronation, found himself in something of a quandary. If he were now to lay a crown on the head of
this Corsican adventurer, his reputation with the princes of Europe
would be destroyed. The Austrian emperor, for example: how would
he react to the spectacle of the Pope crowning an upstart rival,
devoid alike of birth and breeding? But there: Pius knew that he
could not refuse and reluctantly set off, escorted by six cardinals,
across the Alps. On his arrival in Paris he found an unexpected
opportunity to assert his authority: Josephine confessed to him that
she and Napoleon had never had a church wedding, and the Pope
refused point-blank to attend the coronation until they had done
so. Consequently, on the afternoon before the great day, and much
to the bridegroom's disgust, a secret marriage service, without
witnesses, was performed by Napoleon's uncle, Cardinal Fesch. But
the emperor soon had his revenge. On the day of the coronation,
2 December 1804, he first kept the Pope and congregation waiting
a full hour and then personally performed the actual crowning, first
of himself and then of Josephine. Pius was allowed to bless the two
crowns, but that was all: for the rest, he was relegated to the role
of a simple spectator. In David's great painting of the occasion the
papal displeasure is only too obvious.

Unlike most coronations, this one was held in wartime. The
Treaty of Amiens had lasted just fourteen months; France was again
at war with England, and Napoleon was again planning an invasion,
massing a formidable army at Boulogne – the core of what was later
to be known as the Grande Armée. But his problem was the same
as ever – the Royal Navy, which had the seas firmly under its control.
'I do not say', remarked the First Lord of the Admiralty, 'that the
French cannot come. I say only that they cannot come by water.' It
had at one moment been thought possible for French ships to attack
the West Indies, obliging London to send enough vessels to the
Caribbean to make an invasion possible after all; but the British

naval victory off Cape Finisterre in July 1805 and Trafalgar three months later meant that the navy was never again challenged by the French fleet in a major engagement.

It was several weeks before Napoleon received the news of Trafalgar; he had by now given up all hope of invading Britain and had taken his army into Europe, where a navy was unnecessary and where a coalition of states, including Austria and Russia, had been assembled against him. Determined to destroy the Austrian army before its Russian allies could arrive, he led 200,000 French troops across the Rhine and scored a victory at Ulm, which allowed him to enter Vienna in November. Ulm, however, was of minor importance compared with the battle that followed – Austerlitz, fought on 2 December, the greatest triumph of his career, in which he defeated the armies of Austria and Russia, both led by their respective emperors, Francis II and Alexander I. And so the battles continued, in central Europe and later in the Iberian peninsula, victory after victory – over the Prussians at Jena, over the Russians at Friedland, over the British at Corunna, over the Austrians at Wagram.

But then, on 24 June 1812, Napoleon made the biggest mistake of his career: with an army of over 600,000 men, he invaded Russia. Wisely, the Russians avoided pitched battles whenever possible; instead they drew him deeper and deeper into their country, fully aware – in a way the French could never have been – of the power of the Russian winter. There were a few minor skirmishes at Smolensk, but the first real engagement was at Borodino, just outside Moscow, when the Russians made a desperate attempt to defend their capital. Of all the battles of the Napoleonic Wars, Borodino was the bloodiest: a quarter of a million men were engaged, of whom some 70,000 were dead by nightfall. Technically the French were victorious, but it was once again a pyrrhic victory. The French army – or what was left of it – advanced to Moscow, where Napoleon fully expected Tsar Alexander to sue for peace, but the Tsar did nothing of the sort: instead of surrendering the capital, his governor, Feodor Rostopchin, burned it to the ground. Napoleon remained there for five weeks – another disastrous mistake. It was early November when the Grande Armée began its retreat, and by that time winter had set in; on the single night of the 8th/9th, nearly 10,000 men and horses froze to death. By the time the army crossed the Berezina river towards the end of the month, it numbered less than 40,000. Soon after that, the emperor climbed into a sleigh and – for the second time in his career – abandoned his men, leaving them to find their way home as best they could.

Napoleon never recovered from the Russian debacle. In October 1813 there was another calamitous defeat at Leipzig, involving nearly 600,000 men, making it the largest European battle until the First World War. Now, with his back to the wall, the Emperor was obliged to return to Paris and, on 4 April 1814, to abdicate. By the Treaty of Fontainebleau the allies exiled him to Elba, an island of about 12,000 inhabitants off the coast of Tuscany, allowing him complete sovereignty over it and a personal guard of 600 men. Of this he took full advantage: during his nine-month stay he transformed the island – creating a small army and navy, instituting various social and economic reforms, building roads, developing the iron mines and issuing decrees on the modernisation of its agriculture. Meanwhile he watched and waited.*

From his point of view, the situation on the mainland was distinctly encouraging. The Count of Provence – the executed king's younger brother – had proclaimed himself King Louis XVIII, and had arrived in Paris with what he called a charter. This was effectively a bill of rights, including such guarantees as equality before the law, religious toleration, liberty of the press, protection of private property and the abolition of conscription. Following the British pattern, it also provided for a bicameral legislature, consisting of a Chamber of Deputies and a Chamber of Peers. But old Louis – he was already in his sixtieth year – was far from popular. The shrinkage of what had so recently been a great empire to its former borders had caused a good deal of dissatisfaction among the French, who resented the high-handed way Louis and the other returning Bourbon princes

---

* It was while he was on Elba that he heard of the death of Josephine. He had divorced her in 1810 because of her childlessness, and had married the Austrian princess Marie Louise (whom he would never see again); but on hearing the news of her death he locked himself in his room and refused to emerge for two days.

were treating the people in general and the veterans of the Grande Armée in particular. Moreover the great European powers, who were meeting in Vienna to redraw the map of the continent, seemed to be almost continually at loggerheads. What of a possible return to France? He was not closely guarded: escape should not be all that difficult. And then, surely, the soldiers returning from Russia, Germany, Britain and Spain would rally to his colours and provide him with an army far stronger and better trained than anything rustled up by his enemies. And so he took his decision. On 26 February 1815 he slipped out of the harbour in a French brig, *L'Inconstant*, together with as many men as he had been able to muster, landing at Golfe-Juan, between Cannes and Antibes, on 1 March. Knowing that a royalist army would be sent to prevent his reaching Paris and that it would take the obvious route down the valley of the Rhône, he chose the mountain route to the east, through Sisteron and Grenoble, still known today as the Route Napoléon.* The Hundred Days had begun.

It was an extraordinary journey, Napoleon's numbers swelling every day as more and more soldiers joined him. On 5 March, the nominally royalist 5th Infantry Regiment at Grenoble came over to a man; they were joined two days later by the 7th, which had been specifically ordered to intercept him on the road. Napoleon dismounted and walked forward towards them, ripping open his coat. 'If any of you would shoot his Emperor', he cried, 'here I am.' There was a loud chorus of *'Vive l'Empereur!'*: it was all he needed. A few days later, one of his former marshals, Michel Ney – who had earlier remarked that he should be brought to Paris in an iron cage – came over to him with 6,000 men; and on 20 March, in the last stages of exhaustion but triumphant nevertheless, Napoleon arrived at the Tuileries, from which King Louis XVIII had hurriedly departed a few days before.

By this time the Congress of Vienna had declared him an outlaw, and on 25 March 1815, Britain, Russia, Austria and Prussia formed yet another coalition – in fact it was the seventh – against him.

---

* We can still follow every step of his journey. The houses at which the emperor stayed each night are all still standing, each marked with a commemorative plaque.

This set the stage for the last battles of the Napoleonic Wars – which ended, as the world knows, at Waterloo. The hostilities were now directed not against France – where King Louis was now recognised as head of state – but against the person of Napoleon Bonaparte. Rather than leaving the initiative to his enemies, the emperor (as in his own eyes he remained) decided to attack them individually, before the arrival of the Russians and while they were still unprepared for a combined and coordinated invasion. Thus, on 15 June, he led his *armée du nord* across the Belgian frontier, aiming to drive a wedge between the Prussian army under Field Marshal Gebhard von Blücher to the east and the Anglo-Dutch under the Duke of Wellington to the west. There were two preliminary battles, both fought on the 16th. At Quatre Bras Marshal Ney, with 25,000 troops, missed his chance – through a misunderstanding with his chief – of winning a decisive victory; his casualties were fractionally fewer than those of the allies, but the result could only be counted a draw. At Ligny, on the other hand, victory went squarely to the French. Napoleon, with an army of 77,000, successfully dislodged Blücher from the town, forcing him away from Wellington. The field marshal himself lay trapped for several hours under his dead horse but, after having his wounds bathed in a liniment of rhubarb and garlic and further fortified by a liberal dose of schnapps, he was soon able to rejoin his men. The Prussians lost 28,000, including some 12,000 who deserted during the night. French casualties totalled 11,500.

Finally, on 18 June, Waterloo. An hour or two before, there had been a thunderstorm of monsoon proportions; the battle was delayed for several hours while the ground dried out. At 11 a.m. Napoleon promised his officers that they would sleep that night in Brussels, twelve miles away; but six hours later the French had still not managed to drive Wellington from the escarpment on which he stood. Blücher, who had been seriously delayed by Marshal Grouchy – as part of Napoleon's plan to keep the allies separated – arrived in the late afternoon, in spite of his age, his recent wounds and the consequent difficulty of remaining for hours on horseback. Bernard Cornwell writes:

'Forward!' he was quoted as saying. 'I hear you say it's impossible, but it has to be done! I have given my promise to Wellington, and you surely don't want me to break it? Push yourselves, my children, and we'll have victory.' It is impossible not to like Blücher. He was seventy-four years old, still in pain and discomfort from his adventures at Ligny, still stinking of schnapps and of rhubarb liniment, yet he is all enthusiasm and energy. If Napoleon's demeanour that day was one of sullen disdain for an enemy he underestimated, and Wellington's a cold, calculating calmness that hid concern, that of Blücher is all passion.*

With the fate of the battle hanging in the balance – 'a damned close-run thing', as Wellington put it – Blücher and his Prussians saved the day, drawing off Napoleon's badly needed reserves and steadily crushing the French resistance. Their relentless pursuit of the retreating Grande Armée did the rest. But there was another factor too: Napoleon's state of health. There is plenty of evidence that throughout the Hundred Days he was far from being his usual self. He was listless and withdrawn, and by the time he reached Waterloo he seems to have been a good deal worse. He is known to have suffered from excruciating piles, which made it impossible for him to sit for any length of time on a horse. At Waterloo he did indeed ride out on several occasions; but he is said to have spent much of the day sitting in his headquarters, his head in his hands. Had he been at the top of his form, might the battle have gone the other way? We shall never know.

Returning to Paris – Napoleon was not the sort of man to remain in the field with his shattered army – he saw that the game was up. His position was untenable; both the legislature and the people had turned against him. On 22 June he abdicated for the second time – though legally by now he had nothing to abdicate from – in favour of his three-year-old son by Marie Louise, on whom he had conferred the title of King of Rome. He left Paris three days later and settled briefly at Malmaison, Josephine's house on the Seine; on the arrival of the coalition forces a week later he fled to Rochefort

* Bernard Cornwell, *Waterloo: The History of Four Days, Three Armies and Three Battles.*

on the Atlantic coast, in the hope of escaping to America – only to find that, together with all the other Atlantic ports, it was blocked by British ships. In the morning of 15 July he surrendered himself to Captain Frederick Maitland of HMS *Bellerophon*, to whom he entrusted a letter to the Prince Regent:

Rochefort, 13 juillet 1815

Altesse Royale,

En butte aux factions qui divisent mon pays, et à l'inimitié des plus grandes puissances de l'Europe, j'ai consommé ma carrière politique. Je viens, comme Thémistocle,* m'asseoir sur le foyer du peuple britannique; je me mets sous la protection de ses lois, que je réclame de Votre Altesse Royale, comme celle du plus puissant, du plus constant, du plus généreux de mes ennemis.

Napoléon†

What a magnificent letter it is: proud, courteous, tragic and brief – with a note of genuine poetry and a resonance that lingers long after one has finished reading it. And how sad that the Prince Regent did not think it worthy of a reply.

The *Bellerophon* took Napoleon to England, but he was not allowed ashore. Instead, he was transferred to HMS *Northumberland*, which soon afterwards carried him to St Helena. There he was to live for five years in considerable discomfort – the island was rainswept, windswept and hideously damp – dying, probably of stomach cancer, on 5 May 1821.‡

He was only five and a half feet tall, and far from good-looking; for sheer charisma, on the other hand, he was unequalled; and to

---

* Themistocles (524–459 BC) was *archon* – technically head of state – in Athens, but was later ostracised, and entered the service of Persia.

† Your Royal Highness: Exposed as I am to factions which divide my country, and to the hostility of the greatest powers of Europe, I have completed my political career. I come, like Themistocles, to settle at the hearth of the people of Britain. I place myself under the protection of its laws, which I beg from Your Royal Highness, as the most powerful, the most constant, the most generous of my enemies. Napoleon.

‡ There was for many years a popular theory that he was murdered by arsenic poisoning, but recent studies have shown this to be unlikely.

this he added two other vital requirements for greatness, boundless energy and invincible self-confidence. No one in history – not even the dictators of the twentieth century – enjoyed such a reputation. There are old people living still today – the author is one of them – who can still remember being warned as a child: 'If you don't behave, Boney will come and get you!' The Duke of Wellington said that his presence on the battlefield was worth 40,000 soldiers. At the Battle of Auerstadt in 1806, the Prussian forces under King Frederick William III outnumbered the French by more than two to one; but on hearing that the emperor was personally in command the king ordered an immediate retreat that soon turned into a rout. He later discovered that he had been misinformed: the emperor had not been there at all.

Napoleon was not entirely heartless; he loved both his wives, and wrote constantly to Marie Louise from Elba imploring her to join him – little knowing that her family had deliberately provided her with an outstandingly glamorous lover★ to prevent her from even wishing to do so; and he loved his baby son. Yet it cannot be forgotten that twice, first in Egypt and then again in Russia, he abandoned his entire army, leaving it on both occasions to face considerable danger, to say nothing of unspeakable weather conditions; while the number of deaths for which he was personally responsible defies all computation. And yet, in spite of everything, his men loved him and, even when sent to destroy him, rallied unhesitatingly to his cause.

Finally, has any single man had a greater long-term impact on Europe? In France, faced with the chaos and confusion caused by the Revolution and the Terror, he quickly restored peace, political equilibrium and a strong economy; he established religious freedom, while the concordat, which he signed with Pope Pius VII in 1801, restored good relations between Church and state. He maintained low prices for the basic foods; and he created the Code Napoléon of 1804, which remains the basis of French civil law and that of

---

★ Count Adam Albert von Neipperg, who wore a devastating patch over one eye and was to give her three children, the first two while she was still legally married to Napoleon.

nearly thirty other countries as well. In Europe, he left a trail of pillage and destruction; but he also spread the revolutionary ideals of liberty, equality and fraternity the length and breadth of the continent, where such concepts were new and challenging indeed.

16

The Perfect Compromise
1815–48

Do you not feel . . . that the earth is trembling again in Europe?
Do you not feel . . . a whiff of revolution in the air? Can you
be sure what will happen in France, a year, a month, perhaps a
day from now? You cannot; but what you do know is that there
is a tempest on the horizon, and that it is bearing down on you.

Alexis de Tocqueville, to the Chamber of Deputies

I T WAS SAID of the returning Bourbons that they had learned nothing
and forgotten nothing. In many cases this was very largely true, but
it did not altogether apply to King Louis XVIII. He would doubtless
have voted for absolute monarchy if he had had the chance – during
the *ancien régime* he had employed a domestic staff of 390 – but
twenty-three years of exile, first in the Low Countries, then in
Koblenz, Verona, Blankenburg in Brunswick (where he occupied a
two-bedroom apartment over a shop), Courland (in modern Latvia),
Warsaw, Sweden and Hartwell House in Buckinghamshire had taught
him that absolute monarchy had gone for good. His first return to
post-Empire France had been cut dramatically short by the Hundred
Days; his second was something of a triumph. He was welcomed
at Calais by an enthusiastically cheering crowd – which included,
for some unaccountable reason, a party of virgins in white – after
which he boarded his carriage and was pulled, not by horses but
by the local populace, to a service of thanksgiving in the cathedral.*

---

* Considering that he already weighed well over seventeen stone, this was no mean
achievement by the populace. The Prince Regent, fastening the Garter round his leg
three days before, had said that it was like buckling it around anyone else's waist.

On that first return, with his arrival at Cambrai on 26 June 1815, Louis had issued a proclamation promising that those who had served Napoleon during the Hundred Days, 'apart from the instigators', would not be punished. Three days later the Duke of Wellington, then British ambassador in Paris, received a delegation proposing to put a foreign prince on the French throne, but he quickly sent them packing. 'Louis XVIII', he maintained, 'represents the best way to preserve the integrity of France.' And when the king entered his capital on 8 July he was given another rousing welcome, to the point where the duke complained testily that the continuous cheering prevented him from hearing a word His Majesty said. After his second return Louis was determined to stick to his Charter of 1814, but resigned most of his duties to his council. All he wanted was a nice quiet reign, with regular supplies of sufficient food and drink and ample opportunities to swap risqué stories with his friends. To ensure this he was perfectly happy to accept the constitution – though he drew the line at the tricolour cockade – and was delighted to have as his prime minister Prince Talleyrand, who had stood up so brilliantly at the Council of Vienna to champion his defeated country.

If only Louis's family and friends had been like him; alas, they were not. After a quarter of a century in obscurity they longed for vengeance. Talleyrand was succeeded by the Duc de Richelieu, who was accepted by the royal family despite the fact that he had formerly governed the Crimea under his close friend the Tsar. The king's younger brother, the Duc d'Artois, surrounded himself with a fanatical court of his own, his two sons, the dukes of Angoulême and Berry, talking treason from morning till night. Berry was especially vindictive towards Napoleon's marshals: 'Let's go marshal hunting,' he used to say.* Many of the king's friends would have welcomed a return of the Terror, with the gallows of the Old Regime substituting for the guillotine of the Convention, and there were indeed all too many executions. 'If these gentlemen had full

---

* Marshal Michel Ney, 'bravest of the brave', who had had five horses killed under him at Waterloo, was executed by firing squad on 7 December 1815 on a charge of treason. Marshal Brune, Napoleon's Governor of Provence, was butchered and thrown into the Rhône, where his body was used for target practice.

freedom', the king remarked, 'they would end by purging me as well.' This wave of violence was particularly prevalent in the south, where there were at least three hundred lynchings and where, in Marseille, a regiment of Napoleon's Mamelukes preparing to return to Egypt were massacred in their barracks. Meanwhile, in January 1816, all members of the House of Bonaparte were banned from entering France or owning property in the country.

The situation was made more desperate still by the attitude of the allies. The Treaty of Paris that was signed in November 1815 demanded a retraction of France's borders to those of 1790, costing her much valuable territory in the north and east. Then there was to be an army of occupation, to remain for at least three years and possibly five, for which she would be obliged to pay some 150 million francs a year. The French saw the treaty in much the same light as, a century later, the defeated Germans of 1919 would see the Treaty of Versailles. 'After what I've consented to,' remarked the Duc de Richelieu after he had signed it, 'I deserve to go to the scaffold.'

Nobody – except the tiny minority of ardent royalists – liked the monarchy much; but the people of France were prepared to put up with it simply because they were exhausted, and by now sickened by the seemingly constant bloodshed which had left relatively few families in the whole country untouched. Like their ruler, they wanted a quiet life; and a wise government would have given them just that. But the royalists could not bear to see men trained by the Revolution and the Empire occupying high positions in the state – and performing their duties, in all probability, a good deal more efficiently than their royalist predecessors. For some time Louis, assisted by his enlightened chief minister Elie Decazes, was able to keep them under control; but then, on St Valentine's Day 1820, the Duc de Berry was stabbed to death as he emerged from the Paris Opera. The assassin proved to be 'a little weasel-faced mongrel' and rabid Bonapartist who had worked in Napoleon's stables on Elba; and the 'ultras', as they liked to call themselves, were instantly up in arms. The true assassins, they claimed, were those who had bestowed governmental office on the enemies of the Bourbons and the hirelings of Bonaparte.

With all his immediate family in an uproar around him, Louis realised that Decazes would have to go. He bestowed on him a dukedom and appointed him ambassador in London. Richelieu returned to power, supported by the ultras, and immediately clamped down on individual liberties and the freedom of the press. But not even he could last long; when, seven months after the death of her husband, the Duchesse de Berry gave birth to a posthumous son – thus further securing the future of the Bourbon dynasty – the jubilant royalists forced his resignation. They were led by the Comte d'Artois, the king's brother, who had previously promised Richelieu his support; when Richelieu complained, Louis replied: 'What did you expect? He plotted against Louis XVI, he plotted against me, he plotted against you. Soon he'll be plotting against himself.'

Louis was to last another four years, during which a little more sunshine was brought into his life by a lady named Zoé Victoire Talon, Comtesse du Cayla, who visited him every Wednesday.* But in the spring of 1824 his health began rapidly to fail; he was by this time fatter than ever, and a martyr to gout. In the summer his legs were attacked by gangrene, and his neck became so weak that it could no longer support the weight of his head. He was obliged to rest it instead on a cushion in front of him on his desk, which made it difficult indeed for him to maintain the royal dignity during audiences. He died on 16 September – he was the last French monarch to die while still on the throne – and the Comte d'Artois became King Charles X.

The new king was already sixty-seven. He had been the close friend – some said the lover – of Marie Antoinette, with whom he had regularly taken part in the amateur theatricals staged in her private theatre at Versailles. With the beginning of the Revolution he and his family had hurriedly left France at the insistence of his brother the king, and after the death of his wife (Marie-Thérèse of Savoy) in 1804 had spent his years of exile in Edinburgh and London†

---

* It was rumoured that he inhaled snuff from her bosom, a fact which earned for her the nickname of *la tabatière* – the snuffbox.

† There is a blue plaque on the London house at 72 South Audley Street where he lived from 1805 to 1814.

with his mistress Louise de Polastron, generously funded by King George III. The moment he heard of Napoleon's abdication in 1814 he had hurried back to France. He arrived there nearly three months before Louis, for whom in the interim he had acted as Lieutenant General of the Kingdom. During that time he secretly created an ultra-royalist secret police, which was to report back to him, without the king's knowledge, for the next five years.

From the very outset of his reign, it was clear that Charles X was a disaster. Whereas his brother had had the good sense to realise that the days of the *ancien régime* were gone for ever, for Charles it was as if not only the last thirty-five years but the last several centuries had never happened. On 29 May 1825 he had himself anointed in Reims Cathedral, a ceremony which Louis XVIII had scrupulously avoided; and he and his prime minister, Joseph Villèle – ditchwater-dull but ever prepared to do his master's bidding – then retreated so far into the past that even the most ardent of the ultras were moved to protest. When, for example, the proposed law of sacrilege made the theft of sacred vessels punishable by the severing of the hand from the wrist before execution, the historian Chateaubriand remarked on the idiocy of governing as though it were still the year 800, pointing out that if the monarchy continued to make mistakes on such a scale, a republic would surely result. The government grew more and more unpopular until it was beaten at the polls and Villèle had to resign. 'Your forsaking Monsieur de Villèle', the dauphin told his father, 'means that you are taking the first step down from your throne.'

In January 1830 the political situation in France still seems to have been sufficiently stable to allow a foreign adventure, this time a military expedition to Algeria – ostensibly to put an end to worsening piracy in the Mediterranean, but in fact to distract attention from domestic troubles. (There was also an unfortunate incident in which the Turkish viceroy, furious at the French failure to pay debts arising from Napoleon's Egyptian expedition, had struck the French consul in the face with his fly-swatter.) French troops invaded the country and on 5 July 1830 hoisted the tricolour over Algiers; they were to remain there till 1962.

But Charles had other things on his mind. At a meeting of the Chamber of Deputies on 18 March 1830, 221 of its members – a majority of 30 – voted in favour of an address expressing the nation's anxiety at the course the government was taking. The king replied on the following day by dissolving the Chamber, calling for new elections, and shortly afterwards by suspending the constitution. Then, on 25 July, from his residence at Saint-Cloud, he issued four ordinances which further censored the press, dissolved the new Chamber that had just been elected, changed the electoral system in the government's favour and called for further elections in September. Anyone except himself and his prime minister, Jules de Polignac – who claimed to be receiving regular visits from the Virgin Mary – could have seen that this was political suicide: 'still another government', as Chateaubriand put it, 'hurling itself down from the towers of Notre Dame'.

Chateaubriand was proved right all too soon. When *Le Moniteur Universel*, the government newspaper, published the ordinances on 26 July, a rival paper, *Le National*, defied the censorship and published a call to revolt. It was signed by forty-eight journalists from eleven newspapers, led by *Le National*'s founder, a certain Louis-Adolphe Thiers. Born in Marseille in 1797 and only an inch or two over five feet in height, Thiers had first qualified as a lawyer; but his extraordinary energy, combined with his intelligence, his wit and his way with words, made him a natural journalist. In 1823 – by which time, at the age of twenty-six, he had already written the first two volumes of his *History of the French Revolution** – he had met Talleyrand, who had given up all hope for the Bourbon restoration and who saw in the young man a kindred spirit whom he could shape, he believed, into something like his own image. We can imagine him following with interest and approbation the events to follow.

On 28 July the king – who seemed to grow more idiotic with every day that passed – instructed the prefect of police to close down *Le National*, and one of the last survivors of Napoleon's

---

* Another eight volumes were to follow four years later.

former marshals, Auguste Frédéric Marmont,* to re-establish order; but neither command could be carried out. The prefect arrived with workmen who dismantled the printing presses and locked the building; but as soon as he left, the same workers unlocked it again and quickly put the presses back into service. Meanwhile crowds gathered in the gardens of the Palais-Royal; barricades were raised; a group of students unfurled the tricolour on the towers of Notre-Dame. Soon the insurgents had gained control of the entire eastern end of the city. Marmont, receiving no orders or supplies, was powerless; 40,000 of the best French soldiers were away in Algeria and a steady trickle of those under his command was going over to the other side. On the morning of the 29th two regiments followed, and in a few hours the whole army was in flight, from the Tuileries to Saint-Cloud. From his house in the Rue Saint-Florentin on the corner of Place Louis Seize – now the Place de la Concorde – the seventy-six-year-old Talleyrand contemplated the steady procession up the Champs-Elysées. He took out his watch, and announced to his companions: 'Twenty-ninth of July, five minutes past noon: the elder branch of the House of Bourbon has ceased to reign.'

It was in fact not till 2 August that Charles X, surrounded by his family, wrote out his abdication. Even then, he had not entirely given up hope for the future of his line: he appended a proposal that his ten-year-old grandson, the posthumous son of the Duc de Berry, should be immediately proclaimed King Henry V while the Duke of Orléans, as Lieutenant General of the Realm, should act as regent. To this suggestion he received no answer. A considered reply would perhaps have been more polite; but the fact was – as anyone but Charles would have seen – that after the events and the bloodshed of the past three days another Bourbon king would have been out of the question. Even if Orléans had accepted the proposal, the inevitable clashes between the two sides of the family would have made his task impossible; and if the boy had died during the

---

* Perhaps the king should have worried a bit about Marmont. The marshal had recently lost all his money in a hare-brained scheme that involved sewing sheep into overcoats.

Louis XIV reigned for seventy-two years. Despite his many faults, he set his stamp on France as no king had ever done before. Portrait by Hyacinthe Rigaud, 1701.

Louis XV (left) came to the throne at the age of five in 1715. An unimpressive young man, he did not deserve his mistress, Madame de Pompadour (below), on whom he relied absolutely for her intelligence, wise political advice and sparkling wit. Portrait by François Boucher, c.1758.

'We must hope that this game will soon be over.' In a caricature of 1789 satirising the inequality of taxation, an old peasant is depicted as being overburdened by the nobility and the Church.

'Ugliness is power.' Comte de Mirabeau, the most brilliant speaker in the Estates General. Portrait by Joseph Boze.

Fall of the Bastille, 14 July 1789: the Revolution begins.

'The sea-green incorruptible' and the face of the Terror: Maximilien de Robespierre. Contemporary portrait.

Georges Danton, a man of enormous presence and intellect but, like all those pictured on this page, a victim of the guillotine. Contemporary portrait.

Marie Antoinette, a vapid, uneducated princess who – largely because she was Austrian – the French never took to their hearts. Portrait by Elizabeth Vigée Le Brun, 1778.

Louis XVI could have saved the monarchy but made the fatal mistake of identifying with the privileged and ignoring the increasingly influential bourgeoisie. Portrait by Antoine Callet, 1786.

The young Napoleon Bonaparte during the successful Italian campaign of 1796–7. Portrait by Antoine-Jean Gros.

The Battle of the Pyramids, 21 July 1798, was decisive victory against the ruling Mameluke of Egypt. Painting by François Wattea

The consecration of the Emperor Napoleon and the coronation of Empress Josephine (an extremely unhappy Pope Pius VII to the right), 2 December 1904. Detail from a painting by Jacques-Louis David.

Creating the Avenue de l'Opéra, Paris, c.1865.
Georges Haussman and the Emperor Napoleon
together transformed the capital.

The Emperor Napoleon III and the
Empress Eugénie, c.1865.

During the siege of Paris, balloons were used
to communicate with the outside world. Here
one is being inflated in the Place Saint-Pierre,
Montmartre, 23 September 1870.

Captain Alfred Dreyfus. Wrongly accused of treason, he was arrested in January 1895 – the affair was to rock France to its foundations. He was not officially exonerated until 1906.

Parisian taxis waiting to take troops to the Battle of the Marne, September 1914

Delegates negotiate the Treaty of Versailles, May 1919.

Adolf Hitler greets Marshal Philippe Pétain, Montoire-sur-le-Loir, 24 October 1940. (Between them Paul Schmidt, interpreter.)

The bombardment of the French fleet at Mers-el-Kebir, 3 July 1940. The Royal Navy considered this to be the most shameful operation it had ever been called upon to perform.

Winston Churchill and General de Gaulle, Paris, 11 November 1944.

The liberation of Paris: General de Gaulle, 26 August 1944.

regency he would instantly have been accused of poisoning him. A fortnight later the former King Charles X and his family left – hotly pursued by their creditors – for England, on a packet steamer put at their disposal by his successor.*

Louis-Philippe d'Orléans was only a remote cousin of Charles; to find a legitimate royal antecedent we have to go back to Louis XIII, who was in fact his great-great-great-great-grandfather. He was the son of Philippe Egalité, who during the Revolution had voted for the execution of Louis XVI but whose own life had subsequently ended on the guillotine. Louis-Philippe himself had fought with conspicuous courage at Jemappes and later at Valmy, rising to the rank of lieutenant general. The years of exile had not been easy for him. In 1793 he had been obliged to take refuge with his commander, General Dumouriez, in the Austrian camp;† inevitably – though quite unjustly – his reputation had suffered. With his father and two brothers he had kept to the shadows, first in Switzerland and then in Germany, where he had taught at a boys' boarding school at Reichenau on the upper Rhine. This he had to leave in something of a hurry (having made the school cook pregnant‡) and so in 1796 he moved to Scandinavia, staying for almost a year in a remote village in Lapland as the guest of the village priest and travelling widely within the Arctic Circle. There followed four years in the United States, visiting Philadelphia (where he was reunited with his two brothers), Nashville, New York and Boston, during which he met Alexander Hamilton and even George Washington.§

In the autumn of 1797 the three brothers decided to return to

* They went first to Lulworth Castle in Dorset, but soon moved to Holyrood Palace in Edinburgh. In the winter of 1832–3 Emperor Francis I invited them to Prague, but after his death in 1835 they made their way to Gorizia on the Mediterranean. It was there that Charles died of cholera on 6 November 1836.
† See p.213.
‡ So far as we know, this was the only casual affair of his life.
§ He also became friendly with an Indian chief, who accorded him the highest honour the tribe could bestow – sleeping in the chief's wigwam between his grandmother and his aunt.

Europe and travelled to New Orleans, planning to sail first to Havana and then on to Spain. Stopped in the Gulf of Mexico by a British warship, they were taken to Havana anyway – but were quite unable to find a passage onwards to Europe. After a year in Cuba they were expelled by the Spanish authorities, and eventually found a ship bound for Nova Scotia; from there they had to return to New York, from which, finally, they were able to reach England, arriving in January 1800. There they were to stay for the next fifteen years. Louis-Philippe had hoped to marry the Princess Elizabeth, the sixth child and third daughter of George III; but her mother Queen Charlotte drew the line at a Catholic son-in-law so he had to settle for Princess Maria Amalia of Naples and Sicily. The choice was a little awkward perhaps, since she was the niece of Marie Antoinette; but it proved the happiest of marriages. She was to bear him ten children in swift succession.

But Maria Amalia was not the only woman in Louis-Philippe's life. There was another, a good deal closer and perhaps even more important: his sister Adélaïde. She was by no means a beauty, and never seemed much interested in marriage; but she was every bit as intelligent as her brother, and possessed quite remarkable political judgement. For the first fifteen years of their exile the two had been separated, but in 1808 – the year before his marriage – she had made her way to England to find him, and for the rest of their lives they were seldom apart. By an almost incredible stroke of good fortune, Maria Amalia liked her from the start, and the two became best friends; whenever he was away from home, they kept each other company and he would write joint letters addressed to them both.

The question that now arose was a simple one: was he or was he not prepared to accept the position proposed for him by King Charles X? He was not, and for one reason only. He knew that there was no conceivable future for the Bourbons; he would – he must – be king himself. But in such a case, as the monarchists, the republicans and even his own wife and sister objected, he would be a usurper: one who had been trusted to preserve the throne for the rightful king but who had pilfered the crown for himself. Perhaps they were right; but as he persuasively argued, France needed a king, it needed a strong one, it needed him now – and there was no one else available. Besides, he would be a different sort of king, a king without a court. He would not even be King of France; he would be King *of the French*. (Just who, asked his enemies, had consulted the French about this?) But he knew that he was by no means without support. Since the Revolution there had grown up a new and vocal middle class, a class of industrialists, bankers and businessmen, intrigued by the prospect that the franchise was to be doubled to 200,000 and perhaps even seeing themselves with seats in the newly constituted House of Peers provided for in the Charter.★ They, he was sure, would back him to the hilt.

He had one especially valuable champion: Adolphe Thiers, who had already been active in the removal of Charles X and was now convinced that Louis-Philippe of Orléans was the only man to succeed him. Thiers carefully drew up an eight-point manifesto, and plastered it on posters all over Paris. It read as follows:

> Charles X can never again enter Paris; he has caused the people's blood to be shed.
>
> A republic would expose us to dreadful divisions; it would embroil us with Europe.
>
> The Duke of Orleans is a prince devoted to the cause of the Revolution.
>
> The Duke of Orleans has never fought against us.
>
> The Duke of Orleans was at Jemappes.
>
> The Duke of Orleans has carried the tricolour under fire; the Duke of Orleans can carry it again, we want no other.
>
> The Duke of Orleans has declared himself; he accepts the Charter as we have always wanted it.
>
> It is from the French people that he will hold his crown.

Only the penultimate claim was a little premature. Louis-Philippe had not declared himself – so Thiers leaped on his horse and rode off then and there to the duke's house in Neuilly. He has left his own account of what followed. He was disappointed to find the duke absent, but the duchess and her sister-in-law made him

★ See p.241.

welcome and he put the question to them. It was Adélaïde who made the all-important reply: 'If you think that the adhesion of our family can be of use to the Revolution, we give it gladly.' 'Today, Madame,' he replied, 'you have gained the crown for your House.'

The following afternoon Louis-Philippe rode on a snow-white horse in a short procession from the Palais-Royal to the Hôtel de Ville, from which the municipal commission and the seventy-five-year-old Lafayette – whom many were pressing to accept the presidency of a new republic – were acting as the provisional government of Paris. He was, as he well knew, risking his life. The crowds were dense – denser still as the ride went on – and by no means all were friendly. They doubtless contained royalists, republicans and Bonapartists, many of whom would be only too pleased to have done with the House of Orléans for good. More by good luck than anything else he reached the Hôtel de Ville without incident, to find Lafayette on the steps waiting to receive him and to lead him into the Great Hall; but there again his reception was little more than lukewarm, while ominous shouts of '*Vive la République!*' and '*A bas le duc d'Orléans!*' could be heard from the windows looking out on the Place de Grève. It was Lafayette who came to the rescue. With his unfailing gift for the dramatic gesture he seized the corner of a large tricolour flag, gave the other end to Louis-Philippe, and the two advanced side by side on to the balcony, where they warmly embraced each other. It was all that was necessary: Lafayette's towering reputation did the rest. Instantly, the shouts changed to '*Vive le Roi!*' The game was won. Then and there, Louis-Philippe was acclaimed by the people as King of the French.*

During these stirring events Maria Amalia and Adélaïde were still at Neuilly. Clearly they had now to set off for Paris without delay. But the journey was still not without risk, and risks at such a moment were not to be taken. As soon as it was dark, therefore, they and the children crept out of the park at Neuilly and hailed a passing omnibus, on which there was little or no chance of their being

---

* Though he did not technically become king until he took the oath in the Chamber of Deputies on 9 August.

recognised. They arrived safely at the Palais-Royal just before midnight. It was perhaps the only recorded occasion when the family of a man just acclaimed as ruler has used public transport to rejoin him.

There could have been no greater contrast between Louis-Philippe and his predecessor. Charles X had been every inch a king – an absolute monarch, even though a disastrously unsuccessful one. Louis-Philippe had never known a court worthy of the name; all he had known was war, exile and poverty. But just for those reasons he saw himself as the perfect answer to France's present dilemma: a citizen king whose father had voted for the execution of his fourth cousin Louis XVI and then himself ended on the guillotine, he was clearly the perfect compromise between the Revolution and the monarchy. Elaborate protocol and splendid uniforms he avoided as far as possible; he preferred the idea of strolling down the streets with an umbrella, raising his hat to his subjects as he went. It was what we should now recognise as the Scandinavian style, appearing in Europe for the first time; if bicycles had existed, he would surely have ridden one.* He believed in peace, and wanted no more foreign adventures, in Algeria or anywhere else.

A foreign policy, on the other hand, was essential; and that, for Louis-Philippe, meant the closest possible friendship with Britain. It was not just that he had lived there for years and spoke almost perfect English; more important, Britain was exactly what he wanted France to be – a constitutional monarchy founded on liberty. Most of his leading collaborators agreed with him; so did the most venerable of them all, Prince Talleyrand. Talleyrand had represented the revolutionary government in London some forty years before, and several of his old English friends were still alive; now, at the age of seventy-six, he was appointed ambassador, and London gave him an

---

* Alas, the idea did not work in practice. The poet Alfred de Vigny saw him return from a trial walk: 'He arrived . . . in a dreadful state, with his waistcoat undone, his sleeves torn off, and his hat battered by the greetings he had exchanged in the depths of the crowd that submerged him.'

enthusiastic welcome.* He differed from other French ambassadors, however, in one important respect; apart from his official despatches, he also kept up a long private correspondence with Adélaïde, knowing that she would show his letters to the king. Successive foreign ministers objected strongly to this arrangement, but there was nothing they could do.

Talleyrand arrived in London in September 1830 – and immediately found himself in the middle of a crisis. Belgium, which had been combined with Holland by the Congress of Vienna, rose in revolt and demanded independence;† at a conference held in November in London, dominated by Talleyrand and Lord Palmerston, the separation of the two countries was recognised. But now a problem arose: a new country needed a new king. Louis-Philippe wisely refused the suggestion that the crown should go to his own son the Duc de Nemours; the rest of Europe, he knew, would never stand for it. The other leading contender was Prince Leopold of Saxe-Coburg-Saalfeld, whose candidature was not helped by the fact that he was a widower who had been married to the daughter of George IV, and was consequently the uncle of Princess Victoria, heir to the British throne; but objections were at least partly silenced when Talleyrand suggested that Leopold should marry one of Louis-Philippe's three daughters. None of them was particularly keen, but the eldest, Louise, took the plunge and eventually presented her husband – who was twice her age – with two boys and a girl. Leopold was duly selected, and the future of the Belgian royal family was assured.

The two completely separate events of 5–6 June 1832, one tragic and one comic, may not have been particularly important in the history of France, but are perhaps still worth briefly recording here.

---

* His old club, the Travellers, took pity on his increasing infirmity and built him a special banister up the main staircase. It is marked by a brass plaque, and can still be seen today.

† The revolt had begun with a performance of Auber's opera *La Muette de Portici* at the Théâtre de la Monnaie in Brussels. It dealt with the rebellion of Naples against Spain in 1647, and featured a stirring hymn to liberty. The audience began to riot as soon as they left the theatre, and the riot developed into a rebellion. It must be the only case in history of an opera having such an effect.

The 5th saw the funeral of the radical nationalist deputy, General Jean Maximilien Lamarque, who had died a few days before of cholera – an epidemic was then raging in Paris – and the extreme left-wing opposition decided on a public demonstration in the hopes that it might lead to something more. They were not disappointed. The situation soon got out of hand, and for the next two days Paris was virtually under mob rule.* The king hurriedly left Saint-Cloud for Paris, where he distinguished himself by his courage; two days later the situation was once again under control, but at the cost of 150 lives. Meanwhile on 6 June, 300 miles away in the Vendée, another insurrection occurred, engineered almost single-handedly by the quixotic and mildly ridiculous Duchesse de Berry – now disguised as a male peasant – on behalf of her son. Not surprisingly it failed to ignite and the duchess sought refuge at a house in Nantes, in a secret room behind a fireplace. Unfortunately the police who were tracking her down lit a fire in it, and she was forced to surrender. She was then imprisoned in the castle of Blaye on the west coast, where she was almost immediately discovered to be pregnant. The birth of her first child had delighted the monarchists; the imminent arrival of her second embarrassed them considerably and rather put paid to their attempt to portray her as a romantic martyr. But her honour was saved when she was allowed to invent a secret marriage to a chivalrous young nobleman from Naples – to which city she was consequently deported.

The reign of Louis-Philippe was never as calm and peaceful as he had hoped it would be. There were several more insurrections, in Paris, Lyon and elsewhere, all of which were put down without too much difficulty but with inevitable loss of life; there were constant changes of government – in the seven months between August 1834 and February 1835 France had five prime ministers – and on 28 July 1835 the king narrowly escaped assassination. He was riding out

* This is the battle of the barricades described by Victor Hugo, who was caught up in it and made it the climax of *Les Misérables*.

from the Tuileries to review the National Guard, accompanied by his three eldest sons and several of his marshals and ministers, and had reached the Boulevard du Temple when a volley of bullets was fired from an upper window. Eighteen people, including several bystanders, were killed outright; another twenty-two were wounded. Old Marshal Mortier was shot through the head, covering Thiers's white trousers with blood; the Duc de Broglie, then prime minister, was hit in the chest and saved only by his Legion of Honour star. The king himself, however, received nothing but a light graze on the forehead and with his usual courage insisted on continuing the procession. Only at the end of the review in the Place Vendôme, when he fell into the arms of his wife and sister, did he burst into uncontrollable tears.

Meanwhile the National Guard had smashed its way into the house from which the shots had been fired, to discover a rack of twenty-five musket barrels, mounted on a wooden frame so that they could all be fired simultaneously. The assassin had fled, but was quickly found and arrested. He was Joseph Fieschi, a thirty-five-year-old Corsican Bonapartist who had joined forces with two republican terrorists, and had been seriously wounded in the head★ by his own mildly ridiculous weapon, subsequently described by the press – in a phrase that has become almost a cliché in both French and English – as a *machine infernale*. After a show trial that was attended by Talleyrand himself, all three were publicly guillotined before a cheering crowd.

In January 1836 the government of the Duc de Broglie fell, largely because nobody could bear him. By this time Louis-Philippe had gone through seven prime ministers, including a count and four dukes; now at last his choice fell on the man who stood – if only figuratively – head and shoulders above all his predecessors, the commoner Adolphe Thiers. Still only thirty-nine, Thiers had completed the last eight volumes of his *History of the Revolution* in 1827; it had been much praised by Chateaubriand and Stendhal, but

---

★ His head was subsequently examined by a brain specialist; a particularly unpleasant painting of it now hangs in the Musée Carnavalet. No. 50 Boulevard du Temple bears a commemorative plaque.

had found rather less favour in England.* Politically, he started with a major disadvantage: he had no vote. To qualify for the franchise, a man had to pay taxes of at least a thousand francs a year, which meant owning a quite considerable property. Fortunately Thiers was able to arrange for a loan of 100,000 francs, with which he bought a suitable house. In October 1830 he was elected to the Chamber of Deputies where, despite the heavy Provençal accent that he never lost, he developed into a superb speaker; according to Lamartine, 'there was enough gunpowder in his nature to explode six governments'. In 1833 he was elected to the Académie Française at the almost unheard-of age of thirty-six.

But he failed to endear himself to the king. In June 1836 Louis-Philippe survived another assassination attempt – there would be seven altogether during his reign, something of a record – as a result of which he was persuaded not to be present at the inauguration of the Arc de Triomphe, begun by Napoleon but only just completed. The ceremony was performed by Thiers on 29 July,† by which time the relationship between the two men was becoming seriously strained, largely because of the king's insistence on conducting his own foreign policy. Thiers wished France to follow the example of Britain, where the prime minister was responsible for all diplomatic and military affairs, but Louis-Philippe would not hear of it; Thiers felt that he had no choice but to resign – which, the following August, he did.

His two successors, Count Louis-Mathieu Molé and François Guizot, were also outstanding figures, though very different in character: one a Parisian Catholic, the other a Protestant from Nîmes. Molé had been a staunch Bonapartist in his youth, while Guizot – if only because he was six years younger – had escaped that taint and was a committed royalist. During the years of the

---

* The historian George Saintsbury wrote in the *Encyclopaedia Britannica* (11th edition): 'Thiers's historical work is marked by extreme inaccuracy, by prejudice which passes the limits of accidental unfairness, and by an almost complete indifference to the merits as compared with the successes of his heroes.'

† Louis-Philippe's first public appearance after the assassination attempt was on 25 October, when the great obelisk from Luxor, gift of the Khedive Mohammed Ali, was erected in the Place de la Concorde.

Empire he had stayed well clear of politics and devoted himself to literature, becoming professor of modern history at the Sorbonne and producing a translation of Gibbon's six-volume *History of the Decline and Fall of the Roman Empire*; during the Hundred Days he had followed Louis XVIII into exile in Ghent. There was, however, one formative experience that he shared with Molé, and shared also with their sovereign: all three of their fathers had died on the guillotine.

Soon after Molé had succeeded Thiers as prime minister, in April 1837, the engagement was announced between the king's eldest son, the Duke of Orléans, and Princess Helena of Mecklenburg-Schwerin. Blond and blue-eyed, the groom was unusually handsome, and despite somewhat aggressive political ambitions was a good deal more popular than his father. The betrothal was celebrated by an amnesty of all political prisoners and by the reopening of the Palace of Versailles. The building had been sacked during the Revolution and most of its contents sold by auction; it was now restored (and where necessary rebuilt) at the king's personal expense, its completion celebrated by a banquet for 1,500 guests. The marriage proved an outstandingly happy one, and over the next five years the princess was to bear her husband two sons, thus ensuring the Orléans line. But all too soon came tragedy. On 13 July 1842 the young duke, still only thirty-one, was killed in a carriage accident. The family never really recovered from the blow. 'It should have been me!' the king would murmur over and over again.

The year 1840 saw the second ministry of Thiers – who had by this time married the daughter of his creditor and so expunged his 100,000-franc debt. Like his first ministry, it was short-lived, lasting only seven months, but it gave rise to one magnificent event – the return to France of the body of Napoleon Bonaparte. Guizot, who had recently been appointed ambassador in London – all his life he had been a passionate anglophile – was instructed to obtain permission from Lord Palmerston to bring it back from St Helena. To Palmerston the idea seemed mildly ridiculous, but he could hardly refuse; and on 7 July the Duc de Joinville, Louis-Philippe's third son, was despatched in a frigate to the island to fetch it. After the ship docked at Cherbourg the coffin was loaded on to a black-painted barge and carried slowly up the Seine as far as Courbevoie, where it was transferred to an immense carriage draped in purple velvet and hung with battle flags. On 15 December it was trundled slowly down the Champs-Elysées to the Invalides, where the king was waiting to receive it. Twenty years later the work was completed in the crypt beneath the dome, where the gargantuan sarcophagus can still be seen today, magnificently out of proportion to the pint-size body resting within it.

Guizot's embassy in London proved all too short. He was recalled to Paris in October to join a government headed by the seventy-one-year-old Jean-de-Dieu Soult; but Soult, after a magnificent career that had taken him from being one of Napoleon's marshals – he had been chief of staff to the emperor through the Waterloo campaign – to three times prime minister, was now declining fast, and within a short time Guizot, though technically only minister for foreign affairs, was effectively in control. It was he, therefore, who was responsible for the arrangements for the visit of Queen Victoria in September 1843 – the first time a British sovereign had set foot on French soil since the Field of the Cloth of Gold. After Princess Louise's marriage to Prince Leopold there had been two more alliances between Louis-Philippe's children and members of the House of Coburg, so the families felt closely related; and to emphasise the personal and domestic nature of the meeting it was agreed that Victoria and Albert should not even go to Paris; they stayed at Louis-Philippe's country house, the Château d'Eu near Le Tréport. The visit lasted for five full days and was a huge success, to the point where the king actually suggested that it should become an annual event, which it very nearly did. He himself visited England in 1844 – the first time a French king had stepped on English soil since the captive John II had been taken there as a prisoner after the Battle of Poitiers in 1356 – and Victoria was briefly at the Château d'Eu again in 1845. Then, however, the exchange stopped. Events were closing in.

In Paris, and indeed in France as a whole, dissatisfaction was once more on the march. With increasing age the Citizen-King, as he still liked to call himself, was veering further and further to the right, determined as always to govern as well as to reign and to choose his own ministers. Thanks to men of the calibre of Thiers and Guizot and to the extremely limited suffrage – which meant that he had the voters on his side – he was able to limp on for a little longer, but citizen-kings are almost by definition devoid of charisma and somehow he had never been really popular. Now, with the republicans, the royalist supporters of the Bourbons and the Bonapartists all clamouring for his abdication, he was beginning to fear that his reign could be approaching its end. It might have been thought that with Napoleon now dead for nearly a quarter of a century and his son for some fifteen years, the Bonapartist threat had diminished; but Louis-Napoleon, the Emperor's nephew,* had already attempted two coups d'état, the first in 1835 and another in 1840. He had then been sentenced to life imprisonment; but in 1846, with his political ambitions as firm as ever, he had escaped to England – where he could be trusted to stir up trouble. That same year France had suffered a serious financial crisis and a disastrous harvest. The still rudimentary railway system hindered rather than assisted attempts to provide aid, and the peasant rebellions that followed were mercilessly put down. Perhaps a third of Paris was on the dole, and writers like Pierre-Joseph Proudhon ('Property is theft!') were not making things any easier.

For Louis-Philippe personally, the greatest blow – and one that may well have lost him his throne – was the death, on the last day of 1847, of his sister Adélaïde. She was just seventy. As may be imagined, he was devastated. The two had met every evening in his study for long discussions on the problems of the day. For eighteen years he had relied implicitly on her wisdom, her courage, her unfailing political instincts; now, just when he was to need them most, they were gone. He was still in shock when, just six weeks later, the storm broke.

The year 1848 was the year of revolutions; that which was about

---

* He was – or was assumed to be – the son of Napoleon's brother Louis and Josephine's daughter Hortense de Beauharnais.

to occur in Paris would be one of at least fourteen in Europe.★ But for some time Louis-Philippe found it hard to understand that a kingdom like his own, itself founded on a revolution, should be overthrown by another. In the event of a genuine uprising, on the other hand, he was far from certain of his ability to deal with it. He worried in particular over the loyalty of the National Guard. This was separate from the army and was used for policing and for a military reserve. It had previously enjoyed his total trust – having performed magnificently, for example, during the riots of 1832. But times had changed: although the National Guard was much as it had always been, popular feeling had swung against the monarchy and the Guard had swung with it.

And there was another problem. Because political demonstrations had been prohibited, the various opposition parties had begun to hold a series of fund-raising 'banquets' – which also of course provided a legal outlet for criticism of the regime. So dangerous did these occasions become that in February 1848 they too were banned. For the Parisians this was the last straw. At noon on 22 February they swarmed out into the streets, shouting, '*A bas Guizot!*' and '*Vive la Réforme!*'. It was not long before fighting broke out. On the following day Guizot resigned, and a large crowd gathered outside the Foreign Ministry. An officer tried to block their path, but those in front were being pushed by those behind. He then gave the order to fix bayonets, and while this was being done a soldier, possibly accidentally, fired his musket – at which his fellows lost their heads and began firing into the crowd. Fifty-two people were killed. And now the barricades went up, and chaos reigned. Just as the king had feared, the National Guard began to crumble; and it became clear to him that if he were to save his throne he must order the army to fire on the Guard – a step which would effectively lead to civil war. This – like Louis XVI in 1789 – he refused to contemplate. The only alternative was to abdicate, which on 24 February 1848

★ The first was in Palermo in January. In Italy alone, revolutions then occurred in Naples, Rome, Venice, Florence, Lucca, Parma, Modena and Milan; in northern and central Europe, apart from Paris, there would be uprisings in Vienna, Warsaw, Cracow and Budapest.

he did – in favour of his nine-year-old grandson the Comte de Paris.

He had hoped to retire to the Château d'Eu; but early the following morning he was told that his grandson had been rejected and a republic proclaimed. What his own position would be in this republic he had no idea, and no intention of finding out. He and Maria Amalia, with their daughter-in-law the Duchesse de Nemours and her children, and only fifteen francs between them, arrived that evening at Honfleur where, under impenetrable aliases and with the help of the British Consul in Le Havre, they boarded a ship for England. There, within hours of their arrival at Newhaven, they received a message from Queen Victoria offering them Claremont House in Surrey. They were shortly afterwards joined there by nearly all the rest of the family and their troubles seemed to be over; but all too soon tragedy struck again. The house had been uninhabited since 1817, and over the past thirty years the lead piping had poisoned the water supply. Nearly all the inhabitants were severely affected and to three members of the household the contamination proved fatal. The king lived another two years, but his health was by now declining fast. He died at Claremont on 26 August 1850. Maria Amalia survived there for another sixteen years, finally expiring in 1866, aged eighty-three.

Louis-Philippe, it comes as something of a surprise to realise, was one of the best kings France ever had – a king who deserved from his country far more than he ever received. He succeeded where all his predecessors had failed, presenting France with a viable constitutional monarchy which lasted for nearly twenty years and might well have endured a good while longer; he had given the French some of the happiest years in their history. His reward was exile, never again to see the country that he loved and for which he had worked so hard. Sadly and strangely, he has also been neglected by history: compared to Napoleon I and III, there are few books devoted to Louis-Philippe and Adélaïde. Those last two words are important: his sister's contribution was always vital, to the point where arguments still continue as to whether, if she had lived, she might have saved the kingdom, giving her brother an injection of hope and strength at the moment when his confidence failed. We shall never know, but the question is academic. All that can be said is that their country owes the two of them a huge debt – and that that debt has been ill repaid.

17

'A symbol of national glory'
1848–52

Because we have had a Napoleon the Great, must we now have
a Napoleon the Little?

Victor Hugo

THE OVERTHROW OF Louis-Philippe left France once again in
a quandary: who or what was to be put in his place? The
Second French Republic was duly proclaimed, in the name of a
provisional government, by the poet and statesman Alphonse de
Lamartine, but from the beginning it was split down the middle
into two hostile groups: the *National*, based at the Palais Bourbon★
and represented by Lamartine himself, who wanted a normal republic
based on traditional institutions, with early elections to decide who
was to run it; and the *Réforme*, based at the Hôtel de Ville and
headed by the extreme left-wing Louis Blanc, who sought something
a good deal more drastic – a proto-communist reform of society,
with an equalisation of wages and a merging of personal interests
in the common good. They also wanted elections to be delayed
while plans for this new order were worked out. The *National* called
for the retention of the Tricolour; the *Réforme* for the adoption of
the Red Flag. Tension grew, until in June there was a minor three-day
civil war between the eastern and the western quarters of Paris, with
the inevitable loss of life. 'France needs a Napoleon', wrote the
Duke of Wellington, 'but I cannot yet see him.'

In fact he was nearer than the duke knew. After the failure of his
second attempted coup Prince Louis-Napoleon had spent six years

★ Now the Assemblée Nationale.

in prison at the fortress of Ham, fully aware that the popularity of his uncle was once again increasing. Huge crowds had gathered in Paris when the emperor's remains were returned to the capital in December 1840 and received by Louis-Philippe; the time was clearly soon coming when he must make a third attempt at power – and this time he would be successful. On 25 May 1846, with the help of friends outside, he disguised himself as a labourer and simply walked out of the prison. A carriage was waiting to drive him to the coast, where he had arranged for a boat to take him to England.

The moment he heard of the 1848 revolution and the abdication of Louis-Philippe, he decided to return to France: the two actually passed each other in mid-Channel. On arrival he wrote at once to Lamartine, saying that he was in France 'without any other ambition than that of serving my country'. Lamartine replied politely, asking him to stay away from Paris until the city was calmer, 'and on no account to return before the elections'. At this point Louis-Napoleon had no intention of making trouble and obediently took ship back to England; but by the early summer he was in France again to stand for the elections on 4 June, when candidates could run in several departments together. He was elected in no fewer than four, though in Paris he was narrowly beaten by Adolphe Thiers and Victor Hugo.

Lamartine's reaction to this news was somehow symptomatic of the hopeless confusion that the Second Republic was never able to overcome. He announced that the law of 1832 banning Louis-Napoleon from setting foot in France was still in effect, and ordered his arrest if he appeared in any of the departments for which he had been elected. Once again the prince backed down, declining to take his seat. 'My name', he wrote, 'is a symbol of national glory, and I should be sincerely grieved if it were used to worsen the disorders and divisions of the nation.' His advisers all told him that he was being unduly cautious; he had been legally elected and the government could hardly have prevented him taking his seat. Once again, however, he was proved right: in June there was yet another insurrection, when it was announced that the government intended to close the National Workshops, recently created by Louis Blanc to provide work for the countless unemployed. (They had been a failure from the start, providing only dead-end jobs that brought in barely enough money for survival.) The National Guard under General Louis Cavaignac was called out to quell the rioters – which it did, but only at enormous cost. Killed and injured amounted to 10,000, while some 4,000 of the insurgents were deported to Algeria. And that was the end of the *Réforme*.

Louis-Napoleon's absence from Paris saved him from connection either with the uprising itself or with the brutality with which it was put down. He was still in London when new elections for the National Assembly were held, but nevertheless stood as a candidate for thirteen departments. He was elected in five, in Paris receiving 110,000 votes, the highest number gained by any candidate. He hurried back to the capital on 24 September,* and this time took his place in the Assembly. In just seven months his situation had changed from that of an exile in London to being one of the leading figures on the French political scene.

The new constitution of the Second Republic called for a president elected not by the Assembly but by popular vote through universal male suffrage. The winning candidate would serve for four years, after which he could not be immediately re-elected. The elections were scheduled for 10–11 December 1848, and Louis-Napoleon at once declared himself a candidate. There were four contestants – they included Lamartine, who had previously considered himself a certainty, but whose popularity was by now much reduced – and his only serious rival was General Cavaignac, who was serving as temporary head of state. Cavaignac was optimistic for his own chances. The prince was a poor speaker: his slow monotone was distinctly soporific, and the faint German accent that he never lost – the legacy of his childhood years in exile in Switzerland – did little to endear him to his audiences. 'He's a turkey,' murmured one of his enemies, 'even if he does think he's an eagle.' He was in any case unlikely to gain more than 50 per cent of the votes, in which case the election would be referred to the Assembly, where Cavaignac was certain to prevail.

* So hasty was his departure that, when his landlord came to take back the house he had rented in King Street, St James's, he had found the bed left unmade and the water still in the bath.

But the general was in for a surprise. When the results were counted, Louis-Napoleon was found to have won 74 per cent of the total, over 5.5 million. (Lamartine scored just 17,000.) He moved at once to the Elysée Palace, where in the Grand Salon he hung a portrait of his uncle in coronation robes. To every Parisian the symbolism was clear. The kings of France had lived at the Tuileries; the Elysée had been occupied by the emperor, and was now occupied by his nephew and successor.* Louis-Napoleon was, he announced, to bear the title of Prince-President; he was to be addressed as *Altesse* (Highness), or alternatively as *Monseigneur*.

And the Elysée had another advantage too: it enabled the bachelor prince-president to install his beloved mistress in a nearby house at 23 Rue du Cirque. He had first met Harriet Howard at a party given by Lady Blessington in London in 1846. The daughter of a bootmaker and the granddaughter of the owner of the Castle Hotel in Brighton, she had been left a considerable fortune by a former lover, and soon became not only Louis-Napoleon's mistress but his principal financial backer. And she was even more than that: she provided him with a home. The Elysée was cold, impersonal and lonely: three minutes could transport the prince-president to the Rue du Cirque, where he could settle down with Harriet and, quite often, one or two other close friends – including his American dentist, Dr Thomas Evans, of whom we shall be hearing more in the next chapter – doing all the things that relaxed him most: smoking a cigarette, drinking coffee, talking English and playing with his dog.

All too soon, however, he had an international crisis on his hands. The year of revolutions, 1848, had proved disastrous to Austria. Her chancellor, Prince Metternich, had resigned and taken to his heels, leaving the country in chaos. The Italian patriots and champions of unification had seized their chance: now was the moment to free northern Italy once and for all from Austrian occupation. In Milan,

---

* The Tuileries Palace was to be burnt down during the Commune in 1871. Since 1873 the Elysée has been the official residence of the President of the Republic.

the great insurrection known to all Italians as the *cinque giornate* – the five days of 18–22 March – had driven the Austrians from the city and instituted a republican government. On the last of those days, in Turin, a stirring front-page article had appeared in the newspaper *Il Risorgimento*, written by its editor, Count Camillo Cavour. 'The supreme hour has sounded,' he wrote. 'One way alone is open for the nation, for the government, for the King. War!'

His king, Charles Albert of Savoy, responded at once, as did Grand Duke Leopold of Tuscany and King Ferdinand of Naples. Pope Pius IX, on the other hand, was appalled. How could he possibly condone a policy of such naked aggression, against a Catholic country too? In any case, the last thing he wanted was a united Italy; apart from anything else, what would then become of the Papal States? Obviously he must make his position clear. He did so in his so-called Allocution of 29 April 1848. Far from leading the campaign for a united Italy, he declared, he actively opposed it. God-fearing Italians should forget the whole idea and pledge their loyalty once again to their individual princes.

The news of the Allocution was received with horror by all Italian patriots. The Pope's popularity disappeared overnight; now it was his turn to look revolution in the face. For seven months he struggled to hold the situation; but when on 13 November his chief minister, Count Pellegrino Rossi, was hacked to death as he was entering the Chancellery, Pius realised that – not for the first time – Rome was no longer safe for its pope. On the 24th, aided by the French ambassador and disguised as a simple priest, he fled to Gaeta – which was in Neapolitan territory, and where King Ferdinand gave him a warm welcome. His hurried departure took Rome by surprise. When he refused several appeals to return, Count Rossi's courageous successor Giuseppe Galletti called for the formation of a Roman Constituent Assembly, of 200 elected members, to meet on 5 February 1849. Time was short, but 142 members duly presented themselves on the appointed day. On the 9th, at two o'clock in the morning, the Assembly voted – by 120 votes to 10, with 12 abstentions – to put an end to the temporal power of the Pope for ever and to establish a Roman republic. The debate was dominated by a forty-one-year-old adventurer named Giuseppe Garibaldi.

Born in Nice – which would be ceded to France only in 1860 – Garibaldi was a Piedmontese, who had started his life as a merchant seaman. Always a man of action, in 1834 he was involved in an unsuccessful mutiny, and a warrant was issued for his arrest. Just in time he managed to escape to France; meanwhile, in Turin, he was sentenced in absentia to death for high treason. In December 1835 he sailed for South America, and a few years later was put in charge of the Uruguayan navy, also taking command of a legion of Italian exiles – the first of the so-called redshirts, with whom his name was ever afterwards associated. By now he had become a professional rebel, whose experience in guerrilla warfare was to stand him in good stead in the years to come.

The moment he heard of the revolutions of 1848, Garibaldi gathered sixty of his redshirts and took the next ship back to Italy. His initial offers to fight for the Pope and for Piedmont having both been rejected – Charles Albert, in particular, would not have forgotten that he was under sentence of death – he headed for Milan and immediately plunged into the fray; then, on hearing of the flight of the Pope, he hurried at once with his troop of volunteers to Rome. He was elected a member of the new Assembly, and it was he who formally proposed that Rome should be an independent republic.

At first the Piedmontese army had enjoyed a measure of success. On 24 July 1848, however, Charles Albert was routed at Custoza, a few miles from Verona. He fell back on Milan, with the old Austrian Marshal Josef Radetzky★ in hot pursuit; and on 4 August he asked for an armistice. Two days later the Milanese also surrendered, and the indomitable old marshal led his army back into the city. The first phase of the war was over, and Austria was clearly the victor. It was not only that she was back in undisputed control of Venetia-Lombardy: the forces of the counter-revolution were triumphant across mainland Italy.

★ Radetzky was now eighty-three. He had taken part in the very first Austrian campaigns against Napoleon more than half a century before, and had been chief of staff at the Battle of Leipzig in 1813. He had fought in seventeen campaigns, had been wounded seven times and had had nine horses shot from under him.

In Gaeta on 18 February 1849, Pope Pius addressed a formal appeal for help – to France, Austria, Spain and Naples. By none of the four was he to go unheard; to the Assembly in Rome, however, the greatest danger was France – whose response must clearly depend on the complexion of the recently formed French republic and, in particular, on its newly elected prince-president. Nearly twenty years before, Louis-Napoleon had been implicated in an anti-papal plot and expelled from Rome; he still cherished little affection for the papacy. But it was clear to him that Austria was more powerful than ever in Italy; how could he contemplate the possibility of the Austrians now marching south and restoring the Pope on their own terms? If he were to take no action, that – he had no doubt at all – was exactly what they would do. And having done it, why should they stop at Rome? The Kingdom of Naples, already tottering, might prove an irresistible attraction.

He gave his orders accordingly, and on 25 April 1849 General Nicolas Oudinot – the son of one of Napoleon's marshals – landed with a force of about nine thousand at Civitavecchia and set off on the forty-five-mile march to Rome. From the start he was under a misapprehension. He had been led to believe that the Roman republic had been imposed by a small group of revolutionaries on an unwilling people and would soon be overturned; he and his men would consequently be welcomed as liberators. His orders were to grant the Assembly no formal recognition but to occupy the city peacefully, if possible without firing a shot.

He was quickly disillusioned. There was no welcome awaiting him; the Romans were preparing themselves for the fight. Their own forces, such as they were, consisted of the regular papal troops of the line, the *carabinieri* – a special corps of the army entrusted with police duties – the 1,000-strong Civic Guard, the volunteer regiments raised in the city, which amounted to 1,400 and – by no means the least formidable – the populace itself, with every weapon it could lay its hands on. But their total numbers were still relatively small, and great was their jubilation when on 27 April Garibaldi rode into the city at the head of 1,300 legionaries he had recruited in the Romagna. Two days later there followed a regiment of Lombard *bersaglieri* with their distinctive broad-brimmed hats and swaying plumes of black-green cocks' feathers. The defenders were gathering in strength, but the odds were still heavily against them and they knew it.

The first battle for Rome was fought on 30 April. The French defeat was due entirely to Oudinot's ignorance and misunderstanding of the situation. He had brought no siege guns with him, nor any scaling ladders; it was only when his column, advancing towards the Vatican and the Janiculum Hill, was greeted by bursts of cannon-fire that he began to realise the danger of his position. Soon afterwards Garibaldi's legion swept down upon him, swiftly followed by the *bersaglieri*. For six hours he and his men fought back as best they could, but as evening fell they could only admit defeat and take the long road back to Civitavecchia. They had lost 500 killed and wounded, with 365 taken prisoner; but perhaps the humiliation had been worst of all. Rome was clearly going to be a much tougher nut to crack than they had expected.

Nevertheless, they were determined to crack it. Little more than a month later – during which time Garibaldi with his legionaries and the *bersaglieri* had headed south to meet an invading Neapolitan army – Oudinot had received the reinforcements he had requested, and it was with 20,000 men behind him and vastly improved armament that, on 3 June, he marched on Rome for the second time. Now, it was clear, the city was effectively doomed. The defenders fought back bravely, but by the end of the month they could continue no longer. On 30 June Garibaldi appeared at the Assembly, covered in dust, his red shirt caked with blood and sweat. Surrender, he declared, was out of the question. So was street fighting: when Trastevere – the area of Rome lying west of the Tiber – was abandoned, as it would have to be, French guns could simply destroy the city. The defenders could only take to the hills. '*Dovunque saremo,*' he told them, '*colà sarà Roma.*' ('Wherever we are, there shall be Rome.') At last the Pope could safely return, but he did so only on the understanding that the prince-president left a French garrison to protect him. Louis-Napoleon had taken on a huge new responsibility – one that he would bitterly regret.

★

At home, much of the prince-president's time was devoted to consolidating his position, not just in Paris but all over France. This meant showing himself in as many cities and towns – and even villages – as he could. He travelled the length and breadth of the country, quite often by train (the railway network was expanding with astonishing speed), opening new stretches of line, visiting hospitals and schools, presenting colours to regiments, constantly building up his image as the new Napoleon and inwardly rejoicing when – as was happening with increasing frequency – he heard shouts of '*Vive l'Empereur!*' In October 1849 he felt strong enough to dismiss his prime minister and take over the job himself. 'The name of Napoleon', he wrote in a message to the National Assembly, 'is in itself a programme. It means: at home, order, authority, religion and the welfare of the people; abroad, national dignity.'

But there was, as he well knew, trouble ahead. The constitution of the Republic allowed him only a four-year term, which was not immediately renewable. He would have to resign the presidency in 1852, whether he liked it or not. Since he had no intention of allowing this to happen, there were only two alternatives open to him: either to have the law changed, or to take over with a coup d'état. Anxious to cause as little disturbance as possible, he naturally favoured the first and made a formal appeal to the Assembly. The debate was long and heated, but the motion was lost. A coup, in consequence, it would have to be. Plans were carefully laid; the date finally decided upon was 2 December 1851, the anniversary of Napoleon I's coronation in 1804 and of his triumph at Austerlitz a year later.

The element of surprise was complete. On 1 December Louis-Napoleon held his usual Monday-evening reception at the Elysée. At about half-past ten, when the last of his guests had departed, he retired to his study with perhaps half a dozen of his most trusted supporters, to whom he handed the texts of three different proclamations. Their message was simple enough. The Assembly was trying to seize the power that the prince-president held directly from the people of France. It was his duty to protect and preserve the Republic. He had re-established universal male suffrage (which the Assembly had drastically reduced eighteen months before) and now proposed to hold a plebiscite in two weeks' time so that the people – the only sovereign he recognised – could decide for themselves on their future. These announcements, he ordered, were to be pasted up all over Paris by morning. And that would be all. Louis-Napoleon shook hands with each in turn and went to bed.

The next morning all went like clockwork. At about ten o'clock, some 300 deputies arrived at the Palais-Bourbon to find it closed. They moved on to a local town hall to protest, but in vain: before long the police arrived and arrested the lot. At eleven the prince-president rode out of the Elysée on a huge black stallion, with Jerome, former King of Westphalia and Napoleon I's youngest brother, riding beside him. Jerome was now sixty-seven, and of all the brothers looked most like the emperor – an effect still further increased by his habit of keeping his hand tucked into his waistcoat in true Napoleonic style. Cries of '*Vive l'Empereur!*' were now more frequent than ever.

The coup d'état was almost over, but not quite. The opposition – Victor Hugo among them – continued their protests and a few barricades appeared in the time-honoured fashion; but the protesters were for the most part of the middle class, and they failed utterly to persuade the mob to join them. On 4 December the Bonapartists struck: 30,000 troops marched into Paris and smashed the remaining barricades. If anyone objected, he was shot on the spot. It was unfortunate that in the afternoon the firing got out of hand; the soldiers and the artillery somehow panicked and ransacked two of the most popular cafés on the Boulevard des Italiens, killing nearly a hundred perfectly innocent customers. The *massacre sur les boulevards* made a sad ending to an otherwise remarkably bloodless operation.*

As for the promised plebiscite, the result was by now a foregone conclusion. It was, as expected, a landslide: over 7 million for the prince-president and less than 600,000 against. France was still technically a republic, but with every day that passed Louis-Napoleon

---

* Not so bloodless in the provinces, alas, where there were peasant risings in the south and south-east, as a result of which over 9,000 were deported to Algeria and 239 to French Guiana. Some 27,000 alleged protesters were arrested and tried. In 1859, when an amnesty was at last declared, 1,800 were still serving their sentences. Louis-Napoleon never forgave himself for such pitiless repression.

was becoming more imperial. On New Year's Day 1852 he moved from the Elysée to the Tuileries; the initials *R.F.* (République Française) were replaced on the state box at the Opera with *L.N.* (Louis-Napoleon); new coins bore his profile; and a few sharp eyes noticed that the official flagpoles were now once again topped by the imperial eagle. On 7 November the Senate – now composed entirely of his supporters – passed a resolution appointing him emperor, and his heirs after him. One senator only voted against: his brother's old tutor Nicholas Vieillard, who wrote him a regretful letter explaining that his conscience would allow him to do nothing else. Louis-Napoleon's answer was typical; he invited him to lunch.

On 21 November, yet another plebiscite approved the Senate's resolution by 7.8 million to 253,000, and ten days later the President of the Legislative Assembly Adolphe Billault led a procession of two hundred coaches to Saint-Cloud, where Louis-Napoleon and Jerome were waiting to receive him. 'Sire,' he solemnly declared, 'the whole of France delivers itself into your hands.' Louis-Napoleon replied with equal solemnity, ending with the words, 'Help me, Messieurs, to establish a stable government which will have for its basis religion, probity, justice and respect for the suffering classes.' (*Les classes souffrantes* – a typical Napoleonic touch.) Then on 2 December 1852 – that same anniversary once again – he signed the decree proclaiming the Empire and himself as 'Napoleon III, Emperor of the French by the Grace of God and the Will of the People'.

It was a remarkable achievement – and he was still only forty-four. The Empire was his – and he intended to enjoy it.

18

A Sphinx without a Riddle
1852–70

The Empire is peace . . . I wish to draw into the stream of
the great popular river those hostile side-currents which lost
themselves without profit to anyone. We have immense
unploughed territories to cultivate; roads to open; ports to
excavate; rivers to be made navigable; canals to finish; a railway
network to complete . . . We have ruins to repair, false gods
to tear down, truths which we need to make triumph. This is
how I see the Empire . . .

Louis-Napoleon, Bordeaux, 9 October 1852

THE NEXT STEP was to marry: the future of the Napoleonic line
must at all costs be assured. (The emperor had already nominated
Jerome as his heir, but Jerome was twenty years older than he was
and Jerome's son Prince Louis-Napoleon – universally known as
'Plon-Plon' – was a faintly laughable figure who would never make
an emperor in a thousand years.) Harriet Howard, the prince's
mistress – 'Lizzie', as she was always known – was out of the running.
She was, frankly, a courtesan, and courtesans could hardly be
empresses. On the other hand, it was no good thinking about the
great royal or imperial families of Europe – Habsburgs, Hohenzollerns
or Romanovs – nor even about the relatively modest House of
Hanover: the British would feel the same as the others, and would
anyway never countenance a Catholic. To all of them Napoleon III
– as he must now be called – was nothing but a jumped-up adventurer, even worse than his uncle. He would obviously have to lower
his sights.

His choice finally fell on a remarkably beautiful Spanish girl: Doña

María Eugenia Ignacia Augustina de Palafox y Kirkpatrick, in her own right 15th Marchioness of Ardales and 16th Countess of Teba, daughter of the late Count of Montijo. Not quite the top drawer perhaps, but certainly an upper one and anyway the best he could hope for. And there was another point in her favour: he had fallen passionately in love with her at first sight. His immediate entourage was horrified. 'We have not made the Empire for the Emperor to marry a flower-girl,' said his close associate the Duc de Persigny, who actually went so far as to circulate scurrilous pamphlets against her. And Persigny was not alone. 'To hear the way in which men and women talk of their future Empress is astonishing,' wrote the British ambassador, Lord Cowley, to the Foreign Office. 'Things have been repeated to me . . . which it would be impossible to commit to paper.' But Napoleon refused to be shaken, and married Eugénie, as she was henceforth to be known, on 29 January 1853 at Notre-Dame. As for Lizzie, she was made Comtesse de Beauregard, given a beautiful château and granted a more than generous pension. In fact her last goodbye to the emperor proved to be nothing of the sort: within a month she was back between the sheets. But not for long. The empress soon heard about it and presented her husband with the time-honoured ultimatum: he must choose one or the other; he could not have both. This time it was final. Lizzie returned to London, then after a brief and unsuccessful marriage she shut herself away in her château and led a life so secluded that she became known as 'the hermit of Beauregard'. She died in 1864, of cancer. She was forty-two.

Eugénie had won, but she knew that there was a long and probably painful climb ahead of her. She was by no means the adventuress and *intrigante* that the Parisians liked to imagine; she had, however, grown well accustomed to adversity. The beginning of her life had been unusual enough: she had been born on 5 May 1826 in a tent, in which her family had taken refuge after a severe earthquake in Granada, her home city. Her father, having spent many years under house arrest, had died when she was thirteen; and her highly ambitious mother had trailed her and her sister through all the smartest watering-places of Europe in search of suitable husbands, but without success. By the time she caught the emperor's eye she was already twenty-six, well past what was generally considered marriageable age; but once she was his wife she was to be empress for the next sixty-seven years.

It is hardly surprising that Eugénie should have modestly welcomed the emperor's advances; but she made it absolutely clear from the start that there was to be no question of sex until they were married. There was to be little enough of it afterwards: she proved the coldest of cold fishes, making no secret of the fact that she thought the whole process *dégoûtant* – disgusting. In the summer of 1855, however, she took a deep breath, and the following March presented her husband with a single son. There were no more children – and, quite probably, few attempts to have one.

Fortunately, Napoleon had other interests to pursue. Something, he believed, must be done about the state of his capital, much of which was still as described by Balzac★ – winding narrow streets and alleyways and squalid, overcrowded tenements, all deeply insanitary and riddled with vermin. In the summer of 1853 he summoned the Prefect of the Department of the Seine Georges Haussmann, and ordered him to create a new Paris, worthy of the new Empire. He knew just what he wanted: a series of long, broad boulevards, which would enable carriages to pass rapidly from one *quartier* to the next and would lend the city the dignity and distinction it deserved. It would also, he readily agreed, greatly facilitate the swift movement of troops in the event of a sudden insurrection (in Paris, always a possibility). But such considerations were of secondary importance; the emperor's main purpose was to create a city of which every Parisian – indeed, every Frenchman – could be proud.

Haussmann, although his family came from Alsace, had been born and brought up in Paris and knew it like the back of his hand. He had originally intended to be a musician, but realising that he was simply not good enough for the concert stage had joined the provincial administration. He was selected as the man for the job by the emperor's Minister of the Interior, Victor de Persigny, who later remembered:

★ Honoré de Balzac (1799–1850) is considered by many to be the greatest French novelist of the nineteenth century.

Strangely, it was not his talents and his remarkable intelligence that appealed to me; it was the defects in his character. I had in front of me one of the most extraordinary men of our time: big, strong, vigorous, energetic, and at the same time devious and resourceful. It seemed to me that he was exactly the man I needed to fight against the ideas and prejudices of a whole school of economics, against equally devious people from the stock market. Whereas a gentleman of straight and noble character would inevitably fail, this athlete, full of audacity and skill, capable of opposing traps with cleverer traps, would surely succeed.

For virtually the whole of the emperor's reign and for a decade afterwards, Paris was one vast construction site. Hundreds of old buildings were demolished and eighty kilometres of new avenues were cut through to connect the key points of the city. Haussmann and the emperor together transformed the capital. We owe to them the Rue de Rivoli, running from the Place de la Concorde as far as Rue Saint-Antoine; Boulevard Saint-Germain, Avenue de l'Opéra, Avenue Foch, Boulevard de Sébastopol, and (of course) Boulevard Haussmann. Among the new buildings were most of the principal railway stations, the Palais Garnier (then the largest opera house in the world) and the central market of Les Halles. It was also at this time that the first two of Paris's great department stores sprang up – the Bon Marché in 1852, the Printemps in 1865. And all this is to say nothing of the new parks, gardens and squares – and, last but not least, a complete reconstruction of the sewage system. Napoleon did not quite follow the example of the Emperor Augustus, who boasted that he found his capital stone and left it marble; but he certainly transformed Paris more radically than any other monarch, before or since.

The Crimean War, which broke out in October 1853, was a ridiculous affair which should never have occurred at all. It began with a quarrel between the Greek Orthodox and the Roman Catholics over their always contentious sharing of the Church of the Holy Sepulchre in Jerusalem. The Tsar predictably supported the Orthodox;

Napoleon, who for all his peaceful protestations felt he needed a war to consolidate his power and reputation, took an equally strong stand on behalf of the Catholics. The Ottoman Sultan first of all dithered, and then came down on the side of the French; but within six weeks his navy had been utterly destroyed by the Russians, so it hardly mattered. Nobody wanted a Russian presence in the eastern Mediterranean, so the British, Protestant as they were, came in with the French. In March 1854 they declared war and landed in the Crimea.

Meanwhile the emperor had made it clear to Lord Cowley that he would much appreciate an invitation to visit England on a state visit. The British government was largely in favour; the principal drawback was the attitude of Queen Victoria herself. Already in the autumn of 1853 one of the emperor's ministers had raised the question with Cowley, who had referred it to the Foreign Secretary, Lord Clarendon. The queen's reply had been swift:

> The Queen hastens to answer Lord Clarendon's letter, and wishes him to inform Lord Cowley that there never was the slightest idea of *inviting* the Emperor of the French and that Lord Cowley should take care that it should be clearly understood that there was and would be no intention of the kind, so that there should be no doubt on the subject. The Queen feels sure that the Emperor has had these reports put in [*sic*] himself.

Gradually, however, relations improved. The situation in the Crimea having apparently reached a stalemate, in September 1854 Napoleon invited the Prince Consort to visit him at his military camp at Boulogne; and Albert accepted. He found the emperor far more relaxed and intelligent than he had imagined, particularly admiring his excellent German. After his guest's return Napoleon spoke with rather overdone enthusiasm of the prince, 'saying', reported Clarendon to the queen, 'that in all his experience he had never met with a person possessing such various and profound knowledge . . . His Majesty added that he had never learned so much in so short a time.' Such flattery went straight to Victoria's heart. She immediately felt better about the emperor, and when she heard that Albert himself had spoken of a state visit, her resistance crumbled. But she was not yet ready to be gracious; the emperor, she said, could come if he liked, and she suggested the middle of November. She obviously expected him to leap at the chance, and when he asked for a postponement she did not take it well: 'The Emperor Napoleon's answer to Lord Cowley with reference to this visit to England . . . is almost a refusal now, and has not improved our position. The Queen would wish that no anxiety should be shown to obtain the visit . . . His reception here ought to be a boon to him and not a boon to us.'

The war was still not going particularly well, and in April of the following year Napoleon announced that he intended to sail personally to the Crimea to assume command of his army. The queen was horrified. The idea of a nephew of Napoleon I leading his troops into battle alongside her own men,★ only forty years after Waterloo, shocked her to the core. What if he succeeded in making some *grand geste*, led his French troops to a brilliant victory, and stole all the British thunder? Clearly this must be prevented at all costs, and Clarendon hurried to France to try to dissuade the emperor from any such plan. He found that Napoleon's enthusiasm had somewhat cooled, and believed that it would not take very much to induce him to change his mind: a state visit, he thought, might be just the thing. And so the arrangements were made: the visit would take place from 16 to 21 April 1855.

It did, and proved a greater success than anyone could have hoped. There were a few inevitable hitches: the empress's trunks had been held up somewhere between Dover and Windsor, and for the first crucial night she had to improvise. But this was perhaps the best thing that could have happened: the queen was charmed by her simplicity and lack of ostentation. Eugénie, she realised, was by no means the femme fatale of Lord Cowley's initial reports; on the contrary, she had an only too well-deserved reputation for chastity, and Victoria was delighted when she learned of the empress's admiration of the high moral tone of the English court. As for the emperor,

---

★ Relations between the two allies were distinctly chilly, largely owing to the fact that the British commander, Lord Raglan, who had last seen action in the Napoleonic Wars, insisted on referring to the enemy as 'the French'.

she was at first struck by his size. 'He was extremely short,' she noted, 'but with a head and bust which ought to belong to a much taller man.' But she soon forgot his bust. Napoleon III was famous for his charm, and he turned the full force of it on his hostess; within minutes she was captivated. He must, she immediately decided, be awarded the Garter. '*Enfin je suis gentilhomme*,'* he joked after the ceremony. The queen was more enchanted than ever. On the fifth and last day of the visit she summarised her feelings:

> The Emperor is *very* fascinating; he is so quiet and gentle, and has such a soft pleasant voice. He is besides so simple and plain spoken in all he says, and so devoid of all phrases, and has a good deal of poetry, romance and *Schwärmerei* [enthusiasm] in his composition, which makes him peculiarly attractive. He is a most extraordinary, mysterious man, whom one feels excessively interested in watching and knowing . . . All he says is the result of deep reflection; and he sees in trifles and ordinary occurrences meanings and forebodings which no one else would find out . . . He is evidently possessed *of indomitable courage, unflinching firmness of purpose, self-reliance, perseverance and great secrecy*;† to this should be added great reliance on what he calls his *Star*.

The return visit five months later was every bit as successful. The climax was a pilgrimage – in a violent thunderstorm – to Napoleon I's tomb. 'It was touching, and pleasing in the extreme, to see the alliance sealed so completely . . . And to see old enmities wiped out over the tomb of Napoleon I, before whose coffin I stood (by torchlight) at the arm of Louis-Napoleon III, now my nearest and dearest ally.'

In less than two years, she had come a long way.

Perhaps in some measure owing to that state visit – Victoria too could be quite persuasive when she tried – the emperor never went to the Crimea. Nor did he need to. In September 1855, after a seemingly endless siege, the French army under General – soon to be Marshal and later President – Patrice MacMahon stormed the

---

* 'At last I'm a gentleman.'
† The queen's underlinings.

Malakoff fortifications guarding the land approaches to Sebastopol. '*J'y suis, j'y reste!*'★ bellowed the general as, at the head of his troops, he clambered over the battlements – an exclamation that has entered the French language, and perhaps the English one too. It was the turning point of the war; in February 1856 the Russians sued for peace, and the subsequent negotiations took place in Paris. For the emperor, this was a triumph in itself; and though the Crimean War had little or no long-term impact on the future of Europe – apart from significantly reducing its population† – he milked it for all the glory he could get. Few Parisians today could in all probability tell us much about Alma, Malakoff or even Sebastopol; but the Place, the Avenue and the Boulevard ensure at least that their names will not be forgotten.

It is not often that an unsuccessful attempt at assassination of a ruler leads to a radical change in foreign policy; but it could at least be argued that Napoleon III was an exception to the rule. The attempt took place on 14 January 1858, when bombs were thrown at his carriage as he and the empress were on their way to the Opéra for a performance of *William Tell*. Neither was hurt, though there were a number of casualties among their escort and the surrounding bystanders. The leader of the conspirators, Felice Orsini, was a well-known republican who had been implicated in a number of former plots. While in prison awaiting trial he wrote the emperor a letter, which was read aloud in open court and published in both the French and the Piedmontese press. It ended: 'Remember that, so long as Italy is not independent, the peace of Europe and Your Majesty is but an empty dream . . . Set my country free, and the blessings of twenty-five million people will follow you everywhere and for ever.'

Although these noble words failed to save Orsini from the firing squad, they seem to have lingered in Napoleon's mind; and by

★ 'Here I am, here I stay!'
† The siege of Sebastopol alone is thought to have cost the lives of 115,000 allied soldiers. Russian losses were estimated at 250,000.

midsummer 1858 he had come round to the idea of a joint operation to drive the Austrians out of the Italian peninsula once and
for all. His motives were not wholly altruistic. He did have a genuine
love for Italy and would have been delighted to present himself to
the world as her deliverer; but he was also aware that his popularity
and prestige were declining. To regain them he desperately needed
another victorious war, and Austria was the only potential enemy
available. The next step was to discuss the plan with Count Cavour,
now Chief Minister of Piedmont; and in July 1858 the two met
secretly at the little health resort of Plombières-les-Bains in the
Vosges. Agreement was quickly reached. Piedmont would engineer
a quarrel with the Duke of Modena and would send in troops,
ostensibly at the request of the population. Austria would be bound
to support the duke and declare war; Piedmont would then appeal
for aid to France, which would immediately respond. In return for
French help, she would cede to France the county of Savoy and the
city of Nice. The latter, being the birthplace of Garibaldi, was a
bitter pill for Cavour to swallow, but if it was the price of Austrian
defeat, then swallowed it would have to be.

To set the seal on the agreement, the two men agreed on a
dynastic marriage: Victor Emmanuel's eldest daughter, the Princess
Maria Clotilde, should be espoused to the emperor's cousin, Prince
Louis-Napoleon. When the engagement was announced there were
many – especially in Piedmont – who threw up their hands in
horror. The princess was a highly intelligent, pious and attractive
girl of fifteen; her fiancé, the mildly ridiculous 'Plon-Plon', was a
raddled old roué of thirty-seven. Victor Emmanuel, who had apparently not been consulted in advance, made no secret of his displeasure
but left the final decision to Maria Clotilde herself. It says much
for her sense of duty that she agreed to go through with the marriage
– which, to everyone's surprise, proved to be a not altogether unhappy
one.

The wedding ceremony took place at the end of January 1859,
while France and Piedmont were actively – and openly – preparing
for war. Soon afterwards Napoleon III had second thoughts about
the whole affair – to the dismay of Cavour, who knew that his small
country could not possibly tackle Prussia alone. He was saved by

Austria itself, which sent an ultimatum to Turin on 23 April demanding Piedmontese disarmament within three days. Austria had now declared itself the aggressor; the emperor could no longer hope to wriggle out of his commitments and did not attempt to do so. He ordered the immediate mobilisation of the French army. Of its 120,000 men, one section would enter Italy across the Alps while the rest went by sea to Genoa, which was at that time part of Piedmont.

Cavour was well aware that all this would take time. The Austrians were already on the march; for at least a fortnight, the Piedmontese would have to face them alone. Fortunately he was saved again – this time by torrential rains, together with dissension over strategy among the Austrian general staff. The consequent delay gave the French the time to arrive. They were led by the emperor himself who, landing at Genoa on 12 May 1859, for the first time assumed personal command of his army. It was on 4 June that the first battle took place – at Magenta, a small village fourteen miles west of Milan, where the French army, fighting alone under MacMahon, defeated an Austrian army of 50,000. Casualties were high on both sides, and would have been higher if the Piedmontese, delayed by the indecision of their own commander, had not arrived some time after the battle was over. This misfortune did not however prevent Napoleon III and Victor Emmanuel from making a joint triumphal entry into Milan four days later.

After Magenta the French and Piedmontese were joined by Garibaldi, full of all his old ardour and enthusiasm. His death sentence long forgotten, he had now been invited by Victor Emmanuel to assemble a brigade of *cacciatori delle Alpi* – Alpine hunters – and had won a signal victory over the Austrians some ten days before at Varese. Army and *cacciatori* then advanced together, to meet the full Austrian army on 24 June 1859 at Solferino, just south of Lake Garda. The ensuing battle – in which well over a quarter of a million men were engaged – was fought on a grander scale than any since Leipzig in 1813. This time Napoleon III was not the only monarch to assume personal command: Victor Emmanuel did the same, as did the twenty-nine-year-old Emperor Franz Josef of Austria. Only the French, however, were able to reveal a hitherto secret weapon:

rifled artillery, which dramatically increased both the accuracy and the range of their guns.

The fighting, much of it hand-to-hand, began early in the morning and continued for most of the day. Only towards evening, after losing some 20,000 of his men in heavy rain, did Franz Josef order a withdrawal across the Mincio river. But it was yet another of those pyrrhic victories; the French and Piedmontese lost almost as many men as the Austrians, and the outbreak of fever – probably typhus – that followed the battle accounted for thousands more on both sides. The scenes of carnage made a deep impression on a young Swiss named Henri Dunant, who chanced to be present and organised emergency aid services for the wounded. Five years later, as a direct result of his experience, he was to found the International Red Cross.

Nor was Dunant the only one to be sickened by what he had seen at Solferino. Napoleon III had also been profoundly shocked, and his disgust for war and all the horrors it brought in its train was certainly one of the reasons why, little more than a fortnight after the battle, he made a separate peace with Austria. There were other reasons too. The German Confederation was now mobilising some 350,000 men; were they to attack in support of Austria, the 50,000 French soldiers remaining in France would probably be slaughtered. And then there was the situation in Italy itself. Recent events had persuaded several of the smaller states to think about overthrowing their former rulers and seeking annexation to Piedmont. The result would be a formidable power, immediately across the French border, covering all north-west and central Italy: a nation which might well in time absorb some or all of the Papal States and even the Two Sicilies. Was it really for this that those who fell at Solferino had given their lives?

And so, on 11 July 1859, the emperors of France and Austria met at Villafranca, near Verona; and the future of much of Italy was decided in under an hour. Austria would keep her two fortresses at Mantua and Peschiera; the rest of Lombardy would be surrendered to France, which would pass it on to Piedmont. An Italian confederacy would thus be established under the honorary presidency of the Pope. Venice and the Veneto would be a member of this confederacy, but would remain under Austrian sovereignty.

The reaction of Cavour when he read the details of the Villafranca agreement fortunately falls outside the bounds of this history.

Our scene now shifts, briefly and surprisingly, to Mexico. Until 1821 the country had been, like most of Central and South America, a colony of Spain. In that year, led by a charismatic young army officer named Agustín Iturbide, it had declared its independence, and in 1822 Iturbide had proclaimed himself Emperor Agustín I. He was to remain on his imperial throne for just three years before being executed by a firing squad. For the next forty-odd years Mexico had been ruled by a succession of hopelessly corrupt military presidents, all of whom were of Spanish origin and deeply conservative, who together ran up a vast quantity of debts, principally to France, Spain and Great Britain. According to normal practice in the power politics of the nineteenth century, these three countries decided in October 1861 to despatch a joint naval force to the port of Vera Cruz and to take over the customs administration until they were paid the debts owed to them. They would then return to Europe.

They had failed to understand, however, that a new spirit was abroad. Just a year before, in October 1860 after a three-year civil war, Mexico had been taken over by a dour and incorruptible young lawyer of pure Indian stock named Benito Juárez. The whole allied plan proved unrealistic and unworkable. The British and Spanish troops left empty-handed after a few months, but the French unwisely remained. In May 1862 they were routed by Juárez's army at Puebla, on the road up to Mexico City. At this point, the only sensible decision would have been to summon the army back to France and call the whole thing off; instead, another 25,000 French troops were landed at Vera Cruz in the autumn.

Why should the French have involved themselves in a distant adventure, which was bound to cost them many times more than the debts they were owed? Largely because of the emperor's ambition. In September 1861 a certain José Manuel Hidalgo, a Spanish-Mexican childhood friend of Eugénie, had proposed to Napoleon that he should be the founding father of a great Catholic

empire, to be established first in Mexico but with the possible prospect of spreading over much of Latin America. The emperor was
intrigued, for three reasons. First, because the idea naturally appealed
to his ambitious and adventurous spirit; second, because it would
prevent the predominantly Protestant United States from becoming
too powerful in the region. Normally President Lincoln would have
done all he could to prevent the enterprise, citing the Monroe
Doctrine of 1823 whereby any attempt by the European powers to
extend their influence in the Americas would be regarded as a threat
to his nation's security and dealt with accordingly; but Lincoln was
now involved in a hideous civil war of his own, and had more than
enough on his hands.

The third reason was unrelated to the other two; it concerned
the most obvious candidate for the new empire, the Austrian emperor's brother Maximilian. Now Maximilian suffered acutely from
that complaint all too well known among royal families, the younger
brother syndrome. What were younger brothers meant to do? His
wife, the Princess Charlotte of Belgium, felt the problem even more
strongly. When the idea was first put to them, Maximilian was deeply
hesitant; there was clearly a very large degree of risk involved.
Charlotte, however, was thrilled. Daughter of one king, Leopold I
of the Belgians, and granddaughter of another, our old friend Louis-
Philippe, she longed to reign herself; and it was probably her
influence – together with steady pressure from Napoleon III – that
led her notoriously weak-willed husband eventually to accept the
Mexican invitation.

And so, at last, Maximilian allowed himself to be persuaded. In
April 1864 he formally renounced his rights to the Austrian throne,
and a few days later he and Charlotte boarded the Austrian frigate
Novara. The rest of their story can be very briefly told. They both
did their best and, given a chance, the Mexican Empire might
have been a success; but it was not given a chance. Maximilian
made one serious mistake. On 3 October 1865 he signed what was
known as the Black Decree, according to which any individual
belonging to an armed band existing without legal authority would
be court-martialled and, if found guilty, condemned to death by
firing squad within twenty-four hours. As a result, Juárez is said

to have lost more than 11,000 of his men – and he did not forget it.

Meanwhile, despite his losses, he grew steadily stronger. By the beginning of 1866, for the imperial couple the writing was on the wall. Maximilian seemed not to understand the seriousness of his position and continued to travel cheerfully round the country, carousing with the local peasantry and leaving his governmental responsibilities to Charlotte. She presided at the cabinet meetings, until it finally became clear that without outside help she and her husband were doomed. Thus, in the autumn of that year, she returned alone to Europe to appeal to anyone who would listen. Her first port of call was Paris; it was after all Napoleon III who was responsible for the whole disastrous enterprise. At first his guilty conscience made him reluctant to receive her, but Eugénie insisted. The interview was short, for her hosts quickly realised that under the immense strain she had suffered the young empress had lost her reason. When a footman appeared with a tray of lemonade she swept it out of his hands, declaring the drink to be poisoned. She was quietly removed from the imperial presence and escorted back to her lodgings.

It was much the same story when she appealed to the Pope. According to one account she burst in on Pius IX while he was having breakfast and seized his cup of chocolate with the words: 'At least *this* won't be poisoned!' This time they succeeded in getting her out of the building only by suggesting that she visit the Vatican orphanage. Always the empress, she accepted at once, and on entering the kitchen, now ravenously hungry, plunged her hand into a cauldron of hot soup and was badly scalded. Fortunately she fainted with the pain, and while still unconscious was put on a stretcher and returned to the Grand Hotel. There she remained for several days – keeping several chickens tied to the chairs in her room and eating only eggs, oranges and nuts, which she could see had not been tampered with – until her brother, summoned from Belgium, arrived to take her home. She never saw her husband again and lived, hopelessly insane, in Belgium for another sixty years, dying in January 1927.

As for Maximilian, he was captured by Juárez's men on 16 May

1867, court-martialled and sentenced to death. Many European crowned heads and other distinguished figures including Garibaldi and Victor Hugo appealed for clemency, but to no avail: Juárez could not forget the Black Decree, and on 19 June the second and last Emperor of Mexico met his death bravely by firing squad. He was thirty-four.

There is a curious if somewhat hypothetical epilogue to this tragic story. General Maxime Weygand, who distinguished himself in both world wars before unwisely throwing in his lot with the Vichy regime, claimed that he never knew his parentage. He had studied at the French military academy at Saint-Cyr, where he had been financed by the Belgian court; and there is a strong possibility that, born as he was in Brussels on 21 June 1867, he was the son of the Empress Charlotte, not by Maximilian but by Colonel Alfred van der Smissen, who commanded a small Belgian contingent in Mexico. A comparison between portrait photographs of the two men certainly shows a striking resemblance. If this theory is true, it would do much to explain Charlotte's breakdown; an illegitimate pregnancy was, at that moment, the last thing she needed★ and would have added vastly to her anxieties.

For some time Napoleon III had been increasingly worried about the activities of Otto von Bismarck, the Prussian chancellor. Bismarck had visited him in October 1865 at Biarritz, and in long walks along the Atlantic shore had sketched out to him what he had in mind. He would find some pretext to declare war against Austria – the last major barrier to German unity – and, having successfully defeated it, would create that unity under the leadership (of course) of Prussia.†

★ During the Second World War my old friend Costa Achillopoulos found himself sharing a tent with Jean Weygand, the general's son, and asked him one night whether Charlotte was indeed his grandmother. He replied that he had no proof, but that his father had always believed the story to be true.

† Germany needed unity even more than Italy did. At the beginning of the nineteenth century a traveller from Brunswick to Paris would have to pass through twenty-two frontiers – those of six duchies, four independent bishoprics and one free city. The number of these tiny states fluctuated; its maximum was 348.

He had no doubts that he would be victorious; but Austria was twice the size of Prussia and he had to be sure that France would not take her side.

And the emperor, astonishingly, gave his word. Why he did so we shall never understand. He seems to have forgotten his fears of a huge and potentially threatening new state on his eastern frontier. It did not even occur to him to demand a substantial quid pro quo – which Bismarck would surely have been happy to offer. True, if all went according to plan a defeated Austria would be obliged to surrender Venice and the Veneto, the penultimate missing piece in the Italian jigsaw. This might give Napoleon a good deal of personal satisfaction; but it would be of no conceivable advantage to France.

Bismarck, at any rate, was now free to go ahead, and his strategy worked perfectly. In June 1866 Prussian troops invaded Saxony, bringing the Prussian army to the frontier of the Austrian Empire. The newly formed Kingdom of Italy joined in for obvious reasons, and just six weeks later the whole thing was over. For the Prussians, a single battle was enough. It was fought at Sadowa – to the Germans and Austrians, Königgrätz – some sixty-five miles east of Prague, and it engaged the largest number of troops – a third of a million – ever previously assembled on a European battlefield. (It was also the first battle in which railways and the telegraph were used on a considerable scale.) The Prussian victory was total, and the treaty that followed duly provided for the cession to Italy of Venice and the Veneto. Austria was firmly excluded from Germany and left to fend for herself; the North German Confederation was founded, and was joined by several previously independent states. It adopted King William I of Prussia as its president, and Bismarck as its chancellor.

But why – we must return to the question – was Napoleon so unaccountably weak in his dealings with the chancellor? It has been suggested that his health might have been at least partly to

Napoleon I got them down to a couple of dozen, but the Council of Vienna decided to restore a few of the dynasties he had abolished. When Bismarck assumed power there were about forty.

blame; though still only fifty-seven, he was clearly not the man he used to be; and he had moreover recently been suffering agonies from a kidney stone. But that had been dealt with by a minor operation a few weeks before; he was no longer in pain and, as we have seen, perfectly capable of taking long walks with his guest. We are left with the conclusion that he was, quite simply, outsmarted. Bismarck, certainly, had been left unimpressed with his intelligence. The emperor, he had declared after his return to Berlin, was 'a sphinx without a riddle'; Eugénie was 'the only man in his government'.

The state of his health and morale was obvious to everyone, and as the months passed became a matter of general concern. He never recovered from Sadowa, for which he had been, he knew by now all too well, in a large part responsible. The worry brought on a second kidney attack; he was forced to leave Paris and to spend several weeks at Vichy, where the waters afforded some relief. When old Adolphe Thiers commented, 'It is France who was beaten at Sadowa', he spoke no more than the truth. A month after the fateful cabinet meeting, Lord Cowley – no longer ambassador but still a friend – called on the emperor at Fontainebleau. He found him 'aged and much depressed', and suspected that he might even be considering abdication. His successor, Lord Lyons, agreed. He reported to Lord Stanley, the Foreign Secretary, on 11 August:

> It is even asserted that he is weary of the whole thing, disappointed at the contrast between the brilliancy at the beginning of his reign and the present gloom – and inclined, if possible, to retire into private life. This is no doubt a great exaggeration but, if he is really feeling unequal to governing with energy, the dynasty and the country are in great danger.

He was certainly in no state to accompany Eugénie when, in November 1869, she attended the opening by the Khedive Ismail of the Suez Canal. The ceremony was not without a moment of serious embarrassment. The khedive had graciously invited the empress, in the French imperial yacht, the *Aigle*, to be the first to pass through the canal. On the night before the opening, however, HMS *Newport*, under Captain George Nares RN, slipped without lights through the mass of waiting ships till it was in front of the *Aigle*. When dawn broke, the French were horrified to see that the *Newport* was already in the mouth of the canal and that there was no way it could be removed – so it was the *Newport* that went through first. Nares became perhaps the only British naval officer simultaneously to receive from the Admiralty an official reprimand and an unofficial note of congratulation on a spectacular piece of seamanship. The *Aigle* was consequently only the second vessel to sail from Port Said to Suez. She was followed by forty-five more vessels, bearing the khedive, his official guests, foreign ambassadors and other important dignitaries. When, on the morning of the 20th, she emerged in the Red Sea, cannon were fired in salute and her ship's band struck up with 'Partant pour la Syrie'.* It was not, perhaps, the most appropriate of titles; but it is unlikely that many people noticed.†

On 30 September 1868, the Spanish army having been defeated by revolutionary forces at the Battle of Alcolea, Queen Isabella II of Spain boarded a train with her children at San Sebastián and trundled off into exile. For two years the country was without a monarch, while various candidates were considered; in 1870 the throne was offered to Prince Leopold of Hohenzollern-Sigmaringen. Had the prince rejected the offer at once, there might have been no Franco-Prussian War and Napoleon III might have ended his days still on the throne; alas, he accepted. France was appalled. How possibly

* 'Leaving for Syria', a popular song with music by Josephine's daughter Hortense de Beauharnais. The 'Marseillaise' was banned during the Second Empire, and this became the unofficial national anthem.

† There is a popular misconception that Giuseppe Verdi wrote *Aïda* to celebrate the opening of the canal. In fact the historic event seems to have left him cold; he even turned down an invitation to compose an inaugural hymn for the occasion. It was not until early 1870 that he was sent a scenario set in ancient Egypt that appealed to him. He began work at once. It had been agreed that the opera should open in Cairo; unfortunately the scenery and costumes, which were prepared in Paris, were severely delayed by the Franco-Prussian War and the consequent siege of the city. The Cairo opening finally occurred on Christmas Eve 1871. Verdi was not present.

could she accept being the sausage in the middle of a German sandwich? Typically, Bismarck – in his determination that France should declare war – published what became known as the 'Ems telegram', which claimed to be the report of a recent conversation between King William and the French ambassador. In fact their conversation had been perfectly friendly, but Bismarck had craftily edited the telegram in such a way that each nation felt that it had been insulted and ridiculed by the other, dangerously inflaming popular sentiment on both sides.

On 19 July, France declared war, just as Bismarck had intended that she should. The German states saw her as the aggressor – which technically she was – and rallied to the side of Prussia; France was thus left virtually without an ally. It was no use looking to England for help; relations with Queen Victoria had long since cooled, and Thomas Carlyle was probably reflecting – if perhaps exaggerating – public sentiment when he wrote: 'That noble, patient, deep, pious and solid Germany should at length be welded into a nation, and become Queen of the Continent, instead of vapouring, vainglorious, gesticulating, quarrelsome, restless and oversensitive France, seems to me the hopefullest public fact that has occurred in my time.'

To the emperor, there was no question about it. Despite the fact that he was in constant pain – and occasional agony – from a stone in his bladder 'as big as a pigeon's egg', and that he was almost incapable of mounting a horse or even riding in a jolting carriage, he was determined to take personal command. And so, on 28 July, he and his fourteen-year-old son, the Prince Imperial, climbed into a train drawn up at the small private railway station in the grounds of the palace of Saint-Cloud and steamed off to join their army at Metz.

The Franco-Prussian War was a walkover. Bismarck had by now built up the Prussian army into a superb war machine, and though the combined population of Prussia and the Northern Confederation – some thirty million – was considerably less than that of France, together they were able to raise an army of 1,183,000 within eighteen days of mobilisation. The French army by contrast was undermanned, unprepared and dangerously short of vital equipment. There were no ambulances or baggage carts. The generals found they had plenty of maps of the German side of the frontier but none of their own;

in consequence several of them had considerable difficulty in finding the units that they were supposed to command. The German artillery made mincemeat of the French cavalry, demonstrating beyond any doubt that the days of mounted men on the battlefield were over for good. On 27 August Napoleon saw that he could no longer take the risk of his son – on whom the survival of the Empire depended – being killed or captured; regretfully, he sent him back to Paris and thence to England.

The end came – mercifully – on 1 September, near the little town of Sedan. Knowing already that all was lost, the emperor – his cheeks heavily rouged to conceal how ill he was – somehow mounted his horse. Apart from two occasions when he had to relieve himself and another when he was obliged to dismount and fling his arms around a tree in order to deal with the pain, he was in the saddle for five hours. It was only around six o'clock that evening, with the sun already low on the horizon, that the white flag was hoisted and a French officer rode out with a letter from the emperor to King William:

Monsieur mon Frère,
Having been unable to die in the midst of my troops, it remains only for me to place my sword in Your Majesty's hands. I am Your Majesty's good brother,
Louis-Napoleon.

Bismarck, after a quick consultation with the king – who was also present on the battlefield – replied:

Monsieur mon Frère,
Regretting the circumstances in which we find ourselves, I accept Your Majesty's sword, and I beg you to name one of your officers furnished with full powers from you to negotiate the capitulation of the army which has fought so bravely under your orders. For my part, I have designated General Moltke for this purpose. I am Your Majesty's good brother,
Wilhelm.

That night the emperor wrote to Eugénie: 'It is impossible for me to say what I have suffered and what I am suffering now . . . I would have preferred death to so disastrous a capitulation; and yet, in the present circumstances, it was the only way to avoid the butchering of sixty thousand people . . . I think of you, our son, and our unhappy country.'

He was taken to one of the king's castles, Wilhelmshöhe, near Kassel, where he spent the next six months in fairly comfortable captivity.★

When the news of the surrender reached Paris, however, the city exploded with rage. Immediately streets were renamed, and all outward signs of the Empire obliterated. Eugénie at first refused to believe that her husband had surrendered, declaring again and again that he was dead. When she finally accepted the truth she buried her head in her hands in shame. Meanwhile the Third Republic was proclaimed at the Hôtel de Ville, and within hours a crowd estimated at some 200,000 had gathered around the Tuileries Palace, where the imperial flag at the masthead showed that the empress was still in residence. Even now she was reluctant to leave. She had no fear of death, she assured those around her; she feared only the dishonour of being stripped or raped. At last she agreed to go, and together with Prince Richard Metternich and the Italian ambassador took the narrow underground passage leading from the Palace to the Louvre, at the far end of which the party hailed a passing cab. They eventually found refuge with the emperor's old friend, his dentist Dr Thomas Evans. Early the next morning she and Dr Evans left for Deauville, arriving there at three o'clock the following morning. Some hours later Evans went down to the harbour, where he saw a yacht flying a British flag. It proved to belong to an Englishman, Sir John Burgoyne, to whom he explained the situation. Unhesitatingly, Burgoyne put his vessel at the disposal of the empress. It set sail at once, and in the early morning of 8 September landed at Ryde on the Isle of Wight. From there Eugénie went on to Hastings, where, at the Marine Hotel, her son was waiting for her.

The emperor had surrendered; the French had not. The Franco-Prussian War was by no means over, and while it continued Napoleon

---

★ There is a superb description of these events in Emile Zola's *La Débâcle*.

III remained a prisoner and was confined to Wilhelmshöhe. Meanwhile Eugénie and her son settled at Camden Place, near Chislehurst in Kent, a rambling building reminiscent more of a French château than an English country house, which the emperor had quite possibly acquired – though there is no proof of this – some years before in case he were to need it in a hurry. There, on 20 March 1871, he was eventually able to join them. For some time, freed at last of all the anxieties of recent years, his health notably improved: by the end of the year he was even back again on his horse, riding for pleasure rather than duty; but by the autumn of the following year the pain had returned and as Christmas approached he fell seriously ill. On 2 January 1873 Sir Henry Thompson – the country's most famous renal surgeon – operated on him at Camden Place. He found a large stone in the bladder, but was able to remove only half of it. Another operation four days later accounted for a good deal more, but there remained a few remnants, and it was accepted that a third operation would be necessary to wash them out once the emperor – if he could still be so described – had recovered his strength.

But he never did. He died suddenly at 10.25 a.m. on Thursday 9 January 1873. His last intelligible words were addressed to another doctor, his old friend Henri Conneau, who had followed him to England: '*N'est-ce pas, Conneau, que nous n'avons pas été des lâches à Sedan?*'* Eugénie, who seems to have grown gradually to love her husband, collapsed in tears by his bedside. He was buried temporarily in the local churchyard; but in 1880 she moved to a huge and hideous house near Farnborough,† a few hundred yards from which she commissioned the French architect Hippolyte Destailleur to build an abbey and monastery dedicated to St Michael. There, in a magnificent marble crypt, the tombs of herself and her husband can still be seen, together with that of their son Louis, the Prince Imperial.

The story of the prince's death is curious indeed. In 1872 his parents sent him, then sixteen years old, to the Royal Military Academy, Woolwich, to learn gunnery. (The Bonapartes had always

---

* 'We weren't cowards at Sedan, Conneau, were we?'
† It is now a Catholic girls' school.

been artillerymen.) He passed out seventh in his class of thirty-four, but was first in horsemanship. Then, in 1879, came the outbreak of the second Zulu War, when the prince saw all his friends and colleagues departing for Africa. He of course was not among those summoned, but was determined to join them anyway. He appealed to his mother, pointing out that he could never regain the throne if he remained just a pretty face; he must show that he possessed the strength and courage worthy of his family, and here was the perfect opportunity to do so. Eugénie had no desire to see her only son risk his life in Africa, but when he insisted she reluctantly promised to discuss the possibility with the queen. Victoria proved no more enthusiastic than she was, but eventually gave in. Yes, she said, the boy could go to Zululand; but he must remain safely behind the lines; on no account was he to be allowed anywhere near the action. She would give instructions to the commander-in-chief, Lord Chelmsford, to that effect.

The first Zulu War had been a disaster; on 22 January 1879 a British army of about 1,800 had been attacked at Isandlwana by a Zulu force of perhaps 20,000. The Zulus were equipped mostly with assegais and cow-hide shields; the British were armed with state-of-the-art Martini-Henry rifles and two 7-pounder field guns, but were disastrously short of ammunition. They were therefore quickly overwhelmed, leaving 1,300 dead on the field. Chelmsford had no choice but to withdraw from Zululand while he repaired his stricken forces. It was during this period of recovery that further detachments arrived from Britain, the Prince Imperial among them. Meanwhile, a new plan of campaign was drawn up: the army would re-enter Zululand on 1 June.

The prince, who had been obliged, much to his disgust, to join the Intelligence Unit, was soon bored. On the evening of 30 May he suggested to his commanding officer that he should go in advance of the main force to reconnoitre the first ten miles – a day's journey, given that the army relied on ox-carts for transport – and select a suitable place for the first night's camp. A former scouting party, he pointed out, had already declared the area to be free of Zulus, so there would be no conceivable danger. Almost incredibly, permission was given – on the understanding that he would be accompanied by three or four other junior officers, under the command of Captain Jaheel Brenton Carey. The group rode out early the following morning, and by lunchtime had found the perfect stop, overlooking a small wadi, a dry river bed. Dismounting, they left their horses free to graze and settled down to a cup of coffee and a cigarette when suddenly they heard a fusillade of shots: an impi* of Zulus sprang out of the long grass a few yards away. There could be no question of resistance; their only hope was to grab their horses and spur them to safety. This the rest all managed to do. The prince, who was almost certainly the best horseman of them all and who normally thought nothing of leaping on to his mount as it galloped past him, tried to seize the pommel but caught only the map holster of his cheap African saddle; it came away in his hand. The remainder of the party succeeded in making their getaway, and drew up their horses on a small hillock a few hundred yards distant – only to see the prince's rider-less horse galloping up to join them. At once they knew that there was no hope; they could only ride back to staff headquarters and report the tragedy.

The reaction of headquarters can well be imagined. The queen herself had given orders that the prince's life must on no account be put at risk; and there he was, the very first casualty of the new campaign. A search party rode out at once to the wadi; they soon found his body, naked but for one sock, with eighteen wounds, all in front. One thing was clear: for a disaster of this magnitude, a scapegoat must be found; and it was on the luckless Captain Carey that the blow fell. He was accused, most unfairly, of deserting a fellow-officer in time of need, court-martialled and cashiered.†

Queen Victoria was, predictably, furious at the news. Eugénie was heartbroken – she had worshipped her son – but took the blow bravely. He was a soldier, she said, and it was in the nature of soldiers to get killed. On the first anniversary of his death, however, she was herself at the wadi – the difficulties of her journey there can barely

---

* The old-established collective noun for Zulus, applicable, so far as I can gather, to any number. In this case we are probably talking of a hundred or so.

† There was fortunately such an outcry when the news reached England that the queen ordered an enquiry and Carey was reinstated. He died in India in 1883.

be imagined – where she kept an all-night vigil. With her she had brought cuttings from the trees at Farnborough, which she planted as near as possible to the spot where her son had died. That spot was soon to be marked by a small monument in dazzling white marble erected by command of Queen Victoria. It is still there, surrounded by a curious little copse of obviously English trees: a little touch of Hampshire in the veldt.*

* For the centenary in 1979 I made a television documentary of the story for the BBC. It had been fully covered at the time by the *Illustrated London News*, which had included a series of striking woodcuts made from the photographs taken immediately after the event. In the past hundred years there had been no changes at all in the surroundings, except for the empress's trees and the queen's monument. In the wadi itself, one could even identify the individual stones and pebbles that had appeared in the woodcuts a century before.

19

The Last Manifestation
1870–3

I have just come from Paris . . . The sight of the ruins is
nothing compared to the great Parisian insanity. With very rare
exceptions everybody seems to me fit only for the strait-jacket.
One half of the population longs to hang the other half, which
returns the compliment.

Gustave Flaubert to George Sand

AFTER THE EMPEROR'S surrender, Bismarck and the Prussian
commander-in-chief, General von Moltke, had asked him to
sign the preliminary documents of a peace treaty, but he had refused.
He was, he said, no longer empowered to do so; peace negotiations
would be the responsibility of the French government, now headed
by the regent, the Empress Eugénie. But this government too had
ceased to exist, and on 4 September the French Third Republic was
proclaimed by the deputy Léon Gambetta at the Hôtel de Ville.
Meanwhile the war was still on. With the knowledge that the
Prussian army was now marching on Paris, which would consequently
very soon be in a state of siege, a Government of National Defence
was established under the presidency of General Louis Jules Trochu,
with Gambetta as his Minister of the Interior and Minister for War.
To defend the capital they needed every man they could get: together
they assembled a force of about 60,000 regular soldiers who had
returned from Sedan, some 90,000 *mobiles* – essentially territorials –
and a brigade of perhaps 30,000 seamen, to which could be added
350,000 untrained members of the National Guard. The total must
have been something around half a million.

The city's own defences consisted principally of what was known as the Thiers Wall, twenty-five miles long, built between 1841 and 1844 under a law enacted by the Thiers government and following a route similar to – though a little shorter than – the present Boulevard Périphérique; there was also a ring of sixteen fortresses, also dating from the 1840s. But it soon became clear that Moltke had no intention of trying to take the city by storm. He did not even seek a quick French capitulation, which would leave the new French armies undefeated and allow France to renew the war. He was putting his faith in attrition: Paris, he was determined, would be starved into surrender.

In the capital morale was still high; but the situation was now grave indeed, and the Parisians knew it. On 7 September, Jules Favre, Trochu's vice-president and minister for foreign affairs, begged the American minister Elihu B. Washburne to 'intervene to make peace', and two days later he sent Thiers to London in the hopes of rallying British support. Thiers travelled on from London to Vienna, St Petersburg and Florence – then the temporary capital of the new united Italy – but nowhere did he receive much more than polite sympathy. Favre then asked for an audience with Bismarck himself. Their conversation, held in the vast Rothschild palace of Ferrières some twenty miles east of Paris, continued long into the night but once again got nowhere, with Bismarck constantly and deliberately puffing smoke from his Meerschaum pipe into the face of Favre, a non-smoker. Prussia's demands, he said, were simple: Alsace, and most of Lorraine. 'I am certain', he added – and how right he was proved to be – 'that at some future time we shall have a fresh war with you, and we would wish to undertake it with every advantage.' Favre replied that no French government, if it yielded to such a demand, could hope to survive. 'You wish to destroy France!' he exclaimed, and burst into tears.*

When he returned to Paris and reported the interview, the government was outraged. Immediately Gambetta telegraphed to the Prefects of Paris: 'Paris, incensed, swears to resist to the end. Let the provinces rise up!' The only question was, how were they going

---

* Bismarck was unmoved. 'He probably intended', he wrote later, 'to work upon my feelings with a little theatrical performance.'

to do so? How were provincial armies to be raised, trained and organised, and who was going to lead them? Clearly a member of the government must be made responsible for any resistance there might be, but how was he to leave Paris? The Prussians had already taken Versailles, making it their headquarters. The encirclement of the city was now complete and the siege had begun, under the direction of Count Leonhard von Blumenthal, hero of the battles of both Sadowa and Sedan. Paris was now virtually sealed, cut off from the rest of France.

Suddenly a possible solution appeared. Somebody found an old hot-air balloon, a *montgolfière*, which had been one of the attractions of the International Exhibition of 1867. It was called the *Neptune* and was now patched up to the point of something approaching airworthiness. It took off on 3 September, and after a three-hour flight landed safely at Evreux. The blockade was, if not broken, at least cracked. Then came the next question: who, among the senior ministers, was prepared to risk his life on a flight to the outside world? There proved to be just one. As Trochu admitted with commendable frankness, 'Monsieur Gambetta was the only one of us who could regard without apprehension the prospects of a voyage in a balloon.'

Gambetta, however, was possessed of a lot more than physical courage. He was still only thirty-two. Born in Cahors, the son of an Italian grocer, he was described as 'inclined to thinness, with long black hair, a Jewish nose, and an eye which protruded so terribly from its socket as to lead one to fear lest it should escape altogether'. His morals were deplorable, and we are credibly informed that some of his personal habits were worse; but he was a superb speaker, passionate in his sincerity and capable of stirring the blood of all those who listened to him. He was, in short, just the man for the job. At eleven o'clock in the morning of 7 October in the Place Saint-Pierre, Montmartre,★ before an excited and admiring crowd, he clambered into the open wicker basket looking, as everyone agreed, pretty nervous. As well he might: apart from all the other risks, there was also the possibility that the huge bag of highly

★ Near where the Sacré Coeur now stands.

inflammable coal gas above him might be punctured by a Prussian bullet and explode in a ball of flame. As the balloon rose into the air, he unfurled an enormous tricolour; and so it climbed over the Parisian rooftops and slowly disappeared from view.

A balloon factory was quickly established at the Gare d'Orléans together with a training school for pilots, and within a short time balloons were taking off at the rate of two or three a week; henceforth getting messages out of the city was no longer an insuperable problem. Getting them in, however, was a good deal harder, and it was soon accepted that there was only one effective way: carrier pigeon. Fortunately the government was able to find an expert in micro-photography, who was sent to Tours with all his equipment in two balloons: one of them – fortunately the one in which he was not travelling – came down and was seized by the Prussians; but he himself arrived safely and set up his equipment. Official despatches were now photographically reduced to an infinitesimal size, to the point where 40,000 of them – probably the length of the average book – could be carried by a single pigeon. If and when they arrived in Paris, they were projected by a 'magic lantern' and transcribed by regiments of clerks. Personal messages of twenty words or less could also be sent, though the French Post Office was careful to disclaim responsibility for non-delivery. It was just as well that it did, because the system proved a good deal less reliable than the balloons. In the course of the siege 302 pigeons were to be despatched, of which only 59 reached Paris. The remainder were taken by birds of prey, died of cold and hunger, or were shot and consumed by hungry Prussians.

The Parisians, however, were a good deal hungrier. On 5 December, Edmond de Goncourt recorded in his diary: 'People are talking only of what they eat, what they can eat, and what there is to eat. Conversation consists of this, and nothing more . . .' 'I sigh', wrote Minister Washburne, 'for doughnuts.' Already by October, horsemeat had become a staple; in the past it had been eaten only by the poor; now it was eagerly seized by everyone. To a young lady who had unaccountably refused to dine with him, Victor Hugo wrote:

J'aurais tué Pégase, et je l'aurais fait cuire
Afin de vous offrir une aile de cheval.*

Cats and dogs were next. Henry Labouchère, correspondent of the London *Daily News*, wrote in mid-December: 'I had a slice of spaniel the other day', and a week later of how a man he had met was fattening up an enormous cat, which he hoped to serve up on Christmas Day, 'surrounded with mice, like sausages'.† Rats and mice were in fact consumed much less often than horses, cats and dogs. They tended to carry diseases, and tasted revolting; the elaborate sauces needed to make them palatable were hugely expensive; they were thus eaten, paradoxically, by the rich rather than the poor. So, as the grim days wore on, were the animals from the Zoo. Lions and tigers were spared: nobody ate carnivores if they could help it. Spared too were the hippopotami, simply because no butcher could face the challenge. But the Zoo's two elephants, Castor and Pollux, were not so lucky. A few menus survive from enterprising restaurants; one, for Christmas Day, offered stuffed donkey's head, elephant consommé, roast camel, kangaroo stew, antelope terrine, bear ribs, cat with rats, and wolf haunch in deer sauce. Another, rather more ambitious, included *brochettes de foie de chien maître d'hôtel*, *civet de chat aux champignons*, *salamis de rats, sauce Robert*, and *gigots de chien flanqués de ratons*. Tommy Bowles of the *Morning Post* noted in early January: 'I have now dined off camel, antelope, dog, donkey, mule and elephant, which I approve in the order in which I have written . . . horse is really too disgusting, and it has a peculiar taste never to be forgotten.' In the last days of the siege the government introduced a new type of bread, named *pain Ferry* after the minister who thought it up. It was composed of wheat, rice and straw, and seemed, according to one brave Parisian, 'to have been made from old Panama hats picked out of the gutters'.

Two days after Christmas the bombardment began. It had not

---

* I'd have slaughtered Pegasus and had him well cooked
In order to serve you the wing of a horse.
† For these anecdotes – and much else in this chapter – I am greatly indebted to my late friend Alistair Horne and his superb book *The Fall of Paris*.

originally been part of the Prussian programme, but Bismarck and Moltke both felt that the siege had gone on long enough. It is almost a cliché to point out that sieges are often as bad, or even worse, for the besiegers as for the besieged. That may not have been entirely true of 1870–1, but the Prussian soldiers – most of whom were confined to the flimsiest of tents – were beginning to suffer, and if the siege lasted much longer there was felt to be a serious danger of epidemic. When the attacks started the shells came over at the rate of between three and four hundred a night, normally between ten o'clock and two or three in the morning. The right bank of the Seine was fortunately out of range, but the Rive Gauche suffered badly. The domes of the Invalides and the Panthéon made irresistible targets, as did the church of Saint-Sulpice. The Salpêtrière Hospital was also hit repeatedly, to the point where it was suspected that the Prussians were deliberately aiming at it.* A direct hit on the balloon factory at the Gare d'Orsay was another blow: the factory was obliged to move hastily out of range to the Gare de l'Est.

The bombardment was bad enough; but Wednesday 18 January 1871 saw what was, for many a patriotic Frenchman, the worst humiliation of all: in the Hall of Mirrors of the Palace of Versailles, where only fifteen years before Queen Victoria had danced with Napoleon III in all the splendour of the Second Empire, King William I of Prussia was proclaimed Emperor, or Kaiser, of the Germans. 'This', wrote Edmond de Goncourt, 'truly marks the end of the greatness of France.' It was, on the face of it, a purely gratuitous insult: one that only Bismarck could have dreamed up, and one that was to poison Franco-German relations for many years to come.

The Parisians soon got used to the shelling, in much the same way as, seventy years later, Londoners were to grow accustomed to the Blitz. But starvation was far worse, and by late January 1871 the capital was coming to the end of its tether. Occasional attempts

---

* Trochu protested to Moltke on this point. Moltke's reply, that he hoped soon to push his guns close enough to be able to spot the Red Cross flags, hardly inspired confidence.

at a breakout had been markedly unsuccessful – one at Buzenval had cost 4,000 in dead and wounded – and discipline was rapidly breaking down, particularly among the National Guard. On 22 January there was another serious uprising, after which Favre noted 'civil war is a few yards away; famine, a few hours'. On the following day he summoned Captain d'Hérisson,⋆ one of Trochu's former staff officers, and entrusted him with a personal message to Bismarck. A ceasefire was quickly arranged, but Favre's own presence was required at the negotiations. He and d'Hérisson crossed the Seine in a rowing boat which, owing to a number of bullet holes, proved far from watertight: witnesses much enjoyed the sight of the vice-president, in his top hat and frock coat, frantically bailing with an old saucepan.

When he met Bismarck, the chancellor's first words were: 'Ah, Monsieur le Ministre, you have grown greyer since Ferrières.' Later he reported to the Crown Prince that Favre had shown a 'perfectly wolfish hunger' and had eaten a dinner that would have sufficed for three. The talks continued till the 27th when a three-week armistice was declared, during which it was agreed that no Prussian troops would enter Paris. The French army, apart from a single unit, was to surrender its weapons; France would pay an indemnity of 200 million francs. A new assembly would be elected, and would meet at Bordeaux to discuss on what terms it could accept or reject a peace treaty. The Prussians promised meanwhile to do all they could to assist and where possible to accelerate the revictualling of the capital.

Many Parisians – including the Mayor of Montmartre, a young man named Georges Clemenceau – were furious at the capitulation. (So, far away in Bordeaux, was Léon Gambetta, who bitterly complained that he had not even been informed in advance† and resigned on the spot.) But although the most disastrous war in French history was over at last, Paris took some time to recover:

⋆ Captain Hedgehog – an unusual name.

† In fact Favre had sent him a message by balloon, but the pilot had failed to stop at Bordeaux and had come down in the Atlantic. The reason remains a mystery.

the government was found to have gravely overestimated the quantity of food remaining in the city, and for two weeks after the armistice – despite Prussian promises – the supplies grew worse instead of better, to the point where Kaiser William himself ordered that 6 million army rations should be sent to the near-starving Parisians. Supplies also flooded in from Britain: in Deptford, twenty-four great ovens blazed away night and day baking bread, and the Lord Mayor's relief fund could hardly keep pace with donations. The United States was equally quick to respond, sending 2 million dollars' worth of food; but such generous gestures were not always well repaid. The appearance of the first British supply wagons at Les Halles★ provoked a riot, with disastrous results; vast quantities of chickens, eggs and butter were trampled underfoot. And when the American relief ships reached Le Havre, days passed before anyone could be found to unload them.

By mid-February the situation was gradually returning to normal. Except among the poorest of the poor – for whom survival had always been a struggle – great hunger was a thing of the past. Psychologically, however, the wounds were still deep. France was a defeated nation; and as Ernest Renan pointed out, previous victorious races had always had something to offer – their art, their civilisation or their faith – while Bismarck's Germany offered nothing except brute force. In the hearts of all too many Parisians hatred, bitterness and resentment lingered on. They had somehow lost interest in life: they were bored, and boredom made them ill-humoured. It would take very little to arouse their anger – as they were all too soon to show.

Meanwhile the national government, still in Bordeaux, called for the new elections provided for in the armistice. They were held on 8 February 1871. The vast majority of electors in France were rural, conservative and Catholic; consequently it came as no surprise that the vote was overwhelmingly for a return to constitutional monarchy. The voters were however split between supporters of the Bourbon

★ Paris's central food market.

line and the Orléanists, and so the final choice for first minister went to the old republican Adolphe Thiers, now seventy-three but as energetic and vigorous as ever. His first task was to conclude the peace treaty with Prussia. He did his best to negotiate, but Bismarck was adamant, making it clear that if the treaty were not signed at the end of the armistice period, hostilities would be immediately resumed. His principal demands were unchanged: Alsace and most of Lorraine, including the key cities of Metz and Strasbourg. The financial indemnity was higher even than that which he had mentioned during the armistice negotiations: 500 million francs, though the figure was subsequently reduced to 400 million. Until that sum was paid, France would have to submit to partial occupation. Thiers had no alternative. With the greatest possible reluctance, he signed on 26 February.

When he presented these conditions for ratification by the Assembly in Bordeaux, the delegates were appalled; but there was little they could do. Gambetta and the deputies from Alsace and Lorraine resigned in a body, as shortly afterwards did Victor Hugo. The Assembly's last act was to agree to reconvene on 20 March, but where? Paris, they all agreed, would be impossible: too inflamed, too disordered, too radical, too atheist. It was better that they should meet at Versailles. The decision was, as things turned out, a wise one, as was shown on the very day Thiers signed the treaty by an unpleasant incident that took place in Place de la Bastille.

Units of the National Guard had already been demonstrating there for two days in protest against suspected government plans to disarm them, and on 26 February they staged a mass march, which lasted from 10 a.m. to six in the evening. About 300,000 Parisians took part, and at some point the Guard appropriated some 200 government cannon and hauled them up to Montmartre. The atmosphere was already highly charged, and the seizure of the cannon seemed a further act of aggression. In the space of a few hours, the balance of power in Paris changed. On 8 March, Thiers ordered the army – of which one unit only had been allowed to keep its weapons – to recover the guns; the National Guard resisted; and chaos ensued. The horses needed to move the guns failed to appear; the army was soon surrounded by a hostile crowd. General

Claude Lecomte, who was in command, was seized by mutinous guardsmen and dragged off to their local station at 6 Rue des Rosiers; later that afternoon he was beaten into insensibility and shot in the back.

Unlike the army, the National Guard had not been disarmed – in order, ironically enough, that it should be properly equipped to keep the peace in Paris. On paper it now numbered nearly 400,000 men – though effectively there were a good deal fewer – and in mid-February they began to take power into their own hands. On 15 March the Commune, as it was called, created a Central Committee, whose first action was to refuse to recognise the authority of the general recently appointed by Thiers as their commander – or of the Military Governor of Paris. On the same day, at around five in the afternoon, another general, Jacques Léon Clément-Thomas, was spotted in civilian clothes. Though now retired, he had always been deeply unpopular; but he hardly deserved the fate that awaited him. He too was taken out into the little garden of the house in Rue des Rosiers and shot, not by a properly formed firing squad, but by an uncontrolled bunch of guardsmen who riddled him with some forty bullets. At this moment Georges Clemenceau arrived, shouting '*Pas de sang, mes amis, pas de sang!*'* – only to learn that he was too late. When he saw the bodies of the two generals he broke down and wept.

That evening and throughout the night, the National Guard gradually took control of the city. Twenty-four hours later, 20,000 guardsmen were encamped in front of the Hôtel de Ville, and a red flag – rather than the tricolour – flew above it. The Central Committee meanwhile sent a delegation of the mayors of each *arrondissement*, led by Clemenceau, to negotiate with Thiers at Versailles. They asked for nothing less than a special independent status for Paris, allowing it effectively to govern itself. Meanwhile they reintroduced the revolutionary calendar, abolished the death penalty and military conscription, and passed a resolution to the effect that membership of the Paris Commune was incompatible with that of the National Assembly. Later there would be more

---

* 'No bloodshed, my friends, no bloodshed!'

decrees, including the abolition of night work in bakeries (surely, for the French, this spelt disaster) and the remission of rents owed for the entire period of the siege.

But perhaps the most draconian decree concerned the Church, which the Committee publicly accused of 'complicity in the crimes of the monarchy'. It declared the immediate separation of Church and State, confiscated state funds that had been allotted to the Church, seized the property of religious foundations and ordered the secularisation of all church schools. Over the next seven weeks some two hundred priests, monks and nuns were arrested and twenty-six churches were closed. Certain members of the National Guard even went so far as to stage mock religious processions and obscene parodies of Christian services.

By far the most spectacular of the Commune's actions, however, was the felling of the great Napoleonic column in the Place Vendôme, built in 1806–10 to celebrate the victory of Austerlitz. Its destruction was largely due to the painter Gustave Courbet. 'Inasmuch', he wrote, 'as the Vendôme column is a monument devoid of all artistic value, tending to perpetuate by its expression the ideas of war and conquest of the past imperial dynasty . . . Citizen Courbet expresses the wish that the government of National Defence will authorise him to dismantle it.'

His wish was granted, and on 16 May at around six o'clock in the evening the column came crashing to the ground. But his triumph was short-lived. When, after the defeat of the Commune, the decision was made to re-erect the column, Courbet was required to pay the full cost, estimated at 323,000 francs, in annual 10,000-franc instalments. The French government seized and sold his paintings, while he himself fled to self-imposed exile in Switzerland, where he was to spend the rest of his life.

In Versailles, Thiers was meanwhile planning the recapture of the capital, and working hard to reassemble a new and reliable regular army. Fortunately there was a large number of returned prisoners of war, released under the armistice; and many other fighting men were coming in from all over France. To command this new army, he chose Patrice de MacMahon, now sixty-three; the old marshal had been quite seriously wounded at Sedan, but was now recovered. Highly popular with everybody and still full of his old spirit, by mid-May 1871 he was ready; and on the 20th, now virtually at the city walls, his artillery opened fire on the western districts, some of the shells almost reaching the Etoile. By four o'clock in the morning of Sunday the 21st, 60,000 soldiers had occupied Auteuil and Passy, and two days later much of the centre of the city was effectively theirs; the *communards*, with little discipline or coordination and lacking a proper central command, were decisively outnumbered and could not hope to put up more than token resistance. But the government forces were not to have it all their own way: the following seven days were to become known as *la semaine de sang* – the week of blood – owing to the unspeakable violence and cruelty shown on both sides. Thus, when Montmartre was taken on the 23rd, the soldiers seized forty-two guardsmen together with several women, took them to the same house on Rue des Rosiers where Generals Lecomte and Clément-Thomas had been executed, and shot them all. On Rue Royale, the army captured the immense barricade surrounding the church of the Madeleine and there took another 300 prisoners, all of whom suffered a similar fate.

On the same day the National Guard began setting fire to public buildings. Dozens of houses and offices in the Rue du Faubourg Saint-Honoré, the Rue Saint-Florentin and the Rue de Rivoli, and on the left bank the Rue du Bac and the Rue de Lille, went up in flames, as did the Tuileries Palace. The Richelieu Library in the Louvre was also destroyed, the rest of the building saved only by heroic action by the museum staff and the local fire brigades. Jules Bergeret, the local *communard* commander, sent a message to the Hôtel de Ville: 'The last vestiges of royalty have just disappeared. I wish the same would happen to all the monuments of Paris.' The very next day, the Hôtel de Ville itself was reduced to a charred skeleton. And meanwhile the executions continued, hundreds a day, including that of Georges Darboy, Archbishop of Paris. On the evening of 25 May, Charles Delescluze, now leader of the Commune, put on his red sash of office, walked unarmed to the nearest barricade, climbed to the top and showed himself to the soldiers. He was promptly shot dead, as he intended to be.

Two days later, the capture of the Père Lachaise Cemetery marked the end of the *semaine sanglante*. The Commune was finished, but the executions went on. No one knows how many there were: at least ten thousand, quite possibly twenty. Gustave Flaubert wrote to George Sand: 'Austria did not go into Revolution after Sadowa, nor Italy after Novara, nor Russia after Sebastopol. But our good Frenchmen hasten to pull down their house as soon as the chimney catches fire.'

On 24 July 1873 the National Assembly voted for the construction of the Church of the Sacré Coeur in Montmartre, at the highest point of Paris. It is generally believed to have been dedicated to the memory of all those who lost their lives in the war and the siege, and if it were indeed a monument it would be a superb one – unforgettable and unmistakable in outline, and visible from all over the city. Technically, however, it is not a monument at all: the Assembly's decree is careful to specify that its purpose is 'to expiate the crimes of the Commune'. Now, a century and a half later, the point hardly matters; we can only be grateful for what is just about the only good thing to emerge from the sad and shameful years that this chapter has had, alas, to record.

20

'J'accuse!'
1873–1935

We believe that if Germany, far from making the slightest effort
to carry out the peace treaty, has always tried to escape her
obligations, it is because until now she has not been convinced
of her defeat . . . We are also certain that Germany, as a nation,
resigns herself to keep her pledged word only under the impact
of necessity.

Raymond Poincaré, December 1922

THE THIRD REPUBLIC had actually come into being on 4
September 1870, when it had been proclaimed by Gambetta
from the balcony of the Hôtel de Ville; but as France slowly pulled
itself together after war, siege and commune, it began to look as
though it might not last very long. Thiers and Gambetta, both
convinced republicans, had formed a reluctant alliance; but there was
trouble looming – and that trouble was the monarchists. For a long
time they had believed that the principal obstacle to the return of the
monarchy was the rivalry between the two branches of the House of
Bourbon. The Comte de Chambord, posthumous son of the Duc de
Berry and therefore grandson of Charles X – he was already calling
himself Henry V – had no direct progeny; why should he not reign
and be succeeded by the Orléanist Comte de Paris? Thiers seemed
to be riding high; but monarchists and Bonapartists together decided
to get rid of him. They finally unearthed a leader, the Duc de Broglie,
whose father had been minister under Louis-Philippe; he also happened
to be, on his mother's side, the grandson of Madame de Staël.★

★ See p. 188.

319

He set himself up against Thiers, and on 24 May 1873 won the election.

That same evening old Marshal MacMahon was elected President of the Republic. He was a monarchist through and through, and saw no reason not to have Chambord as King of France. But there was a reason, and a good one: Chambord had made it clear from the outset that his sympathies were well to the right of his grand-father. He would not come to terms with any assembly, nor would he accept the tricolour; it would be the white flag of the Bourbons or nothing. And so it turned out to be nothing. 'Nobody will deny', remarked Thiers, 'that the founder of the French Republic is Monsieur le Comte de Chambord.' At this point one might have expected the monarchists to turn to the Comte de Paris; but they apparently felt that they could not do so until after Chambord's death;* instead, they agreed to accept MacMahon as a sort of uncrowned monarch, a 'Lieutenant General of the Realm' who would stand above party political strife. The term of his personal mandate was accordingly fixed for seven years, after which he might stand for re-election. This article was approved in the Assembly by 353 votes to 352. The fate of the Third Republic had been confirmed by a single vote; it was to last another sixty-seven years.

In 1886 the prime minister, Charles-Louis de Saulces de Freycinet, made the cardinal mistake of appointing General Georges Boulanger as his Minister for War on the recommendation of Georges Clemenceau, who had been the general's fellow-pupil at the lycée in Nantes. Boulanger was an able administrator, but he was also a natural showman, with a bottomless talent for self-advertisement. A law had recently been passed forbidding entry into France to the head of any family that had previously reigned; the holding of any office or commission by other members of those families was also banned, but the law had never been intended to apply to those already on active military service. There was accordingly something of a sensation when Boulanger struck from the active list both General the Duc d'Aumale, the fifth son of Louis-Philippe who was

---

* Chambord lived on until 1883, by which time enthusiasm for the monarchy had faded. Two years later the crown jewels were broken up and sold.

then Inspector General of the Army, and the Duc de Chartres, Colonel of the 7th Chasseurs. He also introduced a series of radical reforms of the army, acquiring a reputation for his respect and concern for the simple soldier, whose food and lodging he considerably improved. He was arrogant and insufferably bumptious, but the general public took him to their hearts; many indeed saw him as a new Napoleon, who would rescue France from a series of ineffably dreary republican governments and lead her back to greatness and glory.

In 1887 Boulanger received 100,000 votes for an election in the Seine department, despite the fact that he had not stood for election. His supporters were jubilant, crying: 'To the Elysée!'; many members of the Assembly, however, thought very differently. The minister of the interior, Charles Floquet, is nowadays remembered only for his taunt when Boulanger entered the Chamber: 'At your age, Sir, Napoleon was dead!' This, and other similar remarks which Boulanger took very much to heart, eventually led to a duel with Floquet, in which the general was slightly wounded. Then, quite suddenly, his confidence seemed to desert him. In particular, he became seriously – and probably quite unnecessarily – alarmed by new measures introduced by the government to deal with threats to the safety of the state. He was terrified of arrest, above all because it would separate him from his beloved mistress, the already consumptive Marguerite de Bonnemains. On 1 May 1889 the two of them fled to Brussels; his career was over, Boulangism was finished. When Marguerite died in his arms in 1891, he was utterly heartbroken. Two months later, he shot himself on her grave.

Then came the Panama scandal. Ferdinand de Lesseps had done a splendid job with the Suez Canal, and when he announced that he intended to dig another one through the isthmus of Panama there was no shortage of investors. Work began on the site on New Year's Day, 1881. De Lesseps's original intention was to build a sea-level canal as he had at Suez, and he had paid several visits to Panama to reconnoitre the site. All his visits, however, had been in the dry season, which lasts only four months of the year. He and his men were thus totally unprepared for the eight-month rains, during which the Chagres river became a furious torrent, rising by

35 feet and causing constant landslides. The only hope was to build locks, at vast additional expense. The jungle through which the canal had to run was alive with poisonous snakes and spiders, and by 1884 malaria and yellow fever together were claiming over two hundred victims a month, while the steel equipment rusted almost as soon as it was unpacked. It was never like this at Suez. De Lesseps kept the project going as long as he could, but in December 1888 the Panama Canal Company declared itself bankrupt. Some 800,000 Frenchmen lost their investments, which amounted to some 1.8 billion gold francs.

And worse was to come. In 1892–3, 510 deputies and several ministers (including Clemenceau) were accused of taking bribes, either from de Lesseps and his son Charles in return for authorising further stock issues, or from the Panama Canal Company to hide its financial position from the public. Of these 104 were found guilty. De Lesseps and his son were both sentenced to long periods of imprisonment, as was the engineer Gustave Eiffel,* who had been made responsible for the design of the locks. Their sentences were eventually remitted; but one of the ministers served three years in gaol and Baron Jacques de Reinach, who handled the government's relations with the Canal Company, committed suicide.

Before his death Reinach, though himself Jewish, gave a list of all those implicated in the affair to the violently anti-Semitic *La Libre Parole*, which overnight became one of the most popular and influential newspapers in the country. This list was published every day in very brief instalments, so that for months hundreds of deputies had to live on tenterhooks. It was unfortunate that Reinach's principal collaborator, Cornelius Herz, and several other of their associates were also Jewish – giving the *Parole* plenty of opportunities for scurrilous articles, which may well have had their effect on the events which were shortly to follow.

For the dust of Panama had scarcely settled when there came another disastrous affair – one, this time, which was to rock France to its foundations. French intelligence employed a cleaner working at the German Embassy, who was instructed to watch carefully for

---

* Eiffel had completed his magnificent Tower in 1889.

any documents that might look to her suspicious. Thus it was that in September 1894 she found in the waste-paper basket of the military attaché, Colonel Maximilian von Schwartzkoppen, a document – it was known as the *bordereau* – torn into six pieces, which strongly suggested that a French officer of the General Staff was acting treasonably. Because of a *dissimilarity* in handwriting★ – but also because of the fervent anti-Semitism that was rife in the French army – suspicion fastened on Captain Alfred Dreyfus, a thirty-five-year-old artillery officer of Alsatian-Jewish descent. He was arrested, and on 5 January 1895 was brought before a court-martial. Since, throughout the proceedings, he was denied the right to examine – let alone to question – the evidence against him, he was not surprisingly found guilty. He was then forced to appear in the courtyard of the Ecole Militaire before silent rows of soldiers, while his sword was broken in front of him and his badges of rank, buttons and braid stripped from his uniform, after which, still fervently proclaiming his innocence, he was transported to spend the rest of his life on Devil's Island off the coast of French Guiana.

In the following year, thanks primarily to an investigation ordered by the head of counter-espionage Colonel Georges Picquart, new evidence came to light identifying the real culprit as a certain Major Ferdinand Esterhazy. But the army, reluctant to admit that it had been responsible for so serious a miscarriage of justice and having first silenced Picquart by transferring him to the deserts of south Tunisia, suppressed as much of this evidence as it could: after a trial lasting only two days, Esterhazy was unanimously acquitted. Already, however, rumours were widely circulating to the effect that an innocent man had been deliberately framed and that the army had been guilty of a cover-up; and these suspicions were most forcibly voiced in '*J'Accuse!*', a vehement open letter to the president of the Republic by the novelist Emile Zola, published in January 1898 by Clemenceau's newspaper *L'Aurore*.

Since the clamour refused to die down, in 1899 the army brought Dreyfus back from his exile for a further court-martial, at which still

---

★ The graphologists' assertion was that 'the *lack* of resemblance between Dreyfus's writing and that of the *bordereau* was a proof of "self-forgery"'.

more accusations were to be thrown at him. By this time, Paris was talking of little else. Families were split down the middle; old friends swore never to speak to each other again; furious guests left dinner-parties, slamming the door behind them. The Dreyfusards included Georges Clemenceau and Henri Poincaré, the writer Anatole France and the actress Sarah Bernhardt; the anti-Dreyfusards comprised most of the Catholic Church and its journal *La Croix*, most of the military, much of the aristocracy and a large number of journalists – notorious among them Edouard Drumont, publisher of *La Libre Parole*. There were also some 60,000 members of the so-called League of Patriots, a proto-fascist organisation founded by General Boulanger and the rabble-rouser Paul Déroulède, and another large group from the recently founded Catholic, monarchist and anti-Semitic Action Française. This new trial was, from the point of view of the army, a grave mistake. Resulting, as it was intended to result, in another conviction and an additional sentence (although the previous sentence was for life) it simply showed up the duplicity and dishonesty which had ruined a perfectly innocent man. Dreyfus never returned to Guiana; instead, that same year, he was offered – and accepted – a pardon by President Emile Loubet. He thus regained his freedom – but that, he declared, was nothing to him without his honour, and in the eyes of the law he was still a traitor. Yet still the government dithered; it was not until 12 July 1906 that he was officially exonerated, readmitted into the army and promoted to the rank of major. A week later, he was made a Chevalier of the Legion of Honour. After twelve years, the *affaire Dreyfus* was over at last.*

Through much of the Dreyfus case, the President of the Republic was Félix Faure. He had been elected in January 1895 – largely because he was the only candidate who offended no one – and remained at the Elysée Palace until his sudden and somewhat

---

* Though by then in his mid-fifties, Dreyfus was to fight in the First World War and to live on until July 1935. There is a statue of him, holding his broken sword, in the Boulevard Raspail, outside the Notre-Dame-des-Champs metro station; a second was erected in 1988 in the Tuileries Garden and a third is under construction in his home town of Mulhouse.

embarrassing death on 16 February 1899. This occurred as the result of an apoplectic stroke, which he suffered in the Salon Bleu of the palace while *in flagrante* with one of his several mistresses, Madame Marguerite Steinheil. His secretaries, who were in the room adjoining and who were perfectly well aware of what was going on, were alerted by the lady's screams and burst into the room. They found her hysterical, unable even to extricate herself since the president's convulsed hands were inextricably tangled in some of her hair; she had to be cut free before she could get dressed.* She was then hastily removed from the palace before the presidential widow could be informed. (The story goes that Madame Faure sent at once for a priest, in case her husband had some life left in him and could be given extreme unction. On the priest's arrival the door was opened by the butler, to whom he breathlessly asked: '*Monsieur le Président, a-t-il encore sa connaissance?*' '*Non, monsieur,*' replied the butler. '*On l'a fait sortir par la porte du jardin.*')†

Finding a priest in a hurry had not been so easy; the Church was having a hard time. Much of the hierarchy were fervent monarchists and came from aristocratic families; it was thus only natural that the republicans should see the Church as a threat, both to republicanism and to progress. Already in 1882 religious instruction in schools had been suppressed, and members of religious orders were forbidden to teach in them. Civil marriages only were permitted, divorce was introduced and chaplains were removed from the armed services. The situation became even worse when Emile Combes was elected prime minister in 1902. Almost immediately after taking office he

---

* Rumour had it that they were engaged in oral sex. For ever after Mme Steinheil was known as the *pompe funèbre* (funeral).

† This pun is untranslatable, since *connaissance* can mean 'friend' or 'consciousness'. It was not the last time that Mme Steinheil screamed for help. On 31 May 1908, the police were called to her house to find her husband and her stepmother dead, the former by strangling, the latter by choking on her false teeth. She herself was found gagged and tied, most inexpertly, to a bed. Her evidence about four black-robed strangers was palpably untrue, and she was arrested. Her subsequent trial for murder was the cause célèbre of 1909. She was acquitted and subsequently came to England, where she married the 6th Lord Abinger. Having passed the last forty-five years of her life in unshakeable rectitude, she lived in Hove – where I once met her – until her death in 1954.

closed down all parochial schools. He then banned every one of the fifty-four religious orders that existed in France at that time; about twenty thousand monks and nuns left the country, many of them settling in Spain. There was a further crisis in 1904 when Emile Loubet, who had succeeded Faure as president, paid a state visit to King Victor Emmanuel, only to evoke a strong protest from Pope Pius X, who did not recognise the Kingdom of Italy. Combes replied by withdrawing the French ambassador to the Holy See. In 1905 the Assembly declared that 'the attitude of the Vatican' had rendered inevitable the separation of Church and State, and in December another law was passed to this effect. For the Church, there was one advantage: it could no longer be dictated to, and could henceforth elect its own bishops without government interference. But a quarter of a century of what effectively amounted to persecution had left it gravely weakened, and it has never entirely recovered.

The second half of the nineteenth century, and particularly its last two decades, saw the spectacular growth of the second French Empire. The first, consisting of the colonies in North America, the Caribbean and India, had been subsequently lost; France had started again with the capture of Algiers in 1830; she had subsequently absorbed Algeria to such a point that it had become three French *départements*; technically, it was part of France. This time she concentrated on Africa and its outlying islands – notably Senegal, Tunisia, Mauretania, Mali, Ivory Coast, Chad, Gabon, Morocco (a protectorate), Madagascar and Réunion; on Indochina – Vietnam, Laos, Cambodia; and on the South Pacific – New Caledonia, the Marquesas Islands and much of Polynesia. The Republicans had originally opposed the whole idea of territorial expansion, but when Germany began her own programme they changed their minds; and before long, as trade with the new colonies developed, the empire was seen as a powerful force for good, spreading Christianity, French culture and the French language and generally acquiring prestige for the motherland – what was known as 'the civilising mission', *la mission civilisatrice.*

As for the British, who were of course the principal rivals in the business of empire-building, they viewed the steady French expansion with equanimity and perhaps a moderate degree of admiration. Even when Napoleon III had built fifteen powerful new propeller-driven battlecruisers, the French navy remained smaller and palpably inferior to their own; and besides, the two spheres of influence seldom seriously overlapped. Perhaps the most dangerous moment came in 1898, when a French expedition to Fashoda on the White Nile tried to gain control of the whole river basin, blocking Britain from the Sudan. On the spot the British – ostensibly acting in the interests of the Khedive of Egypt – outnumbered the French by about ten to one, and the two sides remained perfectly friendly; but in London and Paris tempers ran high. At last the French backed down, realising just in time that Germany was growing ever more powerful and that in the always-possible event of another war they would be lost without British friendship; but they could not conceal the fact that they had been publicly humiliated, and it was to be several years before the 'Fashoda affair' was forgotten.

In the first years of the twentieth century, France's foreign policy was dominated by a fear of Germany – whose larger size and faster-growing economy she could not hope to match – combined with a determination to recover what she considered her birthright: Alsace-Lorraine. (Since 1871 the statue representing Strasbourg, capital of Alsace, in the Place de la Concorde had been draped in black.) In an attempt to isolate so dangerous a neighbour, France entered into alliances with Britain and Russia, giving rise to the Triple Entente of 1907. Six years later the prime minister, Raymond Poincaré, was elected president of the Republic. Determined to make the presidency something more than purely ceremonial, he was an enthusiastic supporter of the Entente, having made two visits to Russia to strengthen strategic ties; he was not, however, as anti-German as is often believed – indeed in January 1914 he was the first French president to enter the German Embassy.

Two months later, however, he was involved in a serious scandal which almost cost him his position. A former prime minister, Joseph Caillaux, now minister of finance, threatened to publish letters indicating that the president had been engaged in secret talks with the Vatican – a revelation that would have outraged the deeply anti-clerical left. Fortunately, Caillaux was himself vulnerable: the editor of *Le Figaro*, Gaston Calmette, possessed documents showing that the minister had been having an affair with his future second wife while still married to his first. An arrangement was thus easily made: Caillaux would agree not to publish Poincaré's letters after all; Poincaré in return would put presidential pressure on Calmette similarly to remain silent. All would have been well had not the second Madame Caillaux, fearful for her own reputation, walked into Calmette's office on 16 March and shot him dead. Astonishingly, she was acquitted four months later on the grounds of *crime passionel*. Poincaré's secret remained safe.

On 28 June the president was at the Longchamp races when he heard of the assassination of Archduke Franz Ferdinand in Sarajevo. He ordered an aide to send a letter of condolence and returned to his race-card – and why not? It was not after all the assassination that triggered the war, but the Austro-Hungarian government's decision a day or two later to make it a pretext for hostilities with Serbia, through Serbia with her ally Russia, and consequently with the Triple Entente. France contemplated the outbreak of war with mixed feelings. The intellectuals on the whole welcomed it as an opportunity at last to avenge the humiliating defeat of 1870; so, it need hardly be said, did Déroulède's infamous League of Patriots, which had been agitating for a *guerre de revanche*, a war of revenge, since the 1880s. The socialists had long opposed war as a matter of principle; but when their pacifist leader Jean Jaurès was assassinated by a deranged fanatic in a Paris restaurant on 31 July, they changed their tune. On 4 August Poincaré addressed a message to the French people: 'In the coming war, France will be heroically defended by all its sons, whose sacred union will not break in the face of the enemy.'

The Germans had hoped that the war would be short and sharp: they invaded from the north-east, and advanced through central Belgium to enter France near Lille – the site of much of the heavy industry – counting on striking a mortal blow to French steel and coal production within a matter of months. Their basic strategy was to turn west near the Channel and then south to cut off the French retreat; the French army would be surrounded and Paris left without defence. But then, in early September, when their army was only some thirty miles from the capital, and just after the government had left Paris for Bordeaux, came the Battle of the Marne. By this time the German forces were exhausted; some of them had marched more than 150 miles. They had also – like Caesar almost two thousand years before – dramatically underestimated the French spirit: they found all bridges demolished, all the railways disabled. But their morale remained high; their ultimate victory was never in doubt.

Their proximity to the capital was alarming indeed for the French; but it had its advantages. The Marne is the only battle in the history of the world in which some three thousand of its combatants arrived by taxi. On the evening of 7 September General Joseph Gallieni gathered about six hundred Paris cabs at the Invalides, to carry the soldiers to the front. Each cab carried five men, four in the back and one next to the driver. Only the rear lights were lit: the drivers were ordered to follow those of the cab ahead. Obedient to the city regulations, they dutifully ran their meters; the total of 70,012 francs was reimbursed by the Treasury – a small price to pay for a story that has now become a legend, and for the first use of motorised infantry in battle.*

The Battle of the Marne was a victory. How complete a victory is still a matter of dispute – the French suffered a quarter of a million casualties and Germany gained a large part of the industrial north-east – but it was victory enough: it saved Paris. It was followed by a 'race to the sea', during which both armies moved towards the north-west, each trying to side-step the other. Despite fierce battles, the race was lost by both sides; the front was eventually stabilised from the North Sea to the Swiss border. Meanwhile, the armies had dug into the ground to such an extent that it became little more than a double network of trenches, separated by an occasionally almost non-existent no-man's-land.

Thus it was that the French – and the British – were condemned to four years of attrition, causing unspeakable devastation and the death of one and a half million French soldiers – one Frenchman

---

* The other hero of the Marne was Gallieni's commander-in-chief, Marshal Foch, remembered chiefly for his famous telegram: 'My left is broken; my right is weakening; the situation is excellent: *J'attaque!*'

in twenty – with, at least until the beginning of 1918, virtually no territorial gains or losses for either side. It had, of course, its milestones. There was, for example, the second Battle of Ypres in April and May 1915, which saw the first use (by the Germans) of poison gas. This was directed against a French unit, consisting mostly of colonial troops. At about 5 p.m. on 22 April, French sentries noticed a greenish-yellow cloud moving towards them. A British rifleman remembered:

> I saw . . . the dusky warriors of French Africa; away went their rifles, equipment, even their tunics that they might run the faster. One man came stumbling through our lines. An officer of ours held him up with a levelled revolver, 'What's the matter, you bloody lot of cowards?' says he. The Zouave was frothing at the mouth, his eyes started from their sockets, and he fell writhing at the officer's feet.

The battle was indecisive, though of the city of Ypres there was barely one stone left on another. And after that, the gloves were off: 'the war to end wars' became increasingly terrible.

Virtually all 1916, from February until December, was given over to the Battle of Verdun. This time the British were not directly involved: the fighting was between the French and the Germans. Its 303 days made it the longest and perhaps the costliest battle in human history; the French lost 377,000, the Germans almost as many. It was at Verdun that the world first heard of General Philippe Pétain,* who commanded fifty-two divisions, which he rotated after keeping them only two weeks in the front line. He also organised day-and-night transport by lorry, bringing a constant stream of arms, ammunition and troops into the town. '*On les aura!*' was his order of the day: 'We shall get them!' Known as the 'Hero of Verdun' and a Marshal of France, he was, between the wars, one of the most respected Frenchmen alive; it must be left to the following chapter to record his decline and fall.

Despite the appalling losses, Verdun was technically a French

---

* At the beginning of the battle, he is said to have been fetched during the night from a Paris hotel by a staff officer, who happened to know with which of his countless mistresses he could be found.

victory; but it was far more than that. In French minds it has come to represent the entire war – and not only the war but all the suffering and sacrifice that the war entailed. In the 1960s the battle-field also became the symbol of Franco-German reconciliation; there is an intensely moving photograph of President François Mitterrand and Chancellor Helmut Kohl in the Douaumont cemetery, their heads bowed, holding hands in the driving rain.

During the fighting at Verdun the British army was engaged, between July and November, at the Battle of the Somme – which saw, incidentally, the first appearance of a new and formidable weapon: the tank. Few battles have been bloodier: out of more than three million combatants, a million were killed or wounded. On its very first day the British army alone suffered 57,470 casualties; never before had such a figure even been approached. By November the French had lost another 200,000. The battle had been planned jointly by General Sir Douglas Haig – who had recently replaced Sir John French as the British commander-in-chief – and his French opposite number General Joseph Joffre, affectionately known by the army as 'Papa'. Joffre had had an adventurous early career, with battle honours ranging from Madagascar to Timbuktu; on his promotion to supremo in 1911, however, he had never commanded an army and cheerfully admitted that he had no knowledge of staff work – a fact which was all too soon to show: already by the end of 1914 Gallieni – who had once been his superior – was being tipped to take his place. Joffre's relations with Haig, however, were poor, and there were constant rows: when Haig suggested that the Somme offensive should be delayed until August to allow for more training and more artil-lery, Joffre shouted that in that case 'the French army would cease to exist!', and had to be calmed down with 'liberal doses of 1840 brandy'. He was in fact to be replaced (by General Robert Nivelle) at the end of the year, but was promoted to the rank of marshal of France to make up for it.

And what, after those five nightmare months, did we and the French have to show for the massacre of the Somme? Precious little. For some time after the war it was seen as a hard-won victory, which robbed the German army of its strategic initiative and led to its eventual collapse. More recently, historians have been less sure.

In any event, it has become for the British something like Verdun for the French; and the six footling miles gained of German territory – the most since the Battle of the Marne – serve only to emphasise the obscenity of it all.

In April 1917 Pétain became commander-in-chief of the French army, just in time to deal with a series of mutinies. They were hardly surprising; even among the survivors, Verdun and the Somme had taken their toll. The cold, the rain, the mud, the rats, the whole misery of the trenches had simply become too much. The soldiers were exhausted, many of them severely shell-shocked. On the whole Pétain dealt with them sympathetically. Although some 35,000 soldiers were involved, he held only 3,400 courts-martial, at which 554 men were sentenced to death but over 90 per cent had their sentences commuted. The mutinies, it need hardly be said, were kept secret from the Germans; full details were revealed as recently as 1967.*

That same month of April saw the entry of the United States into the war, after which it made substantial contributions in terms of raw materials and supplies, though it was not till the summer of 1918 that the arrival of vast numbers of fresh, rested American troops changed the whole balance of the war and was largely responsible for the German defeat. In July there was a last despairing assault on the Marne, but the offensive was crushed by about forty French divisions, assisted by British and American units. After this the war was as good as over; and on 11 November, as all the world knows, the armistice was signed.

The following year saw the peace conference in Paris, culminating with the Treaty of Versailles. The terms of this agreement, essentially drawn up by the Big Four – David Lloyd George, Woodrow Wilson, Vittorio Emanuele Orlando of Italy and our old friend Georges Clemenceau, now seventy-eight and prime minister, who drove the hardest bargain of them all – were certainly punitive: France took back Alsace-Lorraine and occupied the German industrial Saar basin; the German African colonies were partitioned between France and Britain; Germany meanwhile was

* Guy Pedroncini, *Les Mutineries de 1917.*

largely disarmed, obliged to take full responsibility for the war and ordered to pay savage reparations.★ Although only a small fraction of these reparations was ever paid, France needed every penny of them. The country, already burdened with a heavy public debt, was faced with a vast reconstruction programme to rebuild its coal and steel industries in the north-east and to repair the damage done in Lille, Douai, Cambrai, Valenciennes and those other cities and towns which had been under German occupation throughout the war. Then, in 1918, came the calamitous outbreak of Spanish flu, which devastated the remaining population of Europe and accounted for another quarter of a million French deaths – so many that serious initiatives were set up to increase the birth rate: mothers who raised four or five children 'with dignity' were awarded the bronze *médaille de la famille française*; those with six or seven received the silver; those with eight or more, the gold. France was in serious crisis. Nor was the situation helped by the fact that in 1920 the president of the Republic went off his head.

Paul Deschanel had enjoyed, like all his predecessors, a distinguished political career. For years he had been a member of the Académie Française, and had written a number of well-received books on literature and history. He had been president of the Chamber as early as 1898, and was re-elected in 1912, holding the position until February 1920, when he became president, having beaten Clemenceau to the post. He began his term of office respectably enough; but his staff became a little anxious after some weeks when, being presented by a delegation of schoolgirls with a bouquet, he hurled the flowers back at them one by one. On another occasion he is

---

★ But perhaps Germany got off more lightly than we think. Far from hanging the Kaiser as Lloyd George had advocated, the Allies allowed him to live in comfortable exile for nearly a quarter of a century until his death; barely a dozen German war criminals were brought to trial, and most of them were acquitted; although Germany ceded some 10 per cent of its territory, it lost less than 2 per cent of its native population; and of the 132 billion gold marks demanded, all but 50 billion had been already written off. Germany finally paid only about 2 billion – a tiny fraction of what Hitler would later spend on rearmament.

said to have received the British ambassador wearing nothing but his ceremonial decorations. There was also an extraordinary incident when, late in the night of 24–25 May, he fell out of the window of the presidential train near Montargis. He was found wandering about in his nightshirt by a platelayer, who took him to the cottage of the signalman at the nearest level crossing, where his aides subsequently retrieved him. Later in the summer he walked out of a meeting straight into a lake fully clothed. He resigned on 21 September, and was the only president to have moved straight from the Elysée Palace to a mental home.

It was fortunate for France that for the first decade of the peace her government – if not always her presidency – was in safe and efficient hands, usually those of Aristide Briand★ and Raymond Poincaré, a leader of the so-called Bloc National, a right-wing political coalition whose watchword was 'Germany will pay!' He showed the world that he meant it when in January 1923 Germany defaulted on her payments and Poincaré, then prime minister, ordered the invasion of the Ruhr. He firmly maintained that he did this not only for purely financial reasons, but also because the reparation payments had been a firm undertaking in the Versailles Treaty; if the Germans defaulted on this, it would create the most dangerous of precedents: what then would prevent them from dismantling the rest of the treaty and plunging the world into another war? Germany naturally protested, staging furious demonstrations in Düsseldorf in the course of which 130 civilians were killed. There is a popular theory – which may be partly, though not entirely, true – that it was the Ruhr occupation that led to the hyperinflation which was to destroy the German economy later that year: by November, the United States dollar was worth 4,210,500,000,000 marks.

From the French point of view, the occupation of the Ruhr achieved its object; but France paid a heavy price in foreign disap-

---

★ Briand was eleven times prime minister. He was also famous for his long affair with Princess Marie Bonaparte, later Princess George of Greece. This appears not to have been entirely satisfactory: after it ended the princess devoted the rest of her long life to sexual research.

proval of her conduct, and in a consequent wave of sympathy for Germany. Nothing could be done by the newly established League of Nations, since her action did not technically contravene the Versailles Treaty; she was however obliged to agree to what was known as the Dawes plan, which provided for the withdrawal of her troops and substantially reduced the German payments; the last French military units were to leave Düsseldorf and Duisberg on 25 August 1925.

Briand was a very different sort of man from Poincaré. He was above all a conciliator, and after 1918 devoted his political life to the establishment of lasting peace in Europe. He at first put himself at the disposal of the League of Nations, but the organisation was hamstrung in its very beginnings by the absence of the United States and a marked lack of enthusiasm on the part of Britain. In 1925 he succeeded in negotiating the Locarno Pact, by the terms of which France, Britain, Italy, Poland and Germany mutually guaranteed one another against aggression. This would technically have drawn Britain in against France at the time of the Ruhr occupation; but that was now over, and Briand was fairly certain that it would never happen again. In 1926 he was awarded, with his friend the German statesman Gustav Stresemann, the Nobel Peace Prize; but his own country was to show him little gratitude for his efforts; when in 1931 he stood for the presidency he was easily defeated. He died in 1932, at the age of seventy.

Briand had only recently gone to his grave when France was shaken by the Stavisky affair – not perhaps quite as serious as the Dreyfus case or the Panama scandal, but throwing nevertheless an unwelcome light on corruption among not a few politicians and judges. Serge Alexandre Stavisky – *le beau Sasha*, he was called – was a Ukrainian Jew whose parents had moved to France. His past had been nothing if not chequered: he had been a café singer, a night-club manager, the operator of an illegal casino and a worker in a soup factory. By the 1930s he was running the municipal pawn-brokers in Bayonne. He was also active in the financial world, and his considerable charm had made him several rich and influential friends. He had first run foul of the law in 1927 when he was arrested on a charge of fraud, but his trial was postponed again and again; he was granted bail nineteen times. Meanwhile a judge who claimed to possess secret documents proving his guilt was found decapitated. According to the American journalist Janet Flanner,

> The scheme which finally killed Alexandre Stavisky . . . was his emission of hundreds of millions of francs' worth of false bonds on the city of Bayonne's municipal pawnshop, which were bought up by life insurance companies, counselled by the Minister of Colonies, who was counselled by the Minister of Commerce, who was counselled by the Mayor of Bayonne, who was counselled by the little manager of the hockshop, who was counselled by Stavisky.

In December 1933 Stavisky saw that the game was up and fled. In January the police reported that they had found him in a chalet in Chamonix, dying from a gunshot wound. They claimed that he had committed suicide, but it was widely believed that they had killed him. These suspicions, the revelations of his long criminal record as an embezzler and a confidence trickster, the losses suffered by vast numbers of his victims and his close involvement with several ministers, led to nasty clashes in the Assembly, finally resulting in the resignation in January 1934 of the prime minister, Camille Chautemps. Chautemps was succeeded by Edouard Daladier, and Daladier took immediate action. First, unsurprisingly, he dismissed the Prefect of Police, Jean Chiappe, who was notorious for his right-wing sympathies and suspected of encouraging anti-government demonstrations; then, for reasons rather more obscure, he dismissed the director of the Comédie-Française, apparently for staging an 'anti-democratic' play, which happened to be Shakespeare's *Coriolanus*. He replaced him, equally unaccountably, with the head of the Sûreté Générale.

Indignation, however, refused to die down. People had seen what had happened in Italy and what was now happening over the border in Nazi Germany, and their fears of a fascist conspiracy were real. But so too were the several fascist groups who longed only to follow the German and Italian example. On the night of 6–7 February 1934 they came out on the streets, all of them, left and right together – monarchists and republicans, radical socialists, anti-Semitic reactionaries, together with members of the Action Française, the

Mouvement Franciste and the Croix-de-Feu.* The Palais Bourbon was literally besieged by the mob, and to defend the Concorde bridge the troops were obliged to open fire. Fifteen were killed. Nothing of the kind had happened since the Commune, sixty-three years before. What was it all about? What, exactly, did the demonstrators want? It is hard to say. '*A bas les voleurs!*'† they cried, but there was more to it than that. Many, it now seems clear, were bent on nothing less than the destruction of the Third Republic. Daladier was forced to resign after just ten days in office.‡ He was followed by Gaston Doumergue, who finally succeeded in forming a coalition cabinet.

A trial of twenty important people associated with Stavisky opened in 1935. Among those in the dock were his widow, two deputies and a general. All were found not guilty; but France had been seriously weakened and remained deeply divided for the rest of the decade. This was a tragedy, the more so because in those years the country was called upon to face the deadliest challenge in all its history – a challenge from which it failed, alas, to acquit itself with great distinction.

---

* The Mouvement Franciste, founded in 1933, was a fascist organisation funded by Mussolini. The Croix-de-Feu began as an association of war veterans but later moved steadily to the right. It included among its members the young François Mitterrand.

† 'Down with the thieves!'

‡ He was back again in 1938, in time for the Munich conference – to which he made remarkably little contribution.

21

The Cross of Lorraine

1935–45

I invite the officers and the French soldiers who are in British
territory or who might arrive here, with their weapons or
without their weapons . . . to put themselves in contact with
me. Come what may, the flame of French resistance must not,
and will not, be extinguished.

Charles de Gaulle, 18 June 1940

B Y THE MIDDLE of the 1930s, the German threat was looming
ever darker on the eastern horizon. Adolf Hitler had come
to power in 1933, and was already speaking openly of 'building a
greater Germany'; his book *Mein Kampf* made it all too clear that
among his aims was the destruction of France. This caused the
French still more distress when in 1935 they learned that Britain
– without even bothering to consult them – had signed a naval
treaty agreeing to a substantial increase in the size of the German
navy; and when in March 1936 German troops reoccupied the
Rhineland in flagrant breach of the Versailles Treaty and Britain
lifted not a finger in protest, Franco-British relations deteriorated
still further. Hitler meanwhile grew steadily more confident that
he need no longer fear active European opposition to his policies.
In London, the government of Neville Chamberlain – who had
been an admirable Lord Mayor of Birmingham but had hardly
travelled beyond the Channel and knew next to nothing of foreign
affairs – believed that, if another war were to be avoided, the
Führer must be given all he asked for; only Winston Churchill
and Duff Cooper did their best to alert the world to the dangers
that lay ahead.

The situation was clarified rather than confused by the Spanish Civil War, which lasted from July 1936 to April 1939. Germany and Italy at once joined the Nationalists under General Francisco Franco, Germany in particular using the war as a heaven-sent opportunity to develop new techniques for her air force, which was by now considerably stronger than that of the Allies. Britain and France, by contrast, refused to intervene – Britain because its government feared escalation and a new European conflict, France because she was afraid to act alone.

In March 1938 Hitler, by now convinced that he could do as he liked, annexed Austria, which gave his troops an enthusiastic welcome.* He then announced that he proposed to do the same to Czechoslovakia, on the grounds that the country contained, mostly around its borders, more than 3 million ethnic Germans – the so-called *Sudetendeutsch* – who were properly subjects of the Fatherland. This news caused still further anxiety in France, which since 1924 had been bound to Czechoslovakia by a treaty of alliance. Edouard Daladier, now once again prime minister, consulted Neville Chamberlain and received the expected reply: Britain had no intention of going to war for such a cause.† But Chamberlain was now genuinely alarmed, making his first flights to see Hitler and to discuss the situation in person. He got nowhere. Hitler either rejected his proposals outright or, in accepting them, told him that they were not nearly enough and immediately stepped up his demands.

Negotiations were eventually brought to a head by a meeting in Munich on 29 September, attended by Hitler and Mussolini on one side and Chamberlain and Daladier on the other. Czechoslovakia, the subject of the conference, was not represented: 'About us, without us!' the Czechs complained. Effectively, the agreement handed Hitler the Sudetenland on a plate. Chamberlain, who somehow believed that this would satisfy him and that there would be no more demands,

---

* Already in 1918 the majority of Austrians had voted for union with Germany.
† Chamberlain was to make his feelings – and his almost unbelievable ignorance – clear in a broadcast of September 1938: 'How horrible, fantastic, incredible it seems that we should be digging trenches and trying on gas-masks here because of a quarrel in a far-away country between people of whom we know nothing.'

returned to London, boasting to the cheering crowds who met him at Heston aerodrome that he had achieved 'peace for our time'. He had, as we know, done nothing of the sort. Duff Cooper resigned in disgust – surprisingly, the only member of the cabinet to do so. On 15 March 1939, Nazi troops occupied not just the Sudetenland but all Czechoslovakia. Five months later, on 23 August, Hitler signed a non-aggression pact with the Soviet Union and on 1 September he invaded Poland. Now at last it was borne in on both French and British minds just how wrong Chamberlain had been. No longer could they attempt to prevaricate. On 3 September they declared war.

For the first eight months of hostilities nothing much happened; this was the period the French call the *drôle de guerre*, known to us as the Phoney War and subsequently dubbed by Winston Churchill as the *Sitzkrieg*. Then, in May 1940, everything seemed to happen at once. There was a calamitous campaign in Norway; Chamberlain resigned and Churchill took over the government; German troops invaded France – together with Belgium (which almost immediately capitulated), Luxembourg and the Netherlands – and, by a combination of dive-bombing and constant tank attacks, carried all before them. On Sunday morning, 26 May, the French prime minister, Paul Reynaud, flew to London to inform Churchill that he was already contemplating the loss of Paris. He himself, he said, would never sign a separate peace; but he might well be replaced by someone who would. That same evening, orders were given to launch Operation Dynamo, the evacuation of the British Expeditionary Force from Dunkirk.

The story of Dunkirk – six days during which some 260,000 British and 90,000 French troops were carried over to England, crossing the Channel in anything that could float – is one of the great epics of the Second World War; but it is not ours. What now was happening in France? The commander-in-chief, General Maxime Weygand, still had forty-three divisions to defend the Somme and the Aisne; but they were hopelessly outnumbered and outclassed, and the Germans were infinitely stronger in the air. On the night of 10 June, Mussolini, having allowed Hitler to do the hard work, declared war on France: a 'stab in the back' is how the French ambassador in Rome described it. The reputation of the *Duce* was not enhanced.

The French government decided not to defend Paris; they could not risk its destruction. They first fell back to Tours, but Tours was already under bombardment. There was a suggestion that they should continue the war from Algeria; but North Africa had no factories, few provisions and practically no aircraft fuel. England was already at full stretch, desperately trying to re-equip its own army after Dunkirk. On 13 June, Churchill was in Tours, arguing that the French were wrong and quoting the words of Clemenceau: 'I will fight before Paris, in Paris and behind Paris.' He was answered by the deputy prime minister, Philippe Pétain who, according to Churchill himself, pointed out 'quietly and with dignity' that Clemenceau had had a strategic reserve of sixty divisions; now there were none. Turning Paris into a ruin would not affect the outcome of the war. The next day Pétain read out to the cabinet a draft proposal, in which he spoke of

> the need to stay in France, to prepare a national revival and to share the sufferings of our people. It is impossible for the Government to abandon French soil without emigrating, without deserting. The duty of the Government is, come what may, to remain in the country. If it does not, it can no longer be regarded as the Government.

Philippe Pétain, born in the last year of the Crimean War, was already eighty-four years old. As a military leader his record had been outstanding, particularly during the ten-month Battle of Verdun in 1916, and again in the following year with the mutinies in the French army. At the end of the war, by which time he was commander-in-chief and considered to be one of France's great military heroes, he was presented with his marshal's baton by President Poincaré. In the 1920s he had commanded the French forces in Morocco; in the 1930s he had been Minister for War and in May 1940, after the German invasion, he had been summoned back from Spain, where he was French ambassador, to join the Reynaud government.

Reynaud was a good man with the right ideas. He hated Nazi Germany and was determined to resist. He had however a disastrous

Achilles' heel: his pro-German mistress, the Comtesse Hélène de Portes, who shamelessly interfered in matters of state and, more serious still, persuaded him to appoint several of her like-minded friends to important ministerial positions. In the course of their conversations in Tours, he had asked Churchill what Britain's reaction would be if France were obliged to sign a separate peace. Churchill's reply was one that only he could have made: 'We shall not heap reproaches on an unfortunate ally. And if we are victorious, we assume the unconditional obligation to raise France from her ruins.' He was of course speaking personally, off the cuff and without parliamentary approval; a few days later he received the reaction of the war cabinet: France might make overtures for an armistice, but only if her fleet were first taken to British ports. The cabinet simultaneously put forward another proposal: that there should be established an indissoluble Franco-British union. The citizens of each of the two countries would automatically acquire citizenship of the other; there would be a single cabinet and a single command. Here, surely, was a magnificent conception; alas, it was seen by the French as yet another attempt by *perfide Albion* to take over their country and was rejected out of hand. Reynaud, by now on the brink of a nervous breakdown, saw that there was nothing more that he could do. He handed in his resignation and told President Albert Lebrun that, if he agreed with the general view that France must seek an armistice, he should send for Philippe Pétain. Lebrun did so, and on 16 June Pétain – who was, incidentally, a passionate Anglophobe – assumed the premiership. On 10 July the National Assembly granted him full powers – and the Third Republic came to an end.

The armistice was concluded on 22 June. France had already seen 92,000 of her men killed and 200,000 wounded; nearly 2 million had been rounded up as prisoners of war. The country was now divided into two zones: some three-fifths of it, 'occupied France' to the north and west, was completely controlled by the Germans; the rest, comprising the south-east, would establish its government under Pétain at Vichy. This meant that there would be a semblance of French independence – and even of neutrality, because the Vichy government never formally joined the Axis alliance. Germany, on the other hand, kept 2 million captive French soldiers, most of them subjected to forced labour, as hostages to ensure that Vichy did as it was told – rounding up its Jews★ and paying a heavy tribute of gold, food and supplies to Germany.

What, meanwhile, was to be done about the French navy, which clearly must not be allowed to be taken over by the enemy? It was told that its ships must immediately sail to a British or American port, or possibly to a French port in the Caribbean – Martinique or Guadeloupe. Alternatively, they must be scuttled within six hours. If both these options were refused, 'His Majesty's Government would use whatever force was necessary to prevent the ships from falling into German or Italian hands.' The options were indeed refused. Much of the French fleet was at anchor in the harbour of Mers-el-Kebir, near Oran on the North African coast. On 1 July the French admiral Marcel Gensoul declined to receive the British captain representing Admiral Sir James Somerville, stating only that the French navy would never allow its ships to be taken over and that if the British were to open fire, their action would be interpreted as a declaration of war. Somerville had orders not to delay; he gave Gensoul until 5.30 p.m., hoping that the admiral would change his mind, and it was only at 5.54 that he concluded that he must give the orders that he had hoped and prayed to avoid – to destroy as many ships of his former ally as he possibly could. With sadness and the deepest reluctance he gave the order to fire. Gensoul's flagship the *Dunkerque* and the battlecruiser *Provence* were seriously damaged, while another battlecruiser, the *Bretagne*, blew up and capsized. A total of 1,297 French sailors were killed, and 350 badly wounded. The Royal Navy considered Operation Catapult, as it was called, to be the most shameful operation it had ever been called upon to perform; but there was no alternative, and at least it showed the world that Britain was determined to fight to the last.

No one, British or French, was more dismayed by the tragedy of Mers-el-Kebir than General Charles de Gaulle. A giant of six foot five, he had commanded the 4th Armoured Division and had reached the rank of brigadier-general when Reynaud had made him his

---

★ Some 76,000 Jews were deported during the Occupation, often with the help of the Vichy authorities.

Minister for War. As soon as he heard that Pétain had become premier he had flown to Britain with 100,000 gold francs from secret funds – given to him by Reynaud – and had set about establishing the forces of the Free French. On Tuesday 18 June – the anniversary, incidentally, of Waterloo, and the same day that Churchill made his famous 'This was their finest hour' speech to the House of Commons – only twenty-four hours after his arrival in England and despite the strong objections of the Foreign Office,★ de Gaulle delivered his equally celebrated broadcast to the French people. France, he said, had lost a battle; she had not lost the war.

The Free French were born.

As the Free French increased in numbers in England, so in France did the Resistance. At first it was limited to minor acts of protest – the cutting of telephone lines, the tearing down of posters and the slashing of tyres on German cars and trucks; but after the Special Operations Executive (SOE) was formed in London, with orders from Churchill to 'set Europe ablaze', it was able to supply quantities of arms and wireless equipment to the men and women of the Resistance, both in the towns and in the countryside, where they soon became known as the *Maquis*. Small aeroplanes flew regularly and secretly at night to tiny makeshift airfields all over France, dropping and picking up agents and supplies; and some of us can still remember the messages in French broadcast by the BBC after the nine o'clock news: *Henri a perdu son parapluie* or *la viande est bien cuite* repeated two or three times in slow, sepulchral tones: all of them secret signals, perhaps to begin an operation, perhaps to call it off.

At this point, as we have now entered my own lifetime, perhaps I may be allowed a personal reminiscence. When my father was ambassador in Paris immediately after the war, he would regularly hold investitures, in which he presented awards – usually the King's Medal for Courage – to heroes and heroines of the Resistance. Most

★ Overruled by Duff Cooper, then Minister of Information, who controlled the BBC.

of these were humble men and women from every corner of France, quite often simple peasants who had never before been to Paris. Some had sheltered escaped British prisoners for weeks until they could be provided with false documents and taken across the border into neutral Spain; others had regularly slipped out under cover of darkness to light a landing strip, at which agents or supplies might be picked up; the tiny delivery aeroplanes seldom spent more than five minutes on the ground. Yet others had planted bombs under bridges or blown up Nazi staff cars. All, in doing so, had risked their lives. Some had been arrested and tortured by the Gestapo, but had refused to talk and on release had instantly resumed their old activities. And they were not, for the most part, stalwart young people; far more often they were middle-aged, even elderly men and women who worked on the land, or ran the local garage, or served in the village shop. My father's secretary Eric Duncannon would read the citations, his voice often choking with emotion; then a small, frightened figure would step forward and my father would pin on the medal, tears pouring down his cheeks. These were, he used to say, the most moving moments of his life.

During the summer of 1942, America – which had entered the war in December 1941, after Pearl Harbor – and Britain were preparing Operation Torch, a joint invasion of French North Africa. For some time the Russians, whose army was then the only one that was actually fighting the German army face to face, had been trying hard to persuade them to open a second front, to take some of the pressure off their own troops. The Americans favoured Operation Sledgehammer, a landing in occupied Europe; but the British, aware that the newly arrived American forces had no experience of the Wehrmacht – of which they themselves had had all too much – believed that this would lead to disaster. They proposed instead an operation to clear the Axis armies from the shores of North Africa: an Anglo-American invasion of Morocco, Algeria and Tunisia, all of which were nominally in the hands of the Vichy government. The ensuing deadlock was broken only by President Roosevelt himself, who gave his generals categorical orders to support the British plan.

Vichy had some 125,000 troops in the area, together with a dozen or so warships and eleven submarines at Casablanca. French loyalties were obviously questionable; would they remain loyal to Marshal Pétain and resist, or would they allow the landings, joining the Free French forces themselves? The American General Mark Clark had had a secret meeting with one of the key French commanders,* who had told him the army and air force might perhaps be won over, but the navy, for whom the memory of Mers-el-Kebir was still fresh, would fight to the death.

The landings took place simultaneously at Casablanca, Oran and Algiers on 8 November, just a few days after Montgomery's victory at El Alamein. Most of the invading forces were American, in the hopes that resistance to them might be less than it would have been to the British; but such hopes were disappointed. In Morocco admittedly, the defenders failed to put up any serious opposition, but there the landings were almost prevented by the heavy Atlantic surf: fifty-five American landing craft were lost, and many lives. On the Algerian coast French resistance was a good deal stiffer, but there too the Allies finally prevailed.

As luck would have it the deputy head of the Vichy regime, Admiral François Darlan, had arrived in Algiers the day before the Allied landings, visiting his son who had been stricken with polio. He was identified and captured. He knew that the Germans were on the point of occupying all Vichy territory, and when they did so, on 11 November 1942, he made the Allies an offer. He would order an immediate ceasefire and would further direct all Vichy forces in North Africa to join them; they in return would recognise him as High Commissioner for France in North and West Africa. The senior Allied commander on the spot, General Eisenhower, accepted, and Darlan was as good as his word.

And now, for the second time, the question arose: what was to be done about the warships in Toulon, and how were the Axis powers to be prevented from taking them over. The commander there, Admiral Jean de Laborde, remembered Mers-el-Kebir and, like nearly all French senior naval officers, detested the British even more than he despised Darlan. In spite of the efforts of his superiors

* The United States and Vichy were not technically at war.

to persuade him that the game was up, he refused to take any action. At last the Minister of Marine, Admiral Paul Auphan, gave him firm orders: he was to prevent, without bloodshed, foreign entry into any naval establishment; if this were impossible, he must scuttle all the ships under his command. Having been assured by the German navy that Germany would make no move against either Toulon or his ships, Laborde believed himself to be in a relatively safe position; but with the arrival of SS Panzer troops on 27 November he changed his mind. The scuttling, when it started, was on a terrifying scale: the French navy deliberately destroyed a total of seventy-seven of its own seagoing vessels, including three battleships, seven cruisers, fifteen destroyers and twelve submarines. Seven more submarines ignored their orders and defected to the Free French in North Africa.

Not surprisingly the 'Darlan deal' aroused a storm of protest. General de Gaulle in London was furious. The admiral was an arch-collaborator; how could any responsible Allied officer even speak to him, let alone negotiate agreements? But the storm soon died down, and further discussion became useless when, on Christmas Eve 1942, Darlan was assassinated by a young Frenchman named Fernand Bonnier. It was to be many years before the full truth was established: that the assassination had been carefully planned by the British SOE and the Free French. Few tears were shed, on either side.

Operation Torch changed the whole complexion of the war. At last it looked as though the Allies might be winning; and on 3 June 1943 General de Gaulle met General Henri Giraud in Algiers. Giraud had had an extraordinary career. He had been captured in the First World War (having been left for dead on the field) and had escaped after two months by disguising himself as a roustabout from a travelling circus. In 1940 he had been captured again, escaping this time by lowering himself from a mountain fortress with a hand-made rope, eventually slipping into Vichy France, where he had tried hard – but failed – to convince Pétain that Germany would lose the war, and that he must resist the German occupation. The Americans had tried to enlist him in Operation Torch, but

Giraud had imposed unacceptable conditions, among them that he himself should be commander-in-chief of the operation and that no British should be involved. (He too remembered Mers-el-Kebir.) The Allies brought him to North Africa anyway, and after Darlan's assassination he became commander-in-chief of the French forces.

The two generals had – with considerable reluctance, since they were given only a supporting role and were debarred from the sessions on military planning – taken part in the Casablanca Conference in January 1943. The situation was also more complicated than it need have been owing to their unconcealed detestation of each other. It was only with considerable difficulty that they were persuaded to shake hands for the cameras; even then, their first try was so momentary and so half-hearted that they had to go through it again. Each, however, recognised the indispensability of the other, and in June they together formed the French Committee of National Liberation, in fact a provincial government of Free France, serving jointly as co-presidents. The existence of a true French government on true French territory (Algeria being technically a part of metropolitan France) gave an enormous boost to the spirits of Frenchmen everywhere, and particularly to the Resistance. It was clear, however, that such an unhappy partnership could not continue for long, and no one was surprised when, well before the end of the year, de Gaulle had outmanoeuvred Giraud – whose physical courage was considerably greater than his intelligence – and established single control.

Where the Second World War was concerned, the twelve months between June 1943 and June 1944 were packed with incident. In July the Allies landed in Sicily and Mussolini fell; September saw new landings in south Italy; in October the Italian government declared war on Germany. At the beginning of the new year Leningrad was relieved after a siege lasting two and a half years and the RAF began its nightly bombing offensive on the major German cities; on 4 June 1944 the US Fifth Army entered Rome; and two days later, on the 6th, came Operation Overlord, the long-awaited D-Day landings in Normandy.

Inevitably, these landings created major tensions with the French. General de Gaulle, as everyone knew by now, was virtually impossible to deal with: quick to take offence, ever-conscious of his own dignity, forever seeing insults where none were intended. On one occasion Churchill was speaking to him on the telephone and rapidly losing his temper. De Gaulle pointed out that the French people thought he was a reincarnation of Joan of Arc. 'We had to burn the last one,' the prime minister growled.

The general's relations with the Americans were even worse. President Roosevelt had always distrusted him – he had refused to recognise the French Committee – and insisted that he be kept out of the way during the landings 'in the interests of security'. He was in fact perfectly right to do so. The French continued to use codes that could be broken by British cryptographers in a matter of minutes, but Gallic pride forbade them to adopt British or American systems. On the other hand, as Churchill pointed out to the president, 'de Gaulle . . . despite all his faults and follies, has lately shown some signs of wishing to work with us, and after all it is very difficult to cut the French out of the liberation of France'. He therefore sent two York passenger aircraft to pick up the general from his head-quarters in Algiers – only to find that de Gaulle was refusing to come, having heard that the Americans would not allow a discussion on a later French civil government. Duff Cooper, now Churchill's representative in Algiers, spent an hour trying to persuade him to change his mind, but it was only on the following day that he very reluctantly – and with remarkably bad grace – agreed.

His mood was much the same when he arrived in England. Churchill, who had established his 'advance headquarters' on a train near Portsmouth, welcomed him warmly and invited him to lunch, but then gave mortal offence by allowing him to believe that he had been brought over to deliver a speech for the BBC. Of civil affairs in France, now the general's chief preoccupation, he made no mention. That was bad enough, but it got worse. De Gaulle was now shown the Allied currency, printed in the United States, which was being issued to the invasion troops. This *fausse monnaie*, as he called it, was 'absolutely unrecognised by the government of the Republic'. After lunch, he was taken to see General Eisenhower, the commander-in-chief, and shown the text of the proclamation that had been drafted for him to broadcast. He refused to accept it, and in his indignation announced that he was withdrawing all the French liaison officers who had been allocated to the British and American divisions. Churchill, who was by this time as angry as the general himself, accused him of 'treason at the height of battle' and proposed flying him straight back to Algiers, 'in chains if necessary'.

Such indeed was the state of Franco-Allied relations that it was not until 14 June – more than a week after D-day – that de Gaulle set foot in France. He was accompanied by a large entourage and a quantity of luggage that seemed extraordinary for a one-day trip. General Montgomery had asked him to lunch, suggesting that he might bring two members of his staff with him; he arrived with eighteen, but was made to settle for three. The remainder had to be driven to Bayeux, but when the jeeps arrived there was another row, the general insisting that they should be driven by the French drivers that he had brought with him. No wonder Churchill used to say: 'The heaviest cross I have to bear is the Cross of Lorraine.'*

Over the next ten weeks the fighting was hard; but by mid-August the Allied armies were approaching Paris, and Paris was preparing for them. On 15 August there was a strike of the Gendarmerie, the police and the Metro; on the 19th, as retreating columns of German tanks and armoured cars moved down the Champs-Elysées, members of the Resistance, now known as the FFI (French Forces of the Interior), called for a general mobilisation of all Parisians; and skirmishes continued for the next three days. On the afternoon of the 24th, General Philippe Leclerc, deliberately disobeying his superior, the American Major-General Gerow, sent an advance guard into Paris, with a message that the whole division would be there the following day; and at 9.22 that evening the 9th Armoured Company, led by Captain Raymond Dronne, broke into the city by the Porte d'Italie.

The German commander in Paris was Lieutenant General Dietrich von Choltitz. Hitler had given him orders 'to destroy Paris if the enemy advanced, and to defend it from the ruins'; but brother-

---

* The cross with the double horizontal bar that was the emblem of the Free French.

officers had persuaded him that to do so would serve no military purpose. He delayed his surrender just long enough to satisfy his government that he had capitulated with honour, and on the afternoon of the 25th in the Préfecture de Police, fat, monocled and sweating profusely, he signed the document handed to him by Leclerc. After more than four years, Paris was free.

On Saturday the 26th, a cloudless summer day, it was reported to General Gerow, still seething with anger at Leclerc's disobedience, that the French army was planning a victory parade that afternoon. At lunchtime he sent off a furious signal: 'Direct General Leclerc that his command will not, repeat not, participate in parade this afternoon but will continue on present mission of clearing Paris and environs of enemy. He accepts orders only from me.' Once again his order was disregarded. At 3 p.m. de Gaulle took the salute at the Arc de Triomphe and then set off on foot down the Champs-Elysées, accompanied by Leclerc, his two other senior generals, Koenig and Juin, and the principal leaders of the Paris Resistance. The parade did not pass off entirely without incident: when it reached the Place de la Concorde shots rang out, and in the ensuing mêlée several people were killed.* De Gaulle, however, displaying not a quiver of emotion, stepped calmly into his waiting car and drove off to Notre-Dame. When he reached the cathedral there were further fusillades. The waiting congregation flung themselves to the ground, but the general continued to march slowly, fearlessly and majestically up the nave to his seat just below the altar steps. In a live broadcast, a BBC correspondent reported:

> One of the most dramatic scenes I have ever seen . . . the General walked straight ahead into what appeared to me to be a hail of fire . . . he went straight ahead without hesitation, his shoulders flung back, and walked right down the centre aisle, even while the bullets were pouring about him. It was the most extraordinary example of courage I have ever seen . . . There were bangs, flashes all about him, yet he seemed to have an absolutely charmed life.

---

* Jean Cocteau, who was watching from the Hôtel Crillon, maintained that the cigarette in his mouth was shot in half; but nobody quite believed him.

Paris was liberated; but the war was by no means over. On 15 August a new operation had begun, the landing of 151,000 Allied troops on the Riviera, between Marseille and Nice. The idea was, first to secure the vital ports on the Mediterranean coast – what Churchill insisted on describing as 'the soft underbelly of Europe' – and secondly to increase pressure on the Germans by opening another front. The US Sixth Corps was accompanied by several French divisions under General Jean de Lattre de Tassigny. The weak German forces in the south were soon retreating up the Rhône valley; they tried to dig in at Dijon, but were unsuccessful; it was only when they reached the Vosges that they were able to establish a stable line of defence. Meanwhile the French had occupied Marseille and Toulon, providing a welcome relief for the ports of Normandy, which were having a desperate time trying to maintain provisions for both the British and the American forces. In the space of just four weeks the Allies had liberated most of southern France, inflicted heavy casualties on the Germans and solved their own supply problems. Operation Dragoon, as it was called, had been a magnificent success – on 19 November, de Lattre and his men reached the upper Rhine, and only four days later General Leclerc and his 2nd Armoured Division entered Strasbourg, as he had sworn to do while still deep in the African desert. Meanwhile, on the 10th, Churchill flew to Paris and on the following day joined de Gaulle in another march down the Champs-Elysées. Anthony Eden, who was also present, told Harold Nicolson that the crowd 'yelled for Churchill in a way that he had never heard any crowd yell before'. 'Not for one moment', he added, 'did Winston stop crying; he could have filled buckets by the time he received the Freedom of Paris.'

The day after the Strasbourg victory, de Gaulle flew to Moscow for a meeting with Stalin. This was important to him for two reasons. First, he was determined to keep the French Communist party under control. In this, fortunately, Stalin was only too happy to oblige; the last thing he wanted was a Communist uprising in Paris, which might well have induced Roosevelt to cut off the Lend-Lease arrangement with the Soviet Union. De Gaulle's other concern was for the forthcoming peace conference, which clearly could not be long delayed. He knew that Roosevelt was still as distrustful of him as ever, and he needed Stalin's support to make sure that he would be participating.

The price of the meeting was to endure one of Stalin's hideous banquets in the Kremlin: alarming affairs at the best of times, and made even worse on this occasion by de Gaulle's Foreign Minister, Georges Bidault, who – precisely as his host intended – became embarrassingly drunk. But finally, at four o'clock in the morning, a Franco-Soviet agreement was signed. The general had got what he wanted. The Communist leader Maurice Thorez, who had spent most of the war in Russia and only just returned to France, made no move to call strikes or man barricades; instead, he encouraged the party to increase productivity with one object only – that of defeating Germany. De Gaulle returned from Moscow a happy man, but bad news awaited him: the German army had broken through in the Ardennes and was thought to be heading for the coast.

It was all Hitler's idea. He was far from well; he had narrowly escaped assassination in July and was also deeply depressed, with the Allied armies moving closer towards Germany and the ignominious defeat of the 'thousand-year Reich' staring him in the face. He now planned a surprise counter-offensive. His armies would penetrate the lines of the US First Army, advance to the Meuse and seize Antwerp. The entire operation, he believed, could be completed in just fourteen days. In doing so, he informed his astonished generals, he would split the Allies, trap the First Canadian Army and knock Canada out of action. After that the Americans would be only too happy to discuss peace terms. Here at last would be the turning point of the war.

Field Marshal von Rundstedt, the commander-in-chief, knew this perfectly well to be a pipe dream. But by this time Germany had nothing to lose, and he willingly agreed to lead the proposed offensive. That offensive – the Battle of the Bulge as it came to be called – was launched in mid-December 1944 and continued for the next three weeks. It started off promisingly enough, in that it took the Allies completely by surprise. Thanks to a total radio shutdown, with communications being confined to telephones and despatch riders, Allied intelligence and the ULTRA codebreakers* failed to detect any sign of what was going on, so nobody saw the attack coming. Ultimately, however, it failed: Germany lost the last of her reserves, and what remained of the Luftwaffe was shattered. But the Allies too suffered fearful losses: they had to contend with one of the coldest winters in living memory, and the operation set back the invasion of Germany for a month or more. There was one particularly bad moment from the French point of view, when Eisenhower ordered French troops to evacuate Strasbourg. He had totally failed to understand what Strasbourg meant to every Frenchman; the city, with Alsace and Lorraine, had after all been annexed by Hitler in 1940 and for the past four years had been part of Germany. No one could contemplate the idea of it returning to German hands. De Gaulle indignantly defied the commander-in-chief, saying that 'Strasbourg will be our Stalingrad' and that, if American troops pulled out, the French would remain and die there alone. Churchill backed him up, and Eisenhower was so impressed by the French determination that he relented.

The Battle of the Bulge also saw a sharp deterioration in Anglo-American relations owing entirely to the monstrous ego of General Sir Bernard Montgomery, who on 7 January held a press conference during which, having given cursory credit to the 'courage and good fighting quality' of the Americans, spent the next half-hour suggesting that he had won the battle virtually single-handed – in fact it was overwhelmingly an American victory† – and making no mention of any American general except Eisenhower. Generals Omar Bradley and George S. Patton – both of whom had always detested him – threatened to resign unless he was transferred, and Eisenhower was indeed on the point of sacking him. Only very reluctantly did he allow himself to be persuaded by his chiefs of staff to settle for an apology.

The last months of the war saw a major conference of the Big

---

* ULTRA was the name given to military information obtained by breaking encrypted enemy communications.

† The American losses were 19,246 killed; the British 200.

Three in Yalta. De Gaulle, to his fury, did not receive an invitation and never forgot the insult. The decision to exclude him was once again due to his old enemy Roosevelt. Even though the French army had captured a good deal of southern Germany, the president continued to block French participation in any discussions that would shape Europe and the post-war world. The presence of de Gaulle, he wired both Churchill and Stalin, 'would merely introduce a complicating and undesirable factor'. On the other hand he agreed with Churchill that France should be allowed a zone of occupation in Germany and that, as Stalin insisted, it should be carved out of the British and American zones – and also that it should be included among the five nations that would host the conference to establish the United Nations. This latter concession was of immense import- ance to France, since it carried with it a permanent seat on the Security Council.

Roosevelt – who had been seen at Yalta to be a pale shadow of his former self – died only two months after the end of the confer- ence, on 12 April 1945; less than a month later, on 8 May 1945, the Second World War came to an end in Europe – though it was to continue in the Far East until August. It left France victorious but, after the experiences of the last five years, seriously traumatised. With the pre-war parties and most of their leaders discredited, there was little opposition to the general forming an interim administra- tion; but he refused to move into one of the principal official buildings like the Elysée or the Hôtel Matignon in the Rue de Varenne, the official residence of the prime minister. Instead he settled with his family into a small state-owned villa on the edge of the Bois de Boulogne, ignoring the fact that it had been formerly occupied by Hermann Goering.

Victory, alas, had done nothing to improve the general's character, as he showed in the military review held on 18 June. Typically, he had given orders that only French troops should take part. The procession did however include an ambulance from the unit estab- lished by Lady Spears, whose husband Sir Edward had personally spirited de Gaulle to London in June 1940. Duff Cooper, then British Ambassador in Paris, takes up the story:

The ambulance which Lady Spears had given to the French army had taken part, and she had flown small Union Jacks on her four jeeps, side by side with the tricolour. The eagle eye of the General had spotted the offensive flags, though I, standing close to him, had failed to do so. The result was that the colonel responsible was summoned and ordered to disband the ambulance immediately and repatriate all British members of it. The ambulance, financed by Lady Spears and her friends, had been serving France on all fronts since the outbreak of war and had taken care of twenty thousand French wounded.

The folly and pettiness of de Gaulle pass belief.

Immediately after the liberation, conditions in Paris were if anything worse than they had been under the Germans. Parts of the city were in ruins, public services almost non-existent. There was also a serious shortage of food, the principal difficulties being not those of agriculture but of transport. Railway tracks had been bombed, rolling stock and lorries had been commandeered and taken to Germany; every bridge over the Seine, the Loire and the Rhône had been demolished. The situation of course soon improved, and by the end of 1945 the country was struggling back on to its feet; psychologically, however, France's wounds were to take a good deal longer to heal.

The overriding problems in the early days concerned the identification and treatment of collaborators. First came the leaders of the Vichy government. Pétain, now nearly ninety, was charged with treason, sentenced to death and stripped of all his honours save that of Marshal of France. Clearly his record in the First World War ruled out the death penalty, and his sentence was commuted by de Gaulle to one of life imprisonment. After three months in a fort in the Pyrenees he was transferred to the Ile d'Yeu, an island off the North Atlantic coast. There he remained until he died, hopelessly senile, in July 1951. Weygand, who had been Minister of Defence in Pétain's government and had driven Jewish children out of the schools and colleges, was – almost unbelievably – acquitted. There were in fact only three executions (by firing squad; the days of the guillotine were at last over) of the top Vichy brass: those of Joseph Darnand, who as an SS officer led the Milice paramilitaries who hunted down members of the Resistance; of Fernand de Brinon, third-ranking member of the Vichy regime and enthusiastic supporter of the Nazis, who in September 1944 fled to Germany and became president of Vichy's government in exile; and of Pierre Laval, perhaps the nastiest of them all, also fanatically pro-Nazi, who played an important part in the deportation of Jewish children to Germany, and in a broadcast speech on D-Day forbade his compatriots to offer any assistance to the Allied forces.

Elsewhere, the collaborators were not so lucky. Many were attacked by lynch mobs and beaten to death; countless women accused of sleeping with German soldiers (many of whom had done so only to obtain food for their children) had their heads shaved or were paraded half-naked through the streets. The Resistance partisans alone were said to have summarily executed some 4,500. In an effort to impose order, de Gaulle instituted what he called the *épuration légale*, to punish all traitors and to eliminate as far as possible all traces of the Vichy regime. Some 2,000 former collaborators were sentenced to death, although fewer than 800 were actually executed. (He himself, as head of state, commuted 998 cases, including all the women.) But there remained a large grey area; many, suspected by some of collaboration, were believed by others to have been heroic members of the Resistance. In Paris alone over 150,000 were at one moment or another detained on suspicion of collaboration, though most were later released. They included the industrialist Louis Renault, the singers Tino Rossi, Maurice Chevalier and Edith Piaf, the actor and playwright Sacha Guitry and the dress designer Coco Chanel. At the British Embassy in the early days after the liberation there were several cases of one dinner guest quietly approaching his hostess before the meal to say that, much to his regret, he was unable to sit at the same table with another.

The Second World War thus left France a hotbed of contradictions. She was both defeated and victorious; there had been moments of glory, others of bitter shame; her new leader was one of the greatest men in all her history, but he was also capable of almost unbelievable pusillanimity and small-mindedness. He did however provide her with inspired leadership, together with a degree of discipline which, after all that she had suffered in those five long years, she quite desperately needed. In the years to come there were problems a-plenty to be faced – with Vietnam, Algeria, with a united Europe and, most recently, with the Muslim world; but two thousand years is enough. I am drawing this book to a close with the end of the Second World War because, once I find myself writing about facts I remember from my own life, I no longer feel that I am writing history. And so I leave the story here, at the last major milestone, with a sense above all of gratitude. The history of Franco-British relations has been, over the past twenty centuries, chequered to say the least; but in those centuries France has made a contribution to European culture greater than that of any other nation – and we have been, among many others, the blessed beneficiaries.

Epilogue

Gratitude comes in two kinds. First, there is the gratitude which we should all feel for what France has given the world. We should begin, perhaps, with its language. To those not French-born it will always be something of a challenge – the hardest by far of the Romance languages to learn and, heaven knows, to pronounce. (In fact, I have always believed that a *slight* accent is an advantage: we have no right to lay claim to a foreign tongue and pretend that it is our own. Thanks entirely to my mother's insistence on lessons from the age of four, I barely remember the days before I spoke French pretty fluently; but I would never be taken for a Frenchman, nor would I have the right to be.) The rewards, on the other hand, are immense, and not only for the traveller but for the reader: however brilliant a translation, much of the flavour of the original is inevitably lost, in poetry even more than in prose. And I am thinking not only of the great writers – Ronsard and Racine, Balzac and Flaubert, de Musset and Victor Hugo;[*] I'm thinking also of Simenon and Maigret, of the ravishingly beautiful folk songs that I used to love to sing, and those glorious and totally untranslatable nightclub ballads of Edith Piaf, Charles Trenet, Georges Brassens, Jacques Brel and the like, in the years when the best the British could offer was 'Cruising Down the River (on a Sunday Afternoon)'. Unlike the British, too, the French are proud of their language. Fashionable anglicisms are bound to creep in (from 'le weekend' to 'email') but there is always the Académie Française to raise a warning finger if things are getting out of control.

---

[*] It was André Gide who, when asked who was the greatest of French poets, replied, '*Victor Hugo, hélas!*' (Victor Hugo, alas!)

And then there are the painters; here again the debt is immense. Claude Lorrain, so beloved of Turner, and Poussin go without saying, as do those two splendid portraitists represented in this book, Philippe de Champaigne and Hyacinthe Rigaud; but my own heart remains in the fifteenth century, with Jean Fouquet, the Limbourg brothers – creators of the *Très riches heures du duc de Berry* – and their equally dazzling contemporaries. Their work is also to be found in the preceding pages; and I only wish I could have found an excuse to include a favourite Impressionist or two.

Going on to the world of music, my own personal list would begin with Jean–Baptiste Lully, simply because I believe '*Au clair de la lune*' to be one of the loveliest songs ever written. As for the nineteenth century, I would give first prize to Hector Berlioz, with Bizet, Fauré and Debussy as close runners-up. (Ravel is disqualified for that dreadful *Boléro*.) And that is not to mention the opera composers – Gounod, Massenet, Meyerbeer and Delibes for a start – whose work is all too seldom heard in England, largely I believe because relatively few English and American singers are happy with the French nasalised vowels and the almost ubiquitous feminine ending -*e*, which is a good deal trickier than it looks.

Where architecture is concerned I will mention only the great Romanesque churches – there are particularly lovely ones at Toulouse, Angoulême, Vézelay, Tournus and Le Puy – Chartres Cathedral and the châteaux of the Loire; this game could be continued almost ad infinitum; but here I am happy to rest my case, adding only the reminder that, to those in England, all this – and much more – is on our very doorstep.

The essence of France, however, is a thousand times more than all this; it seems, sometimes, to be in the very air we breathe. In 1964 I drove along the West African coast from Abidjan to Lagos. Though independence had come, it was still very much the colonial world: before reaching Nigeria I drove through the Côte d'Ivoire (Ivory Coast), Ghana, Togo and Benin (then known as Dahomey). The difference between Ghana and Nigeria (formerly British) and the others (formerly French) was astonishing. In Abidjan and Lomé (Togo) I had delicious lunches of *truite aux amandes*, the trout having been flown in from Marseille the night before; there were delightful cafés, populated largely by the French who had stayed on, sipping Pernods and Camparis in their immaculately cut shirts and shorts. And how well I remember my spirits dipping as I approached the Nigerian frontier, staffed by an enormous Nigerian lady in bulging khaki uniform, sitting at a rickety wooden table ringed with circles left by brimming tankards – she was halfway through one herself – and doing the football pools. Oh dear, I thought, oh dear.

And that brings me to the second kind of gratitude – my own – for the France that I have known for more than eight years, living in everything from the grandeur of the British Embassy to a humble Strasbourg bedsitter. Looking back, the memories come crowding in: gypsy stilt-dancers in pre-war Aix-les-Bains; bicycling through Provence on the first anniversary of the Allied landings in the South; singing the old songs at the *Lapin Agile* in Montmartre, which will always be my favourite nightclub; or – particularly vivid half a century on – an al fresco dinner in Arles, during which a large white horse suddenly appeared from around the corner, bearing on its back a man and, behind him, a remarkably beautiful girl, both in full Provençal costume. For all these memories I am grateful, and for many thousands more. And that sort of gratitude is more than gratitude: it is love.

Acknowledgements

My heartfelt thanks go to Georgina Laycock, Caroline Westmore and all those at John Murray who have worked so hard on this book; to Juliet Brightmore, who has done wonders with the illustrations; and to Douglas Matthews for yet another superb index.

Illustration Credits

Alamy Stock Photo: 1 below/StevanZZ; 3 above left/Hemis; 4 below left/Heritage Image Partnership Ltd; 9 centre left/Josse Christophel/ portrait by Quentin de la Tour/Louvre Paris; 10 above left/Josse Christophel/Bibliothèque Nationale Paris. Bridgeman Images: 1 above left, 4 centre right, 10 centre right/all De Agostini Picture Library; 2 above left and 3 below left/Photos © PVDE; 2 centre right; 2 below left and 4 above left/both © British Library Board All Rights Reserved; 3 centre right, 5 centre left and below right, 6 below left, 9 above right, 12 below/all Louvre Paris; 5 above right/ from *Vie des Femmes Célèbres*, c.1505/Musée Dobrée Nantes France; 6 above left/State Collection France; 7 below left/style of Corneille de Lyon/Polesden Lacey Surrey UK; 7 below right/National Gallery of Art Washington DC USA; 8 above left/studio of Frans II Pourbus/ Château de Versailles France; 8 centre, 11 above left and below right, 13 above/all Musée Carnavalet Paris; 8 below left/La Sorbonne Paris; 9 below right/National Galleries of Scotland Edinburgh; 10 below/ Château de Versailles; 11 below left/Private Collection; 12 above left/State Hermitage Museum St Petersburg Russia; 12 above right/ Musée des Beaux-Arts Valenciennes France; 13 below right/photo Nadar/The Art Institute of Chicago USA; 14 centre; 14 below/

Suggestions for Further Reading

There are libraries groaning with excellent histories of France, far longer and intimidatingly more thorough than mine. In the hope that my little book has piqued your interest, however, I simply want to draw your attention to a handful that I have particularly enjoyed over the years, in case you would like to read more.

De Bello Gallico by Julius Caesar (editions too numerous to count)

Paris and Elsewhere by Richard Cobb (John Murray, 1998)

The History of Modern France by Jonathan Fenby (Simon & Schuster, 2015)

The Discovery of France by Graham Robb (Picador, 2007)

Napoleon the Great by Andrew Roberts (Penguin, 2014)

The History of the Crusades, vols 1–3, by Stephen Runciman (Penguin, 1971 etc.)

François I: Prince of the Renaissance by Desmond Seward (Legend, 1973)

And, on a rather lighter note, I did much enjoy this very entertaining romp through a millennium of misunderstandings: *1000 Years of Annoying the French* by Stephen Clarke (Bantam Press, 2010).

Index